SO FAR FROM GOD

JOHN S. D. EISENHOWER

SO FAR FROM GOD

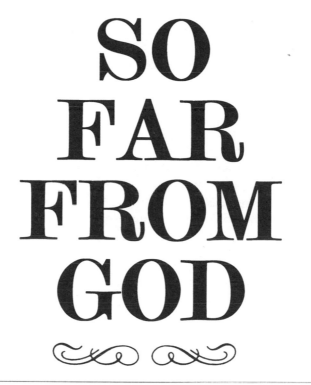

THE U. S. WAR WITH MEXICO
1846 – 1848

UNIVERSITY OF OKLAHOMA PRESS
NORMAN

Library of Congress Cataloging-in-Publication Data

Eisenhower, John S. D., 1922–
    So far from God : the U.S. war with Mexico, 1846–1848 / John S.D.
Eisenhower.
        p. cm.
    Originally published: New York : Random House, c1989.
    Includes bibliographical references (p.) and index.
    ISBN 978-0-8061-3279-2
    1. Mexican War, 1846–1848—Campaigns.   I. Title.

    E405 .E37 2000
    973.6'2—dc21
                                                        00-030257

The paper in this book meets the guidelines for permanence and durability of the Committee on Production Guidelines for Book Longevity of the Council on Library Resources, Inc. ∞

Thanks to *Life Magazine* for permission to reprint excerpts from "My Confessions: The Recollections of a Rogue," by Samuel Chamberlain. Samuel Chamberlain, Life Magazine © Time Inc. Reprinted with permission. Courtesy Life Picture Service.

So Far from God originally was published in 1989 by Random House, Inc. Maps by Arnold C. Holeywell.

Oklahoma Paperbacks edition published 2000 by the University of Oklahoma Press, Norman, Publishing Division of the University. Reprinted by arrangement with Random House Trade Publishing, a division of Random House, Inc., 201 East 50th Street, New York, N.Y. 10022. Manufactured in the U.S.A.

5   6   7   8   9   10

*To a better understanding between
Mexico and the United States*

CONTENTS

THE WAR IN THE WEST

CONTENTS

MAPS

0   100   200   300 Miles

0   500 Kilometers

Pueb

Colorado River

Gila River

Taos

Santa Fe

Albuquerque

Las Veg

Peralta

San Pascual

San Diego

Copper Mines

Socorro

Valverde

Tucson

El Paso

Fronteras

GULF OF CALIFORNIA

Chihuahua

N

Durango

Mazatlán

PACIFIC

OCEAN

INVASIONS OF MEXICO
1846–1848

——— Scott
············· Taylor
——— Doniphan
–·–·– Kearny
– – – – Wool
——— Patterson Quitman
━ ━ ━ Sloat

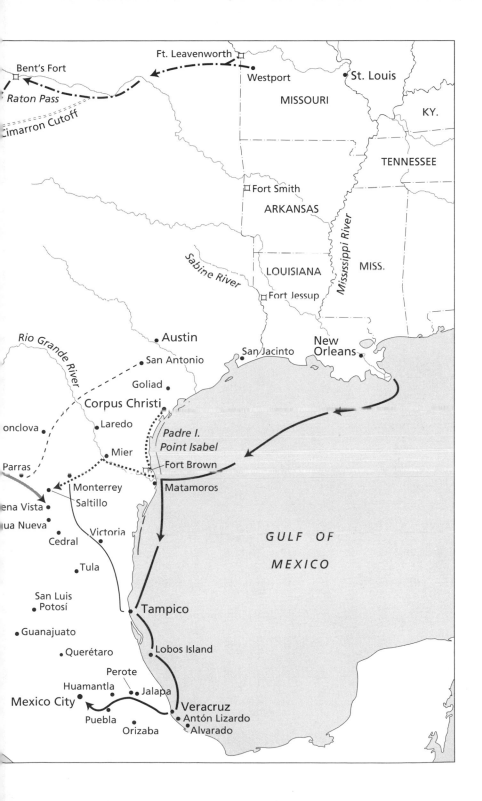

Ft. Leavenworth

Bent's Fort

Raton Pass

Cimarron Cutoff

Westport

St. Louis

MISSOURI

KY.

TENNESSEE

Fort Smith

ARKANSAS

Mississippi River

Sabine River

LOUISIANA

MISS.

Fort Jessup

Austin

San Antonio

San Jacinto

New Orleans

Rio Grande River

Goliad

Corpus Christi

onclova

Laredo

Padre I.
Point Isabel

Mier

Fort Brown

Parras

Matamoros

Monterrey

Saltillo

ena Vista

ua Nueva

Victoria

Cedral

GULF OF

Tula

MEXICO

San Luis
Potosí

Guanajuato

Tampico

Querétaro

Lobos Island

Perote

Huamantla

Jalapa

Mexico City

Veracruz

Puebla

Antón Lizardo

Orizaba

Alvarado

*Poor Mexico! So far from God and
so close to the United States.*

—attributed to General Porfirio Díaz,
president of Mexico, 1877–1911

*From that day nothing was heard but
the cry of "war." Thus succeeded the
scenes of blood and extermination until
the horses of the north arrived to
trample the smiling level fields of the
beautiful valley of Mexico, and the
degenerate descendents of William Penn
came to insult the sepulchres of our
fathers.*

—Alcaraz

*The grievous wrongs perpetrated by
Mexico upon our citizens for a long
period of years remains unredressed;
and solemn treaties have been
disregarded. . . . In the meantime we have
tried every effort at reconciliation.
The cup of forebearance had been
exhausted, even before Mexico passed
the boundary of the United States,
invaded our territory, and shed
American blood upon American soil.*

—President James K. Polk, message to
Congress, May 11, 1846

INTRODUCTION

Overshadowed by the cataclysmic Civil War only thirteen years later, the Mexican War has been practically forgotten in the United States. Through the years, despite our growing interest in Mexico, it is rarely mentioned. And when the subject comes up, it nearly always deals with the questionable manner in which it came about. More specifically, was the United States right in sending Zachary Taylor to the Rio Grande in early 1846, thus provoking war with Mexico? Opinions vary.

Ulysses S. Grant, for one, was certain that the United States was wrong. He did, in fact, call the Mexican War "the most unjust war ever waged by a stronger against a weaker nation. . . . an instance of a republic following the bad example of European monarchies. . . ."[1]

Grant's statement was no passing reference. His words of condemnation, in his celebrated *Memoirs* of 1885, are emphatic. In contrast to much of the text, in which Grant exhibits remarkable serenity, he repeats his disapproval of the Mexican War several times, with heat.

Not everyone agrees with Grant. Indeed, some students of the war have justified the United States' actions with the same fervor. Professor Justin Smith, for example, who was indisputably the most thorough researcher of the war, wrote in 1919, ". . . as a matter of fact, the hostilities were deliberately precipitated by the will and act of Mexico. . . . Mexico wanted [war]; Mexico threatened it; Mexico issued orders to wage it." Smith concludes that when Mexico refused to "apply pacific measures" to the differences between the two countries, such refusal "rendered just the cause which was before doubtful."[2]

But Justin Smith, despite the thoroughness of his research, has not convinced later scholars such as Bernard DeVoto, who considers his judgments "consistently wrongheaded."[3] And without a doubt, the preponderance of American opinion has agreed with Grant that the United States treated Mexico unjustly.

Actually, the issue is not simple, and opinions on it are colored by its role in accelerating the growth of animosity between the Northern and Southern states of the Union which eventually led to the Civil War. The North feared the expansion of slave territory. Thus the facts regarding the conflict that extended the borders of the continental United States from the Rio Grande to the Pacific have been submerged in the slavery issue.

The omission of such events as the Mexican War from the American consciousness does history injustice. Wars as such may best be forgotten, but the period of the Mexican War was an important era, one of upheaval, of passion, of heroism, of bitterness, and of triumph. Respectable men called one another "traitors"; politicians orated; volunteers flocked to the recruiting stations; generals feuded, fumed and grimly disobeyed orders. The cost in American lives was staggering. Of the 104,556 men who served in the army, both regulars and volunteers, 13,768 men died, the highest death rate of any war in our history.[4] The period between 1844 and 1848 was a significant time, not something to be relegated to the attic of memory.

Contrary to common understanding, the war with Mexico was supported with enthusiasm by most of the population for at least the first year, by the end of which the necessary armies were recruited and supplied. Volunteers flocked to the colors to rescue "Old Rough and Ready," Zachary Taylor, from the menace of the Mexicans on the Rio Grande. And as the result of his remarkable series of victories, that same "Zack" Taylor was later elected president, an honor rendered only to victorious generals in popular wars. Boredom and impatience set in among the American population toward the end of the war, but moral disapproval was confined largely to a few New Englanders and some New England settlers in the Midwest.

The fact is that Mexico stood in the way of the American dream of Manifest Destiny. Although that dramatic, pious term was of relatively recent coinage in 1845, the idea of expansion westward to the Pacific had long been in the American mind. As far back as his first inaugural address in 1801, President Thomas Jefferson referred to a vast territory that would provide "room enough for our descendents to the thousandth and ten thousandth generation." And Jefferson did much to make that dream a reality by purchasing the great Louisiana territory from Emperor Napoleon of France and sending exploratory expeditions to the West, first under Zebulon Pike, later under Lewis and Clark.

In the course of the next four decades other expeditions followed, and Americans became aware of the "Oregon territory,"* occupied jointly by the United States and Britain. They also learned of the lands to the southwest, under the shaky control of Spain until 1821 and thereafter under that of Mexico. Migrations of American settlers to the west were well under way as of 1844, when the annexation of Texas, long an objective of American diplomacy, became an acute issue in the United States.

It is generally assumed that the annexation of Texas to the Union, finally accomplished on July 4, 1845, was the cause of the war between the United States and Mexico in 1846. To the extent that the long border war between Texas and Mexico affected American thinking, it was. But the act of annexation itself was an artificial issue, and even after annexation had been accomplished, war might have been averted. True, Mexico had never recognized the "treaty" of Velasco of 1836, in which Mexican President Santa Anna, a captive of the Texans, had agreed to Texan independence; but from that moment the United States and most European nations recognized Texas as a sovereign nation, though domestically no Mexican politician could ever concede that independence. The Mexican government thus broke relations with the United States in 1845, when Congress offered annexation, but war did not come for another year. By that time Taylor's army was on the Rio Grande, occupying territory that many Americans, at least privately, considered Mexican.

During the nine years between the Battle of San Jacinto and the U.S. offer of annexation to Texas, the government of the United States always maintained a proper neutrality between Texas and Mexico. The American people, however, observed no such inhibitions. They openly sympathized with the Anglo-Saxon émigrés whom they now considered Texans; they supplied Sam Houston's army with weapons; and though brutality occurred on both sides, the Americans sided with the Texan version on every controversial issue. As a result the American public grew progressively more antagonistic toward Mexico as a nation. Mexicans came to be considered less than "civilized" people, undeserving of rights generally accorded to Europeans. It is not surprising, therefore, that rationalizing unjust acts against Mexico would become easy.

To the student of today the fate of Mexico is sad, for the Mexicans

---

*Which included what are now the states of Oregon, Washington, and Idaho as well as small portions of Montana, Wyoming, and Canada.

were victims of both their history and Yankee expansionism. But that sadness need not be exacerbated by excessive shame for the conduct of the United States, because Mexico's disorganization, corruption, and weakness created a power vacuum that would inevitably have been filled by some predator—if not the United States, then Britain, less likely France, and even, remotely, Russia. American haste to occupy California, for example, was prompted more by fear of British action than by concern of what Mexico would do. After all, the United States and Britain were threatening war over the Oregon territory just north of California. Mexico's weakness stemmed from nearly three centuries of autocratic Spanish rule and from its own devastating war of independence, not from the actions of the United States.

It may be of some use to the reader to present here a general sequence of events of the Mexican War. As in so many of our wars, the United States entered it woefully unprepared, so much so as to encourage many Mexicans with hopes of easy victory. However, Taylor's quick victories on the Rio Grande removed the immediate Mexican threat to Texas. The United States, therefore, was given time to mobilize, equip, and train a civilian army. Money and volunteers were provided eagerly by a previously reluctant Congress, prodded by an anxious public, mobilized by the announcement that "American blood has been shed upon American soil." It then fell to the President to decide how to use them.

It is important to realize that, from the beginning to the end, President Polk always prosecuted the war with a hope of achieving a negotiated peace. To save American lives and to avoid overly injuring Mexican pride, Polk first pursued limited military objectives. In the beginning he hoped that the occupation of the northernmost provinces of Mexico, coupled with a lack of Mexican will, would bring the two countries to the peace table. Accordingly, Polk sent Taylor from the Rio Grande toward Monterrey (in Nuevo León); General John E. Wool, also from Texas, toward Chihuahua; and Colonel Stephen W. Kearny from Missouri to Santa Fe (New Mexico) and then to California. Occupation of those territories, Polk gambled, might be enough.

That plan, however, failed because it underestimated Mexican pride, determination, and hatred of the gringo. As a result, Polk replaced that limited strategy with a major undertaking, an expedition to seize Mexico City by way of an amphibious landing at the Mexican port of

Veracruz. Only by taking Mexico City itself, he concluded reluctantly, could military force bring Mexico to its knees.*

The strategy worked, but the road turned out to be fraught with hardship and danger. To occupy Monterrey, Saltillo, Santa Fe, Los Angeles, San Francisco, and, later, Mexico City cost dearly, as the statistics show.

The visitor to Mexico—at least, this visitor—is baffled in trying to visualize how Winfield Scott's small army (only six thousand effectives entered Mexico City in September 1847) could ever have conquered a nation of such vast territory, populated by seven million people. But, of course, Scott's army did no such thing. When he first occupied Mexico City, Scott was in fact hard put to maintain order even within its very gates. And even when reinforced to 24,000 men in the next few months he was able only to keep his supply line open to the coast and to occupy Mexico City, Veracruz, Tampico, Cuernavaca, Pachuca, and Toluca.[5] (The last three were within sixty miles of the capital.)

But Scott firmly controlled the parts of Mexico that mattered, and American politics notwithstanding he could continue to do so indefinitely. Such occupation was unbearable to Mexico. Mexico City was not only the main hub of politics and commerce in the country but the soul of Mexico. And Veracruz was the main port, Mexico's window to the outside world. And since the United States was willing to pay $15 million for the territories in the north, over which it had already established absolute control, the terms of the Treaty of Guadalupe Hidalgo in 1848 seemed a reasonable price to sensible Mexicans as the only way of getting rid of the Yankee occupation. But by no means had the United States thoroughly "conquered" Mexico.

Looking back, one is tempted to consider the outcome of the Mexican War as a foregone conclusion, to regard the unbroken string of North American victories as easy. It was not so; the success of American arms represented a remarkable feat. Considering the vast distances, the

---

*The military buff will notice a superficial resemblance between this evolution of strategy and that followed in Europe during World War II. The northern provinces of Mexico would correspond to North Africa; Veracruz would correspond to Normandy.

slowness of transport, the paucity of local resources, and the menace of virulent disease, it is remarkable that Taylor and Scott even managed to reach the scenes of their victories, let alone face the guns of the Mexicans.

Today it is difficult to visualize how slow and tedious cross-country movement was during the 1840s. It required about two months for a messenger to carry a dispatch to Washington from Mexico City and bring back a reply. And hauling supplies was done entirely by muscle power; twenty oxen were needed to tow one large artillery piece. Thousands of animals, all needing water and forage, were required to move even a small army overland. And with sanitation not well understood, the worst enemy was disease. Experienced soldiers recognized some relationship between cleanliness and disease—witness the lower death rate among the disciplined regulars in contrast to that of the casual volunteers. But the exact causes—water pollution, insects, etc.—were not identified. The base troops stationed at Veracruz, therefore, were actually at greater risk over a period of time than were the soldiers in the front ranks of battle.

Logistical factors, then, restricted the amount of force that the United States could deliver to any given point inland. With the size of the armies so limited, American troops were outnumbered in every inland battle fought. Taylor's and Scott's men were much better organized, disciplined, and motivated than their Mexican counterparts; but in some instances, as at Buena Vista, Mexican numerical superiority was so great that decimation of the American force would have been inevitable save for one factor: superior weaponry and the ability to use it.

It is no downgrading of the infantry's claim to be the "queen of battles" for us to recognize that the field artillery made the difference between victory and defeat for the Americans. The Mexican and American infantry were equipped with about the same flintlock and percussion muskets that fired buckshot and ball, which were so ineffective at long ranges that, as Grant put it, "a man might fire at you all day without your finding it out."[6] The artillery arm, however, was a different story. The American artillery had the advantage of a greater range than the Mexican and of much deadlier projectiles. Unlike the Mexican artillery, which fired only solid shot, the American arsenal included both canister and grape.* Of the two, the grape was more flexible because the amount of shot could be varied, but both were deadly. And American artillerists had developed to an advanced state the techniques of quick unlimbering and firing. In the artillery arm, at least, the American army was the peer of any army in the world.

Though every aspect of the Mexican War is interesting, the most fascinating is its cast of characters—the collection of colorful, egotistical, and daring personalities. The 1840s was the age of the individual, in which faceless bureaucrats did not exist. Thus the armies of both nations were both noteworthy for internecine conflicts, far more so than for any lofty unity of purpose. Commanders on both sides disobeyed orders, justifying their acts of insubordination on the basis of "changed situations." The distances from headquarters, of course, accounted to some extent for a local commander's inability to follow instructions to the letter, but that consideration seems often to have excused rather than actually necessitated freedom of action on the spot.

Thus Zachary Taylor justified taking a precarious position at Buena Vista on the basis that Scott and others, who ordered him to pull back to Monterrey, were too far away to appreciate the situation. Robert F. Stockton, in California, argued that a changed situation justified his ignoring presidential orders designating Stephen W. Kearny as governor. Sometimes, especially on the Mexican side, no excuse for insubordination was offered at all. Valencia's defiance of Santa Anna's repeated orders to pull back from Contreras, for example, could offer no such excuse. (Valencia's life expectancy was therefore dependent upon his staying away from Santa Anna for some time after his defeat.) Slavish subservience to authority was not characteristic of the period.

Because of language, distance, and, above all, the paucity of Mexican writing on the Mexican War, this story is told largely from the North American viewpoint. Accordingly, the most vivid characters that emerge are Yankees. Of the Mexicans—Santa Anna, Arista, Ampudia, and Gómez Farías—only Santa Anna, that flawed yet nearly indispens-

---

*A canister was a tin cylinder fused with a powder charge and small shot. Grape consisted of a cluster of balls between two wooden blocks called "sabots." (Lester R. Dillon, *American Artillery in the Mexican War,* p. 14.)

able Mexican leader, stands out. Ambitious, energetic, intelligent, and unprincipled, Santa Anna so dominated Mexican political and military affairs from 1829 to the Mexican War (and later) that other figures seem significant only insofar as they affect the fortunes of Santa Anna himself. Only the idealistic and liberal Valentín Gómez Farías, twice Santa Anna's vice president, appears as a force in his own right. And unfortunately for Mexico, Gómez Farías's domestic political objectives were inconsistent with Mexico's military interests.

Among the Americans the "big three" are, of course, President James K. Polk, General Winfield Scott and General Zachary Taylor. They came together from different directions. Just before 1844, when this story begins, Polk was out of political office, practicing law and politics in Columbia, Tennessee. Scott, as general-in-chief of the U.S. Army, alternated his time between Washington and West Point, where he periodically moved his headquarters at will. Taylor was a soldier-planter, who managed to combine his military duties with farming along the Mississippi frontier, thanks to the generous cooperation of an understanding army. Others of prominence—Senator Thomas Hart Benton, General Stephen W. Kearny, Commodore Robert F. Stockton, Commodore David E. Conner, and Generals William J. Worth, David E. Twiggs, and Gideon J. Pillow—were pursuing separate careers. When the war came, each contributed in an individual, usually individualistic, manner.

On the purely military side, students of the Mexican War have enjoyed making relative evaluations of Winfield Scott and Zachary Taylor. Comparisons between these two men are actually idle, as each had a different set of circumstances facing him.

Of the two, Taylor was by all odds the popular favorite of soldiers and public alike. Rough-hewn, folksy, direct, at the outset self-effacing, Taylor earned the respect and often the adulation of his military subordinates. Professionals such as U.S. Grant and George G. Meade admired him; Oliver O. Howard, later of Gettysburg fame, nearly worshiped him. The political electorate was allowed to see him only at his best. Military officers usually consider him nearly ideal for the job he did, his courage far outweighing the growing insubordination he later developed toward his political masters. Political historians, perhaps influenced by his later career as president, tend to downgrade him. This author admires him.

By contrast, the military competence of Winfield Scott strikes any student of this war as impressive. Not only did Scott visualize the Veracruz expedition—many did that—but he made it work. He calculated the strengths necessary, planned the logistics, approved details such as the designs of the surfboats, coordinated operations with the navy, fought one siege and five bitter battles, and occupied Mexico City within seven months after landing at Veracruz.

The obstacles overcome by Scott were formidable. His highest-ranking subordinate officers were, by fiat of a politically minded president, retreaded volunteers rather than regulars. His army was short of heavy artillery and land transportation. And his progress was halted at Jalapa, a few miles inland, when the enlistments of nearly all his volunteers expired. To cope with his inability to supply his army from Veracruz, Scott felt himself forced to cut off from his base of supply. Without wasting time by awaiting action from Washington, he boldly pushed on and despite some tactical mistakes took Mexico City by relying on the resources of the land. Fascinated military critics, the Duke of Wellington among them, had originally forecast disaster for Scott's campaign into Mexico, but later they heaped upon him lavish praise.

And yet Winfield Scott, who may well have been the most capable soldier this country has ever produced, has never received the credit that was his due. In a way the fame he deserved shared the fate of the war he fought, which was soon cast into the shadows. But his personality also contributed to his historical eclipse. His overbearing manner earned him enemies in important places. His ego often made him appear ridiculous to the press and the public; his talking down to his superiors made him insufferable. Foremost among such superiors was President Polk, who never tired of seeking ways to debase him.

Unfortunately, Scott's personality also divided his army, a flaw that marred the greatness of his campaign. Shortly after the occupation of Mexico City, three of Scott's principal officers were arrested for their unwarranted efforts to degrade him. It is difficult to visualize such personal disloyalty developing among the officers of Zachary Taylor.

So the two generals—Taylor and Scott—played different roles. Probably neither could have done so well in the role of the other.

. . .

President James Polk's reputation among historians and the public alike remained low for decades after he left office, partly because of his unappealing personality but also because of the prejudices of Northern historians, who associated him with the promotion of slavery. Those with a military background are often offended by the contempt that Polk showed for the military in general and for Scott in particular. And Polk's secrecy often gave cause for bitter resentment—especially the questionable way that he managed to present Congress with a "war in being." That incident, in which Polk deprived the Congress of any options regarding war or peace, frustrated many Whigs, whose party produced most of the historians for the next few decades. It also gave rise to the nickname "Polk the Mendacious."

In modern times, however, the growing enchantment with "strong," manipulative presidents has raised Polk's position in the eyes of some historians. Such fashions change, but whatever Polk's fate at the hands of the pundits, anyone must admire his resolve. Despite his guile and his consuming obsession with partisan politics, he was effective as an executive. Manifest Destiny was not Polk's invention, but he was its ideal agent.

The general relationship between Mexico and the United States is beyond the scope of this book. However, the effect of the Mexican War on that relationship has been my preoccupation in writing it. I hope that this effort will assist in an evaluation of the Mexican War as a significant event of history.

BACKGROUND

PRELUDE

〜〜〜

NOVEMBER 1844

I t was getting dark, but General Robert Armstrong decided to remain in his office a little past closing time that evening of Friday, November 15, 1844. Armstrong was postmaster of Nashville, Tennessee, and he usually made his way home by 6 P.M. This evening, however, he had a special reason to stay a little late: a courier just might be coming in with the latest news of the presidential election.

Armstrong was in a gloomy mood. A veteran of the War of 1812, a close friend and protégé of General Andrew Jackson, he had not yet digested the fact that Tennessee had just repudiated Jackson's favored presidential candidate, Democrat James K. Polk. This rebuff was a special blow, for Polk's candidacy held a special meaning for Old Hickory—Polk had always been a Jackson stalwart. Throughout his public life, during which he had been Speaker of the U.S. House of Representatives and governor of Tennessee, he had consistently been such a dedicated Jackson man that he was often referred to as "Young Hickory."

The disappointment from Polk's defeat in Tennessee was made more acute by the fact that the voting margin in Tennessee had been excruciatingly close, only 113 votes. But there would be no recount;

Jackson, the "Old Hero," would never live to see another election; an aged man, growing weaker daily at the Hermitage a dozen miles east of Nashville, he would die with his beloved Tennessee fallen from the graces of the Democratic party.

But the loss of Tennessee did not in itself decide the outcome of the election, close as it was. The results from nearly all the other states had come in, and the tally had been so evenly balanced between Polk and Whig candidate Henry Clay that the entire contest now hinged upon the voting in New York.

Armstrong's patience was rewarded. Just as he began to give up, he heard the clatter of hooves outside, and a messenger entered the room with a packet of mail. Soon Armstrong found what he wanted, and on opening the envelope he jumped jubilantly. Within minutes another horseman was thundering down the forty-mile road to Columbia, where Polk himself waited.

At dawn the Democratic nominee answered the door to receive the message: *"Glorious News!* New York is yours!" Polk put the message away, and walked about town all day without disclosing to a soul that he had been elected president of the United States.

The 1844 election had a special importance: it represented more than a choice of one candidate over another because it was also a referendum on the question of whether or not the Republic of Texas, which had seceded from Mexico eight years before, should be annexed to the United States. Taken one step further, the mandate for annexation assured serious trouble with Mexico.

As the voters of the United States were ushering James Polk into office, Antonio López de Santa Anna, president of Mexico, archenemy of Texas, rode unhappily into Mexico City, his mind beset by many problems. The Mexican people, even his own political backers, had become fed up with him; and now, at the end of the third year of his second term in office, he was about to be ousted once more. As was his wont when in power, Santa Anna had assumed increasing authority, indulging in excessively expensive ceremony, pursuing a hopeless war to regain the lost state of Texas, and otherwise generally neglecting his duties.

But extravagance, poor judgment, and laxity were not unusual in Santa Anna's conduct of affairs. His tenure of office was now in jeop-

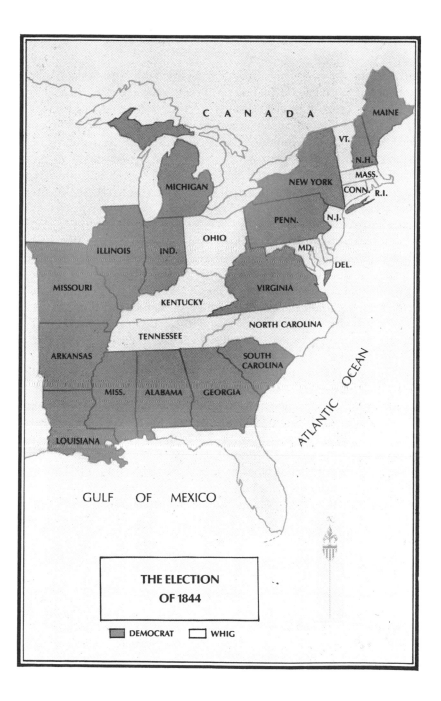

ardy because he had committed two unpardonable sins: he had failed to take care of the men who had put him in power and, more heinous in Mexican eyes, he had shown disrespect for the memory of his wife, Doña Inez de Santa Anna, who was much loved by the people. Doña Inez had died of pneumonia the previous August, and during her lingering illness, Santa Anna had selected her replacement, fifteen-year-old Doña Maria Dolores de Tosta. The people were infuriated because Santa Anna had married Doña Maria only six weeks after Inez's death.

As he arrived now in Mexico City, Santa Anna found the political situation even more serious than he had imagined. General Mariano Paredes, alternately an ally and a rival, had recently decided to defy Santa Anna and had marched with four thousand troops to Querétaro, in the mountains northwest of Mexico City. Santa Anna, still under-estimating his political problems despite the signs about him, decided to deal with Paredes by force. He left the capital on November 22, leaving his acting president, Valentín Canalizo, to deal with the political opposition.

Things went from bad to worse. Unable to corner Parades, Santa Anna now learned that his position in Mexico City had collapsed. The troops in the city rebelled against him, and soon impoverished mobs rose in wrath. They tore down a statue that Santa Anna had erected to himself and then broke into the Santa Anna Theater, causing the director hastily to rename it in order to save it. As a final insult, they broke into the sepulcher where Santa Anna had enshrined his amputated leg and dragged this honored part of his anatomy through the streets. Finally Congress deposed both Canalizo and Santa Anna, appointing the chief of council, General José Joaquín de Herrera, as acting president.

In early January 1845 Santa Anna, admitting defeat, decided to abandon his army and advised its members to submit to Herrera:

Companions in arms! With pride I sustained the loss of an important member of my body, lost gloriously in the service of our Native Land, as some of you bore witness; but that pride has turned to grief, sadness, and desperation. You should know that these mortal remains have been violently torn from the funeral urn, which was broken, and dragged through the public streets to make sport of them. . . . I know your astonishment and that you will be ashamed; you are right, such excesses were unknown among us. My friends! I am going to leave, obeying destiny. There in foreign lands I shall remember you. May you always be the support and ornament of our nation. . . . God be with you![1]

But Santa Anna still had hope of personal freedom. He set out with a small cavalry escort along the National Highway, hoping to make it safely to Veracruz, on the Gulf of Mexico, thence to exile. Soon, however, he concluded that his small bodyguard would never be able to protect him from the fury of the people, so as a last resort he disguised himself as a muleteer, keeping with him only three aides. Suspicious Indians appeared, and the aides disappeared in the woods. Santa Anna's wooden leg not only prevented his following them but also betrayed his identity. His life was saved only when the local priest began ringing the church bell. Religious devotions pacified the Indians, and they turned their prize over to the proper authorities.[2]

By mid-January 1845 Santa Anna had begun a period of imprisonment in the Castle of Perote, petitioning an unsympathetic Congress while being beset on all sides by creditors. Time calmed emotions back in Mexico City, however, and on June 3, 1845, the former dictator, accompanied by his distraught young wife and a small entourage, was allowed to sail from Veracruz to Havana, banished for life.

The sworn enemy of the annexation of Texas to the United States was gone. Santa Anna would no longer dictate Mexican policy.

THE AGE OF
SANTA ANNA

1810–1844

A ntonio López de Santa Anna has been called "the enigma who
once was Mexico." That appellation is no exaggeration, for
the history of Mexico, beginning with independence from
Spain (1821) to 1844 was inextricably tied to the ups and downs of
Santa Anna's career. It would be as difficult to understand Mexico
without Santa Anna during those years as it would be to comprehend
the France of 1796 to 1815 without Napoleon. Nevertheless, the career
of Santa Anna is difficult to follow because of its very eventfulness. It
seems as if this restless, energetic man was involved in a revolution of
some kind almost annually during his early years, and once he had
become the central figure in Mexico he seldom exercised his political
power for any great length of time, and it is possible here only to skim
over the highlights.

Santa Anna has been reviled by many, particularly Mexicans who
decry the fate that befell their country during the first half of the
nineteenth century. Nevertheless, it is difficult to find a man who could
have represented his country better than he did, given the state of
confusion and poverty besetting that unhappy land at the time. Others
more wise lacked his ability to move the masses. And no other leader
possessed the energy and imagination that Santa Anna exhibited. He

was, with all his faults, the best leader that Mexico could produce at that time.

To be sure, Santa Anna's moral flaws were glaring. He was a consummate opportunist who never hesitated to manipulate ignorant masses through his personal magnetism to further his own advantage. A zealous nationalist, his dedication to the glories of Mexico never wavered, but at the same time he was unstable, greedy, and vainglorious.

Santa Anna has been pictured as aristocratic, but in fact he was not. The pomp and panoply he loved to indulge in were the products of the attitudes he learned early in the Spanish army. By nature, he was a populist, and many of his pleasures, such as cockfighting, carousing, and openly womanizing, were attributes of the lower rather than of the more discreet aristocratic classes.

Unfortunately—and this was one of his major deficiencies—Santa Anna was essentially untrained for the responsibilities that would come to him in his spectacular career. He had no formal military schooling, having learned his trade as an apprentice, a product of the Spanish officer class. Santa Anna's career was a symptom, not a cause, of his country's woes.

Santa Anna grew up in Jalapa, a pleasant little city near Veracruz. Nestling in the eastern spur of the Sierra Madre, Jalapa was spared from the heat and disease that prevailed in the lowlands along the Gulf of Mexico. Young Antonio's father was a respected mortgage broker in Veracruz, and the family were native-born Mexicans of mostly but not exclusively Spanish descent.

The atmosphere in Mexico in the early nineteenth century was one of unrest. The privileges exercised by the Roman Catholic Church and the Mexican army were repressive, and the people were destitute; rumblings of rebellion against the Spanish crown, on which this situation was blamed, were therefore becoming audible. The Spanish military force maintaining order in Mexico consisted almost entirely of native Mexicans, with only a few Spanish officers; it would welcome restless, ambitious lads like Santa Anna. With his father's unwilling help, therefore, Antonio López de Santa Anna wangled a commission as a cadet in the Spanish army in 1810 and was assigned to the Spanish regiment that garrisoned Veracruz. He was sixteen years of age.

Santa Anna's military career began, coincidentally, with the first real

Mexican uprising against Spanish authority, that of Miguel Hidalgo y Costilla, and his regiment was soon sent to the field to help suppress the Hidalgo rebellion. By the end of 1813, Santa Anna, nineteen years old, had been exposed to active fighting, in which he had comported himself well. He had participated in the subjugation of the first waves of American immigrants to Texas, who were already defying Spanish authority.[1]

The impressions that this first campaign made on the young Santa Anna were critical. As his biographer Wilfrid H. Calcott put it,

> The whole campaign built up in the mind of Santa Anna . . . two illusions that were to cost him dearly at a later date. One of these was that the way to handle Texas rebels was by terrorization, and the other was that the said rebels were ineffective fighters and could easily be defeated by Mexican troops.[2]

At this point Santa Anna ran into difficulty. He had been decorated for bravery in the San Antonio campaign, but he was also convicted of embezzling three hundred pesos from the unit mess. For a while his career hung in the balance, and charges were dropped only after the Spanish authorities had sold all of his personal possessions to repay the remainder of his debt.

Mexico achieved final independence from Spain in 1821. This revolution, unlike those led by Hidalgo and José María Morelos (both put down brutally), was successful because it stemmed not from the people but from the dissatisfaction of military commanders, who, like their troops, were Mexican by birth. A senior Spanish commander, Agustín de Iturbide, simply renounced his allegiance to Spain and announced the Plan of Iguala, Mexico's declaration of independence. When he was joined by Vicente Guerrero, a true revolutionary rebel, the devastating war of independence was over.

At this time Santa Anna was twenty-six years of age and at the head of a sizable command. His early training, however, had made him a royalist, and he was at first slow to join the revolutionaries, but when he learned that a substantial rebel force was approaching his own weaker contingent, Santa Anna turned coat instantly, and without a qualm.

The year 1829, in which Santa Anna was thirty-five years of age, saw his entry on the center stage of Mexican politics. As it happened, his great opportunity was brought on by an action of Spain. Ever since 1821 King Ferdinand VII had kept a force in Cuba. In July, when President Vicente Guerrero passed a law expelling all Spaniards from Mexico, Ferdinand sent General Isidro Barradas, with three thousand men, to seize Tampico. Alarmed, President Guerrero called on Santa Anna to reduce the foothold that Barradas had established, but, now suspicious of his former comrade's ambitions, he provided Santa Anna with nothing in the way of troops or supplies. Santa Anna, however, rose to the occasion. Drawing entirely on the resources of his home state of Veracruz, he raised an army of two thousand men and armed them by confiscating all weapons in the city and by forcing loans from local merchants. He commandeered five ships, loaded up his force, and arrived at Tampico by sea on August 20, 1829.

The following campaign was no military classic, but, like the dog that can walk upright on his hind legs, it was remarkable because it happened at all. And it succeeded; by the end of three weeks the Spanish commander had surrendered, his army bottled up in the city, his troops starving and suffering from fever.* In exchange for being allowed to depart for Cuba, Barradas agreed to recognize the independence of Mexico in the name of Spain.[3]

Santa Anna was now hailed as a hero, and the nation paid him lavish homage. Veracruz and Mexico City both showered him with expensive gifts; the Congress conferred upon him the title the Country's Benefactor; and Tampico was (temporarily, as it turned out) renamed Santa Anna de Tamaulipas.

President Guerrero, however, was unswayed by the enthusiasm of the crowd. Though of necessity he participated in publicly honoring Santa Anna, he remarked in private that he would "have to hang him yet."[4] Denied a position in the Guerrero administration, a disappointed Santa Anna retired to his hacienda near Veracruz. But by 1833, as the result of elaborate machinations, Santa Anna was elected president of Mexico.

---

*The yellow fever, or *vómito*, at Veracruz was a scourge respected by all. The natives had developed an immunity to it, but outsiders were well advised to avoid the region during its season.

. . .

Santa Anna did not attend his own inauguration. He pleaded ill health and deputized his vice president, Valentín Gómez Farías, to take the oath for him. Nor did he go to Mexico City after the ceremony, but stayed at his ranch near Veracruz and allowed Gómez Farias to run the routine business of government as acting president.

Santa Anna's alliance with the very liberal Gómez Farías proved a disaster. The two men had nothing in common; Santa Anna owed his position to the army, but Gómez Farías, jokingly referred to as Gómez Furioso, was dedicated to reducing the Army's—and the Church's—privileges. One of Gómez Farías's acts had lasting and dire effects on Mexico's future. Unwisely he "secularized" the Spanish church missions along the coast of Upper California. The missions virtually disappeared, and that tie between California and the mother country was broken.

Finally, Santa Anna concluded that Gómez Farías had gone too far. He reassumed office and sent Gómez Farías into exile—to Texas.*

By December 1834 Santa Anna was at the peak of his powers. He had closed down the Congress and had arranged to be officially declared dictator,† thereby offending liberals in Mexico, the United States, and elsewhere.

The next year Santa Anna went even further, replacing the established Constitution of 1824 with the Seven Laws, which (a) abolished the existing states of Mexico in favor of administrative "departments"; (b) set the term of the president at eight years; and (c) limited the franchise to a privileged few. To the average Mexican these measures hardly mattered, but they did matter to the inhabitants of previously self-governing areas far from Mexico City. Foremost among such citizens were the twenty thousand Americans who had moved into Texas during the preceding few years. Those people cared very much.‡

. . .

*Dr. Guadalupe Jiminez-Codinach, of the Library of Congress, says that no hard feelings resulted, that Gómez Farías and Santa Anna met personally before the former's departure.
†The term "dictator" was official. The title had been carried by Simón Bolívar in Venezuela years before. Its powers fell far short of those we associate with dictators in the twentieth century.
‡The term "Texan" will hereafter apply to the American immigrants new to the region.

Texas, with its overwhelmingly American population, would probably
have broken loose from Mexico regardless of the events of 1835. Too
many differences in heritage, culture, and religion separated these
people from the rest of the Mexican nation. Furthermore, these new
Texans were keenly aware that a succession of United States presidents
had made overtures, in one form or another, to buy Texas from Mexico
and they were confident that in the end they would receive assistance
from the United States. But those expectations were not for the near
future; Santa Anna's new restrictions made their disaffection acute.
The law against slavery would now be enforced for the first time, as
would taxes, including duties on goods imported from the United
States. Their very government, the State of Coahuila-Texas, would
cease to exist as a self-governing entity. Such changes, particularly the
practical prohibition of slavery, they found intolerable.

A move for Texan independence from Mexico began in Velasco in
late 1835, led by the legendary Sam Houston. It was heartily encouraged by two prominent radicals from Mexico City (one of whom was
Gómez Farías). On November 3 of that year Texas declared independence. In San Antonio insurgent militiamen forced a Mexican army to
evacuate. The movement was gaining momentum.

Santa Anna now decided to punish the rebels personally. He gathered an army at San Luis Potosí, the area from which invasions of Texas
were usually organized and outfitted, and, with six thousand men,
marched north in early January 1836. So confident was he that he
brought along some 2,500 women and children, colonists to be settled
after he had dispersed the rebels. And he would deal with American
support: he would continue his march, he declaimed, and raise the
Mexican flag over the Capitol in Washington.*

Santa Anna's abortive campaign into Texas, the subject of
volumes, included the storming of the Alamo, in San Antonio, and
the annihilation of all its defenders. From that massacre, which occurred on March 6, 1836, came the famous rallying cry for Sam
Houston's dispirited rebels "Remember the Alamo!" The massacre at
Goliad a few days later was actually the greater outrage: one of Santa
Anna's generals coolly and deliberately executed 350 rebel prisoners

*Santa Anna may not have noticed that the United States government always observed
neutrality. He was aware, however, that the American people unabashedly supported the rebels.

there. Nevertheless, it was the name Alamo that most stirred the rebels' blood.*

The battle of San Jacinto, on April 21, 1836, established Texan independence. It was a brutal episode; Houston's eight hundred Texans caught Santa Anna's inept army taking a siesta, and they visited bloodthirsty revenge on the Mexicans, killing many more than was necessary.[5] After the battle, however, Houston treated Santa Anna with the considerations due his rank as president of Mexico, and though Santa Anna was put in chains for nearly two months in Houston's absence, he was finally allowed to leave Texas—by way of Washington.

President Andrew Jackson received him courteously, as a head of state, on January 19, 1837. While Santa Anna was Jackson's guest in Washington the two men discussed the status of Texas. Their talks ran into difficulties, however, when Jackson insisted on Mexican recognition of Texas as an independent country. The conversations ended on an indefinite note, and Jackson sent Santa Anna home to Veracruz with a United States naval escort.†

Before leaving Texas, Santa Anna had been forced to sign the "treaty" of Velasco, which recognized Texan independence. That agreement, though disallowed by the new authorities in Mexico, was generally recognized abroad, although the United States did not do so until the end of Jackson's term of office. From then on, even though Mexican raids terrorized the Texan settlers along the border, the prospect of actual reconquest was remote.

On arrival back in Mexico, Santa Anna, deposed, underwent three years in the political wilderness. But that period was not devoid of incident. In 1838 Santa Anna, by public acclaim, was temporarily recalled to expel the French, who had occupied Veracruz on a silly pretext. Though the French were soon ousted, Santa Anna suffered a severe wound in the fighting: his left leg below the knee was torn by a shell and had to be amputated. The surgeons did a poor job and two

---

*Santa Anna claimed that his general José Urrea was acting within a law, promulgated by Spain in 1814, which declared that all persons crossing the borders into Texas were to be considered as "pirates." Even Houston acknowledged the legality of Santa Anna's brutalities.

†Robert V. Remini, "Texas Must Be Ours," *American Heritage*, February–March 1986, pp. 45–46.

inches of bone were left protruding. Santa Anna was to live in pain for the rest of his life.

Despite his chronic pain, Santa Anna began planning his return to the presidency. In 1841 he succeeded in a coup remarkable for its speed —it took only twelve days. Santa Anna's main allies, Mariano Paredes and Gabriel Valencia, would later be counted among his bitterest domestic enemies.

During his second presidency, from 1841 to 1844, Santa Anna indulged in a veritable orgy of personal aggrandizement, giving elaborate state dinners with a sea of ornate uniforms. A large body of impressive cavalry accompanied the dictator whenever he left the palace. The National Theater was renamed after him, and a large bronze statue portrayed the Hero, a long finger pointed northward toward Texas (or the Mint, as cynics were prone to point out). And Santa Anna personally supervised the disinterment of his severed leg from its resting place at his ranch and then its relocation to an urn atop a stone column in the Cemetery of Santa Paula.

Despite such preoccupations, Santa Anna was able to achieve some military successes. He subdued the rebellious peoples of Yucatán and Tabasco, and was able to keep the Texans off-balance. In the fall of 1842 he sent a onetime Napoleonic officer, General Adrian Woll, in a raid against San Antonio. When the Texans attempted to retaliate against Santa Fe, Santa Anna's forces captured the entire expedition, imprisoning most of the men in the formidable Castle of Perote. And when more Texans were captured in an abortive raid on the Rio Grande village of Mier, Santa Anna treated them cruelly until he received a request for leniency from the aged Andrew Jackson; he relented in grateful recognition of the courtesies Jackson had rendered him six years earlier in Washington.

Santa Anna's worst mistake as president was to continue the Texas border war. The incursions, killings, and atrocities on both sides were lavishly reported in the United States—always from the Texan viewpoint. This constant flow of war news kept the people of the United States militantly sympathetic to their blood relations in Texas. Many Americans, most of them perhaps, were no longer in any mood to allow the rights of Mexico to have any influence upon the ethics of United States policy.

When Santa Anna was again removed from office, in late 1844, he left a legacy of a nearly impossible situation to his successor, President José Joaquín Herrera.

ANNEXATION!

❦ ❧

NOVEMBER 1844–JULY 1845

With the 1844 presidential election over, the incumbent president John Tyler realized that he still had four months left in office. Rather than simply wait out his time, Tyler resolved that he would continue his efforts, begun in early 1844, toward the annexation of Texas. Achievement of this goal would be the apotheosis of a difficult four years as president.

Many problems, however, lay ahead, not the least of which was the lack of precedent; the United States had never before annexed an independent nation. A treaty of annexation that Tyler had signed with Texan representatives earlier in that year had been rejected by the Senate in June; would it now suffice to make an offer to Texas by simply passing a law?

Aside from the choice of a vehicle, certain practical questions had to be answered, matters such as the future status of Texas once it was incorporated into the Union. Would the former independent nation come in as a territory? A state? Two states? Five states? Slave or free? Even the boundaries of the lands the United States would claim as rightfully Texan remained in doubt.

Though it had been generally assumed that these questions would lie unanswered until Polk's inauguration, Tyler's resolve to meet them immediately met with general approval. The annexation prospect was popular, and the election of 1844 had given it a mandate. Reasonable men were willing to work with Tyler, regardless of how generally unpopular he had been while in office. And political leaders of both parties recognized that the cause of annexation might be irreparably damaged by a delay of four months. The Texans might even lose interest.

Tyler seized the initiative. He began by inflaming American public opinion against Mexico, to which end he appointed an obvious troublemaker as minister to that country in the late fall of 1844. Wilson Shannon, former governor of Ohio, chauvinist and boor, soon clashed with Mexican foreign minister Manuel Crescendio Rejon, a liberal and onetime friend of the United States. Within a month of Shannon's arrival in Mexico City a war of words had begun raging between him and Rejon. Shannon embellished truculent messages from Calhoun, in which the secretary of state castigated Mexico for her "savage ferocity" in the current clashes on the Texan border. Rejon's replies, equally insulting toward the United States, were gleefully forwarded by Shannon to Washington. Calhoun and Tyler were delighted, and the President sent a special message to Congress, appending the Shannon-Rejon correspondence.

At the same time, Tyler sought an emissary to Texas who would promote the best feelings there toward the United States. He found his man in Andrew Jackson ("Jack") Donelson, Old Hickory's nephew and personal aide but one who had earned stature in his own right and was a personal friend of both Polk and Texan President Sam Houston. Donelson accepted the post and by early December 1844 had reached the log-cabin town of Washington-on-the-Brazos, capital of Texas, population five thousand.

On arrival Donelson found the political situation in Texas complicated by the fact that President Sam Houston and his successor, Anson Jones, were both ambivalent about giving up Texas sovereignty. The people, however, though hurt by the senatorial rejection of the annexation treaty in June, were still anxious to join the Union in order to receive protection against Mexico.[1]

Interest in the annexation question was not confined to the Western Hemisphere. The British, always reluctant to see the power of the United States augmented, were watching developments closely, hope-

ful of maintaining Texas as an independent nation. Their capable
chargé d'affaires, Captain Charles Eliot, RN, was sowing the seeds of
confusion among Texans with considerable success.

So effective were Eliot's efforts, at least as the situation appeared to
Donelson, that the American chargé soon sent an urgent message to
Washington. "Let us get annexation," he urged, "on any terms we
can."[2]

Actually, President Tyler, in Washington, was vigorously pushing annexation, encouraged by signs of sympathy in the Northern press.* But
despite favorable national sentiment, passage of specific legislation
would face difficulties in Congress. Any action, for example, would
have to be "politically neutral," since the Democrats controlled the
House of Representatives and the Whigs controlled the Senate. Another problem was slavery.

The first move came when the House passed a measure, sponsored
by Whig Congressman Melton Brown, that called for Texas to be
annexed as a state and for slavery to be forbidden only in the area that
lay north of the Missouri Compromise line. Conveniently, the measure
ignored critical matters such as future Texas boundaries and assumption of Texan debts. Then the Senate passed a bill sponsored by Senator
Thomas Hart Benton that merely appropriated $100,000 to finance a
new negotiation with Texas. Each body now had its own version.

The matter might have died there, but in early February 1845
President-elect James Polk arrived in Washington for his inauguration
and he gave renewed impetus to the issue. Polk maintained a pleasant,
detached manner,[3] but he had a serious purpose, as he wanted annexation settled before he took office. He suggested a compromise to solve
the impasse: Why not let the President make the choice between the
two bills when they were passed together and sent for his approval?

Polk's idea gained many converts, typical of whom was Senator

---

*The New York *Courier and Enquirer* showed the set of the wind by going over to the
administration side. The *Pennsylvanian* remarked: "We are just beginning to awake to the vitality
of the Texas question," that is to say, the loss of a market for Northern manufacturers which the
possession or control of that country by England would entail. At the same time, many still
unfriendly to the measure, perceiving that it was almost certain to be carried through, allowed
themselves to be borne along passively by the rising tide.

William Allen of Ohio, a key member of the Committee on Foreign Relations. So stirring was Allen in supporting the compromise that his colleague Robert Walker shed tears at his performance. Allen's eloquence was given credit for accelerating the passage of the resolution.[4] On the evening of February 27, 1845, the Benton-Brown compromise for annexation passed the Senate by the narrow margin of 27 to 25.

Four days now remained before the end of the Tyler administration, and the work had been done. When the new president was inaugurated, he could choose which of the versions—Brown's or Benton's—should be sent to Texas. All could now turn their heads to the inauguration ceremonies in the days ahead.

All but President Tyler, that is. On Sunday, March 2, Tyler assembled his cabinet to consider whether or not he, with two more days as president, should send the signed resolution to Texas. What did Polk think? To find out, Tyler sent Secretary of State John C. Calhoun to Polk's lodging. Polk refused to answer; he would not be a party to the decision.

On his last evening in office, March 3, 1845, President John Tyler sent a dispatch to Donelson in Texas: the Texans were to be offered annexation to the Union as a single state, the territory north of the Missouri Compromise line to be free of slavery—the House plan.

Tyler's administration was going out of office on a high note. But would Texas now accept his offer? What would Mexico do?

Tyler's successor, James Knox Polk, managed to complicate the issue on his inauguration day by reviving the quarrel between the United States and Britain over Oregon. At midmorning on March 4, 1845, Polk stepped out from the lobby of the Coleman Hotel into a driving rain, climbed into President John Tyler's open carriage, took his seat on Tyler's left, and sat back as the parade slopped down the muddy Pennsylvania Avenue for the rest of the mile to the Capitol. Ten soggy companies of infantry and cavalry provided the escort; the street was lined with drenched spectators. At the Capitol, Polk stood still in the Senate chamber while Vice President George M. Dallas was speedily given his oath of office. Then he led the presidential party out on the specially constructed platform above the East Steps.

The stormy weather did little to dampen the spirits of those who, as at other inaugurations, were happy to set aside party differences for a day in order to share in the new President's victory.

Polk's inauguration address was triumphant but moderate, determined but conciliatory to political enemies. It was well received, though delivered to a "large assembly of umbrellas," as seen by an embittered John Quincy Adams,[5] former president and now representative from Massachusetts.

Polk's assertion that he had been chosen "without solicitation on my part" was perhaps disingenuous, but his personal manner was ingratiating. Most important, he put the world on notice that he subscribed to the expansionist views of the day. He asserted that annexation of Texas would be merely a rectification of the mistake that had been committed in 1819, when the United States had ceded Texas to Spain in exchange for Florida. He further declared annexation to be "a matter between Texas and the United States alone"—an obvious warning to Britain to keep her hands off.

Polk then surprised the audience. He turned to the territory of Oregon, jointly occupied by Britain and the United States, and, ignoring the negotiations then in progress over its boundaries, declared, "Our title to the country of Oregon is "clear and unquestionable." Polk had opened a Pandora's box.

Polk the President would conduct himself much as had Polk the politician. His habits of hard work, attention to detail, indirection, and secrecy had brought him this far, so why change? The end result would prove a mixed blessing, however, because Polk trusted nobody, thus forfeiting any claim for other people to trust him. His secrecy would later isolate him and cost him the public support he would so gravely need.

On the other hand, Polk came to office with firm ideas about what he wanted to accomplish. One day, according to his secretary of the navy, the historian George Bancroft, he outlined the objectives he hoped to achieve during the next four years: the settlement of the Oregon question with Great Britain; the acquisition of California and a large district on the coast; the reduction of the tariff to a revenue basis; and the complete and permanent establishment of an independent Treasury.[6] Bancroft recorded this list of objectives many years after the fact, a circumstance that may account for the omission of Texas. But if Bancroft's memory was good, Polk may have considered that question settled, because to all intents and purposes it was.

Nevertheless, the reaction of Mexico was predictably hostile. Spurred by Tyler's message to Texas the evening before, General Juan N. Almonte, the Mexican minister, promptly delivered a belligerent note to the State Department and demanded his passports. This meant that diplomatic relations between Mexico and the United States were severed.

Almonte's action came as no surprise, as his government had long since warned that it would not stand for annexation. In fact, in 1843 Santa Anna had threatened war, not merely the breaking of diplomatic ties.* Polk, however, still hoped for reconciliation. He knew that four months earlier Santa Anna had been deposed, and hoped the new Herrera regime might prove to be reasonable.

So Polk set to work. As a concession to Mexican feeling, he recalled the objectionable Wilson Shannon as minister to Mexico City and made a point of chiding him in public for the insulting tone of his letters to Rejon and the Mexican government. At the same time Polk sent an emissary, William S. Parrott, who was familiar with Mexico and spoke Spanish fluently, to report on the prevailing attitudes in Mexico City. At the moment Polk could do no more.

During the last days of April 1845 President Polk's attention began to be diverted from the Mexican scene by British reaction to his inaugural address. That reaction had been strong; Prime Minister Sir Robert Peel had responded by sending a frigate to Oregon, but even then the British political opposition was railing against him for being too "reasonable." Even the peace-loving Lord Aberdeen, the foreign secretary, feared that Polk's declaration might "finally lead to War itself."[7] Polk was, in fact, risking two wars—one in the Northwest with Britain and the other in the Southwest with Mexico.

Polk probably did not expect such a strong reaction in Britain. Actually, the statement in his address had been included as a bow to Northern Democrats who had insisted on the unrealistic slogan "Fifty-

---

*"My country is resolved to declare war as soon as it receives information of such an act," said Foreign Minister Bocanagra to the American minister in Mexico, Waddy Thompson, August 23, 1843. Justin Smith, *The War with Mexico,* vol I, p. 84.

four Forty or Fight" during the presidential campaign. But Polk now resolved to stand firm, and he wrote his mentor Andrew Jackson that his position would be maintained "firmly, boldly, but prudently" and he would "not recede" from it.

Jackson approved. The British were simply rattling their drums, he answered, "to alarm us . . . and give strength to the traitors in our country." He warned, "No temporizing with Britain now. . . . England with all her boast dare not go to war."[8] Jackson was adamant on the issue; Britain already possessed Canada, and if permitted to reenter the continent through Texas, he feared—farfetched as that prospect may seem today—that the United States would have to fight to prevent a linkup between British forces in Texas and Canada. But Jackson was also right that economic considerations would make it nearly impossible for Britain to fight at that time. So he insisted that Polk take a strong hand.[9]

But behind the scenes, negotiations over the Oregon boundary remained very much alive, based on the long-standing United States proposal for a settlement extending the line already established from Lake of the Woods, Minnesota, to the Rockies (the 49th parallel of latitude). The only major bone of contention remaining had to do with the disposition of Vancouver Island, in the Strait of San Juan. Other questions, such as navigation rights on the Columbia River, were minor.

Sir Robert Peel's government, fortunately, was disposed to a settlement along the lines of those being discussed in the continuing negotiations. American settlers from the Willamette Valley in Oregon, Peel realized, were daily pouring into the disputed territory, so time was not on Britain's side. So despite the noise in public, the new American minister in London, Louis McLane, was soon talking constructively with Aberdeen. Progress was made when McLane suggested that the United States might be willing to concede all of Vancouver Island.

One snag was encountered, however, when the British minister to Washington, Lord Packenham, inserted himself. When the secretary of state, James Buchanan, handed him a copy of the same proposal that Aberdeen was discussing in London, Packenham rejected it on his own volition, flavoring his note with some caustic comments. It was now mid-July and the tensions were far from receding.

On March 29, 1845, Texan President Anson Jones, still personally ambivalent about annexation, sent a remarkable message to Mexican President José Joaquín Herrera suggesting that, in exchange for Mexican recognition of independence, Texas would be willing to engage that she would not "annex herself or become subject to any country whatsoever."[10]

The British chargé, Sir Charles Eliot, had been the instigator, at the behest of Lord Aberdeen. At the time of the visit Eliot was aware of the "Brown proposal," passed in Washington by the House of Representatives, and the "Benton proposal," by the Senate. Eliot did not know as yet that President Tyler had forwarded the House version (Brown's) to Donelson for presentation to the Texans.

Jones was aware that public opinion in Texas favored annexation but was equally conscious that public opinion could change. So he approved the message to President Herrera on the condition that Eliot himself would be the courier. A tempting proposal from Herrera would allow Jones to give the Texan people a choice: annexation to the United States or Mexican recognition of their independence.

After six months in Texas, Donelson had concluded that the population was overwhelmingly favorable toward the United States proposal, and Polk's private agents, sent to double-check on Donelson, were sending back the same optimistic reports.*

Polk, however, seems by his actions to have desired not only the annexation of Texas but trouble with Mexico as well. That trouble arrived in the form of an American flotilla, commanded by Commodore Robert F. Stockton, who had been authorized to remain at Galveston long enough to "make himself acquainted with the dispositions of the people of Texas toward the United States and Mexico." Actually Stockton was there to do much more.

The flotilla was an impressive formation; its flagship was the vaunted USS *Princeton,* the first propeller-driven warship ever constructed. And its commodore was no ordinary naval officer. Robert F. Stockton, a businessman of wealth and influence, the grandson of a signer of the

*One was Archibald Yell, former governor of Arkansas. The other was Charles A. Wickliffe, a Whig.

Declaration of Independence, a zealous patriot, and a strong supporter of Polk in the recent election, had cut a wide swath in Washington society, lavishly entertaining the capital's elite aboard ship at his own expense. Being a man of influence, his position had been unaffected by the explosion of a gun aboard the *Princeton* in February 1844. President Tyler had been present, and both the secretary of state, Abel P. Upshur, and the secretary of the navy, Thomas W. Gilmer, had been killed. The subsequent court of inquiry had complimented Stockton for his "prudence and loftiest of motives."

Stockton's flotilla arrived early in May 1845, and the people of Galveston immediately began scurrying around to prepare a grand ball in his honor. While they were so engaged, Stockton sent an agent ashore to determine the political attitude of the people. When the agent reported that seven-eighths of the Texans favored annexation, Stockton sent an urgent message to Navy Secretary Bancroft warning that the Mexicans were planning to occupy valuable land on the Texan bank of the Rio Grande. Donelson was away, Stockton went on, and Texan President Anson Jones could not be trusted; therefore he would take matters in his own hands.

And so he did. Within days Stockton had made contact with Major General Sidney Sherman, the adjutant general of Texas; he soon reported that Sherman had raised three thousand men, and that "R.F. Stockton Esq. will supply them in a private way with provisions & ammunition."

Soon an alarmed Donelson wrote to Buchanan rebutting Stockton's reports of a Mexican threat and remonstrated with Stockton himself.

Even after receiving Donelson's stern warnings, Commodore Stockton still seemed bent on initiating hostilities between Texas and Mexico. And President Anson Jones was unable to stop General Sherman from publicly advocating a move by his forces, supported by Stockton's guns, against the Mexican town of Matamoros at the mouth of the Rio Grande. Then, during a three-day conference, Stockton's representative admitted that President Polk himself was interested in stirring up hostilities.[11]

Jones's dilemma was soon resolved, however. On May 30 Charles Eliot returned from Mexico City with a confirmed offer from the Herrera government to recognize Texas provided that Texas would never join any other country. That offer erased Texan nightmares of a Mexican invasion for the moment and permitted the people to choose freely between two options: Accept Mexican recognition or accept annexation to the United States.

The Texans had no reservations. In late June Stockton's flotilla set sail for the United States carrying good news. The Texas Congress had accepted the United States offer of statehood by unanimous vote. Quick ratification by the Texas convention was inevitable.

CONFRONTATION

OLD ZACK

❧⊱ ⊰❧

SUMMER 1845–DECEMBER 1845

Brevet Brigadier General Zachary Taylor,* colonel of the 6th Infantry, U.S. Army, was unlikely material for building a national hero. He was an old soldier by the standards of the day, nearly sixty-one years of age, deliberate and unpolished in manner. Long service in every American war since 1812 had dulled whatever appetite he had ever had for fighting, and somehow he had been able through the years to combine soldiering with his lifelong love of farming. His father, a planter, had moved from Virginia to a ten-thousand-acre plantation in Kentucky the year after Zachary's birth. The son, even while in the army, had purchased one plantation in Louisiana and another in Mississippi.

But despite his homely ways, Taylor had lived a relatively comfortable life between wars, bringing his family and his household furniture with him. After the Seminole (Florida) War in 1840, in which he had earned his brevet promotion to brigadier general, Taylor had

---

*Taylor's "brevet" rank was an honorary title. On the rolls, and for pay purposes, he was a colonel. But since positions exceeded the ranks that Congress was willing to authorize, officers were often assigned, by "direction of the President," to positions according to their brevet rank. All officers were customarily addressed according to their brevet rank, if they held one. The system was a source of much confusion and occasional dispute.

been looking forward to retiring to one of his plantations. It is not surprising that such a practical man should develop a certain immunity to frantic instructions from Washington, as well as a healthy skepticism toward the wild rumors that always permeate armies in the field.

But these characteristics were only one side of Taylor's makeup. In battle he had always been a tower of strength. In 1812, as a captain, he had earned a brevet to major, the first such honor ever bestowed in the army. His record had been creditable in the Black Hawk War and his recent brevet, in the Seminole War, had been awarded for leading 1,100 men through swamp water up to the waist, achieving a surprise victory. Andrew Jackson himself had advised President-elect James Polk that in case of war with the British over Canada, Taylor should be the man to command the American army in the field. Relaxed Taylor may have appeared, even a little bored, but he was still quite fit for arduous duty.

In early June 1845, as Texans were choosing annexation, Zack Taylor was ordered to mass two thousand troops at Fort Jesup, Louisiana— just across the Sabine River from Texas. This Army of Observation comprised about one-quarter of the fighting power of the U.S. Army in 1845. Clearly something was in the air.

Actually, it would have required no genius to deduce the general outlines of Taylor's prospective mission. Nearly three months had passed since President Tyler had sent his annexation offer to Texas, and Taylor's presence was a response to the Texan demand for U.S. protection pending the Texans' acceptance of the annexation proposal. Only the specific future employment of Taylor's army was in question.

A letter order from Secretary of War William L. Marcy, written on May 28, alerted Taylor for action against Mexico. When the Texans accepted the proffered terms of annexation, which the president expected them to do soon, they would then be regarded as "entitled from this government to defence and protection from foreign invasion and Indian incursions." The troops under Taylor's command, therefore, were to be "placed and kept in readiness to perform this duty. . . ."[1]

Without undue haste, Old Zack, also known among his men as Old Rough and Ready, began preparations for a march into Texas. At the moment of receiving that preparatory order, Taylor's small force in-

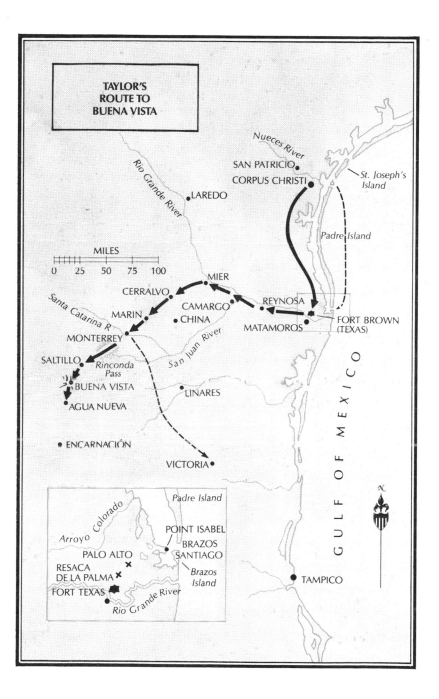

TAYLOR'S
ROUTE TO
BUENA VISTA

Nueces River

SAN PATRICIO
CORPUS CHRISTI

St. Joseph's
Island

Rio Grande River

LAREDO

Padre Island

MILES

0   25   50   75   100

MIER

CERRALVO

CAMARGO
CHINA

REYNOSA

Santa Catarina R

MARIN

MATAMOROS

FORT BROWN
(TEXAS)

MONTERREY

San Juan River

SALTILLO

Rinconda
Pass

BUENA VISTA

AGUA NUEVA

LINARES

ENCARNACIÓN

VICTORIA

GULF OF MEXICO

Padre Island

Colorado

POINT ISABEL

Arroyo

BRAZOS
SANTIAGO

PALO ALTO

RESACA
DE LA PALMA

Brazos
Island

FORT TEXAS

Rio Grande River

TAMPICO

N

cluded two of the army's eight infantry regiments—the 3rd and 4th—and the bulk of one of its two regiments of dragoons, the 2d. (Dragoons were mounted infantry, who served the role of cavalry when on horseback and of infantry when afoot.)

The order promised reinforcement, as it granted Taylor authority to draw upon the state governors for additional forces. That power, to be sure, was nearly meaningless, for only Louisiana could provide any reinforcements in a reasonable time, but Polk and Marcy were sending more regiments from the northern and western frontiers, and in the next few months Taylor's Army of Occupation—as the force had been renamed—would come to include almost the entire regular establishment.

In mid-June 1845, spurred on by Stockton's exaggerated reports, Secretary of War Marcy ordered Taylor to move down the Sabine River or to some other point ". . . as may be most convenient for an embarkation at the proper time for the Western frontier of Texas." Taylor was not to make a landing until certain that the Texas convention, scheduled for July 4, had accepted the terms of annexation—or "until you receive instructions from Mr. Donelson."[2]

By directing Taylor to be guided by Donelson's instructions, Polk was violating established governmental procedure by subjecting a general, a field commander, to the directions of a chargé d'affaires, a member of another department of government. Army General-in-Chief Winfield Scott, in Washington, flew into a rage when he saw that order but could do nothing about it. Donelson, a West Pointer himself, saved the situation. Recognizing its delicacy, he tactfully consulted Taylor rather than trying to direct him.

Taylor, who was probably far less excited over the gaffe than Scott, willingly accepted Donelson's advice to move at once, but only after the Texas Congress had overwhelmingly voted for annexation in mid-June. The two men then conferred and agreed that the Mexican town of Corpus Christi, just across the mouth of the Nueces River, should be Taylor's logical destination. Taylor decided to send the 3d and 4th infantry regiments by water, from New Orleans, but to oblige Donelson's desire for a show of force in the Texas interior, he sent the 2d Dragoons overland by way of San Antonio. A voyage on the sea would be hard on the dragoons' horses, anyway.

In early July Taylor's 3d Infantry, its band playing, marched through the streets of New Orleans to board the steamboat *Alabama*. The rest of the army—the 4th Infantry, the artillery, and supporting troops—would follow on the slower sailing vessels. After an uneventful voyage of about three weeks, Taylor's vanguard arrived at Aransas Bay in Texas on July 25, 1845, Taylor in the lead. The 3d Infantry was commanded by Lieutenant Colonel Ethan Allen Hitchcock, one of the early West Pointers (Class of 1817), grandson of the famous Revolutionary War leader Ethan Allen, erstwhile commandant of cadets at West Point—and egotist extraordinaire. Prolific with his pen, Hitchcock provided the principal account of the difficult landing. His descriptions are self-serving but vivid.

The *Alabama*, Hitchcock reports, could not cross the shoals into Corpus Christi, so Taylor was forced to land first at St. Joseph's Island and then transship his men by smaller craft. The landing met with frustration from the start. The lighters failed to arrive, and the impatient and crowded men fretted aboard the *Alabama* for nearly a whole day. Hitchcock, however, with an eye for the historic and dramatic, procured a small boat in which he sent one of his company commanders ashore to plant an American flag. "The first stars and stripes ever raised in Texas by authority," Hitchcock gloated.[3]

By evening Hitchcock had prevailed upon a Texas revenue cutter to carry three of his companies ashore, and by the next evening he had landed his entire regiment. But troubles were not over. Taylor and his men were stuck on St. Joseph's Island for two more days, and finally, "beside himself with anxiety, fatigue, and passion," Taylor determined to take two companies by lighter down Aransas Bay to Corpus Christi. But the lighter ran aground in the flats, and Taylor's party languished on board the small craft for another full day and night.

It was the thirty-first, five days after arrival at St. Joseph's Island, before Taylor's whole command reached Corpus Christi. The safe landing was "little short of a miracle," Hitchcock grumbled, attributable to the "mere accident" of an exceptionally calm bay.

At least the Americans were greeted by friendly settlers. The worthies of Corpus Christi, who welcomed Taylor's men with "satisfaction," were almost all smugglers, their sole source of illegal goods being the overland trail to the Mexican town of Matamoros, on the Rio Grande. They would profit immensely by the presence of a well-paid

American army. Their head man, "Colonel" H. L. Kinney, was a Texan. His nationality could provide a rationale, though nobody in the army believed it, that Corpus Christi, on the western bank of the Nueces River, was an extension of Texas. By that line of reasoning Taylor's force had not left Texan soil.

Once safely ashore at Corpus Christi, however, Taylor's force was exposed to attack from the Mexican mainland. At the moment he had no cavalry that could warn of impending attack, and he would have none until the three hundred men of the 2d Dragoons, moving overland, would arrive in the nearby town of San Patricio. Taylor knew that the troopers were scheduled to arrive on August 24, and he was in no mood to sit back and wait. In his impatience he set out to meet them, only to have his guide lose his way, and to spend another uncomfortable night, this time in the wilderness. The next day, however, the dragoons appeared, slightly ahead of schedule. Their commander, Colonel David E. Twiggs, had mistaken a thunderstorm over the Gulf for hostile artillery fire and was hurrying to Taylor's relief.

Twiggs brought reports from San Antonio. Great excitement, he said, was being felt in Washington over Taylor's exposed position on the Nueces River, and the President had called for additional troops to reinforce him. "It seems," Hitchcock noted, "that the ridiculousness of the plan to send 800 or 1200 men to make war on a civilized nation of 8,000,000 inhabitants has occurred to others besides me."[4]

Washington was indeed in a state of alarm—and not only because of the situation in Mexico. On August 26, two days after the 2d Dragoons had arrived at Corpus Christi, Polk discussed Packenham's rejection of his 49th parallel proposal with his cabinet. In view of Packenham's rudeness, Polk was determined to withdraw his offer and revert to his basic position. He directed Buchanan to "assert and enforce our right to the whole Oregon territory from 42 degrees to 54 degrees, 40' north latitude," for Packenham, he noted, had submitted no counter proposition. "If we do have war," Polk wrote complacently, "it will not be our fault."

But while Polk was flirting with war along the Northwest frontier he was going on with his plan to reinforce Taylor's position at Corpus

Christi. By the end of October Taylor would have with him a total of 3,554 men.* The Northwest would now be naked.

Taylor's army was remarkable in the U.S. military experience because it was made up entirely of regulars. These were unusual troops —tough, rigorously disciplined, and reliable in a fight. A large number of them, about 42 percent, were foreign-born Germans and Irishmen, soldiering as professionals in the U.S. Army as they would in any other. Yet since so many were not citizens of the United States, they were overly inclined to desert the colors when bored or uncomfortable— Twiggs had lost one man in seven from desertion on his overland march.† But on duty these men accepted hardship, neglect, and too often abuse, conditions that would have caused volunteers to rebel. Their leaders were superior, for Taylor had inherited an excellent set of junior officers, largely products of Sylvanus Thayer's teaching methods at West Point. The infantry officers—Grant, Kirby Smith, Sykes, Sedgwick—would provide discipline and backbone. Artillerists —Sam Ringgold, Ridgeley, Bragg—would provide a decisive weapon in the light artillery. Engineers such as George G. Meade would give expert advice on routes, waterways, terrain, and fortifications.

If this unusual army was in danger, Taylor showed little concern. Part of his confidence—stoicism perhaps—may have stemmed from his experiences with the Indians, who invariably outnumbered whatever force he was commanding. He seemed content sitting outside his tent, ready to receive any and all visitors. One, so the story went, mistook him for an orderly. A certain lieutenant who prided himself on belonging to one of the first families of the State of Virginia went up to

---

*Four infantry regiments (of a total of eight authorized in the entire army), one dragoon regiment (out of two), and all four of the artillery regiments. His army did not need to be so small, even without volunteers. The regular units could have been quickly augmented by filling out the companies and regiments to authorized strength of 42 privates per company. Marcy would ask Congress for 100 per company later in the year; General-in-Chief Scott would have preferred 100. Such an augmentation would have increased the rolls of the regular army by nearly 8,000 men, for a total of nearly 16,000, and would have fleshed out Taylor's army to well over 7,000 overnight. Emory Upton, *The Military Policy of the United States*, p. 198; Matthew Steele, *American Campaigns*, p. 81. Hitchcock was a little off in estimating the population of Mexico.

†One thousand deserted throughout the army every year, according to the Adjutant General's Office Records, National Archives.

headquarters to obtain a glimpse of the general. Seeing an old man cleaning a sword in a bower, the officer went in and addressed the bronze-faced old gentleman hard at work in his shirt sleeves: "I say, old fell', can you tell me where I can see General Taylor?"

The old "fell'" without rising replied, "Wull, stranger, thar is the old hoss's tent," pointing to the headquarters.

"Lieutenant, if you please," said the F.F.V. "And by the way, my old trump, whose sword is that you are cleaning?"

"Wull, Colonel," replied the old man, "I don't see there is any harm in telling you, seeing's you're an officer. This sword belongs to the general himself."

The lieutenant took off his sword and said, "My good man, I would like to have you clean my sword, and I shall come tomorrow to see the general and then I will give you a dollar."

The lieutenant was on hand the next day, and seeing his old friend of the day before standing under an awning conversing with some officers, he beckoned to him to come over. The old gentleman came out, bringing the lieutenant's sword. The lieutenant was profuse in his thanks and, giving the old man a poke in the ribs, said, "Come, old fatty, show me General Taylor and the dollar is yours."

The "old fatty" drew himself up and said, "Lieutenant! I am General Taylor"—he turned slowly around—"and I will take that dollar!" The next day the general had the lieutenant introduced in due form.[5]

Others had similar impressions. When Lieutenant George Meade reported for duty in mid-September, he found the general "a plain, sensible old gentleman, who laughs very much at the excitement in the Northern States on account of his position, and thinks there is not the remotest possibility of there being any war." And, Meade volunteered, "He is said to be very tired of this country, and the duty assigned to him, and it is supposed will return on the arrival of General Worth." Taylor was also rumored to be "a staunch Whig, and opposed *in toto* to the Texas annexation."[6]

But Meade was seeing only what Taylor wanted to show the world. Hitchcock harbored another suspicion, that Taylor was actually "succumbing to ambition." Hitchcock sneered when Taylor casually mentioned "going to the Rio Grande." Such a thought, wrote Hitchcock, was "singular language for one who originally and until very lately denounced annexation as both injudicious in policy and wicked in fact!" Taylor, he finally concluded, wanted "an additional brevet, and would strain a point to get it."[7]

Whatever Taylor's true motivations, morale among his troops and officers was high during the late summer months at Corpus Christi. Compared with winter duty in the snowdrifts of Minnesota, conditions were comfortable; the weather was not too hot, and the breezes kept the camp free of all diseases except for mild diarrhea caused by drinking the brackish water. Granted, firewood for cooking was scarce, a lack that prevented the hunters from fully enjoying the venison and wild turkey they shot on freely granted hunting expeditions, but the mess was adequate, even though the mainstay was pork and beans.

A family atmosphere existed among the officers; many West Point graduates were seeing familiar faces for the first time since graduation. Typical was Captain Ephraim Kirby Smith, commander of a company of the 5th Infantry, who described his arrival in camp during a thunderstorm. He had stumbled past the campfires, he wrote, "greeted frequently by cordial welcomes from the well-known voices of old companions, whom I had not met for years." And like the others, he sensed opportunity. "Our companies are strengthened by fifty recruits. . . . I shall have a pretty command for a captain, and if there is anything to be done, I think I shall have a chance." And, as a dedicated regular, he fairly burst with pride: soon "The Camp . . . will be the largest body of regulars . . . which has been assembled since the Revolution."[8]

On first arriving at Corpus Christi the soldiers conducted themselves better than might have been expected. They were veterans, and a camp in one place was much the same as a camp in another. Little excitement could be found in the small trading post, and they believed that this expedition would be over soon; it would doubtless turn out to be just another foray.

With the passage of time, however, the small trading post began to grow, and soon the population reached two thousand. Few women were among them, other than a few Texan wives and those present as "laundresses." Drinking saloons began to proliferate. Soon after the arrival of the 2d Dragoons, "disgraceful brawls and quarrels" and even "drunken frolics" became commonplace. One dragoon captain resigned from the army to avoid trial, and two others were tried for fighting over a woman. The disorder worsened as time went on.[9]

Taylor himself realized that the army could not remain at Corpus

Christi indefinitely, but the decision to stay or leave was out of his hands. So he did what any prudent commander would do: he prepared for all contingencies. In anticipation of a forward move he sent reconnaissance parties to scout the territory between the Nueces River and the Rio Grande. These parties were usually headed by members of the Corps of Topographical Engineers, among whom was George Meade.

Meade's letters home reveal both the situation and the man. Kirby Smith may have been struck by the beauty of the interior lands, but Meade, even in personal correspondence, would dwell on the topography: the impassable roads, the soft soil, the limited visibility due to the high chaparral. He was intrigued by a place called the Brazos de Santiago, "an arm of the sea, which juts in near the mouth of the Rio Grande, and approaches within twenty miles of the Mexican town of Matamoros." Meade expected to head a hundred-man party to that critical location, but the mission was canceled and he was disappointed.

The reason for the cancellation of that mission probably was word from Washington that the Army of Occupation would remain at Corpus Christi throughout the winter. For most of the winter they did stay there, feeling the bad weather and developing bad tempers. Some of the officers, Hitchcock and Captain William W. S. Bliss (Taylor's adjutant) among them, formed a study group to read Spinoza, Schiller, Kant, and Socinus, but others were less constructive.

In late autumn a nasty quarrel cropped up among the higher commanders over the question of brevet rank. Two fine soldiers—Colonel (Brevet Brigadier General) William J. Worth, Taylor's second in command, and Colonel David E. Twiggs, commanding the 2d Dragoons—were the antagonists. They were very different men. Worth cut a dashing figure—the Ney of the Army, a paper called him—commandant of cadets at West Point (just before Hitchcock), and in 1812 an aide to Winfield Scott. Twiggs was a large, bullnecked, white-haired man, unappealing in personality but forceful and aggressive. This was not a good hour for either of them.

When Taylor called a review one day, he designated Twiggs as commander of troops. Twiggs had been granted no brevet but, as a regular colonel, was senior to Worth. The vain Worth was incensed at this supposed affront, and he made his fury known. Soon the camp broke up into two factions, each supporting its own views of the priority to be accorded to brevet versus regular rank. Taylor became exasperated, so rather than go through with a ceremony that would cause dissatisfaction, he canceled the review and sent a message to the President requesting a resolution of the problem. The request was intercepted by General-in-Chief Winfield Scott, and in his capacity as senior professional in the army he published a circular declaring that brevet should take precedence over regular rank.

Scott's ruling soon became common knowledge at Corpus Christi, and a group of officers, headed by Hitchcock, drew up a petition, ten pages long, to be sent to the president of the Senate, signed by 158 officers. It was sent on December 19, 1845, and pending a reply the emotionally charged issue would remain unresolved.[10]

Autumn rolled on to the New Year, 1846, at Corpus Christi. That New Year's Day would differ little from any New Year's Day anywhere at any time, with drinking, horse racing, gambling, theatrical amusements, and a ball that evening. The one formal observance was a required official call on the senior officers of the camp, who provided eggnog and cake. According to Meade, the theater hosted a "company of strolling actors, who murder tragedy, burlesque comedy, and render farce into buffoonery, in the most approved style."[11]

But the days of boredom were nearly over for Zachary Taylor's little army. The year 1846 would provide all the excitement that they had bargained for—and more.

MISSION OF "PEACE"

SUMMER 1845–JANUARY 1846

Zachary Taylor was drilling his troops hard down on the Nueces River, but his men were leading lives of frivolity compared with that of the single-minded austerity of their commander-in-chief back in Washington. Not that Polk and his wife were recluses—far from it—but every activity of the day and evening was directed toward furthering the objectives of Polk's administration. The Polks would give two or three dinners each week, but the guests, restricted to those people who could promote Polk's aims, would be ushered out early enough for the President to work afterward.

Sarah Polk, as First Lady, was a force in her own right. Following the customs of the rural South, she forbade dancing—but not alcohol—at all White House functions. And, except in cases of emergency, she closed the doors of the mansion to all callers on Sundays. In person she outshone her husband. She, too, had an inner reserve, but she presented to the world a surface charm that warmed political friend and foe alike, and she dressed expensively.* The official portrait of Mrs. Polk, which shows her as a hatchet-faced, forbidding woman, is mis-

---

*She ordered a Paris wardrobe to the tune of a staggering $600. Sellers, *James K. Polk*, p. 307.

leading; her personality overcame nature's omissions, and was such that she remained much admired even when her husband's political stock was low.

Social regulars of Washington were also pleased to see the White House being refurbished inside, an event that had not occurred since the administration of James Monroe. Out of spite the Congress had refused John Tyler any funds for redecorating, but it was generous with the Polks, so much so that Polk soon announced that he would spend only half the amount allotted. The interior was completely redone, and for a while the Polks were forced to take refuge in the nearby Cole-man's Hotel to escape the heat and the smell of fresh paint.[1]

"Polk's religion," it has been said, "was politics, and the Democratic party was his church."[2] Much truth lay in those words, for Polk seemed to live politics twenty-four hours a day. He had never joined a conven-tional church, nor had he hobbies. He indulged in no sports, confining his exercise largely to morning and evening walks. He took pride in this self-denial. "My time has been wholly occupied in my office, in the discharge of my public duties," he wrote in his diary. "My confinement to my office has been constant and unceasing, and my labours very great."[3] No wonder that three years after writing those words he left office broken in health.

Polk's principal problem in his cabinet was James Buchanan. It had been so from the start and it would get worse. For a while, however, the differences between the two did not reach a personal level because they were always kept out in the open; Polk held to a harder line than Buchanan thought wise, but Buchanan followed orders dutifully.

In the fall of 1845, however, Polk and Buchanan had their first confrontation when the death of Justice Henry Baldwin created a vacancy on the Supreme Court, a vacancy that some thought would be filled by Buchanan. Buchanan pretended not to desire that appoint-ment, but when he paid a call to so assure Polk, he volunteered that his home state of Pennsylvania was "disappointed" in Polk's actions regarding the tariff and that resentment was discomfiting him as a member of Polk's cabinet—Polk might ease the situation if he could just "transfer" Buchanan to the Supreme Court.[4] Polk would have none of Buchanan's double talk; the tariff only remotely affected foreign policy, he said, and he was quite satisfied with Buchanan's performance as secretary of state. To Polk, the matter appeared to be resolved for the moment.

Polk's relations with the Congress were far more touchy because there, especially in the Senate, he was forced to deal with ambitious men who held him in no awe—and over whom he had no control. The most prominent of these were Benton, Calhoun, and William Allen, chairman of the Foreign Relations Committee. Polk needed the support of the Senate on both Oregon and Mexico, but no single policy could satisfy all three of these congressional leaders at the same time. Calhoun and Allen seemed to balance each other. Calhoun, becoming progressively more sectional, favored conciliating Britain regarding Oregon; Allen, by contrast, was rabid in insisting on the casuistic policy of "Fifty-four Forty or Fight." For the moment, therefore, Polk settled for making his peace with Benton, who might be more balanced.

In late October 1845 Polk invited Benton to the White House for their first visit since the Democratic convention of 1844. Polk was pleased to discover that "Colonel" Benton, as Polk referred to him, was "pleasant and friendly," as when the two had been in Congress together some years back.

The President opened by denying any probability of settling the Oregon controversy by negotiation with Britain. Benton replied cautiously that he had always supported a settlement along the line of the 49th parallel. Benton was content to admit a clear difference, however, and the two sought areas where they could agree. They did find some, of a short-range nature, that included issuing to the British the twelve months' "Notice" terminating joint occupation of the Oregon territory. Benton also agreed to extending United States laws and jurisdiction over American citizens in Oregon.[5]

The subject then turned to California, an area that was beginning to demand attention. Previously, even the most enthusiastic supporters of Manifest Destiny* had assumed that the flood of Americans into California would, as in Texas, draw that section inevitably into the Union. But that comfortable supposition had been jarred recently by an alarming message from Thomas O. Larkin, the American consul in Monterey. The Hudson's Bay Company, according to Larkin, was

---

*A term apparently coined by John Sullivan, in 1842, according to Dr. Guadalupe Jimenez-Codinach, of the Library of Congress. However, similar terms had been used as far back as Jefferson.

encouraging Mexico City to send an expedition to subjugate the restive population in that wayward region. And British agents were in Monterey with no commercial reasons for being there. That message had coincided with one from Dr. Parrott, in Mexico City, who reported a "great interest in everything Californian" being manifested "in English circles." An Irish priest, he warned, was planning to establish a colony in California.[6]

All this meant that Britain was threatening the United States position all along the Pacific Coast, and Polk confided that he had sent certain instructions to Larkin, to Parrott, and to Commodore John D. Sloat.* Benton appreciated this information but did not commit himself.

But something that Polk left out of his diary had transpired, because a few days later Polk had decided to take some action regarding the situation in California, and Benton was aware of it. By the evening of October 30, 1845, Polk had summoned First Lieutenant Arnold H. Gillespie, USMC, to come to the White House to be sent on a special mission. Three days earlier Gillespie had been designated to deliver dispatches from the State Department to Larkin, but Polk now designated him as a "special agent" and entrusted him to carry a package from Benton to his son-in-law, Captain John C. Frémont, who was leading an exploration mission to Oregon and California. Whatever occurred that evening, Gillespie left the White House convinced that his real mission was to help Frémont encourage the Californios to rise up against the Mexican government.[7]

It took Gillespie over two weeks to depart from New York, as he needed to make elaborate arrangements. The problem he had to contend with was time. As passage from Washington to California directly across the plains and mountains was slow, tedious, and dangerous, Gillespie's only feasible way to reach Monterey was to travel across Mexico. But being seen in uniform would be inviting trouble, so the Navy Department planned to have him assume the guise of a civilian. He would take a commercial vessel from New York to Veracruz, cross Mexico to the port of Mazatlán, thence up the Pacific Coast to Monterey. Secretary Bancroft had arranged a civilian cover as a businessman.

On November 16, 1845, Gillespie was on his way. Off Sandy Hook,

*Sloat commanded the United States squadron in the Pacific.

full of hopes, he sent a last note, by pilot boat, to the secretary of the navy: ". . . I can assure you, you will not regret having named me for this service, & . . . that should I be successful I may . . . receive the only reward a Soldier desires to obtain.[8]

Gillespie was an ambitious man. Just how ambitious would be revealed at the end of his journey.

On November 9, 1845, Polk's special agent, Dr. Parrott, arrived back in Washington, certain that Mexico was anxious to settle the boundary issues dividing the two countries. Polk was not surprised. In anticipation of such a report, in fact, he had just signed the commission of John Slidell, of Louisiana, to be "Minister Extraordinary and Plenipotentiary" to Mexico. He prevailed on a reluctant Parrott to return as Slidell's secretary of legation, though well aware that Parrott, a man disliked in Mexico, would be unwelcome.

At 12:30 P.M. on Tuesday, December 2, 1845, a joint committee of the two houses of Congress called on Polk at the White House to announce their readiness to receive any communication the President might have to make. Then, after making due acknowledgment, Polk sent his secretary to the Capitol, bearing Polk's first State of the Union Message.[9]

Polk's message had been heralded as a reaffirmation of the Monroe Doctrine, second only in importance to the first.[10] Hyperbole aside, it left no doubt where he stood. The text (a) reviewed the many wrongs that Mexico had perpetrated against a patient United States, (b) disclosed the promising report of Dr. Parrott, (c) promised that a minister (not named) would be sent to Mexico, (d) reviewed the terms of the joint occupation of Oregon in accordance with the Anglo-American agreement of October 1818, (e) reviewed the current status of negotiations, and (f) reiterated the interim measures that Polk had discussed with Senator Benton a little over a week before, particularly his intention to send the one year's Notice to Britain.

Polk's discussion of Oregon wound up on a defiant note: "Oregon is part of the North American Continent, to which, it is confidently affirmed, the title of the United States is the best now in existence. . . . The British proposition of compromise . . . can never for a moment be entertained by the United States, . . ."[11]

The courier arrived at the Capitol at 1:10 P.M., and immediately both houses suspended business. A locomotive, steam up, was waiting outside to carry copies to Baltimore, while word of its departure went by the new Washington–Baltimore telegraph. When the document arrived at Baltimore, crowds in the downtown streets heard it read publicly while another waiting locomotive transported advance copies to Philadelphia. In Washington the reading was completed by 4:00 P.M.; by 5:30 P.M. reading began at the Philadelphia post office; by 10:00 P.M. copies had reached New York. Crowds on the streets, in a frenzy of patriotism, declaimed that "Jackson is alive again!"[12]

Even in the more sober councils of state, reaction to Polk's message was remarkably favorable. Lewis Cass, of Ohio, raved, "You have struck out the true doctrine, you have cut the Gordian knot!" Benton was also guardedly favorable.[13] Polk was riding high.

On November 29, 1845, John Slidell, minister-designate to Mexico, landed at Veracruz with an impossible set of instructions; he had been ill-advised to accept them. And if he initially had felt some discomfort regarding his mission, he must have been further disquieted by the reluctance of the Mexican officials to receive him personally. He had been held waiting in New Orleans between September 17 and November 10, 1845, while John Black, American consul in Veracruz, sought to ascertain that an envoy would be received.

On October 13 the Mexican foreign minister, Manuel Peña y Peña, notified Black that he would receive Slidell as a "commissioner" but would not authorize a full-fledged "minister." Meanwhile, Peña insisted, the United States naval squadron off Veracruz must be withdrawn.[14] Informally, Peña requested that such a commissioner be a "conciliatory individual," specifying that Dr. Parrott did not qualify.

These conditions Polk and Buchanan had ignored, by designating Slidell as "minister extraordinary and plenipotentiary," and by returning Parrott to the legation. This cavalier attitude could not have been mere inadvertence; men like Joel Poinsett, a former minister to Mexico City, had warned that "the Mexican Government would not and dared not receive our Minister Plenipotentiary."[15]

The propositions that Slidell was instructed to lay before the Mexicans were likewise harsh. Besides flatly refusing to make reparation for annexing Texas, which would have been reasonable, he was to enumerate the intolerable "injuries and outrages committed by . . . Mexico on American citizens" and to present four alternative boundary adjustments in lieu of cash payment: (a) for a boundary along the Rio Grande and half of New Mexico the United States would merely assume claims of United States citizens against Mexico; (b) for a boundary that would add the rest of New Mexico the United States would assume the claims and pay $5 million; (c) for a boundary including San Francisco Bay the United States would assume the claims and pay $20 million; and finally (d) for a boundary including Monterey (California) the amount paid, in addition to the claims, would be $25 million.[16] A neat shopping list.

Slidell was just the man to do the bullying called for. Though his fluency in Spanish would imply some sympathy with the Mexicans, he gave every impression of holding them in contempt.* And he was hungry for this assignment: it might provide him with the acclaim and status he so craved.

Slidell was a talented man, restless, intelligent, and ambitious. Raised in New York, he had left for New Orleans in 1819, at age twenty-six, under cloudy circumstances,† but once there had assumed the mode of living and the attitudes of his adopted South. A successful lawyer, he was once considered by Van Buren, then secretary of state under Jackson, for a diplomatic post; the idea had been vetoed by Jackson.‡ By 1845 Slidell was a congressman from Louisiana. He had achieved everything except the national recognition he coveted.§

Slidell's arrival at Veracruz provided the trigger for upheaval in Mexico, for at that moment the rebel Paredes was simply waiting for an excuse to rise up against the Herrera government. And he had the means to

*"I have no very exalted idea of the calibre of the Mexican intellect," he wrote immediately on disembarking.
†Slidell's marksmanship in winging the proprietor of the Park Theater in a quarrel over the attentions of a young lady had brought the law on his heels.
‡"Knowing that you had a favourable opinion of Mr. Slidell as well as myself this letter is written to put you on your guard of this man, that you may not break your shins over stools not in your way, and that you may be guarded in any communications you may happen to make with him." Jackson to Van Buren, quoted in Willson, *John Slidell,* p. 13.
§Slidell's mission was, as he put it, "at least a responsible one and should a negotiation be brought to a favourable issue, credit and reputation will be acquired." Wilson, *John Slidell,* p. 15.

do so, for having disobeyed Herrera's orders to march northward the previous August, Paredes had kept seven thousand of Mexico's best troops at San Luis Potosí.

Herrera was astonished when Slidell arrived at Veracruz. The Mexicans had expected a delay while the U.S. Senate was supposedly debating the appointment, but somehow that had not happened. Here Slidell was, in early December! Peña y Peña sent a message to Black imploring him to prevent Slidell from disembarking at Veracruz, but Slidell had already done so and had headed inland before Black could intercept him. Black overtook him at Puebla, but Slidell pushed on, reaching Mexico City on December 6.

Herrera's consternation increased when he learned of Slidell's title of "minister" and his intention to remain in Mexico indefinitely. So Herrera turned the problem over to the Council of Government. Two weeks later the Council answered: Slidell could not be received as a minister. In the meantime an impatient Slidell wrote two notes to Peña y Peña protesting both the delay and the Mexican's failure to address him with what he considered his proper title.

On Christmas Eve Slidell fired off an astonishing protest, which even included a threat of force.[17] He thereupon departed Mexico City for Jalapa, there to await further instructions from Washington. Seven days later General Mariano Paredes occupied Mexico City and took over as the new president.

If events were not pleasing John Slidell in Mexico, they were not doing much better for Polk back in Washington, for following the euphoria of his Annual Message, the world of reality had crept back in. Even his most important recommendation, sending the Notice to Britain, was in trouble.

To heat things up, Lord Aberdeen was again pressing for European arbitration, to which the Americans could never submit. Polk, now seeing the possibility of war, made one concession to the British. He agreed to consult with three or four senators about compromising on a boundary along the 49th parallel to the Strait of San Juan de Fuca, leaving the southern tip of Vancouver to the British. That act would bring the negotiations back to where they had begun.[18]

.   .   .

In early January 1846 Polk received the first message from Slidell since the latter's angry departure from Mexico City. Slidell had given up on reaching a settlement, and his whole objective now was to throw the odium of failure upon the Mexicans.[19]

Slidell's impasse now prompted Polk to make a move. On January 13, 1846, Secretary of War William Marcy sent the following message to General Taylor at Corpus Christi: "Sir: I am directed by the President to instruct you to advance and occupy, with the troops under your command, positions on or near the east bank of the Rio del Norte. . . ."[20]

AMERICAN BLOOD UPON AMERICAN SOIL

❦

JANUARY–APRIL 1846

Polk's order of January 13, 1846, sending Taylor's army from Corpus Christi to "a position on or near the east bank of the Rio Del Norte" was agreeable to Taylor; it was, in fact, based upon a recommendation Taylor had made to the adjutant general three months earlier,* and it left the choice of the actual position to be occupied up to him.

Two paragraphs of Polk's order, however, were written in such a way as to place Taylor in an awkward position. They were delicately worded:

It is not designed, in our present relations with Mexico, that you should treat her as an enemy; but should she assume that character by a declaration of war, or any open act of hostility toward us, you will not act merely on the defensive, if your relative means enable you to act otherwise. . . .

Texas is now fully incorporated into our union of States, and you are hereby authorized to make a requisition upon the Executive of that State

---

*Taylor to TAG, October 4, 1845, Exec. Doc. No. 60, p. 108. Army customs of the day dictated that all field commanders address communications to the adjutant of the next higher headquarters. In this case, the adjutant general of the War Department was Brigadier General Roger Jones. Polk's messages to Taylor were signed by either Secretary of War Marcy or the adjutant general.

for such of its militia force as may be needed to repel invasion or to secure the country against apprehended invasion.[1]

By the first paragraph of that order the President of the United States had placed in the hands of a field commander the power to decide whether or not a state of war existed, a remarkable step. But the second paragraph gave even greater trouble, for the option of calling for militia reinforcements was not the carte blanche it might seem to be. Article I of the U.S. Constitution expressly limits the use of state militia to "executing the laws of the Union, suppressing insurrections, and repelling invasions." Thus, if Taylor were to assume the offensive in case of hostilities (as he was instructed to do), he could not employ militia for that purpose in Mexican Territory.

Considering Polk's secretive nature, it is impossible to determine whether he and Secretary of War Marcy were deliberately placing Taylor in an impossible situation or whether they were committing an honest error. Winfield Scott, the general-in-chief, would have detected at once that the order was unconstitutional. But then Polk had already decided to run the Army without consulting the imperious Scott. Whatever his reasoning, however, Taylor decided to risk sustaining a first battle, should it come, with only his small Army of Occupation.

Taylor's eagerness to move forward from Corpus Christi was motivated partly by concern for the welfare of his troops. When he had first recommended moving, back in October, boredom was already setting in. The constant drilling, no matter how essential, was beginning to gall, and even the most professional of the young officers were complaining of the continual, monotonous drumbeat of the drill field. Further, the weather was deteriorating: the winds from the sea were growing cold and the rains could penetrate the flimsy tents. There was a scarcity of wood for warming cold bodies and for cooking. The camp at Corpus Christi had outlived its habitability.

When Polk's movement order arrived on February 4, therefore, Taylor promised that he would "lose no time" in moving forward to Point Isabel, at the Brazos Santiago, from which base he could be supplied directly from New Orleans.[2]

As it turned out, Taylor required over a month to leave. He lacked a ship on which to send scouting parties to Brazos Santiago (over a hundred miles distant), and a party sent overland would take too long. Further, he needed one or two lightly armed vessels to protect his contemplated base from raids by sea. Taylor had made frequent pleas for these ships, but all had been shunted aside in Washington. The Navy Department, at one point, had made a feeble effort, transferring three ships to the War Department, but none of these were fit for use.* So Taylor delayed.

Help came, finally, from Commodore David E. Conner, commanding the "Home Squadron" patrolling the Gulf. Conner learned of Taylor's predicament in mid-February, and he offered to provide Taylor with "one or two small vessels" to assist in seizing and protecting Brazos Santiago (the bay around Point Isabel). Taylor was grateful.[3]

Despite all the planning, the coming march was successfully kept secret at first. By February 18, however, Taylor's orders were common knowledge, and everyone was in a state of excitement, "hurry-scurry, preparatory for the march." Only the gambling houses and bartenders of Corpus Christi were dejected, and not surprisingly they attempted to prevent Taylor's imminent departure by planting rumors of "a very large Mexican force ready to oppose him."† Taylor, of course, paid these "reports" no heed.

On Sunday, March 8, Taylor's advance guard, consisting of Twiggs's 2d Dragoons with the light artillery, marched out across the direct, overland route to Matamoros. The path was rough but distinctly marked by a well-worn trail that had carried traders and smugglers between Matamoros and Corpus Christi for years. To the Mexicans it had a name, the Road of the Arroyo Colorado.[4]

The next day the 1st Brigade, under the command of Brevet Brigadier General William J. Worth, marched out; on March 10 the 2d Brigade (under Colonel James S. McIntosh), and on March 11 the 3d Brigade (under Colonel William Whistler). Taylor would stay behind to see the 3d Brigade off, march awhile with it, then work his way

---

*In early November, Taylor reported that the *On-ka-hy-e* had sailed from Aransas Bay to Mobile a month earlier and had not returned. The *Harney* had been reported by her commander as "now lying in the Mississippi River," unsafe to go to sea. The *Dolphin* had not been heard of. Taylor to TAG, November 8, 1845, Exec. Doc. No. 60, p. 113.

†George Meade, *Life and Letters,* letter to his wife, February 18, March 2, 1846. On February 14 Taylor had warned Washington: "Many reports will doubtless reach the department, giving exaggerated accounts of Mexican preparations to resist our advance, if not indeed to attempt an invasion of Texas. Such reports have been circulated even at this place, and owe their origin to personal interests connected with the stay of the army here. I trust that they will receive no attention at the War Department."

forward. He planned to catch up with Twiggs before reaching territory where enemy resistance could be expected.

Taylor's total force now consisted of about 3,550 officers and men, followed by a train of 307 oxcarts and mule-drawn wagons. Behind him Taylor left his "sea tail," under Major John Monroe, consisting of a siege train of quartermasters, engineers, artillery, and others. That group would travel from Corpus Christi by water,* timing their departure so as to arrive at Brazos Santiago concurrently with Taylor's overland army. And to make it easy for the adjutant general to reach him, Taylor sent a forwarding address: c/o the Quartermaster in New Orleans.[5]

On March 11 Taylor saw the 3d Brigade off from Corpus Christi. Then, traveling thirty miles the next day, he rode up to join the 2d Brigade, which was "advancing with great regularity." On that day he sent word back to Washington that the brig *Porpoise* had arrived the day before off Aransas, with orders from Conner to render "all the service in his power." Taylor enclosed a letter Conner had written him passing on a report (which Conner discounted) of a large Mexican force moving northward and of general public dissatisfaction with the newly installed Paredes regime. He also enclosed a copy of an anti-Paredes pronunciamento, this one issued by one General Antonio Canales at Camargo, a town on the Rio Grande upstream from Matamoros. The renegade Canales, a hated foe of the border Texans, controlled only one auxiliary regiment, but news of any disruptions in Mexico was still welcome.[6]

The march overland began pleasantly enough for the troops. At first the route ran westward, following the Nueces River over open prairies, sprinkled with little clumps of vegetation, and occasional dense thickets. Kirby Smith wrote home excitedly of a plant, the Spanish bayonet, that grew some fifteen feet tall and sported white flowers some five inches in diameter, protected by glossy green bayonets. This was some-

---

*Taylor had his own transports, such as the *Alabama*. But they were not armed. Hence the need for naval escorts.

thing new to a New Englander! As the march progressed the army turned southwest into the land of rattlesnakes and tarantulas. At one point Smith's men caught a small antelope to supplement their rations. The beast was so pathetic, however, that the soldiers released it.

By now the march had become dirty and hot, and at one point the soldiers went thirty-six hours without water. Taylor, of course, shared the hardships with the rest. Like them, his skin was sunburned, his lips cracked and raw, his skin peeling. Typically, none of his dispatches mention any discomfort, on his part or on that of his men. Veterans such as Smith even seemed to enjoy the long, hot trek.[7]

Taylor expected to traverse the first hundred miles unmolested. However, beyond the Arroyo Colorado, about thirty miles from Matamoros, he could be attacked at any time, so he planned to concentrate his army at that stream. But even if Taylor had not planned it that way, the incident of Thursday and Friday, March 19 and 20, would have alerted him to do so, for when the 2d Dragoons sent out a reconnaissance force to the arroyo late on the nineteenth, a party of irregular Mexican cavalry challenged them from the opposite bank. The Mexicans took no hostile action, but they "made it understood" that crossing the river would be "an act of hostility."[8] Taylor, unable to gauge precisely the strength opposing him, prepared a full-scale river assault the next day.

Early on the twentieth, Taylor placed his dragoons and Worth's 1st Brigade in position at the arroyo, supported by all his available batteries of field artillery. In the meantime, McIntosh's 2d Brigade arrived, and Taylor placed it on the right of the 1st. As Taylor tersely reported, the "crossing was then commenced and executed in the order prescribed. Not a shot was fired. . . ."[9]

Others saw the action in a more dramatic light. Kirby Smith called it "one of the most exciting moments of my life." Everyone in the army, he wrote, "from the General-in-Chief to the smallest drummer-boy, felt morally certain that we were on the verge of a fierce and bloody conflict, yet I saw no one who was not cheerful and apparently eager for the game to begin." Smith admired the perfect order by which four companies, under the command of Captain C. F. Smith, marched into the water. Smith then saw General Worth rush to the head of the column. "We watched them in breathless silence as they deepened in the water, expecting that at every step they would receive a withering fire." When the assault had reached the midpoint of the stream without a shot from the opposite bank, he wrote, "the disappointment of the men was shown from right to left in muttered curses." As the head of the column reached the top of the opposite bank, however, the men cheered, the bands struck up "Yankee Doodle," and they all marched up the hill. In the distance Smith could see a few Mexicans retreating, but "the great battle of Arroyo Colorado was terminated."[10]

On the morning of March 24, 1846, Taylor's force reached a road junction near the Rio Grande. The left fork led to Point Isabel, ten miles away, and the right to Matamoros, about twice that distance. Concerned about the safety of his prospective base at Point Isabel, Taylor decided to see it for himself. So he took the seven companies of Twiggs's 2d Dragoons and turned eastward, sending Worth, with the three infantry brigades, to find a camping ground along the road leading to Matamoros. Worth camped at a pond called Palo Alto.

At Point Isabel Taylor found good news and bad news. His seaborne tail had arrived safely only three hours before his own appearance, and the *Porpoise, Lawrence,* and *Woodbury* were sitting reassuringly just offshore. On the other hand, some of the buildings in the small village of El Fronton had been set on fire, reportedly on the order of General Francisco Mejía, commanding at Matamoros. And a copy of a rousing call to arms published by Mejía portended hostility.*

Taylor did not linger at Point Isabel. Early on March 28 he rejoined his troops at Palo Alto, and before noon his small force, colors flying and bands playing, was marching upstream along the left bank of the Rio Grande in full view of Matamoros.

Here the Americans saw Mexican territory for the first time. Once halted and "at ease," they were able to peer across the hundred-yard river to see the opposite bank lined with sentinels, the Mexican flag flying everywhere in the small town behind. Only a few men and women mingled about, looking nonchalant, but all the boats along the river had been taken to the Mexican side.

At first the atmosphere was not openly hostile. That afternoon, in

---

*Taylor to TAG March 25, 1846. The document actually reached Taylor at the Arroyo Colorado.

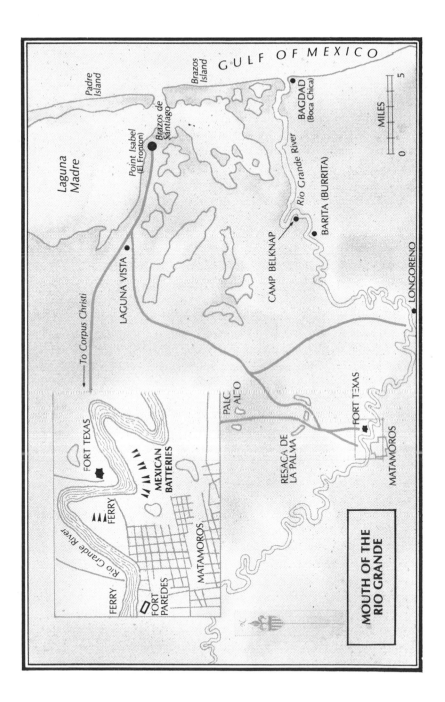

MOUTH OF THE
RIO GRANDE

fact, the Americans were startled by the sight of young women strolling down to the riverside, disrobing without hesitation, and plunging into the stream, ignoring the numerous spectators on either bank. Some young American officers reacted quickly, plunging in from the American side to join them. The Mexican guards forbade them to cross the center of the river, however, "so they returned after kissing their hands to the tawny damsels, which was laughingly returned."[11]

That afternoon, however, the reality of the situation became more apparent. Taylor decided to send a communication to General Mejía, in Matamoros, and to carry it he designated General Worth, whom he treated as his deputy despite Twiggs's higher rank in the regular service. Worth's men displayed a white flag on the American Bank, and the Mexicans, seeing it, sent a small party across in a boat. The members, two cavalry officers and an interpreter, were the same ones who had issued the warning at the Arroyo Colorado.

Immediately, the matter of protocol made things difficult. Mejía, desiring a full-fledged conference between himself and Taylor, refused to treat with Taylor's subordinate, but said he would allow General Rómolo Díaz de la Vega, Mejía's second in command, to represent him. Worth then crossed to the Mexican bank of the river, taking five aides with him. La Vega received him with "becoming courtesy and respect," whereupon Worth produced the dispatch that Taylor had intended for Mejía. La Vega listened as the interpreter read its contents to him.

The positions of the two sides were clear-cut and contradictory. La Vega told Worth that, speaking for Mejía, the Mexicans regarded Taylor's march through the Mexican State of Tamaulipas (between the Nueces and the Rio Grande) as an act of war. Worth replied that the march was not so considered by the United States government and that Taylor's army would remain there, "whether rightfully or otherwise," until ordered by his superiors to withdraw. The matter of the disputed territory would be settled between the two governments. Worth added that he had been sent as a courier, not as a negotiator, and if he could not see Mejía in person, he would withdraw the letter. He had allowed it to be read to La Vega only as a matter of courtesy.

But La Vega insisted on arguing. If Mexican troops were to march into United States territory, how would the United States view the matter? Worth answered with a proverb: "Sufficient unto the day is the evil thereof." He then stated that the Americans would deal with such a situation when it occurred. The interpreter ignored the proverb, but La Vega, who obviously understood English, smiled and shrugged.

But there was a great deal more that Worth wanted to know.

"Is the American consul at Matamoros in arrest?"

"No."

"Then I demand to see him."

No reply.

"Has Mexico declared war against the United States?"

"No."

"Are the two countries still at peace?"

"Yes."

"Then I demand," said Worth, "to see the consul of my government."

At that point, La Vega sent a messenger to Mejía transmitting Worth's demand. He soon returned with a denial of what Mejía called a "request."

To all intents and purposes, that ended the conference. Worth invited the Mexicans to send a courier, who he promised would be received by General Taylor in person. And after La Vega had complained at the sight of the Stars and Stripes flying over Mexican territory, Worth declared that it would remain and that any incursion by Mexican forces on the left bank of the river would be considered an act of war. Worth then returned to the American side.[12]

Two opposing military forces, at peace in name only, now glared at each other across the Rio Grande. Conflict seemed inevitable.

On Friday, February 13, 1846, an unusual visitor called on President James Polk at the White House. He was Colonel Alejandro José Atocha, a Spaniard by birth but a naturalized citizen of the United States. Atocha had paid his respects to Polk some months earlier, but that meeting had not been memorable; this one would be.

Atocha represented himself as a friend of the deposed Mexican president Santa Anna, living in Havana since his escape from Mexico a year earlier. A month previously Atocha had seen Santa Anna, who, Atocha confided to Polk, was expecting soon to return to power. Atocha even intimated that the recent Paredes coup in Mexico City had actually been a front for Santa Anna himself.*

Santa Anna, Atocha claimed, wanted to bargain. In exchange for the sum of $30 million , he would accept a boundary between the United States and Mexico running along the Rio Grande to the Colorado River in the West, thence through the Bay of San Francisco to the Pacific Ocean—essentially ceding to the United States all of present New Mexico and northern California. The money, Santa Anna believed, would pay off the most pressing Mexican debts, support the army, and place the government on a stable footing.

Santa Anna was surprised, Atocha continued, that the United States had previously accommodated the tottering Herrera government by withdrawing its naval squadron from Veracruz and had not ordered General Taylor forward from Corpus Christi. The Mexicans, he contended, would never negotiate without the threat of force. Polk did not mention that he had sent Conner back to Veracruz and had sent Taylor forward a month earlier. The meeting ended inconclusively.

Three days later Atocha was back with the same message, further embellished with a warning that no Mexican government could publicly endorse such a proposal as Santa Anna's and survive. The terms, therefore, would have to appear to be forced upon the Mexicans by the Americans. An army on the Rio Grande, a strong naval force assembled off Veracruz, and the departure of Slidell from Jalapa would probably be enough by way of overt action. In particular the archbishop of Mexico City would be placated when he learned that the Mexican government would now be able to pay him the half million dollars it owed him. Atocha closed by quoting Santa Anna: "When you see the President, tell him to take strong measures, and such a treaty can be made and I will sustain it."[13]

Polk was at least mildly suspicious of Atocha, but the visit had inspired him to take some action. At first he was tempted to send a special agent to meet directly with Santa Anna. He brought the matter to his cabinet, whose members demurred, and Polk did not feel strongly enough about the matter to insist. He then considered ordering Slidell to board an American naval vessel, there to await Santa Anna's return.

*James K. Polk, *Diary* February 13, 1846. There is evidence against this. Dr. Miguel Soto, of the Universidad Nacional Autonoma De Mexico, states unequivocally that Paredes was on the Spanish payroll, a stalking-horse for the reestablishment of some sort of monarchical rule. See Soto, "The Monarchist Conspiracy and the Mexican War."

But Slidell's latest note indicated that he was still hoping to be received by the Paredes government. And, since he had learned that the British were preparing for war in Oregon, Polk considered it prudent to do nothing for the moment.[14]

The situation with Britain was indeed heating up. Based on an alarming report from McLane, in London, Polk sent a conciliatory message to Lord Aberdeen reinvoking the old 49th parallel proposal and conceding limited rights for Britain to navigate the Columbia River. If the British agreed, then Polk would consult an executive session of the Senate for its "advice." From his original position of demanding all of Oregon, Polk had backed down a long way.

But Congress was taking initiatives in the matter—or, at least, several factions were pulling in different directions. Calhoun, George McDuffie, and others in the Senate were promoting a resolution directing Polk to settle the Oregon conflict by compromise. Others were demanding the full Oregon territory. So Polk decided to wait. He remained truculent in public but in private was far less so. He would be content if only the Senate would approve his sending the Notice to Britain terminating the joint occupation.[15]

The Senate debate over the Notice raged on for a month, with the British watching every move. Polk could only express his frustrations to his diary: "The truth is that in all this Oregon discussion in the Senate, too many Democratic Senators have been more concerned about the Presidential election in '48 than they have been about settling Oregon at 49 degrees or 54-40."[16]

But finally the logjam broke. On April 23, 1846, the two houses of Congress approved Polk's sending the Notice. Joint occupation of Oregon would terminate in one year regardless of what might happen at the negotiating table. In the meantime, Britain was still arming, and war over Oregon remained a real possibility.

While the Oregon question was boiling Polk was watching Slidell's situation in Mexico. Despite Atocha's tantalizing "offer," Polk and his cabinet remained convinced that they would do best by dealing with the Paredes regime. Nevertheless, the Atocha visit had reawakened Polk's hopes that concessions from Mexico could be exacted more easily by offers of American dollars than by threats of force. If Slidell could be authorized to pay half a million or more dollars on the signing of a treaty, Paredes would survive in power at least long enough for a treaty to be ratified. The cabinet agreed.

This kind of diplomacy, of course, had to be handled delicately. It would be difficult to put the money in Slidell's hands "without exposing to the public and to foreign governments its object." But Polk recalled an 1806 act that had granted $2 million to President Jefferson for the purpose of purchasing Florida. Though the money was never used, the act had set a precedent. So despite the reservations of Buchanan (who considered any idea of Polk's suspect), Polk invited Senator Benton to come to the White House to discuss the idea. Benton, in favor of expansion but against war, needed no convincing.[17] On succeeding evenings Senators Allen and Cass also agreed. Only Calhoun, now back in the Senate, demurred. He was intent on getting the Oregon question settled peaceably before undertaking anything else.[18]

On April 7, however, all hope of any easy purchase of Mexican territory was dashed. Slidell reported that he would definitely not be received. Polk canceled his request for such legislative measures and considered himself committed to asking for a declaration of war against Mexico. Polk was facing a two-front war, one against Britain over Oregon, the other against Mexico on the Rio Grande.[19]

After the first contacts between Mexicans and Americans on the Rio Grande—the friendly swimming party and the hostile parley—the armies on both sides of the river settled down to a period of tense, watchful waiting. During the first night after the American arrival, Mejía's troops began building breastworks and installing a twelve-pounder cannon, placed in a position where it could "rake the front face of the American camp." In response, Taylor placed Captain James Duncan's light artillery battery in a position pointing straight at General Mejía's reported headquarters.* He also began the construction of an elaborate redoubt. Spurred by a sense of urgency, his men began work with an energy that amazed the Mexicans as they looked on.[20] But at first neither side took hostile action.

---

*Philip Barbour, *Journals,* letter to his wife, March 29, 46, pp. 20–21. Taylor's guide, named Chipita, had lived a long time in Matamoros.

The Americans were edgy. Half expecting an attack during the first night, they slept by their arms. At 10 P.M. the alarm sounded; a "large body of Mexican cavalry" had been detected on the American side of the river.[21] As it turned out, these reports were unfounded, originating probably from nervous outposts.

Although Taylor expected Mexican reinforcements to reach Matamoros in the near future, the force already in the town did not seem to present any immediate danger. Three thousand Mexican troops were thought to be on hand* but were described by one spy as "the most miserable beings," who could be whipped by one regiment. The Mexican officers, however, were seen as "polished in their manners and fine-looking fellows."[22] How much danger this combination presented was open to question. Taylor's army was too small to face all of Mexico, but how much of Mexico would be brought to bear? Hitchcock expected an attack; Taylor did not.†

Desertion among the American troops, new only in its magnitude, now became a serious problem. The Mexicans encouraged desertion cleverly, playing on the religious side of the Irish soldiers as fellow Catholics. Further, they gave royal treatment to two dragoons they had captured the day of arrival. The dragoons returned, flushed with glowing stories. The other soldiers listened to accounts of attractive women and congenial people, and the desertion rate became heavy, especially

---

*The estimate was fairly accurate. Ramón Alcaraz, *The Other Side,* p. 36, reports Mexican units as including an engineer company (sappers), the 2d Infantry Regiment (light), the 1st and 10th infantry regiments, the 7th Cavalry Regiment, several companies of the border guards, a battalion of the Matamoros National Guard, and twenty artillery pieces, three thousand men in all. They were reinforced a few days later with the 6th Marine Regiment and a battalion of the Tampico coastal defense troops.

†Kirby Smith, *Letters,* p. 35. Ethan Allen Hitchcock, *Fifty Years in Camp,* p. 218. George Meade, *Life and Letters,* p. 54. The most balanced view was taken by the articulate Major Philip N. Barbour:

In a military point of view General Taylor has committed a blunder, I think, in coming here with so small a force; although I do not apprehend we can be whipped by the Mexican force now on this frontier, yet it is but reasonable to expect that their people will rush in to defend their own firesides, and they might raise an army of 10,000 men in a short time, while we are cut off, not only from retreat, but from all succor. Considering this, it is truly surprising to see with what indifference, not to say contempt, our Officers and men look upon the Mexican batteries frowning upon us. No one seems to think a disaster to our Army a thing possible, and most of the Army are impatient and disappointed that General Taylor does not create a pretext for taking the town. Barbour, *Journals,* letter to his wife, March 30, 1846, p. 23.

the first few days. When fourteen men swam the river one night, Taylor ordered drastic measures: guards were ordered to shoot. After two men were killed, mass desertions began to diminish.[23]

Typical of the deserters was Sergeant John Riley, a tough, handsome Irishman, who had in fact deserted from the British army in Canada, then served for some time as a West Point drillmaster, and was now a sergeant with the 5th Infantry. Claiming later that he had been "seized with the desire to go to church," Sergeant Riley swam the river one Sunday morning and never returned. Possibly he was attracted as much by the Mexican offer of 320 acres of good Mexican land as by the love of God. But whatever the motivation, he had plenty of company; during the static period at Matamoros over two hundred men deserted, many of whom, like Riley, were foreign-born and had never been assimilated into American society. They had joined the army as an escape from an environment they took to be hostile, and now they were leaving that society behind them.[24]

Internal army politics continued to plague Taylor. Days after arrival at Matamoros Taylor received President Polk's ruling on the brevet question: it sided with Taylor and Twiggs by declaring that regular rank would take precedence over brevet. General Worth, that proud, aggressive, vain officer, sulked for five days, then turned in his resignation. Taylor—perhaps to Worth's surprise—accepted it on the spot, and Worth left the Rio Grande on April 8. A disgusted Hitchcock could not help asking himself "what would have been thought of the patriotism of a revolutionary officer who had abandoned his post in the presence of the enemy on an alleged grievance which, in the opinion of almost everybody, is without any proper or defensible foundation."[25] (Ironically, three days later Hitchcock himself applied for leave home on the basis of ill health.)

Materially, the Matamoros site provided little to complain about. It was early spring, before the heat, with clear days and nights, and steady sea breezes. The camping ground, a plowed field, was difficult to walk on, but an abundance of wood was available, and the Rio Grande provided good fresh water.[26] But though the climate was generally agreeable, it was not always calm. About ten days after arrival a violent storm nearly demolished camp. Kirby Smith and his younger brother barely saved their "frail house."[27]

.   .   .

On April 9, 1846, Taylor's army was shaken when Colonel Truman
Cross, Taylor's quartermaster, failed to return from a routine horseback
ride. Cross was a popular officer, and fears for his safety grew when the
army learned that Antonio Canales with his hated "rancheros" (guerrillas) had been detected in the vicinity. As the days dragged on without
news of Cross his fate became an obsession in the camp.

While the Americans grieved for Cross the Mexicans in Matamoros
learned that General Pedro de Ampudia would soon arrive with about
three thousand additional men. Though grateful for the reinforcements, the people of Matamoros were dismayed at the appointment of
this forty-two-year-old Cuban because of his well-earned reputation for
needless cruelty. He had attained the sobriquet of "the assassin of
Sentmanat," because of his execution of one Francisco Sentmanat in
1844, in which he fried his victim's head in oil, the better to preserve
it for display in the public square of San Juan Batista.[28] Moreover,
Ampudia was considered an opportunist and an incompetent,[29] appointed only because he had seconded Paredes's pronunciamento at
San Luis Potosí the previous December. Because of all this, the townspeople of Matamoros immediately wrote to President Paredes, asking
that another general be sent, hinting that General Mariano Arista
might be the man.[30]

Ampudia, unaware of the attitude prevalent at Matamoros, arrived
on April 11, eager to cross the Rio Grande and give battle at once, even
though Paredes would not declare his "defensive" war for another
twelve days. Ampudia began preparations for an attack to be executed
as early as the fifteenth, the day after his reinforcing troops were
scheduled to arrive. In preparation, he sent Taylor an ultimatum threatening war unless there was an American withdrawal to the Nueces
River within twenty-four hours:

> To Don Z. Taylor: . . . I require you in all form, and at the latest in the
> peremptory term of twenty-four hours, to break up your camp and return
> to the east bank of the Nueces River while our Governments are regulat-
> ing the pending question in relation to Texas. If you insist on remaining
> upon the soil of the Department of Tamaulipas, it will certainly result
> that arms, and arms alone, must decide the question; and in that case

I advise you that we accept the war to which, with so much injustice on your part, you provoke us. . . .[31]

Taylor responded, politely but unambiguously: "I regret the alternative which you offer; but, at the same time, wish it understood that I shall by no means avoid such alternative. . . ."[32]

Ampudia doubtless expected such a reply, but as he was preparing to respond, on the evening of April 14, he learned that he was soon to be replaced by General Arista. Desperately, he called a council of war requesting support for going ahead with the attack on the basis that Mexico City was unaware of the situation at the river. Ampudia's officers, though also eager for action, refused to disobey the orders of Paredes. Without the support of any of his officers, Ampudia had no choice but to await the arrival of Arista and then to serve under him.*

On April 15 General Taylor considered the two nations at war by force of Ampudia's ultimatum. Accordingly, he gave orders to the ships Conner had left with him to blockade the mouth of the Rio Grande. The American naval commander at the Brazos Santiago was to stop all vessels and remove all munitions of war and food bound for Matamoros. With six thousand Mexican troops in that small city, rations would soon be short, and the Mexican command would be forced to act.[33]

In the American camp, meanwhile, the urge grew to investigate the fate of Colonel Cross. One individual attempt was suspicious, to say the least: a lieutenant swam the Rio Grande, ostensibly to look for Cross, and was immediately captured, evoking nobody's sympathy. But on the official side, Lieutenant David Porter† set out with a patrol of ten men to the vicinity of Cross's presumed death. The patrol was ambushed, and Porter was brutally murdered. Cross's body was found shortly after that, and nobody had any doubts that he had died at the hands of "a

---

*Alcaraz, pp. 39–41; Cadmus Wilcox, *History of the Mexican War*, p. 43. Mexican commanders, when superseded, usually remained and served under their successors.

†Porter was the son of the famous naval officer whose ships had actually assisted the Mexicans in the revolution against Spain a quarter century earlier.

party from the other side who were hovering around the camp." A thirst for revenge set in among the Americans.*

General Mariano Arista, age forty-three, freckled and sandy-haired, was one of the most respected of the Mexican generals. Some years before, he had fallen out with Santa Anna and had taken refuge in the United States until Santa Anna's fall in late 1844.[34] But despite his connections with the Americans Arista was no less eager to take action against Taylor than Ampudia had been. On April 23, even before he arrived at Matamoros, he sent General Anastasio Torrejón, with 1,600 cavalrymen, to cross the Rio Grande a few miles upstream of Taylor's army. Taylor, in response, sent Captain Seth Thornton, with a patrol of only sixty-three dragoons, to intercept them. The American patrol was ambushed; sixteen men were killed or wounded and all the rest, including its commander, were captured.

On Sunday, April 26, General Taylor reported the action to Washington: ". . . Hostilities may now be considered as commenced."[35]

At the same time he called on the governor of Texas for four regiments of volunteers—not state militia. Those volunteers would be unencumbered by the embarrassing strictures of the Constitution against use in enemy territory.

In Washington President James Polk was preparing to send a war message to a skeptical Congress, though he was not quite certain that Congress would accede to such a declaration. By Tuesday, May 5,

---

*Meade, letter April 22, 1846., pp. 67–68. "I am sorry to tell you the remains of Colonel Cross have been found, and it is now placed beyond a doubt that he was foully assassinated by a party from the other side who were hovering around our camp, and that at the very time General Ampudia replied to General Taylor's letter, denying any knowledge of his disappearance, it is now known he was wearing the watch of the unfortunate victim, and some other officers riding his horse. . . . He will be buried with the honors of war, though his poor son intends taking him to Washington with him. . . . This dastardly act, and the mean lie of the commanding-general on the other side, have inspired us all with a burning desire to avenge the Colonel's murder, and have destroyed all the sympathy that some few did still entertain for a people they deemed unjustly treated. . . ."

Unlike the fate of Cross, however, the officers of the army regarded Porter's death as honorable, "a soldier's fate in so gallant a manner." The fact that he "made three of his enemies bite the dust before he fell," and that the "cowardly" enemy had allowed nine men to escape, seems to have provided more satisfaction than grief. Meade, letter, April 21, 1846, p. 66.

however, he had learned of Ampudia's ultimatum and of Taylor's blockade of the mouth of the Rio Grande, and although there was still no word of actual hostilities, Polk was confident that he had only to wait for such a report.

On Friday, May 8, John Slidell returned from Mexico and called on Polk. Perhaps defensive over the failure of his mission, Slidell was vociferous in insisting that the United States take "redress" of Mexican "wrongs and injuries" and "act with promptness and energy"—by which he meant war. Polk was inclined to agree. The people of the United States, he reasoned, had taken Slidell's rejection as a national insult, which was only the latest in a series at that.* It was "only a matter of time," he told Slidell, before he would "make such a communication to the Congress."[36]

The next day, Saturday, Polk met again with his cabinet. Only Buchanan and Secretary of the Navy George Bancroft were fearful of congressional resistance to war and of hostility from the British. Polk overrode them, declaring that ample cause for war already existed, that he could not "stand in the status quo" any longer, and that he was obligated to submit a war message to Congress by the coming Tuesday —any failure to do so would constitute neglect of his duty.[37] In a final poll, only Bancroft held out against war; even Buchanan grudgingly assented. Polk resolved to submit the message on Tuesday.

At 6 P.M. that evening the pace of events accelerated further. Adjutant General Roger Jones called on the President, and in his hand was Taylor's dispatch of April 26 warning that hostilities had commenced. Late in the day though it was, the Washington *Union* still managed to carry the flash in the evening edition: "American blood has been shed on American soil!" it screamed. And its editor, the loyal Thomas Ritchie, somehow managed to place the blame for Taylor's dangerous position on Taylor himself. Though the general had been authorized to call for volunteers, the news article blandly stated, he had, unfortunately, "not made his call in time to secure himself against all possible contingencies."[38]

Polk then called an evening meeting of the cabinet. This time Polk met no resistance, even from Bancroft; he would now send his war message to Congress on Monday rather than Tuesday.

---

*"The indignity to our minister requires atonement," said the New Orleans *Picayune;* the St. Louis *Republican* declared that the United States owed it to her character and dignity "not to suffer so open an insult to her representative to pass unnoticed." Polk, pp. 81–82.

With that decision, the White House became a center of intense activity. Clerks from the State and War departments scurried across Washington to begin copying the previous correspondence between Slidell and the Mexican government, as well as that between the War Department and Taylor, all of which would be included with Polk's message. Buchanan and Bancroft, the two erstwhile dissenters, stayed on to assist the President in preparing the message. Buchanan, fortunately, had already compiled a "history of our causes of complaint" against Mexico.

The next morning, Sunday, Polk was at his desk again, the excitement on the streets outside constantly reminding him of the need to submit his message the next day. The President suspended his efforts for only a little over an hour, long enough to take his wife, niece, and nephew to church. After lunch his labors were broken only by calls from selected persons, largely members of Congress, whom he had invited to come and share their views. He finished working at 10:30 P.M., later recording piously that he "regretted the necessity which had existed to make it necessary for me to spend the Sabbath in the manner I have."*

Polk's message was a long, exhaustive lawyer's brief. The Mexicans, of course, were castigated, and sorrow was expressed that the "grievous wrongs perpetrated upon our citizens throughout a long period of years remain unredressed." The United States' forbearance, it claimed, had been exhausted, "even before the recent information from the frontier of the Del Norte."† But Mexico had invaded our territory, and had shed American blood. The two nations were now at war, and Mexico was entirely to blame.[39] This viewpoint was a masterpiece of rationalization. The kindest thing that can be said about Polk's message is that he probably believed it himself.

On Monday, May 11, 1846, the House of Representatives sat for an hour and a half while the clerk read Polk's message and the pertinent documents attached. Then, after only a thirty-minute debate, that body voted to approve Polk's recommendations by the one-sided count

---

*Polk, May 9, 10, 1846, pp. 84–86. Callers included Senator Sam Houston, Congressman Barclay Martin, all members of the cabinet individually except Marcy (indisposed), Messrs. Haralson and Baker from the House, and Chief Justice Ingersoll.
†Del Norte was a term frequently used in referring to the Rio Grande.

of 173 to 14. The fourteen votes against the measure, however, would later assume importance, as the dissenters were led by former President John Quincy Adams himself, and the group would later be dubbed the "Immortal Fourteen" in New England. And the man privileged to carry the news of the lopsided vote to Polk, during the late afternoon, was none other than Slidell himself.

The Senate took longer, with Calhoun and Benton stubbornly demurring. For a while it appeared that a small group of Democratic senators might join with a united Whig party to defeat Polk's declaration. But opposition was all bombast; even the Senate could not deny the President the means to conduct a war that already existed. The next evening word came to the White House that the Senate also had approved by a vote of 40 to 2. Calhoun, who had spoken in opposition, had abstained. War with Mexico was now officially a fact.

Polk's determination to manipulate a war with Mexico appears to have had the effect of making Britain more cooperative. By June 12, a month after the declaration, Britain and the United States had agreed on a compromise line for the division of Oregon. The boundary between the United States and Canada would run along the 49th parallel to the Strait of San Juan de Fuca, ceding to Britain all of Vancouver Island and granting her unrestricted navigation of the Columbia River until 1859. On June 15, 1846, Buchanan and Pakenham signed a treaty, and three days later the Senate ratified it by a vote of 41 to 14.

Polk could congratulate himself. The specter of simultaneous wars with Mexico and Britain had been averted. Now he could turn his attentions, with minimal distraction, to the war in the South.

ZACHARY TAYLOR'S WAR

"I WAS GLAD
I WAS NOT
WITH THEM!"

APRIL 26–MAY 17, 1846

Taylor had no time to ponder. A sizable Mexican force, he knew, was on the east bank of the Rio Grande, upstream of his army, though he had no idea of its strength. But of one thing he was sure: he could not afford to sit and await developments. Back at Point Isabel he had left a supply depot without adequate defense; at Matamoros he had a defense without supplies. And a report that three Mexican regiments had attacked Major Monroe's small garrison gave him alarm.* If the enemy was across the river in that strength, he reasoned, he could not afford to send back a train with only the normal security escort; any expedition smaller than his entire army would be seriously endangered. So in the early afternoon of May 1, 1846, Taylor struck his tents at Matamoros. He left the 7th Infantry to hold the makeshift defenses of "Fort Texas" and moved out with his three hundred wagons.

Taylor's was a high-spirited army, conscious of marching to Point Isabel not only for supplies but also for a fight. The men held no hatred for the Mexicans—on the contrary, the account given by Thornton of

---

*Barbour, *Journals*, April 27,28, pp. 49–50. General Antonio Canales, who had come back into the fold since his pronouncement at Carmago the previous winter, had reportedly led an attack of one cavalry and two infantry regiments. The report later turned out to be false.

the considerate treatment accorded him and his men in captivity had brought forth expressions of gratitude.* But they realized that they would not be safe from further such actions until the Mexican army in the area was roundly defeated. And another intangible entered the picture: Taylor's force of regulars knew they would soon become diluted by the influx of thousands of volunteers, who would inevitably receive all the credit for any future victory in which they participated. So Taylor's men were itching to win a victory for which the Regular Army—and the Regular Army alone—could claim the laurels. If that was to happen, the enemy must be met soon.†

The 7th Infantry, left behind at Fort Texas, was a proud regiment, nicknamed the Cotton Balers because of their heroic defense behind bales of cotton in the Battle of New Orleans during the War of 1812. It was commanded by Major Jacob Brown, a fifty-eight-year-old native of Massachusetts, who had signed up as a private thirty years before. An officer of the 7th Infantry ever since, Brown had earned high respect for his military conduct and impeccable integrity. His regiment was reinforced by two artillery batteries of eight guns: one battery consisted of four powerful eighteen-pounders. The other, commanded by Lieutenant Braxton Bragg, included three six-pounders and a mortar. Though Bragg's light artillery would be of limited use in a fixed emplacement, Taylor felt that Major Brown needed the extra firepower. And as if to make the cook taste his own dish first, Taylor detailed Captain Joseph K. F. Mansfield, the engineer who had designed the fortifications and supervised their construction, to remain with Brown also.

Camp women as well as soldiers remained with the regiment. One was to become more famous than most of the combatants. Her name was Sarah Borginnis, better known as the Great Western after a noted steamship of the day. Her legend as one of the most colorful figures of the Southwest had already begun. A strapping, muscular woman six feet in height, she reputedly could trounce any man in the regiment, and once had nearly done so when an unwary soldier made an untoward remark to her back at Corpus Christi. At the Arroyo Colorado she had reportedly offered to cross the stream herself and "straighten out" the entire Mexican army.[1] But despite her strength and pugnacity, she was

---

*Thornton was placed under court-martial to investigate his conduct of the patrol action.
†The unanimity of this feeling is unquestionable. Barbour (p. 47), Kirby Smith (*To Mexico with Scott*, p. 53), and George Meade (*Life and Letters*, p. 76) all express it strongly.

physically attractive, with dark hair and gray-blue eyes, and she could be tender of heart when the situation called for it. She cared for her boys, refusing the easy journey by water from Corpus Christi to the Rio Grande on the basis that they needed her services as laundress and cook. Regulations specified that only married women could accompany an army in the field, but that detail presented no problem to the Great Western, for she was currently the wife of a soldier of the 7th Infantry.* Though officially a noncombatant, she and her like shared the hardships and the dangers of the troops.

Taylor's determination to complete Fort Texas before marching off to Point Isabel caused him to delay longer than he would have liked, but the time was well spent. Situated on a strategic point in the course of the winding Rio Grande, the position dominated the river both upstream and down. Three of its six redans commanded the town of Matamoros to its front. Its eight-hundred-yard perimeter consisted of a wall over nine feet high and fifteen feet thick at its base, surrounded by a ditch eight feet deep. Though of necessity it was built entirely of earth, it was considered secure against twelve-pounders, the largest guns that the Mexicans could bring to bear. Inside, Taylor left the garrison with two weeks' rations and what was assumed to be ample ammunition. The fort should have no trouble holding out pending Taylor's return—given reasonable good fortune.

On May 1, the same day that Taylor left Fort Texas, General Arista left Colonel Mejía with a small garrison in Matamoros and moved the main body of his army downstream of the Rio Grande toward a place called Longoreno, where he intended to cross to the left bank. Torrejón, who was still upstream of Taylor, was thereupon ordered to make a wide sweep around the rear of Taylor's army and join Arista at Longoreno. If all went well, Arista would then have his entire force concentrated in Taylor's rear, between the Americans and their supply depot at Point Isabel. It was a good plan, though perhaps the rough route assigned to Torrejón was too long to allow Arista to calculate the exact time to cover it.

Arista's army was in a strange mood. Conscious of their numerical

---

*One account calls her "Sarah Bourdett." Nevertheless, her accepted name at this time was Borginnis, after her husband of the moment. During the war she changed husbands freely, cheerfully, and informally. See Samuel Chamberlain, *My Confession*, pp. 241–42.

superiority, they marched with careless abandon—but their confidence was brittle, shaken partly by the backbiting and recriminations among the officers. General Ampudia had not taken his relief stoically, and was sowing mistrust of Arista at all opportunities; Arista himself was uncomfortable with the fact that his plan had been pressed on him by the Ministry of War back in Mexico City. His own lack of confidence must have been contagious.[2]

The operation ran into snags from the start. Torrejón's wing moved slower than expected, and when the man reached Longoreno, they found only two boats on hand to ferry them across; twenty-four hours were consumed in carrying the combat elements alone. By the time Arista had drawn his force up on the east bank, scouts informed him that Taylor's force had already passed in the direction of Point Isabel. The Mexicans had moved too slowly; Taylor had slipped out of the trap.

But Arista was not discouraged. He would find a good position and await Taylor's inevitable return. As soon as the guns at Matamoros began to bombard the American fortification on the opposite side, Taylor would feel compelled to leave Point Isabel and return to the aid of the garrison. Then, outnumbered, he would be forced to attack Arista's superior force.[3]

Meanwhile Zachary Taylor was pushing his army hard toward Point Isabel. He was an anxious man, hardly the cool and collected commander depicted in later political posters. Conflicting reports had come from Major Monroe, and he was disturbed to learn that Captain Sam Walker's company of Texas rangers* had lost ten men to a ranchero raid on the night of April 29, which signaled a sobering aggressiveness on the part of the Mexicans. Thus spurred on, Taylor drove his men so ruthlessly that even the tough veterans complained: departure in midafternoon, short sleep with no campfires, moving on at dawn to Point Isabel—nearly thirty miles, over rough country, in less than twenty-one hours. Stonewall Jackson's "foot cavalry" would never do better.

---

*Walker's company, of seventy-seven men at the time, was the only volunteer unit that up to then Taylor had permitted to serve in his army. He consented to employing these irregulars only after the death of Colonel Cross. See Barbour, p. 50.

Taylor arrived at Point Isabel at noon on May 2. Feverishly he began loading his three hundred wagons and strengthening the depot's meager defenses. Fort Polk, as he had named the position, needed much work because it was vulnerable to enemy attack from the mainland side. Shortly after Taylor's arrival his work was interrupted by the sound of artillery fire from the direction of Matamoros and Fort Texas. Forty years later Ulysses S. Grant, would recall: ". . . for myself, a young second-lieutenant who had never heard a hostile gun before, I felt sorry that I had enlisted."[4]

Taylor once more faced a dilemma, torn between completing the defenses at Point Isabel and a strong urge to march back and reinforce his troops at Fort Texas. He knew, however, that he had prepared the 7th Infantry for a two-week siege, and before reacting sent a body of Texans, under Sam Walker, to make contact with Major Brown. Walker was familiar with the territory and was confident that he could get through and return. And perhaps he could partially regain face after the humiliating surprise his rangers had endured a few evenings before.

The evening of May 1 had passed pleasantly at Fort Texas. Then, the next evening, the garrison heard church bells ringing in Matamoros. As the men peered curiously across the river they saw a procession of priests and monks on the opposite bank, moving from one artillery position to another, blessing every gun.

The Mexican cannons opened fire the next morning. But as the bombardment progressed Brown and his men realized that the fort would hold despite the heavy fire. Its design, and the backbreaking labor that had gone into its construction, were paying off. The siege, they knew, would settle down to a test of will; the noise and the fatigue of staying constantly alert—through the next week, it turned out—would tax the endurance of the garrison. One veteran soldier later admitted that he "would rather have fought twenty battles" than have passed through that bombardment.[5]

As of May 5, only one man in Fort Texas had been killed in the artillery storm—Sergeant Weigart, of the 7th Infantry—but his fate was macabre: after Weigart was killed instantly by a shell, his body was then hit by another as it lay on the surgeon's table, and then, after burial, it was exhumed by a third, which exploded on his grave.[6] Several other men were wounded, and Sarah Borginnis, who at one point had a plate of food shattered in her hand, was kept frantically busy. But she took care of the men—and of the women as well.

Walker reported back to Taylor on May 5. Although the rest of his men had been unable to get through, Walker himself had actually reached Fort Texas and conferred with Major Brown. Brown's report was optimistic. The Mexican twelve-pounders had been silenced; the only piece still firing was a single mortar, placed too low to hit. Brown had been abstemious with his ammunition, was in high spirits, and expected to hold out as long as his provisions lasted. Though Walker had heard some small arms firing after his departure, Taylor was reassured and remained at Point Isabel for two more days.*

Taylor's Army of Occupation left Point Isabel on May 7, determined to shoot their way back to Fort Texas. Major William W. S. Bliss, Taylor's adjutant, issued a general order before leaving: the army would march at three o'clock that afternoon, and if the enemy was still on the route, the general would give battle. He had no doubt of the result. Bliss finished with Taylor's watchword: "[The general] wishes to enjoin upon the battalions of Infantry that their main dependence must be in the bayonet."[7]

Taylor's army marched seven miles on the Matamoros road that evening; the next morning they struck out again across the broad, incredibly flat plain. Progress was slow through the sand, but after eleven miles, at the pond of Palo Alto, Taylor's lead scouts uncovered Arista's army, drawn up in a double line a mile in length, barring the Matamoros road.

This was a tense moment, the one that Taylor's men had been training for these last nine months, the one they had been wishing for ever since the Thornton disaster. But the circumstances were awkward. Taylor, not Arista, had been surprised and Taylor knew he must break through a superior force, outnumbered by nearly three to one.

Arista had arrived only that morning, but he had chosen his position well. And despite his superiority in numbers, he was content to defend, for he knew that the pressure was on Taylor. Taylor sent two young

*A great deal of publicity was accorded Walker's exploit in the United States. In a few weeks a ship brought Walker a new horse, a present from the grateful citizens of New Orleans. Walter Webb, *The Texas Rangers in the Mexican War.*

engineers, Jacob Blake and Lloyd Tilghman, to reconnoiter, and they reported that Arista's flanks were secure—one sealed by an impassable swamp, the other by a wooded knoll. The center of Arista's position was flat, but high chaparral limited visibility, as did the fact that the defensive line lay just south of a bend in the road. Moreover, Taylor's massive supply trains—three hundred wagons and hundreds of mules and oxen—were unusually vulnerable to cavalry attack. Since Taylor could not move them into the dense woods for protection, Arista's cavalry might ride around Taylor's column and plunder his lifeline. Taylor protected his wagon park with a squadron of dragoons and a couple of artillery pieces,[8] but protecting that Achilles' heel cost him valuable troops.

The move from the road into a line of skirmishers was done quickly, for Taylor's small regiments, averaging fewer than three hundred men each, could maneuver off the road smartly, and his whole column could pass a point in half an hour. And Arista allowed him to do so. He did not attack; he waited.

Taylor, too, delayed, allowing his men to fill their canteens in the pond, half of them at a time. Then he moved his troops into line. He placed the 8th Infantry on the left (Duncan's light artillery battery supporting), then the 4th, the 3d, and the 5th infantries. Sam Ringgold's light artillery battery was with the 5th Infantry on the right. The heavy eighteen-pounders in the center would fire from the road, between the 3d and 4th infantries. The "long roll sounds, hearts beat, pulses keep time, and knees tremble and will not be still."* Taylor himself sat sidesaddle on his mount, Old Whitey, and contemplated the field, a chaw of tobacco in his cheek.

Old Zack did not have to wait long. Soon the Mexican artillery opened up from a range of seven hundred yards. But the Mexicans lacked high explosive shells, and their artillery balls struck the ground before the Americans, bouncing along so slowly that they could be ducked. Now Taylor's artillery began hitting back, and the day that his young artillerists had waited for was here. Out in front went the batteries of Ringgold, Duncan, Ridgeley, and Bragg,† unlimbering and pouring fire, one round a minute, into the Mexican ranks.

Arista would have liked to attack. His men were falling all around

*Samuel French, *Two Wars.* Past tense in the original.
†Brevet Major Samuel Ringgold, Captains Braxton Bragg, James Duncan, and Randolph Ridgeley.

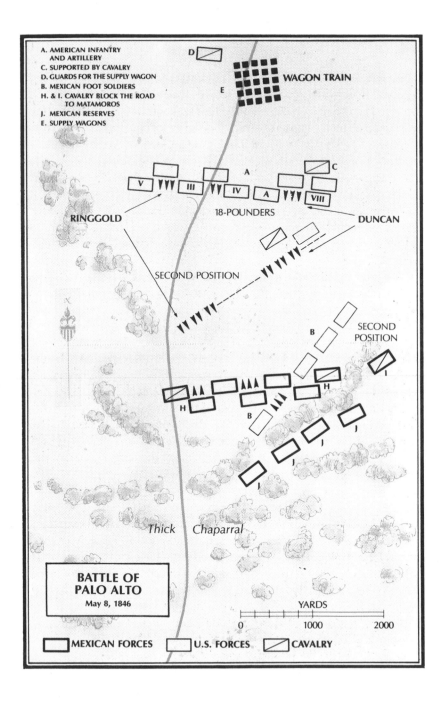

A. AMERICAN INFANTRY
   AND ARTILLERY
C. SUPPORTED BY CAVALRY
D. GUARDS FOR THE SUPPLY WAGON
B. MEXICAN FOOT SOLDIERS
H. & I. CAVALRY BLOCK THE ROAD
   TO MATAMOROS
J. MEXICAN RESERVES
E. SUPPLY WAGONS

WAGON TRAIN

RINGGOLD

18-POUNDERS

DUNCAN

SECOND POSITION

SECOND
POSITION

Thick Chaparral

BATTLE OF
PALO ALTO
May 8, 1846

YARDS

0   1000   2000

MEXICAN FORCES   U.S. FORCES   CAVALRY

him, and the Yankee artillery would have no more effect on his lines up close than it was having back here. But Arista realized that he could never control his infantry through that chaparral, so he decided to attack only with his cavalry. Along Taylor's right flank came the thundering lancers. The 8th Infantry, soon to be surrounded, quickly formed a hollow square, and Ringgold poured fire into the oncoming ranks. Torrejón's men paused. Then they dropped back, leaving many horsemen behind. The U.S. infantry had performed its only maneuver of the day, rotating its right flank forward, not to attack the enemy but to provide a position from which to "sustain Ringgold."*

The two sides paused to catch their breath. Arista tried another cavalry assault on Taylor's left, toward Taylor's exposed train. But his horsemen had lost their zeal, and they also fell back.

By late afternoon neither side had accomplished anything decisive. But maybe the gods were tired of this battle, for they set the grass on fire; bladed prairie grass burned like straws. The smoke blinded both armies—already blind enough from the oppressive chaparral. Many Mexican wounded, lying on the field, tragically burned to death.† When the smoke cleared, Taylor sent a force of dragoons forward on a hard ride toward the Mexican wagon park. But the Mexican trains were covered also. Luckily for the Americans, Arista had no flying artillery to cut them down; they returned nearly unscathed.

Arista's confused soldiers now demanded that the slaughter end. They could not reach their enemy and close in a glorious charge; they were being killed unmercifully at long range. Arista reluctantly complied.

But the battle was indecisive. If rated on points, Taylor could claim victory, as he had lost only four men killed and forty-two officers and men wounded; some five hundred Mexican bodies lay on the field. But he had not broken through; Arista had not fled—he had merely withdrawn a short distance. Taylor would be forced to fight again.

---

*Barbour, p. 55. The exact location of the troops at Palo Alto has been a matter of controversy since it was fought. The most reliable authority had been Mr. A. A. Champion, of Brownsville, who through the years has collected all available accounts and collated them. At one point the U.S. government believed him incorrect because of the large amounts of metal found by engineer mine detector equipment. It turned out that the "battle position" was the impact area of an old artillery firing range, in use long after the Mexican War. Bruce Aiken, interview with author, September 1983.

†Ramón Alcaraz, *The Other Side*, p. 47, puts the timing of the fire before Torrejón's attack on Taylor's right. He also attributes the fire to an American "stratagem."

For the most part, the American casualties at Palo Alto had been minimal. But Taylor had lost two officers, mortally wounded. Sam Ringgold had had both thighs torn out, and Captain John Page had lost his lower jaw to a Mexican cannonball. Both men died slowly at Point Isabel. A particular loss to the army was the death of Ringgold, the pioneer of the invaluable Flying Artillery. But, in a way, Ringgold's greatest service had been performed even before Palo Alto, when he had developed that weapon and had trained the artillerists who would use it in this and later battles.

Arista's men spent a miserable night, mourning their dead and dreading the next day's battle. Portions of the grass fire still raged, its "sinister splendor"9 illuminating the camp. The surgeon to whom the medicine chests had been entrusted had disappeared in the fire that afternoon; the luckier among the wounded were piled into wagons and sent back to Matamoros. Worst of all, Mexican morale had been dealt a devastating blow. After decades, even centuries, of deception on the part of their leaders, Mexican troops had little real trust in them. They could be led into battle only by temporarily instilling in them a contempt for their enemies. Now, with the Americans showing unexpected strength, Arista's army had quickly concluded that "skill and valor could never bring victory." Immediately their thoughts turned to betrayal; even Arista himself was accused of treason. Mexican psychology went even further: they were being punished for the ambition and stupidity of their leaders. The Yankees were merely the agents of evil, sent to Mexico to chastise her.10

The next morning, at 6 A.M., Arista decided to retreat from the field of Palo Alto to a stronger position. His army, conducted by Ampudia, arrived at the new defense four hours later. Taylor did not interfere, so Arista had time to prepare for another battle.

Arista formed his second position at a place called Resaca de la Palma,11 utilizing the empty lake bed itself to bolster his defenses. The feature, typical of the region, was a onetime channel of the ever-changing Rio Grande, resembling what is called a bayou in Louisiana. Though such a formation can be dry or filled, this one was dry, and its configuration made it an admirable obstacle for defense. Arista's reports of that evening exude confidence and optimism.

. . .

On discovering that Arista had left Palo Alto the morning of May 9, Taylor called a council of war to discuss the next move. His own inclination had always been to pursue Arista, but strong arguments existed for breaking off contact. After all, the Mexican army had not been destroyed and was still far larger than his own. Most of his officers at the conference—seven out of ten, it turned out—favored remaining at his present position and awaiting the volunteers that Taylor had called for twelve days earlier. That course might have been wise, considering the odds, but it was not Taylor's style. He heard his officers out and then sided with the minority: "Gentlemen, you will prepare your commands to move forward."*

Taylor's men hit the road. After marching six miles toward Matamoros, they stopped. Taylor's scouts had encountered Arista's pickets, this time just north of Resaca de la Palma. Taylor rode up, scanned Arista's position through his field glasses, and decided to attack. But today he took careful measures regarding his train. He assigned 250 men to protect them, men who were not members of regiments, and bolstered them with the two eighteen-pounders, which he had not found particularly effective the day before. The rest of his men, as he had admonished at El Fronton, could put "reliance on the bayonet."

Taylor would have preferred to repeat his easy victory of the day before by again pounding the enemy with artillery. But the thick chaparral precluded reliance on long range fire; so thick was it that even control of infantry was difficult. The fighting would degenerate into a melee, a collection of small actions.

In early afternoon Taylor galloped forward. There Captain George A. McCall, of the 4th Infantry, reported that the enemy had taken position in the chaparral on both the near and the far sides of the Resaca. Arista's force was occupying a long line, but only a small portion of it counted, the area around the road to Matamoros. So

---

*Versions of the episode vary. Barbour (*Journals*, p. 57) gives credit to McIntosh, Duncan, and Captain Morris for advocating a continuation of the fight. All agree that Taylor was encouraged by the enthusiasm of some junior officer, but the identity varies. Sedgwick, who was not there, holds that it was Duncan, passing by, who volunteered, "General, we whipped them yesterday and we can whip them again." Others say it was Ridgely.

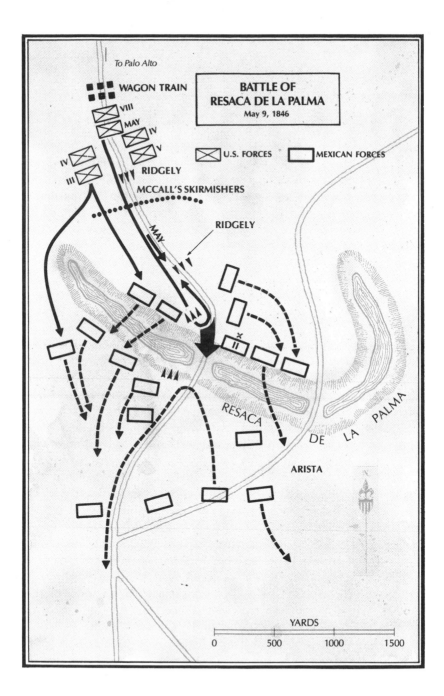

To Palo Alto

WAGON TRAIN

VIII

MAY

IV

V

IV

III

RIDGELY

McCALL'S SKIRMISHERS

MAY

RIDGELY

BATTLE OF
RESACA DE LA PALMA
May 9, 1846

U.S. FORCES   MEXICAN FORCES

RESACA

DE   LA   PALMA

ARISTA

N

YARDS

0   500   1000   1500

Taylor placed his four infantry regiments astride that road, the 5th and the 8th in column on the left and the 3d and 4th on the right.

But first, maybe Ridgely, now commanding Ringgold's battery, could blast a hole through Arista's position. Ridgeley unlimbered within view of the enemy position and fired. But the chaparral hid his view, and he failed to detect a column of Mexican cavalry bearing down upon him until it was almost on top of him. Ridgeley was suddenly in dire straits. He fired one point-blank blast into the oncoming lancers, and then prepared to defend hand to hand. But the fire had had its effect; the lancers fell back. Close fighting continued among the infantry around him in the cruel, ripping chaparral.

Taylor, on hand at the critical point, was determined to move forward. Maybe the dragoons! He sent for Captain Charles May and ordered him to take his company straight against the battery of guns directly ahead. Ridgeley, aware of May's preparations, shouted, "Wait, Charley, until I draw fire!" So saying, Ridgeley let loose a round. The Mexicans answered.

May now knew where the guns were. Forward he galloped, four horsemen abreast, confined to the road, his long black hair flying in the breeze. Like the six hundred at Balaclava some years later, he charged the guns, crossed over, and confronted Mexican General La Vega. But then, finding himself surrounded by enemy infantry—and the Mexican artillerymen returning to their pieces—he turned around and led his dragoons on a wild gallop the quarter mile back.*

Taylor witnessed the action from a vantage point. Now nearing exasperation, he turned to Colonel Belknap of the 8th Infantry: "Take those guns and by God keep them!" Belknap's men charged. They took the guns and kept them. They kept General La Vega as well.

At about this time Arista was belatedly becoming suspicious that the battle was serious. Rushing to the front, he brushed aside the crestfallen Canares, who had had enough fighting, and personally led his lancers in one more vainglorious charge. But a few more rounds—and Mexican casualties—and Arista himself turned back.

Few of Arista's soldiers fought in this battle—they were too spread out. But they could see what was happening, that the heart of their

---

*May was given unjustified credit for having captured General La Vega. Newspapers in the United States carried artists' conceptions of the dramatic moment. May was given a double brevet to lieutenant colonel. Never a popular officer with his peers, his undeserved good fortune brought ridicule upon him. He continued, however, to serve efficiently as a dragoon.

army had been cut out, their line of retreat to Matamoros overrun. Their spirits, already fragile, broke. When they saw the elite Mexican 2d Brigade fall back, panic set in. The rest gave up, fleeing to the rear in droves.

The Battle of Resaca de la Palma now degenerated into a rout. Taylor's army followed the panic-stricken enemy as closely as possible to the Rio Grande. The defenders of Fort Texas, cheering and exultant, watched the fugitives go past; but Mexican batteries across the river made it impossible for them to break out and add to the casualties.

Taylor followed along in the pursuit toward Fort Texas. On arriving, he was shocked to learn that the gallant old Jacob Brown had been hit by a shell while inspecting his positions on May 5, and had died that morning. But otherwise victory was sweet. That night an elated Old Rough and Ready penned a triumphant message back to the adjutant general: "Our victory has been complete."

And it was. Seven pieces of artillery, much ammunition, three standards, and some 100 prisoners, including General La Vega, had been taken. The losses for the two days' battles were, as Taylor reported, 34 Americans killed, 113 wounded. For the Mexicans, he could only guess that 300 were killed; he reported burying 200; Meade later placed their losses at 1,200 killed and wounded, 300 drowned while swimming the river, and between 1,000 and 2,000 deserters.[12]

Now began the grisly task of burying the dead. The soldiers did their best, but the wolves and vultures did much of the job. On the lighter side, the men found great booty in General Arista's tent. Though the silver and valuable luxuries automatically became the property of the U.S. government, piles of his writing paper fell into individual hands, and many a proud note was written home on sheets of it.

On May 17, 1846, General Taylor issued General Order No. 62. Fort Texas would hereafter be named Fort Brown, and the present city of Brownsville would grow up around it.

Years later a ferryman named Ramón would recall early May 1846:

> It took me three days to ferry all the Mexican army over, crossing and crossing back, day and night, night and day. And, oh, I had much desire

to go with the troops. There was *musica,* oh so lively, and there were the *banderas* all flying bright in the air, and the men were all happy and singing. But I did not go, and in three days they were back, but without any *musica* or *banderas* and not needing any ferry-boat. They came in flocks, running and crawling like *tortugas,* and they fell into the water flat on all fours like *tortugas* and never stopped till they were in the brush of the *Republica Mejicana.* They had been at the fight of what we call Resaca de la Palma, and I was very glad that I had not been with them."[13]

"A HASTY PLATE OF SOUP"

⤳⤳⤳

SUMMER 1846, IN WASHINGTON

F ar to the north of the action on the Rio Grande, American public opinion was shifting decisively. Word of the Thornton debacle reached New Orleans several days before it arrived in Washington. As Zachary Taylor was preparing his official dispatch, newspaper reporters on the scene were likewise writing their accounts. Since both types of communication would go on the same ships, the stories destined for the New Orleans papers would be blazing headlines days before the government had any inkling of what had happened. The public, long held in suspense by the dwindling hopes for the Slidell mission, by the fall of the Herrera government in Mexico, by Taylor's move to the Rio Grande, and finally by the murder of Colonel Cross, now reacted like the breaking of a dam. In the Southwest, where the Mexican threat was considered very real, where the Texans of the Alamo, Goliad, and the ill-fated Mier 1843 expedition had been friends and kinfolk, where Mexicans in general and Ampudia in particular had long been seen as "wicked barbarians," men thronged to the banners. They could not stand idle while Taylor's army was in danger.

One officer, writing years later, could still feel the impulse of the moment:

Scattered throughout the country, especially in the Southern and Western states, were many who had taken an active part in the Texan struggle
for independence and returning home were objects of attention, notably
at barbecues and mass meetings, so dear to the American heart, where
their denunciation of Mexican oppression and cruelty, and their descriptions of the heroic sufferings of the Texan martyrs never failed to touch
a responsive chord. There was scarcely a fireside in the land unfamiliar
with the barbarous massacre of Fannin's men at Goliad, of the Spartan-
like defense of the Alamo . . . of the retreat of the Texans across the
San Marcos, Guadalupe, Colorado, Brazos, Buffalo Bayou, halting only
when they reached San Jacinto. . . . There was scarcely a hearthstone
where the details of the ill-starred Mier expedition had not been listened
to with horror. . . . Of Ampudia it was related that in the Yucutan
. . . his adversary, General Santmenal, fell in his hands, and without
. . . a trial he had his head cut off and boiled in oil and his body mutilated
beyond recognition. Naturally, when announced that Thornton, Har-
dee, and comrades had been captured and were in Ampudia's power,
there was . . . common impulse to rush to their rescue."[1]

In New Orleans, old Brigadier General Edmund P. Gaines reacted
as he had "in nearly every disturbance since the war of 1812."[2] Without awaiting word from Washington, Gaines called on the governors
of Louisiana, Alabama, Mississippi, and Missouri for volunteers—all on
his own responsibility. In a remarkably short period he called up and
organized about 12,600 men. Remarkably, he enlisted most of them—
11,000, in fact—for a six-month period, although such a term of service
had no basis in law. Three months was the prescribed maximum for
militia. Before Washington could act to stop him, he actually shipped
out some eight thousand to Taylor's army at Brazos Santiago, where
Taylor had neither space nor use for them.

In Congress the response to the newly recognized war was scarcely
less impulsive. After their two-hour debate of Polk's war message on
May 11, the House of Representatives promptly voted to grant the
President more by way of men and money than he had anticipated. In
his war message, Polk had not specified his exact requirements, merely
asking for authority "to call into the public service a large body of
volunteers, to serve for not less than six or twelve months, unless sooner
discharged" and "a liberal provision for sustaining our entire military

force and furnishing it with supplies and munitions of war."[3] He was actually thinking in terms of twenty-six regiments, some 23,000 men.[4] The House, however, authorized the President, in addition to employing the regular and militia forces in being, to call up and accept "any number of volunteers, not exceeding 50,000" to serve twelve months or to the end of the war.*

In the Senate, however, some members seemed more anxious to avoid the appearance of being railroaded. Prominent among them was Senator John J. Crittenden, a Kentucky Whig, whose first reaction was to question the circumstances under which his friend Zachary Taylor had marched to the Rio Grande. When assured that Taylor had been acting under specific orders from the War Department, Crittenden seemed to feel relieved. Then, after expressing sorrow that we had "entered into war with our nearest neighbor," Crittenden proposed sending a "special mission" of diplomats to accompany Taylor's army.[5] Having thus expressed his disapproval of Polk's actions, Crittenden joined in voting the president overwhelming resources to prosecute the war. This pause for debate prevented the Senate from acting as swiftly as the House—a matter next to treason, in Polk's view—but the delay was minimal; Polk signed the War Bill into law on Wednesday, May 13, 1846.

Considering the haste with which it was passed, the War Bill, with its later amendments, provided a reasonable basis for mobilization. It had two notable weaknesses, however, one of which was that it left the power to appoint the volunteer officers below the rank of brigadier general in the hands of the respective governors even though the men they would command were to be in federal, not state, service. The other weakness, a masterpiece of buck-passing, stemmed from the politicians' unwillingness to set a definite enlistment term for those volunteers. That artful dodging applied to both Polk and the Congress. Thus Polk asked for volunteers to serve for terms of six *or* twelve months—take your choice, Congress. Congress authorized twelve months *or* the end of the war—take your choice, Mr. President. In implementing the law, Polk then asked the governors for a volunteer force to serve "for the period of twelve months *or* the end of the war"[6]—take your choice,

---

*Emory Upton, *The Military Policy of the United States*, p. 203. Other sections of the law required volunteers to provide for their own clothes, horse, and equipment (but not arms), for which they would be compensated by the government.

Mr. Volunteer. As it turned out, few if any signed up for the duration of the war. So after a year new volunteers would have to be recruited, or the war abandoned.

On Wednesday, May 13, 1846, the day that Polk signed the War Bill, Secretary of War William Marcy and General-in-Chief Winfield Scott arrived at the White House for a conference. Scott was no favorite of Polk's: besides being the professional head of the army, he was also considered "in full chase of the presidency"[7]—as a Whig. No worse condemnation could be leveled against anyone in the eyes of Polk.

Further, in terms of personality, Scott was Polk's direct opposite. Big (six feet, five inches), bluff, egotistical, and famous, he tended to condescend to the diminutive, withdrawn Polk. It was Polk who was forced to suppress his personal resentment out of respect for Scott's position as general-in-chief of the army and, even more, for his position as a national hero. Thus, while Polk preferred to turn to such "experts" as Thomas Hart Benton for military advice,* he still could not mobilize for war without the professional help of his highest-ranking soldier.

By 1846 Major General Winfield Scott had already become a legend. Just approaching his sixtieth birthday, he had spent more than half his life as a general officer, having been made a brigadier during the War of 1812 at the age of twenty-eight. He had participated brilliantly against the British at Chippewa and Lundy's Lane, and for his performance in the latter battle he had been awarded a congressional medal† and a brevet to major general. In a war that produced few successes and few heroes, Scott's performance had been a source of national pride, and his military renown had come to rival that of the older Andrew Jackson. Scott had stayed in the army while Jackson had gone on to politics. Thus Scott had been the leading figure in the Black Hawk War (1832) and in "watching" the "nullifiers" in Charleston that same year.

---

*As a staunch Democrat, Benton belonged to the group most offended by the position of Scott, an active Whig. In late March of that year, when Scott had overstepped himself over the "brevet" matter, Benson had advised that Scott be "forthwith ordered to some post on the northern frontier, as a merited rebuke. . . ." James K. Polk, *The Diary of a President*, p. 67.

†Not to be confused with the later Congressional Medal of Honor.

He had commanded during the Seminole War (1837), and in 1838 along the Canadian border. He had further gained stature by executing Jackson's controversial order to move 16,000 Cherokees from South Carolina and Tennessee to reservations west of the Mississippi. His administration of the army, since becoming general-in-chief in 1841, had been marked with precision and reason.

But the road had not always been smooth. In 1809, as a captain in the "flying artillery," Scott had tactlessly referred to his commanding general as a traitor "as great as Aaron Burr." Court-martialed and suspended from command for a year, Scott used the time to study the military profession. He had come off easier in 1817 when he had criticized an order of General Jackson's as "mutinous," this time receiving no punishment except being called in return a "hectoring bully." Twenty years later Jackson finally court-martialed him for lack of success in the Florida war. The court not only exonerated Scott but praised his "energy, steadiness, and ability."

Thus Scott's overbearing manner and his tendency to speak his mind too freely were not, as might be assumed, the result of too many years as a general. They had always been part of his makeup. But he had never been punished severely enough to make him change his ways. In fact, some of the disciplinary actions against him had turned out to be blessings in disguise.

With such a career behind him, Scott had no place to go but the presidency to attain another "brevet"; all other national honors had been his. Not that he allowed this new diversion to interfere with his administration of the army, but it was creeping more and more into his correspondence. His affiliation had always been with the Whigs, possibly stemming from his lifelong competition with Andrew Jackson but more likely from the inbred natural conservatism of most military men.* Scott's name was mentioned in political circles as early as 1839.[8] By 1842 he was taken seriously enough that Pennsylvania put him forward as a sort of favorite son.[9] Henry Clay; however, would be the nominee in 1844.

After Clay's defeat in 1844, Whig leaders, Senator John Crittenden in particular, had decided that Clay could never be elected, and Crit-

---

*One of Polk's problems, at least as he viewed things, was that the three general officers of the army as of May 1846—Scott, Gaines, and Brigadier General John E. Wool—were all Whigs, not to mention Brevet Brigadier General Zachary Taylor and Brevet Brigadier General Roger Jones, the adjutant general.

tenden began to consider both Winfield Scott and Zachary Taylor as possible leaders of the Whig party. And as the only Whig on the Senate Military Affairs Committee, Crittenden was a natural channel of complaint for generals who felt politically mistreated by a Democratic president. Crittenden was good in his role. Described as "the ugly, hard-drinking, whist-playing little senator from Kentucky, dispenser by turns of rough fun, polished oratory, and shrewd political judgment,"[10] he was a born kingmaker. But close association with Crittenden was not something to endear Scott to his commander-in-chief.

Scott's first meeting with the President was short. When Scott outlined his plans for raising the volunteers, something—perhaps his manner—offended Polk, who declared the presentation "incomplete" and demanded a more formal report "during the day." Before the meeting closed, however, Polk did offer Scott the "command of the army to be raised," which Scott, of course, accepted. Polk then recorded that he did not consider Scott "in all respects suited to such an important command."[11]

That day, Wednesday, May 13, 1846, was a busy one for Polk. In his diary he described a long cabinet meeting to discuss the messages to be sent to the heads of the other nations announcing the state of war.[12] But he omitted a meeting with Benton, and made no mention of its follow-up: his orders to a certain brigadier general to take a force westward from Fort Leavenworth, Indian Territory. Neither did he mention a brief message that secretary of the Navy Bancroft sent by his direction:

> *United States Navy Department*
> *May 13, 1846*
>
> *To Commodore Conner, Commanding Home Squadron:*
>
> *Commodore: If Santa Anna endeavors to enter the Mexican ports, you will allow him to pass freely.*
>
> *George Bancroft*[13]

At 8 P.M. the next evening Marcy and Scott called on Polk again for a conference that lasted until midnight. Polk began by outlining his simple, basic war plan, to "march a competent force into the northern provinces" of Mexico and hold them while peace was being negotiated. This plan would be calculated to occupy such large parts of her territory that Mexico would be forced to negotiate a peace. Since that scheme would give the best chance of limiting military action to a small, quick campaign, Marcy and Scott readily agreed. In the course of the meeting Scott proposed to call up twenty thousand of the fifty thousand volunteers authorized by Congress, the initial force to come from the western and southwestern states.* Polk was reluctant to call out such a large force, but he agreed, "not being willing to take the responsibility of any failure of the campaign by refusing to grant to General Scott all he asked."[14] The course had been set, at least for the first stages of the war.

The tense atmosphere in these two meetings precluded open, frank communication. Certainly the conditions under which Polk intended to offer the command of the army on the Rio Grande were misunderstood. Polk, on his part, expected Scott to depart Washington immediately. Scott's presence on the Rio Grande would not, in itself, ensure the safety of the army, but it would be a relief, from Polk's point of view, to get Scott out of daily public view. It would even be in Scott's interest to make his new command a fait accompli, for many Western Democrats in the Senate and elsewhere were pressuring Polk to appoint someone other than the Whig Scott. So Polk wanted action—fast.

Scott, on the other hand, believed that he should stay in Washington for a while, long enough to come to grips with the gigantic administrative task of mobilizing to fight a foreign war. In the course of putting the machinery in motion, he planned to make a trip down the Ohio and Mississippi rivers to ascertain that the shipment of troops was going well. Then at a later time he could proceed to the Rio Grande accompanied by a "cloud of reinforcements." The increase in the size of the force would lend justification to the presence of the General-in-Chief to take command. Under such a circumstance, his arrival would spare Taylor's pride at being replaced.† At that time, of course, nobody

---

*Texas, Arkansas, Illinois, Missouri, Ohio, Indiana, Kentucky, Tennessee, Alabama, Mississippi, and Georgia.

†Scott to R.P. Letcher, 5 June, 1846. Though this letter was written a few weeks later, in a mood of deep self-pity, there is no reason to doubt that these were always Scott's intentions.

in Washington had received any news of Taylor's victories at Palo Alto and Resaca de la Palma. Nevertheless, Taylor had performed well at Corpus Christi and Matamoros and Scott, while anxious to replace Taylor in the field, sincerely desired to avoid the appearance that Taylor was being replaced through any fault of his own. And, additionally, cynics have pointed out, Scott could have seen little attraction in taking over a small army in an exposed position.

On May 19, less than a week after his evening meeting with Scott and Marcy, Polk gave his secretaries of war and the navy a lecture on how the war was to be run. With his usual passion for secrecy—and his mistrust of his generals—he "urged upon both the necessity of giving their personal attention to all matters, even of detail, and not confiding in their subordinates to act without their supervision."[15] In other words, to run their departments as Polk ran his administration. But behind this sermon lay Polk's concern over his first inkling that Scott planned to stay in Washington until the first of September 1846. Such a delay would not be permitted, Polk admonished Marcy, and if Scott did not proceed to his post "very soon," Polk would "supersede" him in command. That would be Polk's policy, but Marcy would at least share the onus for any controversy. He was to "take the matter into his own hands; to issue orders and cause them to be obeyed."*

Marcy took these instructions to heart. The next day he visited Benton on Capitol Hill, and together the two men planned a way to put Scott on the shelf. They could attach an amendment to a pending bill that would authorize the President to appoint two new major generals to the rolls of the regular army (making a total of three) and four brigadier generals (making a total of six). The two additional major generals would allow Polk to promote Taylor (a political necessity) and to appoint another major general who could take command in the field or even become general-in-chief in Washington. That appointment, it was agreed, would go to Benton himself. Although the senator had not been in uniform for thirty years, he had long cherished military ambitions. With the establishment being shaken up by war, this might be his chance. The bill was duly introduced.

---

*Polk, pp. 96–97. Understandably, Scott had another view: according to him, he was "much of the time engaged in doing . . . all the critical work of the Secretary *with my own pen.*" Scott's letter to R. P. Letcher, June 5, 1846, in John J. Crittenden, *Life*, vol. I, p. 245.

Word of this chicanery reached Scott, who "smelt the rat." The
evening after the Marcy-Benton meeting, he confronted Marcy, who
countered by conveying the President's displeasure with Scott's continued presence in Washington.[16] The next day Scott wrote at length
to Marcy. He began with a long description of the problems he was
confronting every day—with the adjutant general, the quartermaster
general, the commissary general of subsistence, the chief of ordnance,
and the surgeon general. Then he declared that he had "learned that
much impatience is already felt, perhaps in high quarters, that I have
not already put myself in route for the Rio Grande." He was "too old
a soldier" not to "feel the infinite importance" of securing himself
against danger in his rear.* He concluded that he did not "desire to
place myself in the most perilous of all positions:—*a fire upon my rear,
from Washington, and a fire, in front, from the Mexicans.*"[17]

That same evening, on May 21, President Polk received an annoying
visitor, a stranger who was requesting a reinstatement of his brother-in-
law to the rank of captain in the army. Apparently to advance his case
by discrediting Scott, the man produced a letter Scott had written the
previous February refusing to recommend an applicant for a position
in the new Mounted Infantry Regiment. Such an action would be
futile, the letter continued, because the proposed riflemen "are intended by Western men to give commissions or rather *pay* to the
Western democrats. Not an eastern man, not a graduate of the Military
Academy and certainly not a *Whig* would obtain a place. . . ."[18] As
Polk was fuming over the political accusation in this letter, Marcy
walked in with the letter he had received from Scott that day. Polk was
now satisfied that Scott was not to be trusted, but he still avoided direct
action. Unless he could secure the approval of Congress to appoint new
generals, he conceded, he might still be forced to send Scott to command in Mexico.[19]

A solution to Polk's bureaucratic problem arrived the evening of May
23, when the New Orleans press reported on Taylor's victories at Palo
Alto and Resaca de la Palma. An elated Polk needed official confirmation before taking action,[20] but by Monday he was sufficiently certain

---

*Bernard DeVoto (*The Year of Decision*, p. 198) describes the letter as "insubordinate and
injudicious . . . but first-rate prophecy."

of Taylor's victory that he called a special cabinet meeting to discuss Marcy's draft of a reply to Scott's indiscreet letter. The final product was a masterpiece—lofty, pained, and magnanimous—treating Scott like a small boy. After referring to the "extraordinary character" of Scott's letter and the "grave issues set forth therein," it concluded that the "President would be wanting in his duty to the country, were he to persist in his determination of imposing upon you the command of the army in the war against Mexico." Scott would be continued in his present position, instructed to "devote your efforts to making arrangements and preparations. . . ."[21]

With relish Polk ordered Marcy's letter to be delivered that day. With Taylor's victories, the country now had a new general, and Scott might fade from the public stage.

Winfield Scott was not accustomed to being treated so condescendingly, and receipt of Marcy's letter put him in a state of shock. When he recovered sufficiently to reply, he characteristically opened his letter on a note of self-pity: "Your letter of this day, received at about 6 P.M., as I sat down to a hasty plate of soup. . . ."[22]

Those twenty words gave Polk and Marcy ammunition to make Scott an object of ridicule. And that they did, ignoring Scott's lame explanation of the terms he had used, as well as a whole paragraph devoted to obsequious praise of Polk.* The correspondence was immediately made public, and the "hasty plate of soup" would haunt Scott for the rest of his life. Polk lost no time in sending a message to Congress nominating Brevet Brigadier General Zachary Taylor to be brevet major general.† With this new rank, Taylor could not legally remain on the Rio Grande, serving under another major general such

---

*"You speak of my interview with the President on the subject of the extended formidable invasion of Mexico. I wish I had time to do justice to my recollection of the President's excellent sense, military comprehension, patience, and courtesies in these interviews. I have since often spoken of the admirable qualities he displayed on those occasions, with honor, as far as it was in my power to do him honor." Polk, p. 652.

†Polk, *Diary*, May 26, 1846, pp. 104–5. In Scott's memoirs, written in 1864, this incident was still a sore subject. His version: "At this period, Scott usually—as always in troubled times—spent from fifteen to eighteen hours a day in his office, happened, on being called on by the Secretary of War, to be found absent. In explanation, Scott hurriedly wrote a note to say that he was back in the office, having stepped out, for the moment, to take—regular meals being out of the question—a 'hasty plate of soup.'" Winfield Scott, *Memoirs*, vol. II, p. 385. This was a plausible explanation except that Scott's letter was not a "note" but a long, pompous epistle.

as Scott. And public opinion would no longer allow him to be brought home.

But Polk was not destined to have his own way completely. Benton's bill authorizing two new major generals and four new brigadiers sailed through the Senate handily but ran into opposition in the House of Representatives. There Garrett Davis, one of the Immortal Fourteen who had voted against the war, took the floor. He dismissed the creation of four new brigadier generals as a device, "obvious enough, to increase his [Polk's] patronage," unnecessary to such a short war with a weak, disorganized nation like Mexico. But the authorizing of two new major generals brought his heaviest attack. This request, Davis charged, had two ulterior motives behind it: "the one to dispose of our present commander-in-chief, . . . the other to supersede General Taylor, and tear from his brow some of the rich chaplet of laurels with which he has lately wreathed it. . . ."

Then Davis suggested that Old Rough and Ready be allowed to manage the war, as the general-in-chief had laurels enough: "It is my wish, Mr. Chairman, that General Taylor should have the chief command in carrying on this war until it is brought to a close."[23]

He called attention to the squib that had appeared in the National *Union* on the evening of May 9, in which Ritchie, under orders, had tried to transfer blame for any impending disasters to Taylor himself.* He then cited every request that Taylor had made for reinforcements, ending with an urgent call for *"speedily sending recruits to this army. . . ."*[24]

Davis's speech was enough to defeat Polk's purpose. Two days later a committee of the House reduced the augmentation to one major general and two brigadiers. Under these circumstances, Polk had no

---

*"It should be understood that General Taylor has been, for several months, authorized to call for any auxiliary forces from Texas, Louisiana, and some other of the south-western states—in fact, for such reinforcements as he might deem it necessary to possess. But, like a gallant officer, believing his force adequate to meet any enemy which might present itself, and to overcome any danger, he omitted to exercise the authority with which he has been entrusted. His sense of security has overcome every other consideration, and *he has not made his call to secure himself* against all contingencies." Quoted in the Congressional Globe.

choice but to promote the new hero, Taylor, to major general. Thomas Hart Benton's military ambitions were temporarily thwarted.

The twenty-ninth Congress had one more task, to clean up some loose administrative matters pertaining to the army. Brigadier General Edmund Pendleton Gaines was reprimanded for recruiting 11,000 illegal volunteers and transferred to an innocuous administrative position. Colonels Stephen W. Kearny and David E. Twiggs would be promoted to the rank of brigadier general. And finally, Polk was granted authority to appoint general officers of volunteers for the duration of the war.[25] Congress adjourned on June 25, 1846.

Thus the "Battle of the Potomac" came to an end. The clear winner was Zachary Taylor, who was promoted to major general, United States Army, and continued in command of United States forces on the Rio Grande. Between Polk and Scott, Polk was the clear winner; Scott, his political reputation in temporary shambles due to public amusement over his letters, was left frustrated in Washington.

Polk's victory was on points only. Scott was not knocked out.

BUILDUP

SUMMER 1846, ON THE RIO GRANDE

Down on the Rio Grande, Zachary Taylor was being afforded no time to savor his victories. Almost immediately after raising the siege of Fort Brown, he was once again headed back to Point Isabel, this time to meet with Commodore David E. Conner. Taylor needed Conner's support in protecting the Brazos Santiago base from the sea and in facilitating his future plans.

Those plans were as yet unformed, as Taylor had heretofore been preoccupied with the threat from Arista's army. His instructions were vague; the last word from Marcy was that of the previous January: "You will not act merely on the defensive." Those words had not been supplemented, but now that the lands claimed by Texas north of the Rio Grande were safe, it was time to think ahead.

In the absence of further orders, Taylor was now planning, as a first step, to cross the Rio Grande and occupy Matamoros. Then, when he could be ready, he intended to move up the river to Camargo to prepare for an ambitious move westward to Monterrey,* capital of the Mexican state of Nuevo León. He could use the Rio Grande as the easiest means

---

*To differentiate, I am using the modern spelling for this city, in contrast to Monterey, as in Monterey, California. Also, despite our tendency to think of Monterrey as being south of Texas, it is nearly due west of Matamoros.

of moving troops and supplies to that advanced location, but to do so he needed the help of Conner in securing boats and crews.

Taylor had never met Conner before, but each man had advance word of the other's reputation. Conner was known to be a formal type, so Taylor, wishing to be courteous, unpacked his wrinkled uniform, with gold braids and epaulets, for the first time since the abortive ceremonial review back at Corpus Christi. On May 13, just four days after Resaca de la Palma, Conner disembarked at Point Isabel, clad in mufti. Once the two recovered from the surprise of their reverse roles, they sat down to make their plans.[1]

In the course of their discussions, Taylor and Conner made new arrangements to improve the flow of men and supplies from the ships forward toward Matamoros. With the Mexican threat to the mouth of the Rio Grande removed, Taylor could bypass Point Isabel by disembarking his troops on Brazos Island and fording them across the shallow inlet directly to advanced bases on the Rio Grande itself. To receive these men and supplies he would establish a series of camps along the river where units could await the opportunity to move into the interior. Fortunate units would travel inland by water; those less favored would march through sand and heat along the banks.*

Taylor put his plans into effect with energy. He completed the arrangements for logistics by May 15 and was immediately back at the newly designated Fort Brown to prepare for crossing the Rio Grande. Thirty years older than most of his officers and men and being spared none of their hardships, Taylor was able not only to keep up with them but to lead them.

On May 17, 1846, Taylor's long-awaited heavy mortars arrived, and Taylor had accumulated sufficient small boats to force a crossing of the river. Just as he was moving forward, he was greeted by an emissary from Arista requesting an armistice. The two armies could suspend activities, Arista proposed, until the respective governments had time to "settle the question" of the boundaries between the two countries.[2] Taylor curtly refused this proposal but said that he would permit Arista's army to retire from Matamoros unmolested, provided the Mex-

---

*This was a more efficient arrangement than the previous one, but it caused an overload on Brazos Island. On the average it seems that a unit during that summer would spend about five days on Brazos Island before departing for one of the camps. At one time there were as many as eight thousand troops on Brazos Island. The pilings of Taylor's port were still visible in 1984.

ican commander left all "public property" in the town. Such sick and wounded as Arista could not take with him would be safe; Taylor was not in the habit of making war on the helpless. Taylor demanded a reply by sundown.[3]

The reply did not come, so Taylor decided to go ahead and force a river crossing just upstream of the town. He waited until daylight and then sent his light infantry across first, followed by cavalry. Once he had safely crossed to the right bank, he encountered a deputation of civil authorities who had come out to meet him. Arista, they reported, had pulled out of Matamoros on the night before. He had taken his equipment with him but had left his sick and wounded, three hundred in all. Taylor would make no concessions to these officials—he had no need to—but he assured them that he would respect their private property and permit their civil laws to remain in effect. Upon taking Matamoros, Taylor kept his units and his headquarters outside the town, and provided medical care for the casualties that Arista had left in the hospitals.[4]

United States policy, with which Taylor concurred, was to treat the people of Mexico as friends.[5] Thus Taylor made every effort to avoid disrupting life in Matamoros. The guard he posted in the streets was light: to patrol a town of four thousand people, only two companies were assigned—and commanders were instructed to pay as much attention to the conduct of American soldiers as to maintaining order among the civilian populace. The members of the guard were, of course, "expected to present a model of discipline and correct deportment."[6] Taylor also strove to prevent making the occupation a financial burden on the people. Any supplies and provisions necessary for his army's use would be paid for at full market value. The price the citizens asked for provisions and fodder often exceeded the "going rate," but Taylor paid it.* And to further promote good feeling, Taylor established a newspaper, printed in both English and Spanish, called *Republic of the Rio Grande and Friend of the People*, the front page of which carried

---

*Not every soldier agreed with such a policy: "Our government was wise enough to suppose that they could conquer the Mexicans by kindness, and force them to a speedy cessation of hostilities, by offering them a ready market for every thing they could raise, and paying an enormous price. . . . How absurd that policy has been, the experience of the campaign has since exhibited." Samuel Reid, *The Scouting Expeditions of McCullough's Texas Rangers*, pp. 43–44.

lessons in the Spanish language and a column in which his soldiers could air their complaints.*

On May 11, 1846, the first of the eight thousand volunteers recruited by General Edmund P. Gaines at New Orleans arrived at Point Isabel; thereafter Taylor's army would assume a new complexion. The newcomers were an unruly lot, and their time aboard ship had done nothing to tranquilize them. A few renegades from their ranks had begun to pillage the environs on the Texas side of the Rio Grande even before Taylor had crossed over. And it was unfortunate that in Taylor's general order renaming Fort Texas in honor of Major Brown, his adjutant found it necessary to issue threats to the new arrivals:

> The commanding general is pained [that] instances have been brought to his knowledge where volunteers have seized private cattle, and sold them for their private benefit. Such conduct will not be tolerated. . . .7

Disorderly conduct, of course, could never be condoned, but in fairness these volunteers had plenty of cause for complaint about the situation in which they found themselves. Taylor completely lacked the facilities to treat them decently, and the camps he was forced to cram them into were miserable and crowded. To make matters worse, the three-month volunteers soon learned that their short enlistments would preclude their accomplishing anything useful during that time. Taylor was aware of their frustration and he was worried.† He took out his own frustration on Marcy by writing to him his complaints. He had requested only eight regiments, a total of five thousand men, he reminded the secretary, and for the record he wanted it understood that "this

---

*This from one soldier: "There was a little bayou . . . to cross and boats to ferry over, but the water being shallow, many chose to wade it. [One volunteer] said, "I'd like to wade this water, but it would be *volunteering*, and I'll never do that again, so help me." *Republic of the Rio Grande*, Matamoras, June 23, 1846 (Courtesy, Bruce Aiken).

†"I fear so many volunteers will come we will hardly find anything for them to do; the enemy's principal positions are so far off, with deserts intervening, that it will be, I fear, impossible to reach them for want of transportation." Zachary Taylor, *Letters*, Taylor to Robert C. Wood, May 19, 1846, p. 3. Taylor had begun an extensive and revealing correspondence with his son-in-law, Surgeon Wood, who remained as a doctor at Point Isabel for several months after Taylor's departure.

reinforcement, beyond the eight regiments, was never asked for by me.[8]

Taylor need not have written, for the officials in Washington were painfully aware of the mess, so much so that Marcy had filed court-martial charges against the cause of the fiasco, Edmund Gaines. And President Polk was well aware that the eight thousand Louisianans dumped on Taylor, though illegally recruited by Gaines for terms of six months, were obligated by the Constitution to serve only three months.[9] He therefore attempted to solve the problem by officially recognizing those eight thousand men as Louisiana's fulfillment of Taylor's request and recommending that Taylor "urge" them to volunteer for twelve months.[10]

No chance. The men who had enthusiastically signed up for three months the previous May had now sweltered at the Brazos Santiago with its mosquitoes and had suffered in the crowded camps along the river. They wanted no part of this life, and only one Louisiana company, Captain Albert C. Blanchard's, volunteered to extend its tour to a whole year.* So aside from Blanchard's "Phoenix Company," the men of Louisiana returned home, all except the 145 of their comrades who had died of disease.†

The volunteers from Texas were a different story. Taylor had requested four regiments from that state, and Texas had produced three, two of them mounted and one of infantry. Together the three had been organized into a division. The Texas governor, J. Pinckney Henderson, had left office temporarily to command them with the rank of major general. When presented with the option of extending their time, the men of the infantry regiment elected to be discharged. Those of the two mounted regiments, however, remained. One of these, under Colonel John C. ("Jack") Hays, came from western Texas and would

---

*The decision to send the "six-month men" home after three months caused bitter resentment. "His Excellency," Isaac Johnson, governor of Louisiana, wrote that the three-month term was harsh and would subject the recruits to the "torture" of choosing between three months and twelve. After all, "The call upon the patriotism of Louisiana . . . left no time for calculating, reflection and none for delay. . . . The judge deserted the bench, the lawyer his clients, the physician his patients, the merchant his counting-house, the mechanic his workshop, the minister of the Gospel his pulpit, to respond to the proclamation for volunteers. . . ." Johnson to Marcy, June 12, 1846, in U.S. Congress, Exec. Doc. No. 60, pp. 309–10.

†Marcy to Taylor, June 26, 1846, Exec. Doc. No. 60, pp. 307–8. Emory Upton (*The Military Policy of the United States*, p. 202), notes that this number was only twenty-five short of all casualties (dead and wounded 170) at Palo Alto and Resaca.

become known as the Texas Rangers, and would leave their names indelibly in the history of this war.

Hays's men were veterans, men who had been fighting Indians and Mexicans ever since Texas had won independence in 1836 though they were not formally organized until February 1845. The regimental organization was loose, and in practice the several companies tended to operate separately. One of them, Sam Walker's, had already participated in Taylor's campaign against Arista; McCullough's and Gillespie's would arrive soon after.

These frontiersmen knew each other, knew the Mexicans, and knew what they were there for. As Walter Prescott Webb noted, they "brought their old sets of enemies with them," the foremost being "the Chaparral Fox," Antonio Canales. Inured to the cruelty of frontier warfare, they felt a contempt for all things Mexican, an attitude that clashed with Taylor's efforts to promote friendship with the populace. But as irregular cavalry they were superb, and even though Taylor would despair of their conduct off the field, he would always strive to retain their services.[11]

About mid-May 1836 Ben McCulloch's Texas Ranger Company arrived at Brazos Santiago. McCulloch had recruited his men in only thirty-six hours, and he had moved them out quickly—there had been no time for issuing uniforms, certainly no time for drill, and, most of all, no time for instilling discipline. To the casual observer these rangers were a ferocious-looking group, most of them wearing long beards and mustaches in an age when most men, certainly soldiers, were clean-shaven. All were contemptuous of any kind of uniform and could be identified only by the standard Texas Ranger slouched hat and the belt of pistols they wore around their waists."[12] But despite their rough appearance and conduct, the ranks of the Texas Rangers included doctors, lawyers, and many college graduates, who chose to set aside their professional status for the time of their enlistment.

McCulloch's company marched from Point Isabel on May 22, 1846, and camped near the water hole of Palo Alto. During the evening they indifferently noted the sound of horses' hooves passing them in the dark. Only later did they learn that the passing party was that of William J. Worth, en route from Point Isabel to Matamoros.

At noon the next day McCulloch's men reached Resaca de la Palma, where hats, cartridge boxes, belts, broken bayonets, and torn and bloody garments of the Mexican soldiers were still lying about. It was a grim sight; "the free fresh air of heaven was tainted by the horrible effluvia arising from the dead bodies of horse, mules, and oxen which lay on every side," wrote one of the men. But cleaning up this debris of battle was none of McCulloch's concern, so he continued his march out of the stench, "leaving the wolves and carrion birds to gorge and fatten undisturbed upon the dainty feasts prepared for their revolting appetites by man."[13]

William Jenkins Worth, who had passed McCulloch's company during the night at Palo Alto, reported to Zachary Taylor on May 23, 1846. Worth was despondent that the newly authorized promotions to brigadier general had gone to David E. Twiggs and to Stephen W. Kearny, but Taylor was not very sympathetic. He disapproved of Worth's leaving the Army of Occupation earlier over the petty question of brevet rank (thereby missing the battles of Palo Alto and the Resaca). He had also received reports that Worth had behaved badly in the United States while under the influence of liquor. Taylor, whose sour judgments of peers and superiors contrasted with his courtly demeanor toward subordinates, viewed Worth with distaste. Worth, he wrote, had been "pampered and bloated for things he never done [sic] or acts he never performed." And even worse, "There are few if any officers in the service who require more from the private soldier to make himself comfortable, or who would put himself to less inconvenience for their benefit. . . ."[14] But though harsh in his judgment of the man's character, Taylor recognized Worth's unquestioned capabilities and was glad to get his wayward subordinate back.

In Washington, war planning remained remarkably vague, even after news arrived of Taylor's victories on the Rio Grande. Polk had ceased to confer with Scott directly, and even Marcy kept the general at arm's length. As a result Marcy and Scott sent separate orders to Taylor, some of which duplicated each other and at times varied in their emphasis. But all instructions from Washington left the ultimate decisions in the hands of Taylor. On June 8 Marcy made his first cautious mention of Monterrey. "It is desirable," he wrote, "that you should maintain yourself in sufficient strength to capture and hold Monterrey with your present force."[15] And four days later Scott was only a little more specific: ". . . it is the wish of the President that, with your accustomed energy, you take up lines of march beyond the Rio Grande, and press your operations toward the heart of the enemy's country. . . . The high road to the capital of Mexico will, of course, be one of those lines. . . ." The "high road to the capital of Mexico" could be interpreted in no way other than the road that led from Monterrey through the eastern range of the Sierra Madre by way of the Rinconada Pass to Saltillo and beyond.

At the same time, however, Polk was sending expeditions to occupy other parts of the northern Mexican territories. As early as June 2 Marcy issued orders to Colonel Stephen W. Kearny to lead a force from Fort Leavenworth, Kansas Territory, overland to Santa Fe. Having secured New Mexico for the United States, Kearny was to continue to California, if he deemed it possible, before winter.[16] At the same time Polk had personally instructed Brigadier General John E. Wool to assemble an army of volunteers at San Antonio, Texas, to march into Mexico and report to Taylor. If Taylor thought it feasible, Wool was to continue westward to the trading center of Chihuahua.[17] Finally, Polk expected that Commodore John D. Sloat's Pacific Squadron would seize the ports of upper California, probably before Kearny's arrival.[18]

These operations were necessary and well advised, as their success would ensure occupation of the territories that President Polk surreptitiously wished to obtain at the end of the war when the two nations signed a treaty of peace. But they were small expeditions compared with that of Taylor, who commanded the bulk of the United States Army. His was the principal effort.

Taylor was realistic as he received successive discretionary orders from Washington. On July 2 he advised that the thousand-mile overland route from the Rio Grande to Mexico City could never support a sizable army, and he recommended that his operations be limited to "cutting off the northern provinces."[19] By the "northern provinces" he meant Nuevo León, whose capital was Monterrey, and Coahuila, whose capital was Saltillo, fifty miles beyond Monterrey.

But long-range strategy was not Taylor's primary concern at this time. He had decided to march on Monterrey but was still uncertain as to which route to follow. He would prefer, if the Rio Grande would take him, to establish his base at Camargo, but the uncertainties of that means of transport necessitated his planning an overland route as an alternative. Specifically, he was eager to learn if the road direct from Matamoros to Monterrey by way of Linares was feasible.[20] In early June, therefore, he sent McCulloch's company of Texans to reconnoiter the Linares route. To help McCulloch, Taylor gave him a fine map that had been found in the tent of General Mariano Arista as the Mexicans had left in haste from Resaca de la Palma. McCulloch's rangers set out enthusiastically, for one bonus of this mission would be the opportunity to hunt for Antonio Canales and also for Blas Falcón, the reputed killer of Colonel Cross. In their quest for Falcón they were nearly successful. On June 12 the rangers fought off a group of Mexicans, who hit and ran. Falcón, they later learned, had been among them.[21]

By June 23 McCulloch was satisfied that the march from Matamoros to Linares would be impracticable for a "large division" because the route lacked sufficient water. McCulloch also learned that Arista was currently at Linares with a thousand infantry and a few squadrons of cavalry. Canales was reported to be hiding in the hills to the west, so McCulloch, his job done, cut off contact with Taylor and took off in pursuit of his personal enemy.[22]

When Taylor received McCulloch's findings, he decided to concentrate on moving his army up the Rio Grande to Camargo. Such a move was possible, as Taylor had succeeded in procuring a number of small boats, but it would not be easy; the river was proving a formidable opponent. The direct distance of a hundred miles was actually four hundred as measured by the course of the winding stream. Furthermore, the current was strong, and the water swirled in the tortuous riverbed. No pilots familiar with the river were available and wood for fuel was short. Nevertheless, he pushed on by moving his army a section at a time.[23] In this effort he called on Worth, the man he trusted most with independent command, and before the end of July Worth had taken most of the 1st Brigade ahead. Advance contingents—the 5th and 7th infantries—were already on hand at Camargo. Taylor himself left Matamoros on August 4.[24]

.   .   .

In late July Captain Luther Giddings, 1st Ohio Volunteers, landed with a group of replacement officers at Brazos Santiago Island. Giddings had been separated from his regiment when he had come down sick in New Orleans after the journey down the Mississippi River. Now recovered, he was attempting to catch up with his comrades.

The scene at the Brazos fascinated Giddings. The island that had recently been a wilderness was now "alive with busy men; soldiers, sailors, artisans, and others, who were running to and fro like ants." But the real work was being done by the Mexican stevedores as they unloaded the vessels, all of the laborers naked except for their great sombreros and seeming not to suffer from the sun. And besides the soldiers and laborers were the sutlers that follow every army. These welcome parasites were displaying their merchandise under awnings, asking for exorbitant prices, and the troops, having no alternatives, were buying their goods.

On one part of the island was a tragic sight—the corner where deathly sick volunteers were trying to find some sort of shade. Suffocating, choked with sand, and parched with fever, they were denied access to the comfortable hospital that housed the wounded of Palo Alto and the Resaca.[25] Such facilities were reserved for the regulars.

Giddings himself was fortunate, for officers traveling individually were detained only a few hours on the Brazos Island. Soon he found himself on a small boat pounding in the rough water toward Camp Belknap, the temporary station of the 1st Ohio Volunteers. On the way, as the boat approached the narrow mouth of the river, Giddings peered at a small collection of mud-and-reed huts on the Mexican bank, a town known to the Americans as "Bagdad." Camp Belknap was located farther up the river on the left, or Texan, bank. Upon arrival Giddings witnessed the same hubbub that had absorbed him the day before at the Brazos. The camp was full of soldiers, sailors, sutlers, clerks, cooks, and camp followers, but again only the Mexican laborers appeared to be really working.

Living conditions at Camp Belknap were miserable. Men and animals were packed together in the mud, and mere survival required extraordinary efforts. For the convenience of the quartermaster, the regimental commissary had been located on the bank of the Rio Grande, but the camp itself lay a mile away on the other side of a swamp. Thus every man was forced to wade daily through the mire in order to draw his provisions. To add to the discomfort, the area teemed with snakes, tarantulas, ants, scorpions, fleas, and spiders. The ants were the most annoying, the tarantulas the most feared.* One out of eight men in the 1st Ohio were on the daily sick report when Giddings arrived, and a month later he estimated that number was one in four.[26]

With tempers short, incidents were inevitable. One involved a dispute between the 1st Ohio and the nearby Maryland Battalion. A Maryland volunteer had been caught stealing a catfish from the tent of the 1st Ohio's commander, and the troops of each command rallied to the support of their respective fellows. In the confrontation, someone had given the order to load live ammunition, which, however, had not been followed and a major catastrophe had been averted, but the respective colonels were now abashedly explaining the circumstances to Taylor himself. The disorder provided absorbing news for the newspapers at home.†

Eventually the 1st Ohio left Camp Belknap by water for Camargo. The trip up the Rio Grande was both novel and perilous. The high water, strong current, and inexperienced pilots delayed the riverboat so much that the four-hundred-mile journey took a whole week. The water overflowed the banks and covered the country for miles; the pilots found it difficult just to identify and stay within the river itself, and sometimes it was necessary for the colonel to send troops ashore to gather wood for the riverboat's boilers.[27]

But the trip had its rewards. The Mexicans along the west bank were friendly. At one stopping point the troops went ashore to mix with the people and to witness a "fandango," which turned out to be an open-air dance involving "a swarthy and sweating crowd, of both sexes, engaged in waltzing, gambling, smoking, and drinking." And one evening the boat moored near the hut of a locally renowned fiddler. The troops

---

*A tarantula bite would cause spasms and delirium sufficient that a victim could be dealt with only by carrying him forcibly to his tent and keeping him there.

†Luther Giddings, *Sketches of the Campaign in Northern Mexico*, p. 38. This "catfish war" was one of the two celebrated confrontations between volunteer units. The other, between the Illinois and Georgia volunteers, actually broke out in fighting. Colonel Edward D. Baker, of Illinois, who would later place Abraham Lincoln's name in nomination for the presidency, was one of the injured. See Taylor, *Letters*, Taylor to Robert C. Wood, September 16, 1846, p. 59.

sought him out and spent the evening with him; some of them made music in their own way, while others danced to the clatter of their heavy shoes. Glad to be released from the crowded quarters of the boat, the men "vied with each other in the extent and singularity of their saltations."[28]

The 1st Ohio arrived at Camargo on Sunday, August 16. The town itself was located up the San Juan River about three miles from its junction with the Rio Grande. The American camp, which eventually held over 12,000 men, was spread southward along the San Juan River. Unfortunately, its water was even less potable than that of the Rio Grande, which Giddings estimated to consist of 20 percent mud. And to add to the health hazard some soldiers were complacently filling camp kettles alongside others doing laundry. Upstream from the Ohio regiment the Texans were washing their horses, and above the Texans were the Mexican women, carrying water away in primitive earthen jars, water far cleaner than that which filled the canteens of the soldiers.[29]

At first Giddings found the camp at Camargo agreeable. With a newfound friend, a volunteer brigadier general, he called on General Taylor himself, who was standing casually outside his tent "dressed in linen coat and trousers, twirling a straw hat between his fingers, and apparently conversing with or dictating to someone within." Benevolent and affable, the stout, gray-haired Taylor greeted his visitors and had a short discussion with them. Then he asked that the two officers pay a call on General Worth, as Worth was formally in command at the camp.[30] The next morning Giddings strolled through the camp of the regulars, admiring its impeccable organization. The infantry, artillery, and cavalry, all located in the same field, were each in place, "their appointments and discipline" perfect.[31] And Giddings wound up his tour of the camp by witnessing the review that Taylor held on August 18. As always, Giddings focused on Taylor, who, though wearing comfortable civilian clothing, was "conspicuous in the glittering group."[32]

Unfortunately, the glitter at Camargo was confined to Taylor and his regulars. For the volunteers the very name Camargo was synonymous with boredom, filth, and tragic death. Diseases took a fearful toll, and the dead march never ceased throughout the day. The large hospital tents were constantly full; the dead were removed at sunrise and sunset. But the nearby troops could hear "the groans and lamentations of the poor sufferers" throughout the night.[33]

The death statistics of Taylor's stay at Camargo are startling. When his army finally marched out, only 370 of 795 Georgians were present for duty; only 324 of 754 Alabamians; 317 of 588 in the 2d Tennessee. An estimated 1,500 men died at Camargo—one out of every eight to encamp there.[34] Taylor was keenly aware of the sufferings of his men, and he was bewildered that the inadequate advance information of the place had caused him unwittingly to select that location as a concentration point. But once there, he was powerless to do anything other than to visit the hospitals, plan to leave as soon as possible, and to write the adjutant general asking for a supplement in medical officers. (The surgeon general, in Washington, dismissed Taylor's pleas and called his medical officers "censurable.")*

About a week before Taylor's planned departure from Camargo the first wave of volunteer generals arrived at his camp from the United States. In this contingent were Major General William O. Butler and Brigadier Generals John A. Quitman, Gideon J. Pillow, Thomas L. Hamer, and James Shields. It was a large contingent, and Taylor was taken aback by the surplus. "There will be no lack of generals," he commented wryly. "I could have myself wished that they had not been quite so numerous."[35]

But considering the political nature of their appointments, it was not a bad group. Butler, of Kentucky, was the most experienced, having served under Andrew Jackson in the War of 1812. Quitman, of Mississippi (whom Taylor sized up as "a gentleman of intelligence"), had also seen military service, having raised a body of troops in 1836 to aid the Texans.

The one destined for dubious fame, Gideon Pillow, of Tennessee, had already made an imprint on history by his efforts in securing James Polk's nomination by the Democrats at Baltimore in 1844. But as a

*Taylor to the attorney general (TAG), September 2, 1846. Exec. Doc. No. 60, p. 414; the surgeon general to Taylor, July 29, 1846, Exec. Doc. No. 60, p. 41, (this letter is an answer to an earlier one from Taylor, which is missing).

soldier, Pillow had little to offer. Though he had long been a brigadier general of the Tennessee militia, that rank had been political and social; he had seen no active military service. That deficiency could be remedied by experience, of course, if such hands-on training would not cost too many lives, but Pillow had a menacing aspect to him: his role as President Polk's secret informant. Taylor was probably unaware of that attribute of Pillow's, and Pillow, for the moment, at least, felt cordial toward Taylor.[36]

By early September 1846 the need to leave Camargo was becoming a matter of urgency. Polk, the press, and the public were becoming impatient. The recent hero of Palo Alto and the Resaca de la Palma was now being called "General Delay." And of course Taylor was yearning to remove his army from the cesspool of Camargo. So he chose to move out before he was completely ready. He would make up for his shortage of wagons by substituting mules.* Further, he would advance with only a portion of his army, all his regulars (about 3,200) and only about 3,000 of his volunteers. And he would take only a portion of the heavy artillery he had available.

On August 19 Worth's 2nd Division set out for Cerralvo, about sixty miles away, to establish a forward base there. Twiggs's 1st Division would follow Worth in a few days, and the "Field Division," Butler's volunteers, would bring up the rear. On a parallel route, to the left (south), Hays's Texas Rangers would march by way of China, presumably to join up with Taylor's main body at Marin.†

Since Taylor had decided that he could take only 3,000 volunteers to Monterrey, out of 7,700 such volunteers on hand, his decision as to which to take was a touchy matter. All of the 4,700 left behind were bound to be bitterly disappointed, as they had signed up to fight, not to die in mud holes. Nevertheless, the decision had to be made, and Taylor's prime consideration, so he wrote the War Department, was

---

*Taylor to TAG, September 1, 1846, Exec. Doc. No. 60, p. 558. Justin Smith, *The War with Mexico*, vol. I, 490, says that Taylor procured one thousand mules from the alcalde of Reynosa.

†Taylor had some doubts as to whether the Texans would show up—their unique six-month enlistments had almost expired—but he had hopes. If they failed to do so, he would go on without them. Taylor to TAG, September 3, 1846. Exec. Doc. No. 60, p. 418.

to draw from "as many States as possible."* Common sense, of course, also meant giving priority to those units least depleted by disease. So he selected, besides the Texans, the Mississippi Rifles, the Tennessee Regiment, the 1st Ohio, and the Baltimore-Washington Battalion. Those left behind were distributed among Camargo, Matamoros, camps in the lower Rio Grande, and the hospital. All left behind were to be under the inevitably loose command of newly arrived Major General Robert Patterson.†

The last of Taylor's force left Camargo on September 6.³⁷ A stirring and dangerous adventure lay ahead for those who would face the guns of the enemy. For them the miserable period of buildup was over.

---

*Taylor to TAG, September 3, 1846, Exec. Doc. No. 60, p. 417. The army was organized as follows: Eight regiments of regular infantry (2,500 men), four regiments of volunteer infantry (2,000 men), four batteries of light artillery (280 men), one battery of heavy artillery (100 men), two squadrons of regular cavalry (200 men), one squadron of volunteer cavalry (150 men), and two regiments of volunteer cavalry (1,000 men). Total 6,230 men. George Meade, *Life and Letters*, vol. I, p. 126.

†Justin Smith, *War with Mexico*, vol. I, p. 493. Distribution was Camargo 2,100 (Pillow and Marshall); Matamoros 1,100 (Clarke); camps below Matamoros (4,500); hospitals (1,400).

THE SOLDIER
OF THE PEOPLE
RETURNS

SUMMER 1846, IN MEXICO

T he Americans had every reason to wonder about the intentions of the Mexican high command. The fact was that the Mexicans themselves had no idea as to what they should do next. General Mariano Arista's dispirited army had suffered more on the retreat from Matamoros than it had in either battle north of the Rio Grande. The road westward to Linares was perilous because it was so desolate. At first the lack of water parched the throats. Then a brief torrential rain appeared to be a "blessing of Providence" until it soaked the roads, turning them into mudholes. The men, already exhausted and hungry, came close to despair. Some committed suicide; others killed and ate their pack animals while the generals used much of the transportation to carry their own belongings. On May 24, however, after a hellish week, the survivors of the army staggered to the Well of Todos Santos. Here supplies were in abundance, and the immediate crisis of survival was past.

But rather than being welcomed as heroes, Arista's men were to suffer still more humiliation, for the Paredes government, now tottering, needed a scapegoat for the sorry situation throughout Mexico. Not surprisingly, the victim was the popular Arista, who was tried by court-martial and dismissed from the army in early July. His successor as army commander was the ineffective and ailing Tomás Mejía, who had originally commanded at Matamoros.[1]

The gesture of punishing Arista, though, could not stave off the day of reckoning for the ill-starred Paredes government. Mariano Paredes was vilified as a product of the army, not of the people, and his lack of popularity engendered indifference toward the war. Aware that his only hope for survival lay in the loyalty of the army, Paredes explored every source of revenue to keep the soldiers paid. His efforts to borrow heavily on the credit of Church property failed, and soon the Monarchial party, on which he relied, let him down. Its leaders balked, and the party itself was weak, without plans for the future and lacking any strong popular following. Personal attacks upon Paredes increased. He was accused of failing to protect the northern frontier against Indians, and when he withdrew the bulk of the army to the vicinity of Mexico City, opponents claimed that he was bolstering his own private bodyguard at the expense of national security.[2]

Revolutionary groups were both plentiful and powerful. A movement to reinstate the exiled Santa Anna had begun as early as February, and by April 15, as Ampudia and Taylor were exchanging threats across the Rio Grande, the cavalry renegade Juan Alvarez had declared his support for a triumvirate of Santa Anna, Herrera, and Rincón. (Canales, it will be recalled, had rebelled even before Taylor had left Corpus Christi.) Paredes imprisoned several political leaders in May, but that act only provoked further discontent. Several pronunciamentos against him were made throughout the country, especially at Guadalajara, in the state of Jalisco, on the twentieth of the same month. Near the end of July Paredes abdicated, and Vice President Nicolás Bravo accepted the reins of government. His term in office would be numbered in days.[3]

On August 16, 1846, Commodore David E. Conner, aboard the *Princeton* off Veracruz, penned a hasty note to Secretary Bancroft. The first part was factual, an account of how he had complied with the May 13 directive from the president. Santa Anna and his officers had just arrived at Veracruz on the English merchant ship *Arab*, he reported, and Conner had "allowed him to enter without molestation." He had been reliably informed that the *Arab* carried no cargo—nor would she be allowed to carry any for her return trip. Conner could easily have boarded the *Arab,* he went on, but had deemed it best not to do so, "allowing it to appear as if he had entered without my concurrence." And then Conner added a bit of personal conjecture:

It is now quite certain the whole country—that is the garrisons of every town and fortress—have declared in [Santa Anna's] favor. But, unless he has learned something in adversity, and become another man, he will only add to the distractions of the country, and be hurled from power in less than three months.[4]

Conners's report described the culmination of many months of plotting on the part of Santa Anna and his friends. At least as far back as February, when Colonel A. J. Atocha had visited President Polk, serious plotting against the Paredes regime had begun. In the meantime Santa Anna had gained the support of J. M. Almonte, formerly his chief rival. The pronouncement of Guadalajara in May provided the excuse for Santa Anna to return to Mexico, so by August 8 he had procured permission to leave Havana and had boarded the British steamer *Arab.* After some difficulties at sea the *Arab* had made it to Veracruz.

That morning of August 16 Santa Anna was met on the streets of Veracruz by a ragged honor guard—the troops in that city had declared their support for him—but the civil population was at best lukewarm. Some of the people were openly hostile, and a sizable gathering demanded that the authorities ask the newcomer for "guarantees" as to his future conduct. When this request was refused, they sent a representative to demand that Santa Anna order his guard of honor to leave the city. The courageous representative, even in the presence of the renowned Santa Anna, reminded the erstwhile dictator that his exile had resulted from his previous failure to carry out the will of the people.[5]

But adversity of this sort had never defeated Santa Anna. He left the dock and traveled over the streets of his boyhood to City Hall. There he delivered a long manifesto that castigated the conduct of affairs since his departure from office in late 1844. He did not, however, commit himself at that point to war or peace with the United States.[6] As had happened many times before, his magnetism won the crowd—for the moment.[7]

Santa Anna knew that the initial hostility he had met with was not to be taken lightly. A master of Mexican mob psychology, he quickly decided that he and his followers could not move to Mexico City immediately; the way must be prepared. Almonte and other supporters, therefore, went ahead to the capital while Santa Anna and his wife returned to his ranch in Veracruz.*

During this period of seclusion at Veracruz, Santa Anna sent volumes of orders and advice (much of which was ignored) to his agents in Mexico City. Then, satisfied that the time was ripe, the Napoleon of the West began his journey. He was right; prospects were now improved. His reception at Jalapa on September 5 was cordial, and in Mexico City the National Theater was suddenly renamed the Santa Anna Theater. During the course of a week statues and portraits of him were brought out of hiding, and the name of Santa Anna appeared once more on numerous street signs. Mobs shouted pro–Santa Anna slogans, and a few threw stones at the house of the former president Herrera. When Santa Anna arrived at the gates of the city on September 15, the new acting president, General J. M. Salas, was there to meet him.

The time favored Santa Anna. Zachary Taylor was now known to be heading for Monterrey by way of Cerralvo, and that threat provided justification for Santa Anna to take immediate command of a great army himself. At Veracruz almost exactly a month before, he had harangued the crowd:

> Mexicans! There was once a day, and my heart dilates with the remembrance, . . . you saluted me with the title of Soldier of the People. Allow me to take it again, never more to be given up, and to devote myself, until death, to the defence of the liberty and independence of the Republic!

Now he would give meaning to that title "Soldier." Gone was any promise of a negotiated peace in which territorial concessions would be granted in exchange for Yankee dollars. Mexico's natural leader was back to drive the hated gringo from her soil.

---

*Wilfrid Calcott, *Santa Anna*, p. 240. Conner to Bancroft, August 25, 1846, Exec. Doc. No. 60, pp. 776–77. The emissaries were, besides Almonte, Juan Alvarez, J. M. Mora, the Gómez Farías family, and Rejon (who had also come with Santa Anna from Havana).

MONTERREY I: APPROACH

༄ ༄

SEPTEMBER 1846

C aptain John R. Kenly, a company commander in the Baltimore-Washington Battalion, was proud of his unit. Not only was it to be "brigaded" with a regular army regiment in Twiggs's 1st Division, but it had also been issued blue army uniforms, regular style, which set it apart from the other volunteer units. Kenly credited this special recognition to the influence of Colonel William H. Watson, the battalion commander.

Kenly regarded the Baltimore Battalion, as the unit was commonly called, as "a little different." It had developed a reputation for disorderly conduct off-duty, but Kenly attributed that failing to the sophistication of its worldly-wise members, former sailors or members of prestigious fire companies and fishing clubs who, in their "regular" army uniforms, tended to "lord it over" their less favored comrades. But in military matters Kenly considered his men "more soldier-like" than the rest.[1]

As the Baltimore Battalion was preparing to leave Camargo on September 1, 1846, Colonel Watson notified his company commanders that they must go through one last ritual: each company must elect from its ranks one additional second lieutenant. Although Kenly questioned this method of selecting officers, he was confident—justifiably, as it turned out—that the man he wanted would be elected. The procedure delayed departure by one day.

The next day, as the battalion fell out to move, Kenly watched fascinated as the Mexican *arrieros* (muleteers) loaded up the mules.* He admired the competence of these humble men as they performed a job that required patience, good humor, and skill. "You have but to know," he later wrote, "that tents, tent-poles, kettles, mess-pans, axes, picks, coffee-mills, boxes of ammunition, etc., were to be daily put on and off a mule's back, to be safely carried over hill and dale, through thicket and through flowing water for miles and miles of toilsome march, to appreciate the knowledge requisite to do the work well." He had developed an affection for both the mule and its keeper, "despite the many annoyances incidental to this species of army transportation."[2]

The Fourth Brigade, of which the Baltimore Battalion was a part, marched out of Camargo by night. By September 4 they had passed Mier, and at Puntiaguda, which they reached on the sixth, they paused to await the rest of Taylor's army. Taylor himself soon arrived, and the brigade covered the last fifteen miles to Cerralvo on September 9. From that point on, the prospect of hostile action would be more immediate, so the army would march by division, not by individual brigades.†

Nuevo León provided a delightful change from the Rio Grande area. Here was well-cultivated country, with clear running streams, gardens and fields blooming with figs and pomegranates. The air was refreshing, and the water that ran from mountain brooks was cool and clear. The roads were good, a welcome change to men who had been "driven in confusion through the lagoons and mire, over sandy deserts and burning plains, from the Gulf to the banks of the San Juan."[3] Spirits were high.

. . .

---

*Two of these animals were assigned to company headquarters to carry the officers' belongings; through the rest of the company they were allocated on the basis of one per eight men. This amount of transport fell far short of what the army considered usual.

†John Kenly, *Memoirs of a Maryland Volunteer*, pp. 81–83, Luther Giddings, *Campaign in Northern Mexico*, p. 108. A concentrated division could defeat any anticipated attack. An isolated brigade might be wiped out.

Not so lucky was the 1st Ohio Regiment, of Hamer's Brigade, Butler's Division, scheduled to march four days after the Baltimore Battalion. Things went awry from the first moment, when the mules failed to show up on time. The delay stretched into hours, forcing the unit to set out in the sweltering midday.[4] The broiling sun made all metal objects impossible to hold, and the inexperienced troops drank the day's ration of water too quickly. Some men soon became feeble from thirst, and at every turn of the road they hoped they would find water, any kind, even "if only in some foul mud-hole." Once, when they sighted a solitary rancho up ahead, all semblance of discipline disappeared. The troops broke and ran for the well beside the hut. "Ah!" Giddings wrote, "deceitful hope! transient pleasure! The house was deserted, and the well contained not 'a drop to moisten life's all gasping springs.'" Each man ran up, refusing to believe the reports of the first, and each stared unbelieving into a dry well.[5]

All order was now lost as the units became intermingled. And after the guides became lost, causing the first companies to double back for two extra miles, only one half of the 1st Ohio arrived at camp before dusk. The rest, with the exception of two, straggled in during the night.[6]

Meanwhile, Captain William Henry, 3d U.S. Infantry, was enjoying a respite at Puntiaguda, having arrived there early on September 5. Henry was not much impressed with this dilapidated town of four hundred souls, but he did appreciate the friendliness of the townspeople, who had been hospitably inviting the visiting American officers to two fandangos a week. So one evening Henry joined a party headed for town. On the way they passed through a crowd of happy Mexican boys, who ran up around his horse, crying merrily, "Fandango! Fandango! Bonita señoritas!" But Henry and his friends were doomed to disappointment that evening. A rain began just before the opening time of 10 P.M., so the fandango was called off. Henry contented himself with observing a little gambling in the town, and returned to camp.[7]

Such entertainments represented the only form of recreation the Americans enjoyed on this march. But as Taylor's men progressed farther southwest toward Monterrey, they noticed a change: the people became less friendly. With increasing frequency the locals, when asked about fandangos, would look hostile and say meaningfully, "Sí! Mucho fandango a Monterrey!" Obviously the fandango they had in mind would be not a dance but a fierce battle.

Butler's division joined the rest of Taylor's army at Cerralvo on September 10. Little time was left for the troops to enjoy this smiling little town, with its white limestone houses and sparkling mountain stream, for their commanding general had more weighty things to think about. His army was now located about halfway to Monterrey, in increasingly hostile territory.

Meanwhile, in the wake of Arista's disgrace and Mejía's incompetence, Pedro de Ampudia was reinstated as Mexico's general-in-chief, Army of the North. As at Matamoros, Ampudia took up command with visions of glory dancing in his head. He knew, of course, that Santa Anna would assume command eventually, but that change would be a long time off. Before that day, Ampudia dreamed that he could defeat Taylor at Marin, twenty-five miles north of Monterrey, and as a result be hailed as a hero throughout Mexico. The numerical odds certainly did favor Ampudia. Three brigades of regulars had just arrived from Guadalajara, and that addition would bring his total strength (as of September 10, 1846) to seven thousand regulars and three thousand rancheros, considerably more than Taylor would have.[8]

On Friday morning, September 11, 1846, Ampudia rode up to Marin to inspect the terrain and meet with Anastasio Torrejón, whose cavalrymen had been hovering around Taylor's army ever since it left Camargo. Two days later he held a council of war, but found to his dismay that his brigade commanders shared none of his zeal to take the offensive; they were, in fact, determined to remain behind the fortifications of Monterrey. As Ampudia could not override them all, he was forced to give in. At least he would have a strong position behind which he would be facing a smaller army.[9]

The city of Monterrey was a veritable fortress. Its buildings were made of stone, with flat-topped roofs and straight streets, making each house a strongpoint. On the west the rugged Independence Hill* overlooked the city, and as long as Ampudia could retain possession of it, he could ensure protection of his supply line, the Saltillo road, which ran westward behind it. The city was further protected on the south and on the east by the winding Santa Catarina River, which, while fordable, made any attack from either direction difficult. Behind the Santa Catarina on the south rose the majestic Sierra Madre, whose first detached ridge, known as Federation Hill, ran parallel to Independence Hill.

Taylor would inevitably approach Monterrey on the Marin road, which ran northeast from the city. To defend that approach, Mexican engineers had constructed two forts, the Tenería (Tannery) in front and Fort Diablo (Devil's Fort) slightly behind.

The entire area was dominated by a monster fortification known as the Citadel. This solid pile of masonry located about a thousand yards north of the city had been built on the foundations of an unfinished cathedral. But it now bore no resemblance to a cathedral; its walls stood thirty feet high, enclosed in a quadrangular, bastioned earthwork, capable of holding thirty guns and four hundred troops. Nearly unassailable, its eight guns could rake the Marin road; in fact they could reach almost any point north or east of the city. It had a dark, menacing look. The Americans quickly—and respectfully—dubbed it the Black Fort.†

Ampudia's position, which appeared impregnable at first glance, actually suffered from a glaring weakness: the individual positions, from Federation Hill to Independence Hill to the Black Fort to the Tenería, were too far apart to make them mutually supporting. Therefore, since Ampudia had decided to man all of them at one time instead of holding part of the army in reserve, he lacked a mobile force with which to reinforce any individual strongpoint that came under heavy attack. So long as he conceded all the territory between bastions to Taylor, Old Zack would be free to pick off each position, one by one, with relative impunity.

Ampudia adopted this tactic—so opposite from attacking Taylor at Marin—because he and his veterans of the Resaca were nervous. And the inhabitants of Monterrey were nervous also. Some fled the city to

---

*Referred to by the Mexicans as the Mountain of Obispado (Bishop's Palace), after the structure at its east end.

†Justin Smith, *War with Mexico*, vol. I, p. 233. Eight guns was all the Mexicans installed out of a total capacity of thirty. Eight would be enough.

escape the coming terror, and the ones who remained were anxious to
help prepare barricades in the streets and at the surrounding forts. This
cooperation from the populace gave the soldiers a touch of confidence.
What soldiers and citizens sensed, but did not yet know, was that the
weakest link in the chain around Monterrey was the commander himself.

For Ampudia, despite his soldierly appearance—large, straight, with
a handsome mustache and goatee—was no more popular in Monterrey
than he had been at Matamoros because it was generally perceived that
his courage—or lack of courage—ranged from bravado to terror. His
weakness and vacillation cost expensive time in building and tearing
down positions such as the Tenería. But the soldiers and citizens
stoically kept working as the fateful hour approached.

As Monterrey braced its defenses, Taylor came inexorably on. By September 11, 1846, he was ready to leave Cerralvo, unimpressed by the
news that Santa Anna had arrived at Veracruz. His final days at Cerralvo were devoted to finding shoes for his horses and mules, a task that
had to be accomplished, for his scouts had confirmed that henceforth
the road would consist of sharp stones.[10] His troops, for their part, were
less interested in logistics than in the possibility of a hard fight at
Monterrey. They knew quite a bit about the area. Henry, for one,
clinically pondered the advanced batteries (Tenería and Diablo), en-
filading fires from the Citadel, and "all sorts of fire from the Bishop's
Palace." Reports of such prospects, he observed, made "even the old
regulars open their eyes, to say nothing of the volunteers."[11] Kenly, by
contrast, based his concern on information about Ampudia's army
provided by one of the arrieros, who had assured him that Ampudia
would fight hard. "I could not disbelieve the positive statements of this
man," Kenly wrote, "his truthfulness was stamped on every lineament
of his honest countenance."*

Taylor's formal march order specified that the army would continue to
march by divisions. Troops would carry eight days' rations and forty

---

*Kenly, p. 84. Given Kenly's professed admiration for the arrieros, his statement is probably
sincere.

rounds of ammunition each.* On September 12, Taylor's advance party of about two hundred men† set out to prepare the roads for the heavy trains. And on September 13 Twiggs's 1st Division marched off, followed on the fourteenth by Worth's 2d Division and on the fifteenth by Butler's Field Division.[12]

From Cerralvo the next major stop would be at Marin, which the head of Taylor's column reached on September 15. Kenly's company of the Baltimore Battalion, still in Twiggs's division, was in the lead. As he was nearing the last crest overlooking Marin, Kenly was allowing his mind to wander to the beauty of the area when his reverie was suddenly interrupted by the sound of horses' hooves coming up from the rear. Kenly turned; it was General Taylor, with a small escort. Dismounting, Taylor extended his hand with a pleasant smile, and recalled their first meeting weeks before, at Matamoros. This friendliness shown by his commanding general flustered Kenly, but he managed to report that his advance guard had seen no living being since leaving camp that morning.

Taylor stopped and gazed down the valley, saying nothing for a minute or two. Then he turned and said, "Captain, move forward cautiously, and if you can, continue your march into that town, and halt on the other side until the column gets up."[13]

Kenly's command was on the march immediately. As it approached the town Kenly could sense that Marin was abandoned. Oppressed by the lonely atmosphere, his men huddled silently together, utterly quiet. The tread of their feet reverberated from the stone walls.

Kenly, in the lead, suddenly came upon a Mexican lying in a pool of blood, feet in a doorway. He was obviously dead, probably just killed, but by whom and why? No clues presented themselves, so after a moment's pause Kenly began leading his men forward again, cautiously. When they finally reached the other end of town, all heaved a sigh of relief that they had not encountered snipers in the town. But

---

*"All surplus arms and accoutrements, resulting from casualties on the road, will be deposited with Lieutenant Stewart . . . who will give certificates of deposit. . . ." Taylor, Orders No. 115, Cerralvo, September 11, 1846. Quoted in Luther Giddings, *Campaign in Northern Mexico*, pp. 119–20.

†Ninety pioneers, protected by one hundred dragoons and twenty-five rangers. At Papa-Gallos they encountered a group of about six hundred Mexican cavalry, who only observed them.

out there before them, about three-fourths of a mile away, stood a body of Mexican cavalry.[14] It was Torrejón, who had been dogging Taylor's steps all along the route. As Kenly watched, the horsemen hesitated, "irresolution apparent in their actions," and then they slowly trotted on.

Kenly remained where he was until the lead battalion of the army came up behind him. It took several hours for the last of Twiggs's stretched-out division to close in for the night.[15]

Taylor paused at Marin, waiting for the divisions of his army to close in. Disappointingly, Henderson's Texas mounted regiments, a thousand men, did not arrive as Taylor had hoped and expected. Perhaps they had gone back to Texas because their enlistments were up; perhaps they had run into trouble. Or perhaps they had set off on a mission of their own. Taylor had no way of knowing. On September 17 he reported that Torrejón's one thousand cavalrymen had been constantly on his front, engaged principally in driving off Mexican citizens and looting their own people. Taylor had always been doubtful whether Ampudia would attempt to hold Monterrey—and he still was.*

Marin was the last location where the army could relax in pleasant surroundings. But thoughts were on the future. The enterprising William Henry, for example, rode into Marin one morning, climbed a spiral staircase up the masonry tower of the cathedral, and surveyed the breadth of the San Juan Valley, about fifteen miles across. Though twenty-five miles away, he could see the town of Monterrey, and even, he thought, the Bishop's Palace itself.[16]

"At dawn on the 18th of September, the slumbering camp was aroused by the gay notes of reveille from drum and bugle. In a few minutes, the thousand tents which had checkered the verdant little valley disappeared, the morning meal was eaten, and the foremost troops began to cross the stream and march towards Monterey, still eight leagues

---

*Taylor to TAG, September 17, 1846, Exec. Doc. No. 60, p. 422. Meade was not so sanguine. On the same day, he wrote, "Well, here we are within twenty-five miles of Monterrey, one day's forced march, and two easy ones, and really know no more of the nature of the reception they will give us, or of their defenses, or of the number of troops they have, than we did at Matamoras, three hundred miles distant." George Meade, *Life and Letters*, p. 130.

distant."[17] Torrejón's cavalry still lurked up ahead, and the prospect of impending battle was making the arrieros fearful of capture by their own countrymen. Some of them tried to escape, but the ubiquitous Kinney, now head of the mule train, quickly brought them back.[18] The army covered eighteen miles that day, and when they arrived at the farm of San Francisco, Taylor was happy to find Henderson's Texans waiting, totally unapologetic for their unauthorized absence. Their presence under any circumstances was welcome; they would make a difference at Monterrey.

This was the last night before Taylor's first major battle, a time for thinking and musing. Most thoughtful men expected the Mexicans to put up a stubborn fight. *"Mucho Fandango at Monterey!* I confess that these words were continually ringing in my ears. . . ."[19] wrote one. And another: "To all ranks, particularly to us raw volunteers, the proximity of our enemy, and the certainty of combat, was strangely exciting. How anxiously did the mind at that hour contemplate the future! How busy, too, was memory of the past! How ineffably pleasing to the aroused senses were all the works of nature then! For ourselves . . . the earth and its 'majestic roof, fretted with golden fire,' seemed more beautiful than ever before."*

The next morning, September 19, Zachary Taylor's Army of Occupation broke camp for its march to Monterrey. At about 9 A.M. the suspense was broken. Taylor, riding with the Texans, spotted a body of lancers between him and Monterrey, which was now about three miles distant. The Texans were eager to charge, but Taylor, well aware that a further advance would place them under the guns of the Citadel, firmly held them back.

The Black Fort then spoke, reverberating from mountain to mountain. Men who had been lagging from the heat were startled. Two more reports resounded. But the missiles, though dangerous enough, were

*Giddings, p. 149. He also wrote (pp. 148–49): ". . . there were but few persons in the army who could regard with indifference such a trial as was then at hand. Officers high in rank . . . may see bright rewards glittering in the dark and dangerous future. In their ears, the weird sisters may whisper mystic promises of the Presidency, the Senate, and Foreign Missions. But *life* is their stake also, and considering the responsibilities as well as the rewards attending rank and station, it is doubtful whether their minds are as much at ease on the eve of battle, as those of the nameless soldiers, abused in the particular, and applauded in the aggregate, who are destined to die unwept, or live unhonored."

only solid-shot cannonballs, not explosive shells. When the third ball struck in front of Taylor and bounced over his head, he and his staff trotted slowly back. He would camp where his men were waiting, at a welcoming grove of pecan trees, Spanish moss, live oaks, and gushing springs. The soldiers immediately—and inaccurately—dubbed the area Walnut Springs. Though misnamed, Walnut Springs would provide a congenial place on which to base the battle that was now upon them.*

---

*William Henry, p. 190. Giddings (pp. 139–40) substantiates this account. The official name of this grove, a favorite recreation area for the Mexicans in peacetime was "Bosque de San Domingo," though it was never anything but "Walnut Springs" to the Americans.

MONTERREY II: "THREE GLORIOUS DAYS"

❧

SEPTEMBER 20–23, 1846

The Mexican cannonballs that belched out from the walls of the Black Fort that Saturday morning signaled the beginning of the struggle for Monterrey. Though his information had been incomplete, Taylor had been planning for this moment, and he already had a tentative plan of action.

The key to the Monterrey position was the Bishop's Palace, on the tip of Independence Hill, possession of which would give an attacker command of the town itself and of the major road running west to Saltillo. A quick seizure of the Bishop's Palace might, in fact, force Ampudia to surrender the town without further contest.

But Taylor could not march his whole army toward Independence Hill. Since he was coming in from the east, he would have to march north of the city to reach it, thus leaving his flanks and rear exposed to fire from the Black Fort. He therefore decided to compromise, sending part of his army, terrain permitting, north and then west of the Black Fort to hit Independence Hill from the northwest, and keeping the bulk on the eastern approach—his present position.*

---

*Taylor's plan conformed generally to what is termed a "turning movement," a maneuver designed to strike the enemy's rear, not just his flank. Under any conditions this method is daring, as it calls for a separation between the two wings of an army, thereby putting them temporarily out of the range of mutual support.

Taylor's decision to split his army in the face of a foe numerically stronger than his own was audacious, to say the least. Such a risk reflected the contempt he held for his enemy, his assumption that Ampudia, even with his superior strength, would remain within the fortification of Monterrey. But the fact remained that attacking Monterrey at all was an ambitious undertaking, especially since the Mexicans could be expected to fight with desperation. Unfortunately for his men, Taylor's underestimation of the Mexicans was unwarranted.

Before putting his plan into effect, Taylor needed to ascertain whether the terrain north of the Black Fort could be traversed by a large part of his army. Immediately upon arrival, therefore, he directed his chief engineer, Major Mansfield, to determine its feasibility. At the same time he sent Captain William G. Williams, Mansfield's assistant, to reconnoiter the defenses on the north and east of the city.

The scouting missions were hazardous, as the country was infested by Mexican cavalry and rancheros. By 10 P.M. that evening, however, Mansfield returned to Walnut Springs with six prisoners and good news: the terrain was passable and the defenses of the city from the west were relatively weak. So Taylor issued orders for Worth's division, with Hays's Texas Rangers, to march out to the west the next day.[1] Twiggs's and Butler's divisions, on the north and east, would divert Ampudia's attention from Worth's effort, and, if fortunate, secure inroads into the city.

In selecting Worth for this independent role, critical to the success of the campaign, Taylor was pointedly ignoring the fact that Twiggs, not Worth, was the senior regular subordinate. But for all his difficult personality, Worth was the best soldier in Taylor's army, and Taylor could afford to take no unnecessary risks. Twiggs apparently raised no protest.

September 20, 1846

By 2 P.M., Sunday, September 20, Worth was ready to go. Hays's regiment of mounted Texans took the road first, followed by Lieutenant Colonel Thomas Staniford's 1st Brigade and Colonel Persifor F.

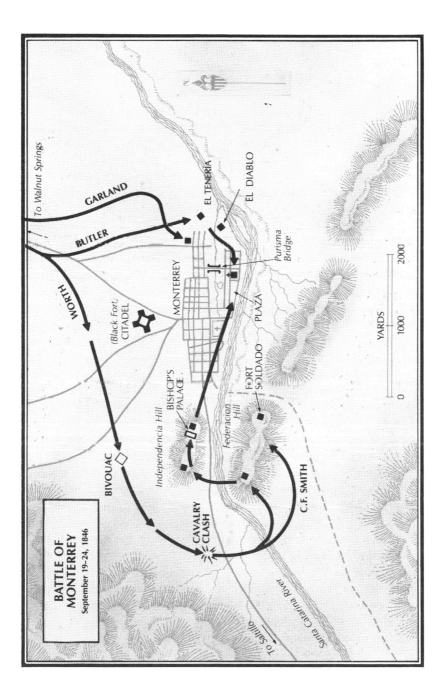

BATTLE OF MONTERREY
September 19–24, 1846

To Walnut Springs

GARLAND

BUTLER

WORTH

EL TENERIA

EL DIABLO

Purisma Bridge

MONTERREY

(Black Fort)
CITADEL

PLAZA

FORT SOLDADO

BISHOP'S PALACE

Independencia Hill

Federacion Hill

BIVOUAC

CAVALRY CLASH

C.F. SMITH

Santa Catarina River

To Saltillo

YARDS

0   1000   2000

Smith's 2d Brigade.* The formation marched as if on parade, "thoroughly military and soldier-like." One notable unit was Childs's "red-legged infantry," artillerymen without their field pieces who insisted on retaining the artillery color down the seams of their trousers. And Worth "the beau ideal of a gallant soldier," rode proud and self conscious at the head of the column.[2] What no witness could perceive was Worth's grim determination to achieve for himself a "grade or a grave."[3]

Mansfield had selected a good route for Worth to follow. For most of the distance his path was shielded from the guns of the Black Fort, but it would have been too much to expect the column to go completely undetected, and soon Mexican scouts on Independence Hill picked it up. Taylor, at Walnut Springs, could see Ampudia's reaction: Mexican reinforcements were being rushed to reinforce the troops on Independence Hill. Taylor attempted to divert attention by ordering a demonstration on the eastern approaches to Monterrey, but that gesture was empty at best.[4]

After four slow and tedious hours, Worth ordered a halt, having covered only seven miles. Anxious to move on, he went forward to check the ground for himself, accompanied by Meade and about fifty Texans. After going about two miles, Worth's party became aware that a large Mexican force was drawing up between them and the Saltillo Road, so they prepared to return. Some of the Mexicans, however, had made their way around to their rear and taken a position by a fence. The Texans opened fire on the would-be ambushers, and while the Mexicans hesitated, Worth and his party were able to gallop to safety.[5] It was now too late to continue the march, however, and Worth ordered his men to make camp where they were. He also scribbled a note to Taylor advising him of the division's position and outlining his tentative plans for the next day.[6] The men of the division spent the night without tents, blankets, or fires. A few made dinners—and sport —of some chickens and pigs belonging to Mexican farmers. But it would be an uncomfortable night.

*Worth report, September 28, 1846, in U.S. Congress, Exec. Doc. No. 4, p. 102. Staniford's brigade consisted of the 8th Infantry, C. F. Smith's dismounted artillery, Child's dismounted artillery battalion, and Duncan's battery. Persifor F. Smith's brigade had the 5th and 7th infantries, Blanchard's Louisiana volunteer company, and Mackall's artillery battery.

September 21, 1846

Monday began early for Worth's men; they moved out at sunrise, Hays's Mounted Rifles once again leading. For about a mile and a half they marched to the west, encountering no resistance in their path but receiving sporadic fire from Independence Hill. Then, at a point about three hundred yards from the Monterrey-Saltillo Road, Hays's scouts encountered the force that had nearly ambushed Worth the night before, some fifteen hundred cavalry and infantry.* In short order Hays's men deployed as skirmishers behind a fence, Childs's two light infantry companies taking position on their flanks.

The engagement was sharp, bloody, confused. McCulloch's company of Texans, caught in the open, turned and fought its way back on horseback. The Mexicans came on at a gallop, led fearlessly by an impressive leader, Lieutenant Colonel Juan N. Najera, pennants of green and red fluttering in the wind. McCulloch's men returned the fire with rifles, pistols, and shotguns while the Texans at the fence poured in a deadly fire. Najera fell in the thick of the fight, still urging his men on.[7] Soon Duncan and Mackall managed to get their batteries unlimbered and began to pour shot over the heads of the embattled Texans.

The Mexican squadron was nearly destroyed; its remnants fled, some toward Monterrey, some toward Saltillo, leaving behind one hundred dead and wounded after a fight of only fifteen minutes. Their gaudy uniforms added to the "wild and ghastly" scene of bodies, lying in all sorts of positions. Having little time for niceties, Worth's men shoveled thirty-two of them into one shallow pit.†

This action opened the way to the Saltillo road, and shortly after 8 A.M. Worth was astride it. In his exultation Worth penned a hasty note to Taylor: "The town is ours."‡ He was a bit premature in his claim, but Ampudia was at least cut off from his only source of resupply and reinforcement.

---

*Accounts vary. Meade estimated two thousand.

†Samuel Reid, *The Scouting Expeditions of McCullough's Texas Rangers*, p. 158, Worth, Report, p. 103. Ramón Alcaraz, *The Other Side*, pp. 71–72. Worth's losses were small, variously reported between one dead and two wounded. At the most, the total came to only a dozen.

‡Justin Smith, *War with Mexico*, vol. I, p. 244. A couple of small trails, through the Sierra Madre, remained. They would not, however, suffice as supply or reinforcement routes.

.   .   .

Worth had accomplished part of his task, "to turn the hill of the Bishop's palace" and "to occupy a position on the Saltillo road." But an important part of his mission remained: "to carry the enemy's detached works in that quarter."[8] He was indeed determined to move on, especially since possession of Independence Hill was essential to reestablishing direct communication with Taylor at Walnut Springs. But to reach the Mexican positions Worth needed to march some distance, as his circuitous route had brought him out some miles to the west.[9]

But which of these parallel ridges should he attack first, Independence on the north or Federation on the south? Both would have to be taken eventually, as the Bishop's Palace was located on the east end of Independence Hill and El Soldada occupied a corresponding point on Federation. Both looked down into the city. Worth, who had mentioned Federation in his note to Taylor the evening before, settled on attacking it.[10] As that ridge was somewhat less heavily defended, it should be the easier to take. And since it extended a little farther east, its possession would place the Americans in a semicircle around Independence, allowing them to concentrate fire on it from three sides. To move against Federation first was logical.

Federation Hill, like Independence, was defended on the western nose by an artillery position, inevitably the first objective. To scale the heights Worth selected a storming party, consisting of Captain C. F. Smith's three light infantry companies and six companies of dismounted Texas rangers, about three hundred men in all. Once the party had seized those two guns, Smith was to continue eastward down the spine toward El Soldada. His command departed at noon.[11]

To reach Federation Hill from Smith's present position, his command would have to cross the Santa Catarina River and make its way along the right bank. But fords were difficult to find, and Smith was forced to move upstream (westward) before he found a place where his men could slosh their way across. Eventually they found a feasible site and forded the stream amid an ineffectual fire of grapeshot from the hill.* Once across and in a hidden position south of Federation Hill,

---

*Reid (p. 162) describes the fire as a "terrific storm of shot and grape." However, nobody was hurt.

Smith set out to reconnoiter. He found that the heights of the hill rose to four hundred feet, were lined with rough chaparral—and were defended. Despite the odds, Smith ordered his men forward.[12]

All this, of course, took time, and soon an impatient Worth, out of touch, decided to send Colonel Persifor Smith's 2d Brigade as a follow-up. This force followed a more direct route, and for some reason escaped being fired upon, perhaps because the Mexican defenders were preoccupied with C. F. Smith's small party. Soon the two Smiths had joined at the bottom of Federation, the men intermingled. Up the hill they all went, regulars competing with Texans, all firing volley after volley, "followed up by the wild cheers and shouts of the men." The defenders of Federation, having no idea of what they were up against, fled in terror, leaving one nine-pounder cannon in-tact.[13] The Americans turned that single gun on El Soldado, at the other end of the hill, and a lucky shot knocked out the lone gun in that position. The Mexican defenders of El Soldado broke and ran.

That ended a successful day for Worth and his men. The victors rejoiced in a wild scene amid the looming mountains on either side, oblivious of sporadic fire from Independence Hill.[14]

   That evening storm clouds rose, this time even worse than before. The men were wet, without shelter, blankets or food. Some men would get a couple of hours of sleep; none would eat. Perhaps it was merciful that the attack the next day would be early.

That twenty-first of September 1846, the day when William J. Worth was covering himself with glory, could well be described as Zachary Taylor's worst in a long career. It began, however, with high hopes.

   Captain John Kenly, of the Baltimore Battalion, was awakened early that morning. Colonel Watson, his friend and battalion commander, had sent for him, and as Kenly, full of anticipation, parted the flaps of Watson's small tent, he found the colonel still dressing. Watson had great news: the Baltimore Battalion would remain brigaded with the 1st Infantry and together they would march to storm Monterrey. Watson was concerned about only one touchy matter: which company he should leave at Walnut Springs to guard the trains against marauding Mexican cavalry.

Actually, Watson had already decided: Captain Robert Bronaugh's company would be so designated. Kenly agreed in the choice but sympathized with the colonel's embarrassment. Bronaugh and his men, who believed they were in Mexico to fight the enemy, would be enraged. And in the manner of volunteers Bronaugh would not hesitate to so express himself. But that scene would have to be borne.

As Kenly was preparing to leave, Watson stopped him and asked lightheartedly which pair of boots he should wear that day, the heavy new ones with the cork soles or a lighter pair, lying on the floor. Kenly recommended the lighter ones; after all, Watson might have to run some that day. But Watson, laughing heartily, said that he, unlike his men, would be riding horseback. Besides, the heavy boots were a gift from his friends of the Baltimore Bar. Kenly admiringly inspected the heavy boots.

Those boots would later provide the only means by which Kenly would identify Watson's remains.[15]

Ampudia's plan for defending Monterrey remained passive. So passive, in fact, that he was prepared to evacuate most of the eastern suburbs of Monterrey north of a small stream that originated in the center of the city and flowed northeastward. The stream was fordable, but its banks were steep, especially where the main road from Marin crossed at the Purisima Bridge. It would provide a strong defensive line, provided Ampudia was willing to let Taylor take the outlying suburbs without a fight.

But the pendulum of Ampudia's resolve had now swung back to the optimistic side, and he had decided to defend those suburbs. To accomplish that defense, his engineers had previously constructed a couple of small redans, beyond which stood the strong fort called El Diablo (or El Rincón). This fortification housed three guns and could accommodate 150 to 200 men.[16]

About four hundred yards beyond El Diablo stood the most advanced of Ampudia's positions. This was the Tenería, a commercial tannery whose walls had been strengthened and whose enclosure could hold about two hundred men. Its flat roof and sandbags made it a formidable position, which could have been even stronger had the approaches been cleared and the ditch completed; nevertheless, even as it was, it would be something to contend with.*

Taylor was familiar with the Tenería, having designated it as "Advanced Work No. 1," or just No. 1. That morning he had sent Mansfield to scout the area leading to it. Nevertheless, Taylor seemed to regard the Tenería as casually as he did the other positions, and in ordering Colonel John Garland to conduct a limited, diversionary attack in that direction, he spoke offhandedly: "Colonel, lead the head of your column off to the left, keeping well out of reach of the enemy's shot, and if you think you can take any of them little forts down there with the bayonet, you'd better do it—but consult with Major Mansfield, you'll find him down there."†

Taylor's main interest at this time centered on trying to damage the Black Fort by artillery bombardment. His two twenty-four-pound howitzers and one ten-inch mortar, protected by a regiment of Butler's volunteers, were already hammering that position, though with no effect. Then the fort returned fire, and the Americans suffered their first casualties. The volunteers were thrilled by the exchange until the surgeons set up for business and "the groans of the first sufferers were heard."[17] Then the soldiers turned away.

Taylor had drawn up the forces on the east end of town with Twiggs's 1st Division (temporarily commanded by Garland) on the left side of the Marin Road; Butler's Field Division he placed on the right. On the left side calm prevailed; on the right, excitement. Soon Garland moved out to execute his "diversionary" attack against the Tenería, the 1st Infantry leading, then the 3d Infantry and finally the Baltimore Battalion. After a half hour of hard marching, Garland's lead elements emerged in a cornfield about five hundred yards from their objective. At that point the three units formed into line of battle, the 3d Infantry on the right, 1st Infantry in the center, and Baltimore Battalion on the left. At once the guns in the Tenería opened up, the first rounds hitting the ground before the feet of the troops and bouncing overhead. Soon the Black Fort, to the right front, let loose with an eighteen-pounder.

---

*Justin Smith, *War with Mexico*, vol. I, pp. 249–50. The incomplete state of the Tenería was due largely to Ampudia's vacillation as to whether to occupy a position in advance of the stream. In fact, it had been destroyed previously and rebuilt frantically only the night before, Sunday.

†Recorded by Garland's aide, Adjutant General's files. Quoted in Justin Smith *War with Mexico*, vol. I, pp. 251, 566. General Twiggs was laid up that morning, apparently from taking an overdose of laxative on the theory that loose bowels were less vulnerable to rifle wounds. See Kenly, *Memoirs*, p. 119.

A few men were hit, and only chance spared many others. But the Americans doggedly pressed on without firing.*

At that point, Garland met up with Mansfield, who was still on horseback. Together they discussed the next move, neither one completely understanding the vague order that Taylor had issued only a short time before. Should they move forward in the face of heavy fire, they wondered, or had they performed their task by putting on a demonstration? They took their answer, apparently, not from Taylor's words but from his personality. Neither man wanted to assume the responsibility of falling back without attacking. So they would press the attack. It was a fateful interpretation of an equivocal order.†

Forward Garland's men marched. When they reached a point about a hundred yards from the Tenería, they could see that one of its gun positions had already been abandoned.[18] Success seemed at hand.

Garland, if he had also noticed the abandoned gun position, ignored it in favor of of the plan he was following. He halted the brigade and laboriously began moving his five hundred men on an oblique slant to the right, obviously intending to take the position in the rear.[19] The troops had now reached the fortified suburbs, and they were being taken under fire by the defenders on the rooftops, the Black Fort, the Tenería, and now El Diablo across the stream. Confusion set in, and officers lost their way in the smoke and narrow streets. They simply had to stand and take it. The aristocratic but popular Major Philip Norbourne Barbour was killed instantly by a ball through the heart. In the confusion the 3d Infantry dashed forward to a point where the buildings shielded them from some of the fire, and Barbour's body was dragged into one of them. Nearby, mortally wounded, lay Captain Williams, the engineer who had scouted the position.[20]

At about this time Braxton Bragg's battery of flying artillery arrived, but his guns were totally ineffective as they fired down the empty

---

*"We were being enfiladed. Still we advanced; another shot from the citadel, and the leg of Lieutenant Dilworth, of the First Infantry, was taken off as he stepped. If the gun which had fired that shot had been aimed the eighth of an inch more to the left, there is no telling how many would have been crippled." Kenly, *Memoirs*, p. 107.

†"To send the troops back without an overwhelming reason . . . and look 'Old Rough and Ready' in the eye, was unthinkable." Justin Smith, *War with Mexico*, vol. I, p. 251.

streets. Now Garland, on Mansfield's recommendation, ordered the division to fall back. Most, but not all, of the units received the order.

One who apparently did not was Colonel Watson, of the Baltimore Battalion. Though his troops had received the order, and were attempting to persuade him to retire, his fighting spirit was up. He took a drink from a canteen and declaimed, "Never, boys! I have too much Irish blood in me to give up!"[21] He would not leave.

Taylor, meanwhile, soon realized that Garland's attack was in trouble, and he sent three companies of the 4th Infantry forward, followed by Quitman's brigade. On the way the second wave passed just to the east of Garland's division, but in the rough ground the two never made contact. But this second force ran into the same hail of fire that was decimating Garland's brigade. Though they sustained "considerable execution," in Taylor's words,* they pressed on toward the Tenería.

Quitman's brigade, consisting of the Tennessee and Mississippi volunteer regiments, were now closing in on the Tenería. On nearing the position they discovered that one company of the 1st Infantry was already there, firing in from an adjacent rooftop. Captain Electus Backus had either failed to receive Garland's retreat order or had ignored it. The Mexicans, alarmed by the willingness of the Americans to take such heavy casualties, began to falter. They were thrown into panic when their commander, a man who had fled at the Resaca, fled once more at the Tenería. A good portion of the garrison followed him.[22] The Americans, volunteer and regular, then stormed into the Tenería, taking some thirty prisoners. The role of Backus had been critical, but the price had been paid by the volunteers, who had attacked in the open. The Tennesseans lost twenty-five killed, seventy-five wounded.[23] The Tenería, once taken, would remain in American hands. Taylor had gained a foothold in his advance toward Ampudia's position.

As a sidelight to history, the feat of taking the Tenería constituted a landmark in promoting the career of Jefferson Davis, commander of

---

*Taylor to TAG, October 9, 1846, in U.S. Congress, Exec. Doc. No. 4, p. 85; Justin Smith, *War with Mexico,* vol. I, p. 252. The 4th Infantry lost a third of its men "almost in a moment." Colonel Watson, separated from his men, joined up with Quitman's men and fell leading a charge with them, away from his own command.

the Mississippians. That ambitious man, onetime son-in-law of Zachary Taylor before the death of his young bride, had been prominent in Mississippi politics and was now seeking to justify his education at West Point and to attain further laurels by feats of military heroism. He achieved that aim by his valiant performance on September 21, 1846.

Meanwhile Butler's other brigade, Hamer's, advanced on the west of Garland toward the Purisima Bridge, the 1st Ohio in the lead. Hamer, Butler, and Taylor himself were at the front, and Taylor, perhaps from habits acquired while fighting the Indians in Florida, took the field as an infantry officer. But the Mexicans, unimpressed by all the rank facing them, beat off the American attacks, Taylor or no Taylor. Ridgely's battery did its best but was no more effective than Bragg's had been. By 5 P.M. Taylor saw that all was useless. He ordered the entire army, except for those occupying the Tenería, to fall back to Walnut Springs.

The American withdrawal was orderly but not without harassment. One unit drove off a squadron of Mexican lancers, but the fire from the Black Fort continued to take its toll. When losses for the day were tallied, the figure came to a staggering 394 casualties.* At that cost Taylor had seized the Tenería, inflicted some casualties, and captured five pieces of artillery. More important, Taylor's wing of the army had definitely diverted Ampudia's attention from Worth's attack on the west; he had been fighting the bulk of the Mexican garrison.†

But even though the results of the day's fighting might have justified the cost, this was the worst day of Taylor's career. For on September 21 the usually composed battle leader lost control. Rather than being precise, he was vague; rather than being determined, he was vacillating; rather than being cool, he lost his head.

What went wrong? Just about everything. What Taylor had intended as a diversion to assist Worth evolved into a major, unplanned attack on a strong, entrenched enemy. On that single day Taylor had lost some 10 percent of those engaged, and an even higher percentage

---

*Taylor to TAG, October 9, 1846., Exec. Doc. No. 4, p. 86. Henry saw a shell from the Black Fort take a man's head off, throwing it and a part of his gun high in the air. Henry, p. 197.
†Mexican reinforcements, under General García Condé, originally sent to reinforce Torrejón that morning, had been called back to the bridge of Purisima. Alcaraz, *The Other Side*, p. 73.

among his officers. At a fearsome cost he had learned that the underestimated Mexicans could fight very well. At the end, tired and discouraged, he had given up most of what he had gained.

It has been so with most great commanders of history. Stonewall Jackson would have his lapse at White Oak Swamp in 1862; Lee would blunder on the third day at Gettysburg; Grant would sacrifice many at Cold Harbor in 1864. In that vein, though on a smaller scale, Taylor floundered on that first day at Monterrey. In common with those other great commanders, he would recover.

September 22, 1846

Taylor's force rested on September 22, the second day of the battle. His men were exhausted physically and morally, hard put even to reorganize themselves. The burden that day fell completely on Worth.

Worth's men were ordered to "fall in" at 3 A.M., before daylight. A new storming party, this time under Childs and Hays, began stumbling some crawled—up the western slope of Independence Hill.* The wind and rain covered their movements, and they crept up within a few feet of the Mexican positions before being discovered. With full surprise, they reached the top of Independence Hill within a few minutes.

But the Bishop's Palace at the eastern end of the hill was capable of holding out against any purely infantry assault. Worth therefore waited while Lieutenant Edward Deas,† with fifty artillerymen, dragged a dismantled twelve-pound howitzer up the eight hundred feet to the top of the hill. At about noon the howitzer was placed inside the earthen entrenchment on the western peak, whence it opened fire upon the Bishop's Palace, far below and at a distance of four hundred yards. It was obviously effective.[24]

Lieutenant Colonel Francisco Berra, inside the Bishop's Palace, was now faced with heavy odds, fired upon by American artillery from two directions, Independence Hill from the west and Federation Hill across the river. The American strength was growing; Childs and Hays had now been reinforced by the 5th Infantry and Blanchard's Louisiana

---

*Smith's light infantry and the Texans had rejoined Worth's force after El Soldado had been taken. Smith's 2d Brigade remained in place.

†Edward Deas should not be confused with the Deas (Lieutenant George Deas) who swam the Rio Grande at Matamoros.

volunteers. Yet Berra had two hundred defenders inside the fort, and the walls had not been breached; if he had remained within the enclosure, he might have held out for some time.*

But such was not in the impetuous Mexican nature, and against Ampudia's orders Berra led his infantry and cavalry in a desperate charge out of the palace into the fire of the waiting Americans. His troops were quickly decimated; Berra had squandered what little chance had been afforded him. His men turned and fled down the hill toward Monterrey below; only a few retired back into the palace.

Soon the palace gate was knocked down by Worth's twelve-pound howitzer, and Americans poured in. The enclosure was large, however, and fighting was not over until Duncan and Mackall unlimbered inside the walls, spreading grapeshot and consternation everywhere. The Stars and Stripes flew over the Bishop's Palace by 4 P.M., and American artillery fire followed the fleeing survivors down the hill and into the streets.[25]

That night, Ampudia, utterly shaken, withdrew all his outposts into the built-up area of Monterrey, abandoning Fort Diablo, the strong defense protecting the Purisima Bridge, and all other outlying positions. His soldiers, still confident, protested to no avail.

Wednesday, September 23, 1846

By the morning of September 23 both sides in the battle for Monterrey were exhausted, the Americans in particular. Worth's men had undergone a grueling physical ordeal, and though their losses had been relatively light (thirty-two killed and wounded during the two days),[26] the long marches, the precipitous hills, and the lack of food and shelter had taxed the limits of human endurance. And on Taylor's end of the city, the heavy losses, disorganization, and emotional shock of the first day's battle had made the men nearly incapable of functioning.

The Mexicans, on the other hand, had undergone a different kind of ordeal. Though not so fatigued as Worth's men—and not so riddled with casualties as Taylor's—they had nevertheless borne the psychological burden of being forced to respond to the enemy's initiatives. But

*Alcaraz, p. 75. The conjecture is mine.

none of them, neither the men nor Ampudia, had any desire to take the offensive. So the situation was quiet.

Taylor was lethargic that morning, seemingly in no hurry to follow up the advantages he had gained. He sent no orders to Worth, who was chafing impatiently in the Bishop's Palace, and sent Quitman up to the Tenería with orders to enter the city at his own discretion, cover his men by houses and walls, and to "advance carefully as far as he may deem prudent." Taylor was unaware that Fort Diablo had been abandoned.[27]

When Quitman relieved Hamer at the Tenería, however, he learned that Diablo had been evacuated, and he sent Davis's Mississippians forward to occupy it and to enter the city. Davis did so, encountering only light opposition. The troops back at Walnut Springs received an inkling of what was happening only when they heard firing as they fell in for reveille. Taylor then ordered up George Woods's 2d Regiment of Texas volunteers, the 3d and 4th infantries, and Bragg's battery. (The regulars were once more commanded by Twiggs.) Taylor himself rode forward to the Tenería.[28]

To Taylor, the morning's action was only a "reconnaissance in force," in preparation for a coordinated attack to be launched the next day. Thus, even though his infantry penetrated deep, to a point only a block from the Central Plaza, Taylor claimed that he was "satisfied" that his men could enter the city with relative ease. He thereupon withdrew them all the way back to the Tenería and Diablo. Meanwhile Ridgely, with a captured artillery piece, pounded the city. That evening Quitman's men were relieved once more by Hamer's.

So it went—according to the general. To those advancing "carefully, covered by houses and walls" the scene was a bit more dramatic. Nevertheless, the Americans this time advanced methodically, instructed by Woods's Texans, who had been fighting in cities for a decade. The troops avoided the streets, advancing from house to house, breaking into each successive building. Using picks and crowbars, the men would beat holes in the common walls and toss six-pound shells, with fuses set, into the next building. The explosion would wipe out what Mexican troops were on the bottom floor—the civilians had long since taken refuge at the Plaza in the city—and the troops would then rush up the steps to the rooftop. There they would set up a base of fire to protect their comrades, who would repeat the process in the next house. And the light artillery, though of limited effectiveness, could at least operate with relative impunity by loading under cover, firing quickly down the street, and yanking the piece back to cover by a rope. Casualties for that day, therefore, were described by Taylor as "small."*

In the course of this action Taylor's troops uncovered grim evidence of the battle two days earlier. In the confusion of September 21, Garland's desperate troops had been forced to abandon many dead and wounded, Colonel Watson, of the Baltimore Battalion, among them. But some of the victims were still alive, tongues horribly swollen by thirst. Most had died, and evidence showed that some had been gnawed by wolves while still alive. The cleaning up would have to wait until the battle was over.

Meanwhile, on Independence Hill, Worth was waiting for orders that never came. At 10 A.M., as the sound of firing in the streets below became heavy, he decided he had waited long enough and determined to attack on his own.† Soon his men were charging eagerly down the hill and into the western edge of Monterrey. At the edge of the built-up area, they slowed down and began employing the Texan street-fighting techniques, working their way to a position only one block from the Central Plaza.[29] The two wings of Taylor's army were now only two blocks apart, yet no communication had been established between them.

At that point Worth heard the fire from the other end of the city stop. He halted his advance and set up the ten-inch mortar that Taylor had sent around to him. From the Campo Santo Cemetery that heavy piece began lobbing shells into the Central Plaza. One round took a piece off the cathedral.

Ampudia was now completely unnerved. Not only was he cut off from Saltillo, but he was fearful that the large mortar would destroy the cathedral. He had reason for alarm, as he was using this house of God to protect his ammunition and (for a while) his own person. A round

---

*Taylor report, October 9, 1846. U.S. Grant, however (*Memoirs*, vol. I, p. 115), claimed years later that the 3rd Infantry lost five officers killed, of twelve present for duty.

†Worth report, September 28, 1846, in U.S. Congress, Exec. Doc. No. 4, p. 105, says that orders must have "miscarried" because of the distance they would have had to travel.

falling into the middle of his cache of explosives would cause unthinkable devastation among the terrified crowds, huddled inside for protection. This possibility weighed heavily on the Mexican commander toward the end of the period that Winfield Scott would later call "Three Glorious Days."

MONTERREY III: TRUCE

SEPTEMBER 24–OCTOBER 12, 1846

Thursday, September 24, 1846, dawned bright and cheerful for Samuel C. Reid, of McCulloch's Texas Rangers. The rains the night before had cooled the air, and the valley of the Santa Catarina "smiled once more in the bright and joyous sunbeams, as if to gladden and cheer on our men to new exertions for victory."[1] McCulloch's men were drawn up near the post office in the western part of Monterrey and were getting ready to attack toward the center of town. A short time before, the pickax of some enterprising ranger had penetrated the solid wall of a house on the opposite corner, and a whole company of terrified Mexican infantry, huddled inside, had tried to escape by the front door. McCulloch's men had poured in a fire so murderous that half the company were dead before reaching the other side of the street. It was, Reid wrote, a "most delightful morning."[2]

The attitude of the civilians reflected low morale. Mexican women were standing in the doors, ignoring the corpses in the streets and offering oranges and other fruit to the Texans. The Mexican cavalry had left during the night, they claimed. They denounced Ampudia as a coward, and predicted that the Americans would certainly carry the city before sundown. The men partook of the women's peace offerings, and just as they were ready to march off, "excited by the noise of the artillery, the shouts of the men, the pace of the infantry, and the clang of arms,"[3] a courier rode up to McCulloch with a message. To the disappointment of his men, McCulloch had been directed to hold up the attack, as negotiations for the surrender of the city were under way. It was still barely daylight.

On the eastern side of the line the troops were better informed. On the preceding afternoon, in fact, Ampudia had sent a message, under a flag of truce, asking that hostilities be ceased until he could remove the women and children from the city. Taylor had refused, much to the approval of his officers.

Actual negotiations for a cessation of hostilities began early that morning of September 25. At 3 A.M. the 1st Ohio, in the Tenería, heard a bugle sound from the Mexican line, and at that moment they sighted a Mexican officer marching down the street with a small escort, the sad expression on his face indicating his purpose. The officer turned out to be Colonel D. Francisco R. Moreno, aide-de-camp to Ampudia. Moreno introduced himself to General Hamer, who immediately provided him with a small escort to guide him back to Taylor's headquarters. On Moreno's departure, the men of the 1st Ohio, who had been maintaining their decorum, broke up and gleefully congratulated each other.[4]

At Walnut Springs, Moreno delivered Ampudia's offer to surrender the city of Monterrey. Showing no sign of fear, Moreno verbally laid down a stringent condition, that Ampudia's troops be permitted to march off with all arms and equipment.[5] In the ensuing discussions he conceded that the Americans might take Monterrey by force, but contended that it would cost Taylor two-thirds of his command to do so. Further, Moreno claimed that commissioners at the governmental level had already been appointed by both Washington and Mexico City to negotiate for peace.[6] Taylor had no way of knowing whether Moreno was telling the truth, but in any case he rejected Ampudia's conditions and simply demanded the total surrender of Ampudia's entire army, along with all public property in Monterrey.[7] He advised that he would resume his attack if Ampudia had not accepted these terms as of noon of that same day. But Moreno's words had made an impression; Taylor held up Worth's attack and awaited the passage of time.

Soon Ampudia sent another message through the lines asking to meet with Taylor in person at Worth's headquarters in the western section of the town, a place more convenient to both sides than Walnut Springs or the barren Tenería. Since Worth's men had made contact with Taylor's main body that morning, Taylor agreed.

The first confrontation between Taylor and Ampudia was brief. Taylor remained adamant, scorning discussion of any subject other than his earlier terms of surrender. He did, however, extend his previous deadline from noon to 1 P.M. Ampudia returned to his headquarters and soon sent word that he had "accepted the basis" for the surrender.*

When the two commanders met a second time, Ampudia built on the foundation Moreno had laid that morning, advising that the Mexican government had "consented to receive commissioners for the negotiation of peace, and had already appointed commissioners on the Mexican side."[8] Ampudia claimed that this development, and this alone, absolved him personally of his obligation to defend the city. But he stuck to his previous demand that he be allowed to evacuate with all equipment and government property.

Taylor concluded that Ampudia was backtracking, as he had earlier accepted Taylor's demand "in principle," and was about to break off the conference when the governor of Monterrey intervened, pleading for a "mixed commission" of Americans and Mexicans to "study" the problem. Taylor hesitated. After some consideration, however, he consented to appoint three Americans—Worth, Henderson, and Davis—to match Ampudia's three.† It was now late afternoon, September 24.

When the commissioners met, neither side expected hostilities to resume, but both maneuvered to obtain the best possible bargain. By now Taylor had made a major concession. No longer did he demand the surrender of Ampudia's army; rather, he would permit it to evacuate Monterrey, but it must leave all equipment except for the officers' side arms. Ampudia would retire beyond the Rinconada pass, and

---

*R.S. Ripley, *The War with Mexico,* vol. I, pp. 239–40. Ramón Alcaraz (*The Other Side,* p. 78) portrays a distraught Ampudia: "Ampudia, enraged, and perhaps repenting of his weakness, protested solemnly, if he had nothing else to offer, he should first be buried under the ruins of the city." Alcaraz further states that Worth traveled the few blocks from his headquarters to Ampudia's to influence Ampudia's acceptance. Worth's report makes no mention of this gesture, nor does any other American source.

†The Mexican commissioners were General García Condé, General Raquena, and D. Manuel María del Llano. Alcaraz, p. 78.

Taylor would undertake not to advance beyond that line for eight weeks, or until the respective governments were heard from.

The predictable refusal by the Mexicans now centered on peripheral objections, specifically to the American demand that they surrender all arms and artillery. Back and forth the arguments went, hindered by the fact that Ampudia's commissioners assumed a stronger position than the general did.

Finally the two sides reached a compromise. The Mexicans would retain one battery of field artillery (liberally interpreted to mean six guns, chosen at random) and twenty-one rounds of artillery ammunition. The cavalry would keep their horses. One final delay stemmed from Ampudia's need to save face by phrasing the document in the most euphemistic way possible. The surrender was duly signed by the respective commissioners during the early morning hours of September 25, 1846.[9]

From the American viewpoint the most important single feature of the truce was the immediate surrender of the Black Fort, the position that controlled the region around Monterrey. At Taylor's prodding, Ampudia sent word to surrender the fort, and the signing ceremony was held that very morning.

Persifor F. Smith, in recognition of his admirable service in the capture of Federation Hill, was designated to command the troops at the surrender of the Black Fort. In keeping with the terms of the truce, the Mexicans fired a salute of eight guns as their flag went down. When the Stars and Stripes were raised above the dark walls, a salute of twenty-eight guns—one for each state of the Union—was fired from Independence Hill. The Mexicans marched out of the fort, and Smith's exultant troops marched in to the tune of "Yankee Doodle."*

So rapidly was the surrender of the fort arranged that the ceremony came as a surprise to much of Taylor's army. The Baltimore Battalion, having replaced the 1st Ohio in the Tenería, got their first inkling of

---

*Henry, pp. 214–15. That flag would be "sacred to every American," Henry was sure. And "when they think by what a loss of noble spirits it has been obtained, they will drop a tear."

a truce about an hour after daylight, when hundreds of Mexican women appeared, "some sobbing, some smiling, to see the prisoners who were confined in the distillery building."[10] And then, when all of Monterrey seemed dead, conflicting rumors began circulating. Around noon, however, fire flashed across the sky, followed by a crash of thunder. The men sprang to their feet, thinking that the battle had been resumed. But as they peered toward the Black Fort they saw the American flag being hoisted.[11] After deafening shouts, the men raised the flag of the Baltimore Battalion over the Tenería along with the Stars and Stripes. The volunteers fired their own salute "in the honor of the storming and capture of Monterrey."[12]

On subsequent days Ampudia's army evacuated Monterrey, a division leaving per day. The Americans watched the Mexican troops with keen interest, concluding that they "were not a defeated army." The infantry, though poorly clad, were "brawny and thick-set." Their cavalry, though mounted on inferior horses, were considered a "fine looking body of men." After the troops the camp followers trudged out, "mounted on everything, from a decent mustang to an humble, uncomplaining donkey." Some were officers' wives, "picturesquely wrapped in their gay-colored ponchos,"[13] but many were devastated townspeople, who found themselves unable to remain among the hated enemy. Many of them abandoned their homes and businesses, carrying their children as they left on foot.[14] Behind them the Mexicans had left a "vast cemetery. The unburied bodies, the dead and putrid mules, the silence of the streets, all gave a fearful aspect to the city."[15]

On September 28 Taylor designated William J. Worth to be governor of Monterrey, and his division moved in. The Americans, all of them, were exhausted and grateful for a respite—the process of rebuilding and refitting their army would take a long time—Taylor estimated six weeks.[16] While little criticism was directed within the army toward the commanding general himself, the shock of the losses—especially those of the first day of battle—weighed heavily on the men. Few, if any, believed that the war would be terminated without further bloodshed.

.   .   .

On the evening of Sunday, October 11, 1846, news of Taylor's victory reached the War Department in Washington. That same evening Secretary Marcy took the message to the White House.

Polk received the news of Monterrey's surrender coolly; far from being filled with pride, he concentrated only on the negative. In particular he disapproved of the truce Taylor had agreed to. In doing so, Polk quickly concluded, Taylor had "violated his express orders." The enemy had been "in his power," Polk claimed, and Taylor should have made prisoners of them all, stripped them of their arms, put them on parole, and pushed on into the country.* He expressed neither pride in Taylor's accomplishment nor sadness at the losses; he focused only on the truce.

The next morning Polk met with his cabinet. Well aware of their chief's predisposition, that group of confirmed yes men joined in the opinion that Taylor had "committed a great error" in allowing lenient terms to Ampudia—he was especially wrong in agreeing to an armistice of eight weeks. Polk contended that if Taylor had made prisoners of Ampudia's army, it "would probably have ended the war with Mexico."[17]

But in public Polk was forced to swallow his bitterness. The country, in its exultation, would brook no overt criticism. Winfield Scott, not bothering to obtain Polk's blessing, publicly termed the battle "three glorious days," and the press, on the whole, agreed.

Although Polk could not face down the tide of public acclamation, he determined to order Taylor to terminate the armistice "in terms neither to approve nor condemn his conduct. . . ."[18] Accordingly the message that Marcy sent Taylor the next day simply expressed the President's regret "that it was not deemed advisable to insist upon the terms first proposed." Conceding that the President was "uninformed" of the circumstances that justified the change, Marcy hit on Taylor's weakest point, his being influenced by Ampudia's talk of a quick peace. In that regard, Marcy's message pointedly advised that "the present

---

*James K. Polk, *Diary*, October 11, 1846, p. 155. As regards Taylor's previous instructions, Polk was essentially correct, although Scott's letter of instructions to Taylor, written on June 12, 1846, contained some room for doubt: "Should continued success attend your operations, you may some time before be met by the proposition to treat for peace, with an intermediate armistice. No such proposition will be entertained by you, without your first being satisfied that it is made in good faith on the part of the enemy. Being satisfied on this point, you may conclude an armistice for a limited time, and refer the proposition to treat of peace to the government here."

rulers of that republic have not yet given any evidence that they [were] 'favorable to the interests of peace.' " Taylor was instructed to "give the requisite notice that the armistice is to cease at once."[19]

Polk's rejection of Taylor's truce was based largely on political considerations, both personal and official. He was quite right, actually, in his objection to Taylor's citing the possibility of an imminent peace as a consideration in granting the truce, for Taylor, if sincere in making that argument, was exceeding his purview as a military commander.

Taylor's real reasons for the truce had been military—and realistic. Taylor's army was depleted, and a final assault would have decimated it. Most of the others in Taylor's army felt the same way. Meade, for example, defended Taylor's action on the basis of the remaining strength in Ampudia's army and the exhausted state of Taylor's. The volunteer force, he wrote, "were beginning to be disorganized, and already regiments were holding back, and individuals refusing to advance," and the "regulars were crippled almost to inefficiency. . . ."[20]

Others felt likewise—Giddings, who blamed the Texans for inciting criticisms of the truce,* and even Reid, the member of McCulloch's company who had been disappointed when the last attack had been called off. Reid was not a man likely to shy away from further combat if such was necessary or advisable.

But foremost among Taylor's defenders was Jefferson Davis, commander of the Mississippi Rifles and one of the commissioners. When the question later came up, he wrote a letter for publication, insisting that he did not believe Taylor "could have made the enemy surrender at discretion." He went further: "Had I entertained the opinion, it would have been given to the commission and to the commanding general, and would have precluded me from signing the agreement."[21]

---

*Luther Giddings, *Campaign in Northern Mexico*, p. 212: "The fault-finders in our army were chiefly Texans. On the night of the 23d of September they had obtained possession of the highest houses in the vicinity of the great plaza, and, unsated with slaughter, they but waited for the morning to avenge signally the hoarded wrongs suffered during their long war of independence. The capitulation of the 24th, of course, disappointed all their sweet and long-cherished hopes of vengeance. Fortunately for the Mexican population the American General knew how to crown a triumph with mercy. It appears from the Mexican 'History of the War,' that some of the enemy were equally dissatisfied with the finale of the siege, and it must be admitted, with better reason. Both parties of malcontents, however, in complaining, sin against humanity."

An idealized portrait of President James Knox Polk. *Library of Congress*

Below: James K. Polk in 1849, at the end of his term. Though Polk was only in his fifty-fourth year, this photograph shows the harsh effect of the office on him. *Courtesy Amon Carter Museum, Fort Worth*

An official photograph of
Antonio López de Santa
Anna, president of Mexico.
Despite Santa Anna's political
prominence over many years,
photos of him in office are
rare. *Library
of Congress*

Santa Anna in old age. *Library
of Congress*

Major General Winfield Scott,
as he looked during the
war with Mexico.
Library of Congress

Major General Zachary Taylor.
Possibly since he was a prime
presidential candidate in 1848,
Taylor had many photos taken
during the war with Mexico.
This is the most revealing of the
man. *Library of Congress*

General Mariano Paredes, who
was not as disagreeable-looking as
he was usually described. *Alcaraz*

Valentin Gómez-Farías, a liberal,
idealistic politician who was
twice miscast as Santa Anna's
acting president. *Benson
Collection, University of
Texas, Austin*

Brigadier General John E. Wool.
Portraits like this one required the
subject to hold still for extended
periods of time, which may
account for the pained expression.
Library of Congress

An idealized portrait of
Brigadier General John E. Wool.
Library of Congress

General Pedro de Ampudia.
Ampudia was only in his
forties during the Mexican
War. *Benson Collection,
University of Texas, Austin*

Mariano Arista. The popular
aristocratic, American-educated
Mexican commander at Palo
Alto and Resaca de la Palma.
*Benson Collection, University
of Texas, Austin*

Senator Thomas Hart Benton.
A fine photograph showing
the senator's strength and
arrogance. *Library of Congress*

Secretary of War William
Marcy. *Library of Congress*

Taylor's camp at Corpus Christi. The impeccable order of the encampments of the "regulars" is confirmed in accounts written by various observers, notably Luther Giddings, of the 1st Ohio Volunteers. *Library of Congress*

Brigadier General William J. Worth. The only photograph showing the strength and vitality of this most egotistical of generals. *Wagstaff Collection*

Brigadier General David E. Twiggs. Lacking the sizable beard usually mentioned in accounts of him, Twiggs is deceptively mild-looking in this photo.

Captain Samuel Walker, Texas Rangers. This image shows a no-nonsense individual, tough but not vainglorious. *Library of Congress*

Gideon J. Pillow. Pillow was known as a handsome man, and this painting, done in the uniform of a major general, bears that out. *Photographic Archives, Special Collections, University of Texas at Arlington Library, courtesy of John R. Neal*

The Battle of Palo Alto. This is one of the better battle paintings, possibly because the field at Palo Alto was restricted enough that it could be shown in one picture. It undoubtedly shows more than what was seen by the soldier in the thick chaparral. *Library of Congress.*

The Battle of Resaca de la Palma. Only the critical point is shown. Though the lines ran for some distance along the resaca, the only severe fighting took place in the middle. *Library of Congress*

New Hampshire Volunteers. This is said to be the only photograph of volunteers marching off to war. These volunteers belonged to one of the later units of the war, as the bulk of the early participants came from the southern and western states. *Beinecke Rare Book and Manuscript Library, Yale University*

Polk and Scott plan the war. An artist's conception after consultation with the author. It well depicts the atmosphere of tension between two men who disliked each other but were forced to respect each other's official position. *Charles M. Tyson, Carlisle, Pennsylvania*

Above: Street fighting, Monterrey. This picture is remarkable for its realism at a time when artists in the United States usually depicted battle scenes in largely formal terms. *Library of Congress. Below:* The Bishop's Palace and Monterrey—obviously the product of someone's imagination. *Library of Congress*

A Mexican family, Saltillo. *Amon Carter Museum, Fort Worth*

Above: Santiago Cathedral at Saltillo, 1846. *Beinecke Rare Book and Manuscript Library, Yale University. Left:* General Wool at Saltillo. *Beinecke Rare Book and Manuscript Library, Yale University*

A standard photograph of Captain John C. Frémont. It provides no clue as to why Frémont's men rendered him such complete—and often unwise—loyalty.
Library of Congress

Commodore Robert F. Stockton. A fine photograph showing Stockton's strength, along with his overbearing arrogance.
Library of Congress

.   .   .

And so the battle of Monterrey came to an end, a costly victory. Taylor had taken an important city, both strategically and politically, in a battle he had hoped would not be necessary. But Ampudia's army had been spared to fight another day. The war would drag on; in fact Marcy's message to Taylor ordering the commencement of operations had been devoted largely to plans for the future. As far as Taylor's army was concerned, the important thing was that it, like Ampudia's, had survived. But morally it had suffered damage. Taylor's principal subordinate, William J. Worth, had received justified praise but a dangerous boost to his ego at the expense of his commanding general.* But nearly as important as these other results was the effect of Polk's repudiation of Taylor's truce with Ampudia. That action would have consequences as yet unforeseen either in Washington or in Monterrey.

*The Honorable Bailly Peyton, a politician volunteer who was serving as aide to Worth and a great Worth partisan, wrote to Crittenden: "He [Worth] requests me to . . . say that you must and shall be the President of the United States; that he has not fully made up his mind as to whether he will accept the office of Secretary of War, which he considers as tendered to him in advance. . . .

"Take him in all, he is the high-combed cock of the army, head and shoulders above the crowd."
John J. Crittenden, *Life*, vol. 1, p. 259.

CHAPTER 14

SECOND
BEGINNING

〜〜〜

OCTOBER–NOVEMBER 1846

anta Anna was too good a politician to be deceived by the lavish reception accorded him as he entered Mexico City. He knew that his followers had engineered the celebration, and he was keenly aware of the prevailing disorder and discontent. The unpleasant incident that had marred his arrival at Veracruz had sobered him. But the Mexicans were united in their hostility toward the Americans, so Santa Anna decided, perhaps by instinct, to exploit that unity for his own ends. He placed governmental administration in the hands of General José Mariano Salas and reassumed his role as his country's military defender. With his customary energy, Santa Anna began organizing the units around the capital into a new army, then hurriedly prepared to march northward. As early as September 28, 1846, he led his small army through the gates of Mexico City, headed for San Luis Potosí. There he would base operations against Taylor in the north.

Santa Anna received his first word of Ampudia's surrender when he had been on the road one day, and he soon began meeting deserters from Ampudia's force. In doubt as to the condition of Ampudia's army, Santa Anna sent orders ahead to Saltillo directing Ampudia to bring the remnants of his army back to San Luis Potosí, meanwhile placing Ampudia under orders for court-martial.[1] Ampudia, in turn, levied charges against about a dozen of his subordinates. That turned out to be a good ploy, because Santa Anna could not follow up. He had more pressing matters to deal with. The defeated commander, though under a shadow, went unpunished.[2]

Santa Anna arrived at San Luis Potosí on October 8, 1846. His obsession at this time was to concentrate, train, and equip an "invincible" army to attack Taylor, whose supply line had become longer with every mile he had ventured from Camargo. Concentration at San Luis Potosí was a sound idea, but Santa Anna carried it to the extreme, recalling the garrisons of all towns and villages throughout Mexico, thus conceding Taylor a free hand in the northern provinces. Even the port of Tampico was to be evacuated, despite the howls of its citizens and despite accusations throughout Mexico of complicity with the Americans. To create his great army, the Napoleon of the West would willingly pay even that price.

Santa Anna's major problem at that time was to attain logistical support for the force he was organizing. At first, while the citizens expected Taylor to descend on them at any moment, they came forth zealously with produce and resources. When that scare passed, however, the public attitude began reverting to normal—that is, apathy. Obtaining recruits from the various Mexican states, especially from the north, became increasingly difficult. Durango demurred on the basis of Indian troubles; so did Michoacán; Zacatecas was already plotting to join with other states to overthrow the new president. But some cooperated: Guanajuato produced five thousand men; Jalisco, two thousand.[3]

Funds, as always, were lacking. At an estimated cost of one peso per day per man, support of an army of 35,000 (the planned total) would come to a million pesos a month. The usual source, customs duties, was dried up by the American naval blockade, so alternative means were sought, including the usual pressure on a reluctant clergy. Santa Anna obtained a loan of fifteen million pesos, secured with Church property, although only ten million were ever realized from that source.[4]

While Santa Anna was thus laboring at San Luis Potosí, the political situation back in Mexico City was becoming more fragmented. Acting President Salas was largely by-passed, and both the Puros (who had ousted Paredes) and the Moderatos looked to San Luis Potosí rather than to Mexico City for signals. Balancing the two factions against each other appeared to keep Santa Anna in the driver's seat for a while, but meetings and plots were common in the capital. In early December the

Senate held a presidential election in which Santa Anna squeaked by, receiving an unimpressive eleven votes (as a Puro) against nine for an unknown. But Gómez Farías, elected vice president, was in position to take over daily administration from Salas,[5] and that development added some stability. Goméz Farías, however, was a poor fund-raiser, so the Mexican government provided Santa Anna's army with a minimum of resources. Fortunately for Santa Anna, the governor of San Luis Potosí declared his unqualified support, and the army was able to depend on local resources.[6]

Santa Anna spent a busy four months at San Luis Potosí. Though he neglected his military activities at times because of his preoccupation with money,* he conducted an effective training program and assembled the strongest force that Mexico would field during the entire war. By the end of January 1847 its rolls came to over twenty thousand officers and men.† It would be, as Santa Anna had planned, a force overwhelmingly superior to that of Taylor.

At Monterrey Zachary Taylor was conveniently immobilized, legally and morally, by the provisions of his truce. He was actually making a virtue out of necessity, for his units needed a full eight weeks to adjust for the loss of their leaders. Henderson's Texans, so prominent at Monterrey, had cheerfully left for home; their replacements, the Tennessee and Kentucky cavalry regiments, would not arrive from San Antonio for some time. Morale among Taylor's men would recover slowly from the unexpected shock of the Monterrey battle, but news of Ampudia's evacuation of Saltillo and rumors of the bad condition of Santa Anna at San Luis Potosí were heartening.[7]

Even in the relative calm, tragedy was not absent. In late October, Captain Randolph Ridgely fell from his horse, struck his head, and died the next day. A few weeks later Brigadier General Thomas Hamer, the

---

*Wilfrid Calcott, *Santa Anna*, p. 249. The old charge of corruption raised its head despite the fact that Santa Anna himself contributed to the army's supply from his own estate.

†Ramón Alcaraz, *The Other Side*, p. 94. It consisted of three infantry divisions (11,616), four separate cavalry brigades (2,437), a regiment of hussars (422), and a "division of observation" (1,655 infantry and 2,121 cavalry). With artillery, engineers, and other supporting troops, the total came to 19,996 men, 1,379 officers, and 162 "chiefs." The "chiefs" must be presumed to be general officers and the numbers of useless hangers-on. The organization was cumbersome, with the cavalry split into five different commands. But it was the best that Santa Anna could do, depending as he did on the various individual states to supply the troops.

man U. S. Grant believed would have been president one day succumbed to a fever after a long illness.*

The relations between the occupiers of Monterrey and those civilians who had remained were cordial. William Henry, for one, found himself entranced with a story of a Señorita dos Amades, who had donned a uniform and, like "a second Joan D' Arc," had led a troop of lancers against the Americans at Monterrey on the afternoon of September 21. Henry had no sympathy, however, for a priest caught urging Americans to desert: "If he gets his desert, he should be hung, in spite of his sanctity." Henry also made an informal visit to a girls' school: "There were some beautiful creatures among them, and with one bright-eyed little one I should most certainly have had a frolic had I been master of her language." And he sympathized with the plight of the poor, who were kept "in utter ignorance, and under blind obedience to their priests."†

President Polk's original war plan, it will be recalled, envisioned the occupation of all the northern and northwestern states of Mexico. Taylor had been charged with the main occupation force, but a respectable auxiliary expedition, commanded by Brigadier General John E. Wool, was also organized to depart from San Antonio and cross the Río Grande to come under Taylor's command. Polk anticipated that Wool would continue five hundred miles westward to seize Chihuahua, but that judgment he left to Taylor. On the east the most important city was Tampico, a port that lay 270 miles south on the Gulf, with the eastern chain of the Sierra Madre separating it from Matamoros. Tampico would be a logical objective for Commodore David Conner's Home Squadron to seize.

Wool's Operations,
August–November 1846

Brigadier General John E. Wool had been in Washington at the beginning of hostilities. He was another of those Whig generals whom Polk mistrusted, but he was known as a capable soldier, and presented

*William Henry, pp. 234, 252. U.S. Grant, I, *Memoirs*, p. 100. Hamer, as a congressman, had appointed Grant to West Point in 1839.
†Henry, pp. 233, 240, 241. Smith mentions the señorita under a slightly varied name, but cites no source.

no political threat to Polk. So on May 28, 1846, Polk had met Wool and instructed him "to proceed to the West and see that the volunteers were speedily raised and marched to the Rio Grande with the least possible delay."[8]

Polk had picked a good man for this difficult task. Wool was a formal, meticulous officer ("Old Fussy," his men called him), who paid close attention to every detail of his command, an ideal personality to organize a mass of volunteers into the semblance of an army. His troops had always complained about his strictness; nevertheless, they had always viewed him with respect.

Wool left Washington without receiving written orders from the War Department. They caught up with him at Louisville, placing him in command of all regulars and volunteers in San Antonio and confirming that Taylor would probably send him to Chihuahua.[9] At Lavaca, Texas, he joined a portion of his future command (including five hundred wagons) and trudged through deep mud to San Antonio, arriving on August 14. There he found the town of two thousand people totally unable to provide the supplies he needed, so he broke his force into two sections and marched 1,300 men out of San Antonio on September 25. The first leg of his journey would take him southwestward 175 miles toward the Presidio del Rio Grande (Eagle Pass). Colonel Sylvester Churchill would command the follow-up echelon of some 1,200 men a month later.*

At the Rio Grande on October 8, 1846, Wool took several days to erect a small pontoon bridge across the swift stream, and then, leaving a detachment to guard the bridge for Churchill's later use, he moved southward a few miles. After a week, during which time he learned of the fall of Monterrey, he continued on to Monclova. The roads were difficult for wagons, but the country was barren of sustenance, and mules would not have sufficed to carry enough rations to see him through.

---

*Justin, Smith, *The War with Mexico*, vol. I, 267–68, 270. Buhoup, quoted on p. 509. Eventually Wool's force would reach about 3,400, of whom only 600 (including squadrons from the 1st and 2d Dragoons) were regulars. "General Wool's division consisted of the 1st and 2d Illinois Volunteers under Colonel J.J. Hardin and Colonel William H. Bissell; Major Bonneville's battalion of the 6th U.S. Infantry; the Arkansas Cavalry under Colonel Archibald Yell; Captain John M. Washington's battery of light artillery; and Colonel William S. Harney's Dragoons; and a "spy" company of Texan Rangers, the whole numbering about 3,000 men and officers" (Samuel Chamberlain, *My Confession*, p. 43).

By the end of October Wool had reached Monclova and had reported to Taylor. Taylor, bound by the provisions of his truce, instructed him to make camp where he was and await instructions. Very well, the respite at Monclova would afford Wool time to drill his men and scout the road to Chihuahua. He could also instill a modicum of discipline. That would prove a trying task. Samuel E. Chamberlain, 1st Dragoons, described the kind of thing Wool was up against:

> One day when I was on the general's guard, he with his staff road into town to dine. As we approached the guard line, a "sucker" on post was seated on the ground with a roguish-looking Senorita, engaged in eating *frijoles* and *pan de maiz*. The sentinel coolly eyed the cavalcade, and with no thoughts of rising to salute, he remarked, "Good day, General, hot riding out I reckon."
>
> The General thundered out, "Call the officer of the guard!"
>
> The man just raised himself on his elbow and drawled out, "Lieutenant Woodson, come here right quick, post nine, for the old General wants you!" He then turned to his companion with a self-satisfied air, as if he had discharged his duty in the most exemplary manner.
>
> The officer of the guard made his appearance without belt or sword, coat unbuttoned and a straw hat on. The general gave him a severe reprimand for his own appearance as well as the unsoldierlike conduct of the guard, whereupon the officer broke out, "Jake Strout, yer ain't worth shucks. If you don't git right up and salute the General, I'll drive your gal away, doggone if I don't."
>
> The gallant sentinel riled up at this and replied that "if the General wanted saluting the lieutenant might do it, he wasn't agoing to do anything of the kind."[10]

Conner at Tampico

On the Gulf coast, the port of Tampico had long been eyed as a possible target for occupation by the United States. As the main city of Tamaulipas, and Mexico's second most important port, Tampico would be a natural prize for a nation that controlled the adjacent waters.

The city had a strange history. Because of its distance from Mexico City, it had, as with the Spanish expedition of 1839, provided a tempting target for foreign invaders. It had also served as a haven for several revolutions. Because of Tampico's proven usefulness as a base for all enemies, therefore, the Mexican government had historically kept its fortifications weak. But after the beginning of hostilities with the United States, Mexico City had decided to defend Tampico, and Anastasio Parrodi, commander of the garrison, had been ordered to fortify it. But now Santa Anna was withdrawing Parrodi's troops to Tula, across the mountains, and they would continue to San Luis Potosí before they would ever return to Tampico. So Parrodi was helpless.

To Commodore Conner, however, an assault on Tampico presented problems. The waters at the mouth of the Pánuco River were difficult, and ships anchored offshore would be vulnerable to the storms that raged around the region. And Conner had already suffered setbacks in similar operations, having tried twice, during August, to seize the port of Alvarado, south of Veracruz.*

Those experiences had convinced Conner that it would be difficult for him to take and hold a fortified port without the help of ground troops. But Conner needed his men aboard his ships, so a land force would have to come from the army.

In September 1846 President Polk became aware of this problem and directed Marcy to send three thousand men from Taylor's army to cooperate with Conner. Marcy selected Major General Robert Patterson to command. The detachment was subject to Taylor's approval, but in order to save time, Marcy alerted Patterson directly at the same time as he wrote to Taylor.†

Taylor did object, strenuously. Since the troops to be taken were those he had left behind on the Rio Grande, it is difficult to see how such a detachment would have interfered with his campaign. But Taylor was becoming touchy, and on the basis of his own prerogatives

---

*The swollen river and Mexican resistance had frustrated his small effort. Insignificant as the actions had been, they represented the only Mexican successes to date; it was even proposed in the capital to confer upon Alvarado the title Heroico. R.S. Ripley, *The War with Mexico*, vol. I, pp. 307–9.

†James K. Polk, *Diary*, September 22, 1846, p. 150. Marcy believed that Patterson was back at Matamoros, a condition that would have made direct communication more compelling.

he managed to stop Patterson's movement and on October 15 protested Marcy's action. Patterson would remain at Camargo, and Conner would have to take Tampico on his own.[11]

At about this time, Conner learned from an agent* that all defenders had been moved from Tampico and that Parrodi himself was scheduled to leave, but he was in the dark as to when that would be. He waited until mid-November, at which time, having received considerable naval reinforcements, he decided to make an effort. As he moved his ships into the harbor a deputation from the city came out to meet him and to plead for a peaceful occupation. The townspeople, they promised, had neither the means nor the disposition to resist. The next morning Conners formally issued a declaration that the city was under United States protection.[12]

But Conner still needed a force to occupy the city, so in the absence of Patterson's infantry, he sent his deputy, Commodore Matthew Perry, to Brazos Island. Patterson, at Camargo, assumed responsibility for sending a small detachment of five hundred men, who arrived by water at Tampico on November twenty-third. The rest of the troops needed to garrison Tampico were sent directly from the United States.[13] American occupation was secure.

Marcy's letter directing Taylor to terminate the armistice of September 25 reached Monterrey on November 2, 1846. Taylor was understandably furious at the rebuke, and possibly as an act of malice sent the same messenger on to Saltillo with the required letter terminating the truce. Calculating the time he expected the letter to reach San Luis Potosí, Taylor considered himself free to resume hostilities as of November 15, 1846.†

---

*Anne McClarmonde Chase, Irish-born wife of the departed American consul, who used her immunity as a British subject to act as spy and planter of false rumors among the Mexicans. David Nevin, *The Mexican War* p. 132.

†"On the 2d of November Major James Graham arrived from Washington as bearer of dispatches to General Taylor. Of course all was excitement until their contents were divulged. The government directed General Taylor to announce to the Mexican authorities that the armistice was broken up, and that we were to commence hostilities with renewed energy. . . . To carry out these instructions, Major Graham, with a small escort, was dispatched, on the

Taylor's anger at Washington was exacerbated by reports of plots against him. In this matter, Scott unwittingly added fuel to the fire. Trying to convince Taylor of his own personal friendship, Scott wrote to him that there were plots afoot to replace him (Taylor) with Patterson.[14] Thus, in the light of Marcy's direct communication to Patterson and the order to terminate the armistice, Taylor was feeling aggrieved. His assessment was fairly accurate:

> There is, I hear from high authority, an intrigue going on against me; the object of which is to deprive me of the command; my only sin for this is the want of discretion on the part of certain politicians, in connecting my name as a proper candidate for the next presidential election, which I very much regretted. . . .[15]

But by this time Old Zack was also beginning to give Polk and Marcy cause for justifiable complaint. In his frustration, Taylor began to write letters to various friends. The principal recipient of these letters was Senator Crittenden, to whom Taylor wrote several times at great length. The two men were friends, and, whether or not Taylor had politics in mind, Crittenden became convinced that Polk and Marcy were treating him unfairly. But Crittenden was discreet; Gaines, by contrast, was not, and he made public one letter that Taylor had witten to him. Washington now had concrete evidence that despite Taylor's disclaimers the "presidential bug" had bit him. This caused Polk to begin viewing Taylor as a political threat, the more so because the Whig newspapers, considering Scott finished in the 1848 political race, had played up Taylor's victories to their fullest. Even the urchins of Philadelphia were singing little jingles:

> *"Old Zack's at Monterey,*
> *Bring out your Santa Anner;*
> *For every time we raise a gun,*
> *Down goes a Mexicaner."*[16]

6th of November, to communicate to the general commanding the Mexican forces the orders of our government. We know he will be permitted to go to Saltillo, but it is extremely improbable that they will permit his further advance." William Henry, p. 239.

Such strains, or similar strains, undoubtedly reached Polk's ears. They could have given little comfort to the man whose "religion was politics."

Irritations were one thing, but stark reality concerning the progress of the war was quite another. By now it was apparent that the strategy of limited war had failed. There would be no quick, cheap victory over a submissive Mexico: the war would have to be carried to Mexico City, or at least to the Gulf ports.

This realization had not come about overnight. Polk and his advisers had been seriously considering a landing at Veracruz for some time, but up to now they had been reluctant to face up to it in view of the concomitant need to call up new volunteers and augment the regular establishment. The decision was forced by the upcoming State of the Union Message.

Polk habitually spent weeks, even months, preparing his annual message, and even though it was to be presented in December, he was working on it as early as October. In a preliminary draft of that message he had anticipated recommending an end to the active prosecution of the war and mere occupation of that portion of Mexico along the current line of contact. This line of action conformed to Taylor's view, expressed earlier in the year, and to the opinions of many, even including such Democrats as Buchanan and Calhoun, the latter of whom proposed to apply his policy of "masterly inactivity"[17] to Mexico as well as to Oregon.

That policy however, changed suddenly when Polk's favorite military adviser, Senator Benton, returned to Washington for the 1846–47 session of Congress. When Polk asked Benton to read over the manuscript of his message, Benton immediately took issue. The policy of "masterly inactivity," he said, ran counter to his nature. He had been contemplating the course of the war during recess and he now felt ready to advocate an expedition to seize Veracruz, to be followed by the advance of a powerful force overland to seize Mexico City. A bipartisan commission of distinguished political leaders (including himself) should accompany that force to offer peace. Only immediate action could prevent the war from overthrowing the Democratic party.[18]

Polk presented Benton's views to his cabinet on November 10, 1846, but he deferred any decision in hopes of first receiving Taylor's thoughts on the matter, which had been solicited in Marcy's letter of September 22. Four days later, however, an impatient Polk asked Benton to attend a cabinet meeting in order to argue for his more aggressive strategy. Benton accepted, and despite the general reluctance to reactivate the war,* he carried the day. As a meaningless concession to Marcy, who was against expanding the war, Polk directed that only nine regiments—instead of Benton's recommended ten— would be called up.†

So the Veracruz operation was decided upon. But organizing an expedition entailed selecting a man to command it. Such a question was bound to be difficult for Polk, who hated delegating such heavy responsibility to anyone, especially to a professional soldier and not one of his own men. It was made even more difficult because Polk, far from being a stranger to the candidates for the command, was well acquainted with them, and he disliked them all. But the issue had to be faced, and soon.

The issue of a commander had been discussed with Benton on November 10, 1846, even before the significant cabinet meeting in which Benton had changed the course of the war. But with the campaign decided on, Polk called for Benton's views again. The discussion began as an exercise in elimination. Taylor, Polk said, was "not a man of capacity enough." Benton concurred. Then Scott? Benton expressed his disapproval by saying nothing. Polk named some others, but Benton liked none of them.

Finally Benton spoke his piece. "There ought to be a lieutenant-general of the army," he said, "who should be general-in-chief." This position, he went on, required a man of talent and resources. Obtaining a peace under these circumstances depended more upon the abilities and energy of the officer than upon mere bravery. The man to take such a command, therefore was obvious: "If such an office was created by Congress," Polk recorded, "he [Benton] would be willing to accept the command himself."[19]

This display of megalomania was not the least bit astonishing to

---

*Marcy, for one, was on public record against calling up more volunteers.

†Benton, *Thirty Years View*, II, 694–95. Benton, according to his account, much enjoyed Calhoun's shock when the final message was later read on the floor of the Senate. Calhoun, Benton claims, had not been previously apprised of this radical change in strategy for the war.

Polk. After all, Benton had been a colonel in the War of 1812, thirty-four years before, and had been considered by President Jackson once as a possible general-in-chief. And the prospect of a Democratic general-in-chief was delightful. After all, the Whigs must not be allowed to use the war as a successful political weapon![20]

Polk therefore assured Benton that even if Congress refused to create the rank of lieutenant general, Benton could still be a major general, for authority for such an appointment existed. Benton politely declined appointment to any such junior grade, but Polk reiterated his promise that the senator could head any peace commission.*

Winfield Scott, meanwhile, had been exercising unaccustomed restraint as he languished in Washington. Nearly bursting with the desire to take command in the field, he nevertheless made no public statements. Possibly to avoid such temptations, he moved the headquarters of the army for a time to West Point, where the air was good for his chills and fever and the distance between him and the secretary of war was great.

At one point, in early September, Scott had made an overture in a letter to Marcy. The newly organized mounted volunteer regiments were now within fifteen or twenty marches of the Rio Grande, he remarked, and (pretending that his assumption of command awaited only their availability) advised that he could reach the Rio Grande personally by the end of the month.[21]

Marcy had answered tersely within two days: ". . . It is not within the arrangements for conducting the campaign in Mexico to supersede General Taylor in his present command by assigning you to it."[22]

Thus put down, Scott's only recourse had been to send copies of the "vulgar and cold-blooded" letter of Marcy's to his old friend Crittenden.†

---

*Elbert Smith, *Magnificent Missourian,* p. 216. One historian gives this theory: "Benton does not seem at any time to have intended personally to take the direction of campaigns and battles but to confine his function to 'the responsibility of plans and movements, while the generals, at the heads of divisions and columns, would only have the responsibility of execution,' and in his speech . . . to the Senate he compared the command . . . to that ordinarily exercised by the President" (Meigs, *The Life of Thomas Hart Benton,* p. 364).

†John J. Crittenden, *Life,* vol. 1, pp. 249–50. Crittenden, known for his congeniality, was a natural avenue for Scott to express his woes. He must have smiled when Scott once alluded to himself in poetry: "True as the dial to the sun, Although it be not shone upon."

But all that had happened before Monterrey. In the light of Taylor's fall from Polk's favor—and the new plans for expanded action in Mexico—the scene had changed. And Scott, while being outwardly correct in his attitude toward Taylor, was doing everything possible to ingratiate himself with Marcy, by preparing plans and showing deference. (He submitted one plan for a Veracruz landing just after Benton first broached the idea to Polk, on November 12, 1846.[23])

Scott's campaign worked. Marcy, who lacked Polk's vindictiveness, was soon convinced that Scott, with all his faults, was the most capable man on the scene. So on Wednesday, November 18, 1846, Marcy formally recommended Scott to Polk, emphasizing that the general had been rendered politically harmless. Besides, Butler had been wounded at Monterrey; Patterson was inexperienced and foreign-born, ineligible to serve later as a presidential possibility. And time was growing short.

Not quite satisfied with Marcy's recommendation, Polk invited Benton back to the White House again. Benton, now reconciled that the position of lieutenant general would not soon be established by Congress, seconded Marcy's choice of Scott. Polk reluctantly consented, though reiterating his promise that the position of lieutenant general, if established, would go to Benton, along with command of the whole force.[24]

The next day Polk sent for Scott. Ordinarily a president derives some pleasure in creating new commands, and in informing the grateful general. Such action is one of the privileges of the position. But Polk derived no pleasure from this meeting, unless he enjoyed watching Scott squirm. Polk played a cat-and-mouse game, discussing the expedition at some length, dwelling upon its importance, to all of which Scott enthusiastically agreed. In an oblique manner Polk then said that if he could be satisfied of Scott's "proper confidence in the administration," he, Polk, was "disposed" to assign him to the command.

Scott, in Polk's terms, was "much affected," and poured forth "that he had the utmost confidence in the administration . . . and would cordially cooperate. . . . He left, apparently the most delighted man I have seen for a long time, and as he retired expressed his deep gratitude to me."[25]

The grateful Scott, bordering on tears, left the President's office. He was blissfully unaware that his chief still hoped to replace him with a future Lieutenant General Thomas Hart Benton.

BUENA VISTA I:
"THE GREATEST
ANXIETY"

NOVEMBER 1846–FEBRUARY 1847

W hile Polk was altering the character of the war in Washington, Taylor, at Monterrey, was going ahead with his own plans. Essentially his views as to the strategy of the war had changed little from those he had outlined in early July, that American forces in his area "should not look to the city of Mexico, but should be confined to cutting off the northern provinces."[1] His views in that regard had not changed, but now he was able to be more specific as to numbers.

Just to reach San Luis Potosí from Saltillo, Taylor believed, would require an American army of twenty thousand men, half of them regulars.[2] And to attack San Luis Potosí and Tampico simultaneously would require some twenty-five thousand to thirty thousand. Taylor was also consistent in his attitude toward Tampico. He had always been in favor of seizing that city, but only as one of a chain of positions to be held pending negotiations for peace. He did not see it as a springboard for future advances.

But Taylor conceded that an amphibious landing near Veracruz and a subsequent march to Mexico City would be necessary if the strategy of occupying the northern provinces should fail to bring peace. That campaign, he estimated, would require an expedition of twenty thousand men, again half of whom must be regulars.[3] Taylor had always considered that campaign with reluctance, but not for selfish reasons. At the time when he expressed those views, he had every reason to expect that he would command such a campaign himself.*

On November 8, 1846, Taylor learned that Wool had arrived at Monclova and was recommending that his force remain as part of Taylor's rather than march to Chihuahua. Wool's scouts had returned to Monclova reporting the route to be devoid of water and too rough for his wagons. Wool recommended marching down to Parras, 180 miles to the southeast, a point that controlled one main road to San Luis Potosí (the other was Saltillo). With Santa Anna known to be forming an army at San Luis Potosí, Taylor was only too glad to add Wool's force to his own. As far as he was concerned, Wool's original mission had been a failure.†

Taylor himself had already decided to move forward to Saltillo. On the same day that Wool's message arrived, Taylor ordered Worth to depart for Saltillo in four days. The morning that Worth was scheduled to leave, however, Taylor received a message from Marcy reflecting the concern prevalent in Washington. Marcy, as usual, worded his orders tentatively, expressing only "serious doubts" in Washington regarding the wisdom of pushing on beyond Monterrey. It directed Taylor to secure his present position and merely keep his line of communications open, if he should "concur in this view."[4]

---

*Taylor to TAG, October 15, 1846, in U.S. Congress, Exec. Doc. No. 60, pp. 352–53. Parenthetically, Taylor reiterated these views in a letter to Edmund Gaines on November 5, 1846, a couple of days after receiving orders to terminate the truce. After a long justification of the truce, he took exception to the Veracruz expedition: "If we are (in the language of Mr. Polk and General Scott) under the necessity of 'conquering a peace,' and that by taking the capital of the country —[then] we must go to Vera Cruz, take that place, and then march on the city of Mexico. . . . But, admitting that we conquer a peace by doing so—say, at the end of the next twelve months —will the amount of blood and treasure, which must be expended in doing so, be compensated by the same? I think not—especially if the the country we subdue is given up; and I imagine there are but few individuals in our country who think of annexing Mexico to the United States." Taylor to Gaines, Monterrey, November 5, 1846. This letter, made public in January 1847 served only to harass and anger Polk. Gaines should not have released it.

†William Henry, p. 241. Wool's peregrinations around northern Mexico gave the mistaken impression to Taylor's men that Wool had been lost. The general was seen as "marching somewhere in the wilderness, hunting for the army of occupation." A standing joke circulated around Taylor's camp: "When did you hear from General Wool?" (John Kenly, Memoirs of a Maryland Volunteer, p. 167.)

Given that latitude, Taylor continued with his plans the next day. Worth led the march with about one thousand men, and Taylor, with two squadrons of May's dragoons, followed him closely.*

The route to Saltillo took Worth and his men nearly thirty miles up the Santa Catarina River, past a village of the same name, then southward into the gorge of the Rinconada Pass, then upward once again, breaking out into a wide valley that led to Saltillo itself. Here in the higher altitudes the vegetation turned from citrus groves to wheat fields. A seventy-mile march brought them from a tropical climate to a temperate one.[5]

Along with the change in scenery, Worth's men could easily detect a hostility in the attitude of the Mexican people. When Worth's advance guard approached within a dozen miles of Saltillo, it met the usual deputation carrying a protest from the governor, who, however, had already departed for San Luis Potosí. Naturally, the protest was ignored, and Worth's men marched on to the Saltillo town square with drums beating and colors flying. Taylor continued and pitched his tent by a stream on the south of the city.[6]

Despite the cold welcome they received, the men found Saltillo to be a fairly agreeable place, about the same size as Monterrey but more compact. The streets were well paved, the houses well built. It boasted four plazas, and its cathedral was larger than the one in Monterrey. Flour was plentiful, but fuel had to be brought in from miles away, and the lack of firewood would make the winter cold. The townspeople at first attempted to charge exorbitant prices for forage, until Taylor threatened to seize what he wanted, paying his own prices.[7]

Taylor had never intended to remain at Saltillo personally, but before returning to Monterrey, he sent a company of his dragoons down the road toward San Luis Potosí to check on its ability to carry an army— Taylor's or Santa Anna's. They returned after having gone thirty miles, reporting that all the water tanks over that stretch had been destroyed. At least the Mexicans would not return by this route—or so Taylor believed.[8]

· · ·

*Justin Smith, *The War with Mexico*, vol. I, p. 264. Troops consisted of Duncan's battery, the 5th and 8th infantries, Blanchard's company, and the eight companies of dismounted artillery, all of whom had been with him during the Monterrey battle.

Taylor's personal leadership had been missed at Monterrey; relations between soldiers and civilians were degenerating. One regiment had sent a detachment back to Marin to exact revenge for the murder of two of their men. That same day a Mexican was shot in his own doorway, and an officer passing by casually watched as he breathed his last. Further, the line of communications with the Rio Grande was reported endangered, as nearly every train along the route was attacked by rancheros. The army needed the reassuring presence of Old Rough and Ready, even though he had been absent only about ten days.[9]

Upon his return, Taylor was greeted with word that Tampico had fallen to Conner's Home Squadron. This time, since he was acting on his own, Taylor responded with alacrity, sending a brigade under Brigadier General James Shields to Camargo, for travel by water to Tampico. Shields would command the garrison in that city pending the arrival of a larger force.* But Taylor needed an overland route from Monterrey to Tampico, and to clear the road through Linares and Victoria, he decided to conduct four thousand men personally to Victoria, about halfway, send part of that contingent on to Tampico, and return to Monterrey with the rest. He began preparations for this move immediately, in late November.

The situation facing Taylor had now changed. With the threat of meeting a large Mexican force deemed remote, he could now occupy strongpoints much as he used to do on the frontier. So he reorganized, abolishing the bulky Volunteer Division, and grouping the Ohio and Kentucky infantry regiments in one brigade (Butler) and the Georgia, Mississippi, and 1st Tennessee regiments in another (Quitman). Taylor would take Twiggs's division, with Quitman's brigade and the Baltimore Battalion, along with him to Victoria, leaving Worth at Saltillo; Wool at Parras; and Butler at Monterrey. Butler, the senior officer, would be in overall command of the various troops left behind. Patterson, currently at Matamoros, would join Taylor at Victoria.†

---

*Henry, p. 247. Taylor was probably unaware of reinforcements being sent directly from the United States.

†Justin Smith, *The War with Mexico*, vol. I, p. 357; letter, Taylor to Crittenden January 26, 1847, in John J. Crittenden, *Life*, vol. I, p. 272. Kenly (pp. 168–69) described his battalion's elation at going to Victoria with Taylor: "I went over to the market this morning to buy some oranges; having made my purchase, I was returning with an armful of the fruit, when hearing the call of 'Captain,' I looked and saw General Taylor sitting on a camp-stool in front of his tent. I approached him, and shaking me by the hand, he gave me a seat; I was so highly flattered that

.   .   .

Back in Washington, Winfield Scott was happily preparing to leave for the Rio Grande, taking special care to preserve his fragile truce with Polk and Marcy. When Taylor's letter protesting the detachment of Patterson reached the President, Scott readily "condemned" it and said that he would demand an explanation from Taylor.[10] (He never did.) He planned to depart from New York by steamer on November 28, a bare ten days after being notified of his new assignment. Polk forbade Scott to inform Taylor of the new strategy, but when Scott reached New York he wrote Taylor a letter that cloaked the new developments only thinly. He was going to Mexico, he wrote, to conduct operations in a new field (which he presumed Taylor could guess). He would be forced to take most of Taylor's troops, but Taylor's victories had given him "such an eminence" that he could afford to act on the defensive for a time. Scott professed to hope that Taylor would be reinforced sufficiently before spring to resume operations. And then:

> I am not coming, my dear general, to supersede you in the immediate command on the line of operations rendered illustrious by you and your gallant army. My proposed theatre is different. . . .
> But, my dear general, I shall be obliged to take from you most of the gallant officers and men (regulars and volunteers) whom you have so long and nobly commanded. . . . But I rely upon your patriotism to submit to the temporary sacrifice with cheerfulness. No man can better afford to do so. . . .
> You will be aware of the recent call for nine regiments of new volunteers. . . . These, by the spring—say April—may . . . be in the field, should Mexico not earlier propose terms of accommodation, and long before the spring (March) it is probable you will be again in force to resume offensive operations.[11]

I hardly knew what I did, except that I gave him an orange. He asked me how we were getting on; I told him. He then said, 'What could have induced Watson, yourself, and others to come so far from home to go through so many dangers and hardships?' I replied. He listened attentively, and when I got through he shook his head, smiled, and said 'he couldn't understand it.' Before I left, General Twiggs came to where we were sitting, and made inquiry of General Taylor as to when they would likely march, and whether he would take the Baltimore Battalion with him. General Taylor turned to me and asked whether I wished to go. I replied, 'General *we* always wish to follow you." He answered Twiggs, 'certainly, take them along.' I waited to hear no more, but ran over to our camp to spread the joyous intelligence."

Scott was careful to apprise Taylor of his own schedule, in hopes that they might meet. He planned to be in New Orleans on December 12, Point Isabel on December 17, and Camargo on December 23. He did not expect to visit Monterrey, and acknowledged that Taylor might be prevented by circumstances from coming to see him. In that case, he would regret not having an opportunity to congratulate Taylor in person for his "brilliant achievements," but he expected to meet him "somewhere in the interior of Mexico."[12]

Scott sailed on the last day of November, but the voyage was slowed by bad weather. After a busy stop in New Orleans he reached the Brazos two days after Christmas, two weeks late.

At San Luis Potosí Santa Anna received word from his agents that Taylor was planning to take the bulk of his army to Victoria. He therefore decided immediately to overwhelm Worth's small garrison at Saltillo, and to that end he sent the bulk of his cavalry northward, intending to follow with his main army as soon as possible. Word of Santa Anna's movements reached Worth on December 16, and he duly notified Butler at Monterrey. Butler sent a messenger to Taylor, who had been on the road to Victoria for four days[13] and had still heard nothing of Scott's new assignment.

When Taylor received Butler's message on December 18, he decided to return to Monterrey with his regulars and to send Quitman's volunteers on to Victoria. All the units still in northern Mexico were to converge on Saltillo. Butler arrived from Monterrey on December 19; Wool, from Parras on the twenty-first. Taylor was following behind Butler.[14]

Meanwhile, Santa Anna's alert scouts brought word that Taylor had changed his plans and was now concentrating a force at Saltillo, so Santa Anna, not yet ready for a major battle, canceled his own northward movement for the moment. A frustrated Taylor learned of the false alarm as he was passing through Monterrey. He therefore turned back once more to Victoria.[15]

Taylor arrived in Montemorelos, forty-five miles from Monterrey, the day after Christmas. Here he received mail from Washington, including the letter Scott had written a month earlier from New York. Since Scott's itinerary had anticipated his arriving at Camargo on December 23, which had already passed, a rendezvous between the two seemed out of the question.* Taylor sent a reply reporting his recent activities and his immediate plans. He would examine the pass between Victoria to Tula, he wrote, and then, when his presence was no longer required at Victoria, he would return to Monterrey, probably in February. He would, he added, be "happy to receive your orders."[16]

On January 4, 1847, Taylor arrived in Victoria, six days behind Quitman. A body of some fifteen hundred Mexican cavalry, in no mood to fight, had fled the town on Quitman's approach. On examination, Taylor concluded that the passes to Tula, where Santa Anna was concentrating part of his army, were impracticable for artillery or wagons. Satisfied that Santa Anna offered no threat from that point, he sent all of Twiggs's division ahead to Tampico. He, personally, could return to Monterrey earlier than his scheduled February date.[17]

At that point the friendship between Scott and Taylor began to break down. The main cause was faulty communications. Scott had arrived at Camargo on January 3, 1847, to learn that Taylor had gone to Victoria. But Taylor's letter of December 26, written at Montemorelos, was waiting, and its cheerful wording seems to have emboldened Scott. In Taylor's absence, therefore, Scott hastily instructed Butler to put most of Taylor's troops in motion for the Rio Grande, and unfortunately Scott saved time by simply sending Taylor a copy of his detailed letter to Butler, accompanied by a brief note. The troops he was taking included the following:

Regular cavalry (1st and 2d dragoons)	500 men
Volunteer cavalry (Butler's choice)	500 men
Two batteries of light field artillery, (Duncan's and Taylor's)	
Regular infantry (Worth, Twiggs)	4,000 men
Volunteer infantry	4,000 men[18]

Insensitive to Taylor's feelings, Scott worded his letter tactlessly, showing a tinge of pique. He regretted, he said, that his letter of November 25 had taken so long, as "it would, I think, have brought you back to Monterey." He added a smarmy reference to the chimeri-

*Scott was two weeks behind that schedule, but he did not realize that Taylor was unaware of his delay. He therefore had reasonable hopes that Taylor might meet him at Camargo.

cal prospect of a further advance, later, by Taylor. And his ending, though reflecting the optimism that any commander needs, was on an irritatingly airy note: "Providence may defeat me, but I do not believe the Mexicans can."[19]

Scott's instructions to Butler were sent to Taylor by two different couriers. One copy was entrusted to a young infantry lieutenant, John Alexander Richey, born in Ohio, graduated from West Point in 1845. With a small escort Richey left on this routine mission, reaching the village of Villa Gran, between Monterrey and Victoria, on January 13, 1847. Upon arrival there, Richey decided to purchase some provisions. He went into town alone, carrying Scott's letter with him, and that evening was lassoed and murdered. At San Luis Potosí a delighted Santa Anna soon was perusing a full-scale blueprint of American dispositions and intentions in northern Mexico.[20] Since the other copy of Scott's letter reached Taylor direct from Matamoros, the Americans would not suspect for several days that Santa Anna was privy to its contents.

But when that other copy reached Taylor at Victoria, Old Rough and Ready reacted furiously. To maintain official decorum, he sent two replies, an "official" one to Scott's adjutant and an angry personal one to Scott himself. The personal letter protested against the amount of force to be removed and the manner in which it was done. Such a decimation of his army, he claimed, had never crossed his mind before, though Scott's letter of November 25 had "hinted" at it. He would never have complained (he claimed) had he simply been relieved of command and assigned as a subordinate to Scott or allowed to go home. But Scott's action had left him with fewer than a thousand regulars, and a volunteer force of new levies, to hold a defensive line with a Mexican army of over twenty thousand approaching from the south. As to Scott's promise that he would later be able to advance toward San Luis Potosí, the idea was "too preposterous to be entertained for a moment."

Nevertheless, Taylor did not resign his position: he would remain in Mexico "however much I may feel personally mortified and outraged by the course pursued, unprecedented, at least in our own history."[21]

Scott brushed off this blast in remarkably good humor. He ignored Taylor's reproofs, and soothingly rejected Taylor's offer to serve under his command. Taylor's present position, he wrote, carried greater responsibility than a post directly under him. But one paragraph, all-important, belied the soft words: ". . . I must ask you to abandon Saltillo, and to make no detachments . . . much beyond Monterey."[22]

That sentence was too much for Taylor, who received it back at Monterrey. He chose to ignore that order—for an order it was—and unloaded his frustrations on his friend Senator John Crittenden, calling Scott's course "outrageous," without precedent. He accused Scott of "the greatest duplicity." Then he reversed himself on the strategy he had recommended only a few weeks before: "I believe much the safest course would have been to have concentrated the whole force at Saltillo . . . and at once marched into the heart of the country." He ended with an ominous postscript:

> Just as I finished this, a report has reached here from Saltillo, sixty or seventy miles in front of this, where there is a considerable force stationed, that one or two companies of the Arkansas mounted men, under Major Borland, of that State, sent in advance, some fifty or sixty miles, to gain intelligence and watch the movements of the enemy, had been surprised and the whole captured; although it comes from an officer of high rank, yet I flatter myself it will prove erroneous.*

By late January 1847 the situation seemed well under control to Taylor at Monterrey. True, his efforts to recover the dispatches on Richey's body had failed, but rumor had it that Santa Anna, as newly elected president of Mexico, had returned to Mexico City and that the San Luis Potosí army was suffering from want of supplies, the Mexican Congress being "unwilling or unable to vote the necessary appropriations."[23]

With the threat apparently eased, therefore, Taylor decided to put his own cherished plan into effect, to concentrate south of Saltillo. He would leave Worth at that city and send the newly arrived Wool down to Agua Nueva, eighteen miles farther on. This he did, and twelve days later he himself was at Agua Nueva, still serene.

Not all news was good, however. A force of Kentucky and Arkansas

---

*Taylor to Crittenden, January 26, 1847, Crittenden, vol. I, p. 273–78. Taylor was unknowingly being unfair to Scott, as the order to pull back from Saltillo had originated with Marcy (Scott to Marcy, February 4, 1847, Exec. Doc. No. 60, p. 876.

cavalry, under Majors John P. Gaines and Solon Borland respectively, had indeed been surprised and taken prisoner at Encarnación, thirty miles south. And a small detachment of Kentucky cavalry under Captain William J. Heady, sent out to find Gaines and Borland, had suffered the same fate. But these were minor incidents, instigated by a Mexican cavalry force that had presumably fallen back. Taylor concluded that "large detachments have been made from San Luis in the direction of Vera Cruz, which I think not improbable."

As to his own intentions, "It is my purpose to hold this position, unless I am positively ordered to fall back by the government at Washington, to which my views and the position of affairs here are fully communicated."[24]

Scott and Taylor had been right in fearing that Santa Anna would soon be in possession of Richey's copy of Scott's letter to Taylor. Scott learned of Richey's fate in early February, but he misjudged how Santa Anna would react. Santa Anna, Scott believed, would now concentrate against Scott's landing at Veracruz, of which he was learning for the first time. Since such a movement would preclude any action on Santa Anna's part against Taylor, Scott planned to write Taylor suggesting a move southward from Saltillo to San Luis Potosí.[25] Scott never sent that letter, but Taylor had come to the same conclusion, that he could move south of Saltillo, though not all the way to San Luis Potosí.

Santa Anna, however, did not react as Scott and Taylor had predicted. From a military viewpoint he would have been sensible to do so, but Santa Anna was more interested in elevating his personal position in the eyes of the Mexican public. He was therefore less concerned with a possible future threat by way of Veracruz than with the shining prospect of overwhelming Taylor. Such a resounding victory over the gringos would raise the Napoleon of the West to unprecedented heights of popularity.

And political pressures were building in Mexico City, whose population was impatient with the lack of action. So Santa Anna undertook to march an army of some twenty thousand men across the desert and mountains between San Luis Potosí and Saltillo to destroy Taylor.

On January 28, Santa Anna's lead units, comprising the artillery, a battalion of engineers, and the San Patricio company of American

deserters, departed San Luis Potosí. An infantry division would follow
on each of the three succeeding days.* Headquarters moved on February 2. Many of the troops had a good idea of what was in store for
them, and though they were determined, they were also sad. In a
resigned fashion they said their tearful farewells.[26] Aside from the
troops, considerable numbers of camp followers also trailed along,
mostly women.

From the very beginning of the march, everything seemed to go
wrong. On the day of departure three men of Ortega's division died
of the cold. Fatigue set in quickly, eased only by the sight of the
American prisoners, taken by Miñón's cavalry, being sent to the rear.†
Freezing rain, unusual for that region, persisted for a week. A respite
came on February 5 with a few hours of good weather, but this quickly
dissipated into excessive heat. Thus, after the troops had left the
cultivated land, which stretched only thirty miles, they encountered
the heat of the desert, which caused thirst and suffering. Poorly disciplined, many men threw away rations and other necessaries to lighten
their loads, and the incompetence of some commanders contributed to
the misery.‡

Pacheco's division, in the lead, reached Encarnación on February 17,
1847, having covered about three hundred miles in slightly less than
three weeks. It was not a rapid march, but Santa Anna himself had
contributed to its hardships some weeks before by destroying all the
water tanks along the route. The remarkable thing, actually, was that
fifteen thousand of perhaps twenty thousand men made it at all. The
rest had died, been abandoned, or deserted. And yet when the doughty
Santa Anna held a review of the survivors at Encarnación, he was
cheered with enthusiastic vivas.[27]

Only the strong had made it. And soon these rugged troops would
be falling on an overextended, greatly outnumbered Taylor.

---

*January 29, Don Francisco Pacheco; January 30, Don Manuel Lombardini; January 31, Don
J. M. Ortega. R. S. Ripley, (*The War with Mexico*, vol. I, p. 377) quotes "Mexican accounts"
as estimating Santa Anna's force at 23,340 with twenty pieces of artillery. This number may have
included the four cavalry brigades sent ahead.

†Ramón Alcaraz, *The Other Side*, p. 115. The prisoners were from Gaines's, Borland's, and
Heady's commands, taken prisoner at Encarnación. Alacaraz does not specify their unit identifi-
cation.

‡At about the halfway point, one division commander decided to rest in a comfortable spot
without notifying the division to the rear. Since each such station could accommodate only one
division, that meant that a full division, on arrival, was forced to march backward a day to retain
proper interval. Alcaraz, p. 117.

. . .

In Washington, Senator John Crittenden was continuing in his role as the pacifier among Whigs. Having received Taylor's bitter letter, he answered with sympathy but also with the hope that the wrongs done to him had been the result of inadvertence only. He also hoped that any further controversy between Scott and Taylor could be avoided unless such were necessary for Taylor's "defense and honor."[28]

But more important things were on Crittenden's mind. He was concerned over Taylor's safety, not only as a friend but as a political asset. Somehow all the events, all the machinations on both sides, had worked to place Taylor in a favorable light with the public. In the public mind the villains who were putting Taylor's force at risk by either incompetence or foul design were Scott and an increasingly unpopular Polk. Crittenden had seldom seen "such a burst of public feeling." Taylor was "the object of universal sympathy and concern," every voice being raised against "those by whom you had been left exposed to such inevitable dangers. . . . The greatest anxiety still prevails."[29]

BUENA VISTA II: "A NEAR RUN THING"

~~~ ~~~

FEBRUARY 22, 23, 1847

S amuel E. Chamberlain, 1st Dragoons, was an exuberant sort of
lad when reporting dramatic events. His evaluations of his contemporaries, however, were usually harsh. Even though he was
a new recruit himself, he had quickly adopted the attitudes of the 1st
Dragoons, a regular army unit, and developed a contempt for the
volunteers that would have been unbecoming even had he been an "old
soldier" himself. And in contrast to most of his contemporaries, who
held Zachary Taylor in affection and awe, Chamberlain's admiration
for his commanding general was grudging at best. His greatest venom,
however, was reserved for Lieutenant Colonel Charles May, who had
been awarded a double brevet some months back for his putative
capture of General La Vega at Resaca de la Palma. Chamberlain never
forgot that May had received unjustified credit for that capture. In
Chamberlain's accounts May is always referred to sarcastically.

As the 1st Dragoons lined up at General Taylor's tent at daylight,
February 20, 1847, Chamberlain felt a surge of pride. The force that
Taylor was sending to reconnoiter the country south of Agua Nueva,
he crowed, "embraced the very elite of the army," three hundred
dragoons, Ben McCulloch's company of Texas Rangers, and a section

JOHN S. D. EISENHOWER   179

of Washington's six-pounders—the best. Unfortunately it was commanded by the "Murat of America," Charley May.[1]

Having reported to Taylor, May led his command south on the San Luis Potosí road, past the pickets of the Kentucky regiment, through the Paso de los Pinos. After six miles the road turned left. After three hours at a trot, the unit stopped and rested for an hour. When a captured Mexican lancer refused to give information of the enemy, he was turned over to McCulloch's men to be "put out of the way."

Several more hours passed. Then Chamberlain's platoon, acting as the advance guard for the command, reached the top of a hill overlooking a long mesa at the base of which stood the Rancho Hediona. As Chamberlain's platoon neared the ranch they sighted men running into a ravine, and in the distance rose the vast clouds of dust that could mean either a large army or simply a herd of cattle. Lieutenant Sam Sturgis, commanding the platoon, turned it over to the second in command with orders to occupy the hacienda. He, with his orderly, went forward to pursue the group of fleeing Mexicans. Shortly thereafter Chamberlain heard shots. The lieutenant did not return.* The Mexicans who had remained in the hacienda were taken prisoner and confined. The cloud to the south fixed Chamberlain's attention; he was certain that it foreshadowed a large army.

Soon May caught up with the advance party and set about preparing to defend the hacienda, although he himself was sure that the dust clouds had been raised only by herds of cattle. The captured Mexicans were put to work preparing breastworks; the artillery was wheeled into place; the horses were unsaddled, groomed, watered and fed; cattle were herded in and killed—the troops ate well for supper.

All of a sudden horsemen appeared on the horizon a mile off, the fading sun glittering on their lances. It was impossible to determine their number, but May, convinced he had come upon Santa Anna's main body, prepared for defense. He ordered the excess animals released and shouted orders—fortunately obeyed—to shoot the captured Mexicans. By ten that evening scouting parties returned without encountering any enemy troops, but reported finding a spot where enemy cavalry had camped. May ordered "To horse!" and the com-

---

*Samuel D. Sturgis was a Mexican prisoner for eight days. He served with distinction as a brigadier general, USV, during the Civil War. See DAB.

mand began moving back to Agua Nueva, the buglers blowing the call in utter defiance of May's orders.

The trip back was not easy. Horses fell in prairie dog holes; the artillery bounced along the rough road; snakes rattled; owls hooted; men cursed. Gunfire rumbled in the distance, and a line of horsemen appeared far off on the Americans' flank, apparently intent on an ambush at the Paso de los Pinos. The only fire that May's men received, however, came from their own frightened pickets. Going through the pass, May ordered the command to take up a gallop. At Agua Nueva the "long roll" beat the alarm; guards fired and ran.

May's four hundred rode straight to the general's tent. Old Zack, standing unconcernedly by a log fire, simply remarked, "Doggone them pickets, I knew it was you that was coming." It was now early morning. The camp would have no need for the usual reveille. Having ridden eighty miles in twenty-four hours without sleep, May's men were given a chance to rest.[2]

The Mexican cavalry that May's force had encountered was part of Miñón's cavalry, scouting up ahead of Santa Anna's army. At the time Santa Anna's main body was concentrating at Encarnación, the next watering hole below Agua Nueva. Aware of Taylor's position, the Mexican general had debated as to which route he should take to attack. As one choice he could take the Hedionda route, which May had scouted, a secondary road leading around to the east of Agua Nueva. Following it would cut Taylor off from Saltillo—a tempting prospect for Santa Anna—but it would be difficult, requiring an extra couple of days to cover the distance. Santa Anna therefore settled on sending Miñón along that route toward Saltillo, keeping his main force on the major road. On February 21 Santa Anna began marching, and his lead elements camped that night at Carnero Pass, six miles from Taylor.[3]

In Santa Anna's haste to leave Encarnación, he and his officers had been too preoccupied to notice a strange presence lurking in the Mexican camp. That figure was Ben McCulloch, who had audaciously managed to blend in with the scene. Slipping off at an opportune moment, McCulloch made his way back to Taylor about midday, February 21, to report that Santa Anna was nearing Pasos de los Pinos. Taylor now knew he had a battle on his hands.

Monterrey had not shaken Taylor's confidence in his ability to fight the Mexicans in the face of numerical odds, and he was ready to battle it out right there in the pleasant valley of Agua Nueva. Though both of his flanks could be turned in that position and the flat ground would allow the Mexicans to exploit their superior numbers, Taylor was reluctant to withdraw. However, Wool insisted that the army drop back to the Angostura (the Narrows), an ideal defensive position just in front of the Hacienda de Buena Vista. Taylor, who respected Wool's ability and his seniority, finally assented. He detached the Arkansas Cavalry to remain at Agua Nueva to pack up his supplies. It was Taylor's only retreat before an enemy in the war,* and it caused him some pain.

The Arkansas Cavalry Regiment, under Colonel Archibald Yell, soon sent for assistance that evening in loading the baggage at Agua Nueva,† so a battalion of Kentucky Cavalry and two companies of the 1st Dragoons were sent. When they arrived at midnight, huge stores of supplies were burning, with long trains of wagons empty. The Kentuckians and dragoons pitched in, and twenty wagons were trundled back to the rear by the time the first of the Mexicans, Miñón's cavalry, descended upon them. The volunteers fled in a near stampede and the dragoons stayed only long enough to set the torch to the remaining supplies and buildings before following the rest in haste. They arrived "in good order" at the Angostura Pass the morning of February 22.‡

---

*"General Taylor was for fighting where we were, not from any military advantage of the place, but because his inflated pride would not listen to anything like retreat. 'No,' he said, 'I'll be d—d if I run away!' . . . General Wool, after a consultation with the leading officers, stated that he would take the full responsibility on himself; that he would not see the army sacrificed but would march them back to Buena Vista, and leave the result to the battle and the War Department. 'Rough and Ready' raved and told General Wool to 'go to h—l in his own way,' and rode off for Saltillo on Old Whitey. . . ." (Samuel Chamberlain, *My Confession*, pp. 110–11). this story, written years later and not repeated by any authentic source, was undoubtedly exaggerated, to say the least. Nevertheless, even Taylor's report treats the withdrawal with a certain apologetic overtone (Taylor to TAG, March 6, 1847, Exec. Doc. No. 1).

†"The Arkansas Cavalry refused to work in loading up the waggons . . ." Chamberlain, p. 111.

‡R. S. Ripley, *The War with Mexico*, vol. I, p. 386. Chamberlain (p. 112), says the Arkansas Cavalry were "panic stricken." However, the same caution regarding Chamberlain's propensity for telling a good story must be exercised here.

. . .

Santa Anna arose at Carnero Pass the morning of February 22, expecting an easy victory that day. If he was angered by the refusal of the women to stay behind at Encarnación, he took no action. And when he discovered the American camp at Agua Nueva in flames, he quickly concluded that Taylor's entire army had panicked. Thus exhilarated, he pushed his parched and exhausted troops on to La Angostura, hardly allowing them time to fill canteens.*

As Santa Anna neared La Angostura, he began to realize that victory would be costly in this restricted valley. At Agua Nueva the ground had been "formed of extensive and broad plains," ideal for exploiting a vigorous frontal attack and making maximum use of his "beautiful cavalry."⁴ But La Angostura would be different.

Once Taylor had decided to withdraw from Agua Nueva to La Angostura, he left the field to Wool and, accompanied by May's dragoons, rode back to Saltillo. Wool was completely capable of organizing the defensive position—probably better at it than Taylor himself—but Taylor was by no means certain that Santa Anna would continue on the main road and hit him frontally at La Angostura. The region, while hilly and even mountainous, afforded many secondary roads, and Taylor had every reason to expect an envelopment in his rear by Mexican cavalry, possibly even by a portion of Santa Anna's main force. As it turned out, the battle of Buena Vista was fought at La Angostura, but the potential battlefield was much larger.†

Taylor remained at Saltillo until, on the morning of February 22, he was convinced that nothing of importance would happen there. He thereupon departed once more for Buena Vista, six miles away.

. . .

*Ramón Alcaraz, *The Other Side*, p. 121. Alcaraz claims that the cavalry went on, without stopping for water, in obedience to Santa Anna's orders.

†The military-history buff will recall that First Bull Run would later be fought in only a corner of the potential battle arena. The same with Waterloo in 1815. And the parallel between Taylor's successful stand at Buena Vista and the unsuccessful stand of Leonidas at Thermopylae (480 B.C.) is striking. In the case of Leonidas, the Persian access to his rear by way of a secret route caused his defeat and annihilation.

John E. Wool, left to establish the position south of Buena Vista, had only some 4,750 men at his disposal, including the sick, organized as follows:

1st Illinois Infantry 580	Col. John J. Hardin
2d Illinois Infantry 573	Col. William H. Bissell
2d Kentucky Infantry 571	Col. William R. McKee
Indiana Brigade 1253	Brig. Gen. Joseph Lane
2d Indiana Infantry	Col. William A. Bowles
3d Indiana Infantry	Col. James H. Lane
1st Mississippi Rifles (Regt) 368	Col. Jefferson Davis
1st Arkansas Cavalry Regiment 479	Col. Archibald Yell
1st Kentucky Cavalry Regiment 305	Col. Humphrey Marshall
1st Dragoons 133	Capt. Enoch Steen
2d Dragoons 76	Lt. Col. Charles A. May
Texas Ranger 61	No commander specified
McCulloch's Spy Company 27	Maj. Ben McCulloch
Battery, 4th Artillery 117	Capt. J. M. Washington
Battery, 3d Artillery (150	Capt. Braxton Bragg
Battery, 3d Artillery (150)	Capt. Thomas W. Sherman
General Staff 41	Taylor/Wool[5]

It was, by and large, a green army. Its artillery, including some eighteen guns,* were all regulars, as were the dragoons; but only 700 of the nearly 4,800 men had seen previous combat—the Mississippi Rifles, the 2d Dragoons, and the artillery.

But the terrain that Wool and Taylor had selected was ideal for defense, and Wool organized it in a masterly way. Essentially, the ground provided only three feasible avenues of approach from the main San Luis Potosí road into the American position: the main road to the front and two ridges leading around Wool's left flank.

Wool's first priority, of course, was the main Saltillo–San Luis Potosí road, along which Santa Anna's army was known to be marching. It was, however, the easiest one to defend, as it necked down to a passageway only forty feet wide, limited on the east by steep bluffs and on the west by a small river sliced up by gullies so steep as to be impassable

---

*Estimate by the author, based on three companies of the standard six guns each. There may have been a few more, as Washington's battery had a total of eight. Justin Smith, vol. I, pp. 388, 450.

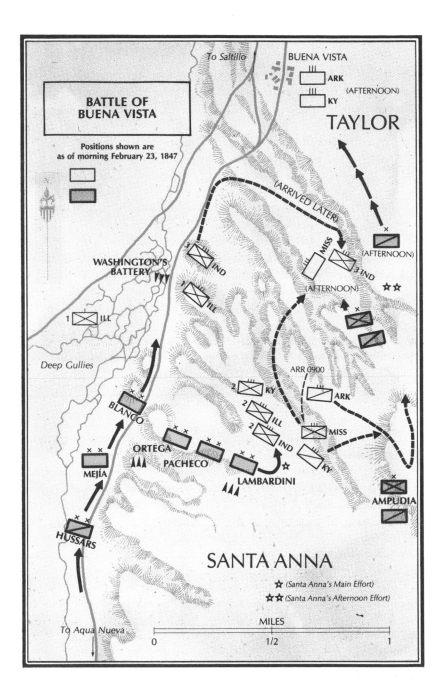

BATTLE OF
BUENA VISTA

Positions shown are
as of morning February 23, 1847

To Saltillo

BUENA VISTA

ARK

KY

(AFTERNOON)

TAYLOR

(ARRIVED LATER)

(AFTERNOON)

MISS

3 IND

★★

(AFTERNOON)

3 IND

WASHINGTON'S
BATTERY

ILL

1 ILL

Deep Gullies

ARR 0900

ARK

2 KY

2 ILL

MISS

2 IND

KY

BLANCO

ORTEGA

PACHECO

LAMBARDINI

AMPUDIA

MEJÍA

HUSSARS

SANTA ANNA

★ (Santa Anna's Main Effort)

★★ (Santa Anna's Afternoon Effort)

MILES

0   1/2   1

To Aqua Nueva

for artillery. (Wool's position faced south, so the bluffs were on his left flank and the river and gullies on his right.) To defend that position, Wool placed three guns of Washington's artillery battery almost on the road, protected by Hardin's 1st Illinois, part of which took position on the nose of the bluff on his left and the rest on a small knoll on his right. To back up that position, Wool placed Lane's 3d Indiana on a small hill just behind Washington's battery.

The second avenue of approach, the most dangerous, consisted of a broad plain to the east of the main road, leading to the nose, occupied by part of the 1st Illinois, overlooking Washington's battery at the Narrows. This plain, known as the Plateau, was wide and flat, standing about fifty feet above the San Luis Potosí road, accessible to artillery and cavalry only by way of a gully about a mile and a half east of the Narrows. Santa Anna could (and actually would) use that gully for access to launch his main attack on Taylor's left flank.

To protect the Plateau, Wool posted, from left to right: Bowles's 2d Indiana Infantry (with three guns from Washington's battery); Bissell's 2d Illinois (with two guns from Bragg); and McKee's 2d Kentucky (with three guns from Sherman's battery). But since these regiments were facing the expected direction of attack in an oblique way, the 2d Indiana would probably be hit first.

The third avenue available to Santa Anna led around Wool's position, straight to Buena Vista in the Americans' rear. This ridge, beyond the Plateau, was relatively narrow (1,500 feet) and long, entailing a journey of some four miles for an attacking force (in contrast to the mile and a half along the Plateau). For the moment, this avenue did not, in Wool's judgment, constitute an immediate threat, and he did not garrison it at the outset.

February 22, 1847

Washington's birthday, an occasion so important to Taylor's patriotic volunteers, would see only the sparring preliminary to the great battle. Santa Anna's men were exhausted by their last sixty-mile march, and not yet in position.* His army was organized about the same as it had

---

*Alcaraz (p. 122) says that some men, rugged though they were, had actually died of fatigue, rather than of thirst or hunger.

been when it had left San Luis Potosí (minus some 4,000 men) except for the appearance of a couple of new formations. Ampudia, his period of disgrace after Monterrey now suspended, commanded an independent brigade of light infantry. And another formation, a reinforced engineer regiment under General Santiago Blanco, had attained the status of a major maneuver element, a fourth division.

Santa Anna's initial plan followed sound military practice. He placed Blanco's division on the left, heading straight down the main road into the Narrows. His main attack, to be executed by Lombardini's and Pacheco's divisions, was to advance down the Plateau, east to west, hitting Wool's left. Ortega's division would follow the main attack along the Plateau. But putting these troops into position took time,* and the main effort was not yet ready by the close of February 22.

In the meantime, however, Santa Anna's scouts had detected that the high mountain east of the Plateau was unoccupied. Possession of those rugged slopes might afford Santa Anna a position for artillery and even set up an end run around the Plateau. Santa Anna, therefore, sent Ampudia's light infantry brigade and Julian Juvera's cavalry brigade around noon to occupy the heights.

At 11 A.M., February 22, Taylor reappeared, and the men cheered. Competent Wool certainly was, but Taylor was their hero. Hardly had Taylor arrived than a messenger came through from Santa Anna under a flag of truce:

> You are surrounded by twenty thousand men, and cannot in any human probability avoid suffering a rout and being cut to pieces with your troops; but as you deserve consideration and particular esteem, I wish to save you from a catastrophe, and for that purpose give you this notice, in order that you may surrender at discretion, under the assurance that you will be treated with the consideration belonging to the Mexican character; to which end you will be granted an hour's time to make up your mind, to commence from the moment when my flag of truce arrives in your camp. . . . God and liberty![6]

Taylor reacted strongly—witnesses say profanely—but his written reply was mild, though tinged with sarcasm:

*Even if his whole army was closed up in a single parade-ground column, four abreast, the time-length of 14,000 men would still be over an hour. And that rough terrain was no parade ground.

In reply to your note of this date, summoning me to surrender my forces at discretion, I beg leave to say that I decline acceding to your request.[7]

The battle began at 3 P.M. that day with the exchange of fire between a brigade of Blanco's division and the Americans at the Narrows. It was of little import. Up on the mountain, however, Ampudia's men were soon scaling the Sierra, and Taylor belatedly dispatched the Arkansas and Kentucky cavalry regiments, plus a battalion of the Indiana infantry brigade, all under the command of Colonel Humphrey Marshall, Kentucky Cavalry. Marshall's men met Ampudia's, and an indecisive firefight sputtered all afternoon. Finally the American force, outflanked, withdrew to the base of the mountain. At nightfall Taylor was satisfied that his position was strong. The 2d Indiana and the 2d Illinois were in place on the Plateau, ready to meet the enemy the following morning—if, as expected, Santa Anna's main attack should come from that direction.[8]

Then, still concerned about his open rear, Taylor rode back again to Saltillo. The first day's battle, such as it was, had ended.

February 23, 1847

After a bitterly cold, windy night, with a slight drizzle at an altitude of six thousand feet, both the Mexicans and the Americans were on edge by morning. The Americans, outnumbered three to one, had the more reason.

In the Mexican camp, Santa Anna ordered reveille to be sounded at a different time for each unit in order to emphasize the impressive size of his army. Then he drew his infantry and cavalry up in one long line while massed bands played religious music. Priests in splendid robes passed benedictions along the lines; the smoke of incense filled the air. Even from that distance the Americans could admire the elaborate Mexican uniforms—red, green, yellow, crimson, and blue—a striking contrast to their own ragged outfits, and the deliberate movements of the Mexican units were impressive. The rolls of vivas portended a battle with a formidable foe.[9]

The day's action began with a simultaneous attack at the Narrows and on the Plateau. At the Narrows Blanco's division was quickly repulsed by Washington's battery and the 1st Illinois, but on the Plateau Santa Anna enjoyed more success. Yell's Arkansas and Marshall's Kentucky cavalry regiments, both of which had reascended the Sierra that morning, soon broke in confusion. Then Pacheco hit Bowles's 2d Indiana, and after some heavy fighting Bowles astonished all by ordering his regiment to withdraw. The volunteers of the 2d Indiana, astonished or not, were unstoppable once they were headed back for the rear. Wool's left flank was now open.

Success now seemed within Santa Anna's grasp, even though disorder reigned in his army also. Manuel Lombardini's division (now commanded by Francisco Pérez, Lombardini being wounded) soon caught up with Pacheco's men and the intermingled forces concentrated on Bissell's 2d Illinois. But the Mexicans passed prematurely around Bissell's left, thus exposing their own flanks to the massing American artillery. A hail of grape halted the Mexican infantry for the moment, though the cavalry continued to pursue the 2d Indiana and the Arkansas and Kentucky cavalry.[10]

At this time, about 9 A.M., Zachary Taylor arrived back on the field, none too soon. When he reached the Plateau, a downcast Wool reportedly remarked, "General, we are whipped," to which Taylor replied, "That is for me to determine." He thereupon ordered Davis's Mississippi Rifles, who had been back with him at Saltillo, to rally the fleeing 2d Indiana and hold the crumbling left flank. Forthwith Wool sent Lane's 3d Indiana to reinforce Davis.*

Davis's men held, and even moved forward, with the attached artillery causing havoc among the Mexican divisions. At this time, however, Mexican lancers passed a full half mile beyond the American flank toward Buena Vista. Taylor dispatched four companies of dragoons, under May, with two companies of Arkansas Cavalry, to intercept them. Passing behind Davis's men, May's troopers reached their destination in time. The combined American cavalry was able to repel and disperse the lancers. And the withering fire of American artillery created such confusion that Pacheco's and Lombardini's divisions with-

---

*Cadmus Wilcox, *History of the Mexican War*, p. 224. The troops Taylor left back at Saltillo were four companies of Illinois volunteers, two companies of Mississippi Rifles, and two 24-pound howitzers (p. 217). The authority for the Taylor-Wool exchange is Lieutenant R. S. Garnett, quoted in Wilcox, p. 223. The threat was Miñón's 1,500 cavalrymen.

drew to the north. Santa Anna, in the vicinity, had a horse shot out from under him. A battery of sixteen-pounders, drawn up on the Sierra by the San Patricio battalion, was no match for Taylor's flying artillery.[11]

Thus ended the first phase of the battle. Santa Anna had (1) enveloped Taylor's left, (2) decimated three units—the Arkansas and Kentucky cavalry and the 2d Indiana, (3) secured an advantageous position at the head of the Plateau, and (4) cost the Americans dearly. Taylor still had an army on the field, however, and he had lost no terrain vital to his defense.

With the Americans strong on the Plateau, Santa Anna determined to send his uncommitted division, Pacheco's, along the third avenue, the ridge on Taylor's extreme left, which would envelop the American position, the Plateau being surrounded on three sides. Taylor saw Ortega, led by cavalry, as it started out, and he immediately sent the Mississippi Rifles and Lane's 3d Indiana to intercept it. Those regiments, with Bragg's artillery, clambered up to the far ridge and awaited the Mexican charge. The two regiments formed up in an inverted V, holding their fire until the Mexicans reached a point only seventy yards away, and then all fired at once. The Mexican lines crumbled. The Mississippians viciously put their eighteen-inch bowie knives to work on the Mexican wounded. The Mexicans recoiled into the adjacent ravine, and only a sudden thunderstorm saved them from suffering more dead than they actually did.

It was now 1 P.M., and Taylor was preparing to attack the cowering survivors of Pacheco's division. At that moment a small group of Mexican officers approached with a flag of truce. Their question was strange: "What did Taylor 'want'?" Puzzled, Wool himself took a white flag and rode forward to the spot where Santa Anna was believed to be. But Mexican fire did not cease, and Wool returned to American lines. The lull had allowed the bulk of Ortega's division to escape.[12]

The Mexicans now seemed vulnerable, and Taylor, in his zeal, ordered an attack. Hardin's 1st Illinois, on the upper reaches of the Plateau, moved forward with six companies. The Mexicans, seeing the small size of the force, stopped and rallied; Bissell (2d Illinois)

and McKee (2d Kentucky) saw Hardin's plight and ordered their regiments forward to his support. At that moment unexpected numbers of
Lombardini's men began emerging from a broad ravine. The Americans fell back, but many of their officers stayed behind. Hardin, of
Illinois, was killed while wielding his saber to the last. Henry Clay, Jr.,
ordered his men to the rear while he, wounded, remained. Clay was
the son of a man whose protest against an aggressive policy
toward Mexico probably cost him the presidency. Ironically, the
younger Clay fought his last, firing a pistol from the ground, in a battle
of which his father roundly disapproved. McKee, Clay's commander,
was also killed.*

Again Taylor was saved by his artillery. As the remnants of the
American infantry fled down the Plateau, Washington's battery, now
redeployed, turned on the pursuing Mexicans, tearing them apart.
Bragg's and Sherman's wheeled around in support. The last attack of
the day was history.

Tuesday Evening, February 23, 1847

Zachary Taylor's army had held the field, but it was in desperate straits.
The men were exhausted; his ammunition was low; he had lost 673
officers and men and some 1,500 or more had deserted.[13] To reinforce
his army he returned a third time to Saltillo, once more taking along
the Mississippi Rifles. (Davis's was the only regiment that had not at
least once turned its back to the enemy.) Taylor planned to leave Davis
to garrison Saltillo while he moved forward the six companies of Illinois
and Mississippi infantry that he had previously left. And other reinforcements were coming in response to previous messages. Two regiments, in fact, reached Buena Vista the night of February 23. With
these reinforcements Taylor's army was now as strong as it had been,
numerically, before the beginning of the battle.† And Taylor's critical
supply situation, much to his relief, would be eased the next morning
by the arrival of forty wagons. So the Army of Occupation would be
ready to fight another day.

*Justin Smith, *The War with Mexico*, vol. I, 393–5. Pérez had been commanding Lombardini's
division, since the latter was wounded early in the day.

†Wilcox, p. 235. Brigadier General Thomas Marshall, previously at Rinconada Pass, and even
Colonel George W. Morgan, of the 2d Ohio, at Cerralvo.

February 24, 1847

As the sun rose behind the Sierra, Taylor's men braced themselves. But they could discern few Mexicans on their front. Soon they discovered that Santa Anna's fires had been kept burning all night but Santa Anna was gone.

A murmur, slight at first, became a shout. Taylor and Wool, tears in their eyes, embraced each other.[14]

Santa Anna had held a council of war the previous evening, the results of which had convinced him that supplies on hand could not sustain another day's attack. He paused at Agua Nueva, rationalizing that he was luring Taylor to more open ground. That may have been so, for he still had superior numbers, even after suffering 2,100 casualties.* But Taylor did not bite.

From Taylor's side the close squeak was soon forgotten, and dispatches to Washington reflected nothing but satisfaction. On March 1, once more at Agua Nueva, he wrote the adjutant general: "No result so decisive could have been obtained by holding Monterey. . . ."[15]

Taylor would have been more candid had he described the Battle of Buena Vista as Wellington described Waterloo: a "near run thing." But his actions said it for him. He fell back on Monterrey and stayed there. He had fought his last battle against Mexico.

---

*Justin Smith, *The War with Mexico*, I, pp. 397–98. Santa Anna's casualties broke down to 1,800 killed and wounded, 300 captured.

THE WAR IN THE WEST

"THE PEAR
IS RIPE FOR
FALLING"

1540–1846

O n May 13, 1846, the day that the United States Congress recognized a state of war with Mexico, President James Polk, it will be recalled, took a little-noticed but far-reaching action, directing Secretary of War William Marcy to send Colonel Stephen W. Kearny, 1st Dragoons, to occupy the Mexican city of Santa Fe, New Mexico. Polk did not anticipate much difficulty in subduing the local population. Therefore, Kearny was to continue on to California if he thought he could do so before the snows fell in the mountains. This move Polk set in motion with an eye to the peace treaty he expected to sign with Mexico sometime in the future.

The dispatch of a force to the West was not a drastic action. Given the small size of Kearny's force, this episode is nearly lost in the current of the great westward movements of American settlers. Indeed, in hindsight it seems likely that the United States would have gained control of the West without fighting for it as the population expansion to the Pacific Ocean had already begun. In 1843, the first of the "great migrations" to Oregon had occurred, followed by an even greater surge in 1845. As historian Bernard DeVoto has remarked, ". . . those years made Oregon American soil no matter what might be said in Congress or Downing Street."[1] The surge was delayed in California and New Mexico, but by 1846 it was beginning.

The fever to take California had now assumed a sort of mystical justification, born partly out of romance, partly out of an idealistic desire to share superior American institutions with those less favored, and partly out of a feeling of incompleteness. Even those like Benton, who disliked infringing on Mexican rights, still seemed to feel that "providence" called for the United States to spread westward to the Pacific.*

Manifest Destiny, in practical terms, was far from unrealistic, for the territories the United States coveted were nearly empty, and the people living in Texas, New Mexico, and California were already enjoying a state of semiautonomy within the republic of Mexico. They constituted the portion of the old Spanish Empire where "Spain's imperial energy had faltered and run down. . . . Here it began to ebb back."[2]

To the American people these lands were called the Great American Desert, only waiting to be filled by an expanding United States.

In 1846 Texas claimed all the land to the north and east of the Rio Grande, territories that even included the city of Santa Fe itself. West of that boundary, generally north of El Paso, Texas, and south of Oregon, was territory claimed by Mexico, theoretically divided into two states, Upper California and New Mexico. The boundary between the two was indeterminate, at least to American mapmakers,[3] though California was generally supposed to extend eastward to a line within a hundred miles of the Rio Grande, and to include the present American states of California, Nevada, Utah, Arizona, New Mexico, and parts of Wyoming and Colorado.[4] In reality, the settled portions of both New Mexico and California were narrow, restricted strips, in New Mexico's case running along the Rio Grande, and in California's along the Pacific Coast. Outside these strips the surrounding territories were

*A group called the Brook Farmers, a literary group located near Boston, wrote in their house organ, "There can be no doubt of the design being entertained by the leaders and instigators of this infamous business, to extend the "area of freedom" to the shores of California, by robbing Mexico of another large mass of her territory; and the people are prepared to execute it to the letter. . . . [It] is to be viewed as monstrously iniquitous, but after all it seems to be completing a more universal design of Providence." DeVoto, *The Year of Decision,* pp. 9–10.

occupied only by Indians, separate from and almost unaffected by these former Spanish colonies.

Of the two, New Mexico had been founded earlier. Coronado's expedition of 1540 in that region had led to no permanent settlements, but before the turn of the sixteenth century, Don Juan de Oñate had established a colony of four hundred men, with a number of women and children, on a site near present-day El Paso, Texas. From there New Spain had sent out exploring expeditions that in turn established a number of smaller missions. The Indians were generally docile, and by 1680 an estimated 2,400 Mexicans were living in various settlements in New Mexico.[5] After an Indian rebellion that caused a gap in the occupation, New Spain reestablished her settlements, still surrounded by the Navajos, Utes, Apaches, and Comanches. By 1800 the population of New Mexico had grown to about thirty thousand, of whom ten thousand were pure-blooded Indians. This number grew to about forty thousand by 1825.[6]

Before Mexican independence in 1821 Spain had prohibited any intercourse between New Mexico and the United States. This was an easy policy to enforce on the Mexicans because of the nearly nonexistent road system. Most people were forced to remain close to home anyway. But Spain exerted the same restrictions on Americans as well. Nearly all who ventured into the forbidden region were arrested. Some, like Lieutenant Zebulon Pike (in 1807), were treated decently and released. Others, like Sylvester Pattie (in 1830), died in captivity.

After Mexican independence, however, the border restrictions were relaxed, and soon trade between the United States and Mexico began to spring up. American traders from St. Louis began traveling the route to Santa Fe, and by 1825 the route along the Arkansas River to Santa Fe, by then called the Santa Fe Trail, was marked and smoothed out. The Bent brothers, William and Charles, established Bent's Fort, an important way station located near present-day Animas, Colorado, and set up a roaring business of supplying and refitting caravans as they passed along the way. Traders from Missouri delivered hardware, cutlery, hats, shirts, calico, linen, shawls, and hose for sale at 600 percent profit—a total of thirty thousand dollars from one caravan load. At Santa Fe they would pick up gold and beaver skins.[7]

Santa Fe was an unimpressive town. It was described as a "prairie-dog capital . . . a collection of brick kilns, a dry-land gathering of Mississippi flatboats." The Palace of the Governors came in for more scorn, described as a "single-story four-hundred-foot straggle of mud along the north side of the plaza, its portico held up by pillars of rough-hewn tree trunks and its doors so low that a tall Missourian had to stoop to enter."[8] The streets were full of donkeys and oxen, the latter drawing two-wheeled carts, Indians, peons, trappers, and teamsters. But in the evening the square reflected the red light of bonfires while men stood around and warmed the seats of their pants as they listened to fiddles and guitars. As at Taos, so the visitors reported, the main amusements seemed to be drinking, fornicating, and gambling. So Santa Fe appeared to the first American traders.[9]

From Santa Fe the caravans from Missouri continued southward on the Camino Real (Royal Highway) to the trading center of Chihuahua. Both the Santa Fe Trail and the Camino Real were well marked, but water and forage were scarce; and the fierce Indian tribes killed and plundered any group of travelers lacking force to resist them. To proceed in relative safety a traveler or messenger planning to go from Missouri to Santa Fe or Chihuahua would have to accommodate to the schedule of the next escort.

The governor of New Mexico in 1846 was one Manuel Armijo, a man of great power who reportedly harbored ambitions to emulate Texas and make New Mexico independent."[10] A man of imposing size and energy, Armijo was shrewd, greedy, and cruel. On the side he was a businessman, and sent his own caravans over the Santa Fe Trail to Missouri. Armijo was reportedly born poor and had achieved his political start by his proficiency in avoiding punishment for sheep stealing.[11] Armijo had been governor off and on since 1837, and by 1846 the Armijo family had accumulated most of the lands around Abuquerque, about sixty miles southwest.

In 1841 Armijo chanced on a golden opportunity to enhance his position. The new Republic of Texas had decided to enforce its claim to lands extending to the northern reaches of the Rio Grande, land that included Santa Fe itself. Having been independent for over four years, the Texans decided to send an expedition, thinly disguised as an escort for merchants, to that town as their military objective. Unfortunately for them, the planners had placed too much stock in reports of New Mexican dissatisfaction with Mexico City, and the Santa Fe expedition was woefully inadequate, comprising only 270 volunteers.

Everything went wrong for the expedition, and physical deprivation, not New Mexican guns, destroyed it. Some members of the expedition surrendered at the town of Anton Chico, and another at Laguna Colarada. Armijo, gloating, officially described the nearly bloodless surrenders as "great victories." Bells celebrated Armijo's victory in Mexico City, and speeches lavished praises on him and also on the recently reinstalled Santa Anna. The Texan prisoners were treated with great cruelty at Santa Fe, though their fortunes improved as they were shipped south of the Rio Grande, and eventually most of them made it home.

The fortuitous circumstances surrounding the destruction of the Texas expedition served to reinforce Armijo's conviction that "it is better to be thought brave than to be so."[12]

Conditions prevailing in the Mexican state of Upper California were similar in most respects to those in New Mexico. The main difference lay in how these states were perceived by the American people. Although there was more interest in California than in New Mexico, the public knew less about it. As a cosmopolitan area on the ocean, California carried a certain mystique, but its allure resembled that of the Orient, not of a territory on the same landmass as the United States.

Americans had been arriving on the West Coast for many years, alone or in small groups, most of them trappers or deserters from the great whaling fleet that periodically put into port at Monterey.* Most of them fit into the California scene. For a long time the emigrants arrived intending to leave or to become Californios themselves.

Political leaders in the United States, on the other hand, had long coveted the region. President John Quincy Adams had advocated its acquisition at one time, and Andrew Jackson, in 1835, had offered $5 million to Mexico to purchase territory north of a line that ran between Monterey and San Francisco Bay.† The offer was spurned, but in the

---

*Estimates placed that fleet as comprising 600 vessels and 17,000 men (Hunt's Merchants' Magazine, January 1845, quoted in Justin Smith, *The War with Mexico*, vol. I, p. 525). It was based largely on Lahaina, in the Sandwich Islands (Hawaii). Before Mexican independence it was illegal, but one John Hudson is recorded as having bought a schooner from the Spainsh king as early as 1805 (interview with William Mason, Los Angeles, December 26, 1985).

†Hubert Bancroft, *History of California*, vol. III, p. 400. The Russians had an interest in the region, and it was said that the Russians feared American influence more than they did the Mexican.

same year Richard Henry Dana made his trip to the region as a seaman and in 1840 his acclaimed book *Two Years Before the Mast* whetted the public interest in that region. Soon newspapers began to print reports of a bountiful land, its hills full of gold. At the same time, they reported evidence of British machinations to seize California and to restrict the United States to the Eastern seaboard. Nevertheless, although Americans were stirred by tales of wonderful California, they still knew nothing of its topography, rivers, ports, or towns—in contrast to their knowledge of the facts regarding both New Mexico and Oregon. The West Coast was just too far away.

The population density of California in 1846 came to only one person per twenty-six square miles. About twenty-five thousand people inhabited the entire area, and of these only some ten thousand were whites. Some five thousand of the others were "semicivilized" Indians, who had been baptized by the missions, and another ten thousand were complete savages. The capital of California, Ciudad de Los Angeles, was an adobe pueblo of only fifteen hundred people;* the region around San Francisco Bay was inhabited by a few people in a group of buildings known as Yerba Buena, founded in 1836. Other settlements existed, most notably at Monterey, San Pedro, and San Diego, but all were trading posts, mere clusters of small buildings.

The native people of California—the Californios—had long since ceased to hold any strong ties with Mexico City, and the political link between the regions has been described as "gossamer."[13] Racially and culturally, the Mexicans and Californios were the same, but time, distance, and circumstance had pulled them so far apart emotionally that Mexicans from home had more difficulty than even Americans in being accepted in California.[14] The most critical of the cultural ties between Mexico and California had been cut in 1834, when Acting President Valentín Gómez Farías had "secularized" the twenty-one missions of the Catholic Church. Those missions had constituted one leg of the Spanish plan for regional settlement, along with the presidios, or military garrisons, and the pueblos, or civil towns, where colonists were granted free land. Of the three types of installations, the missions

---

*Justin Smith, *The War with Mexico*, vol. I, p. 315. Alaska today has one person per 1.3 square miles, about twenty times as dense.

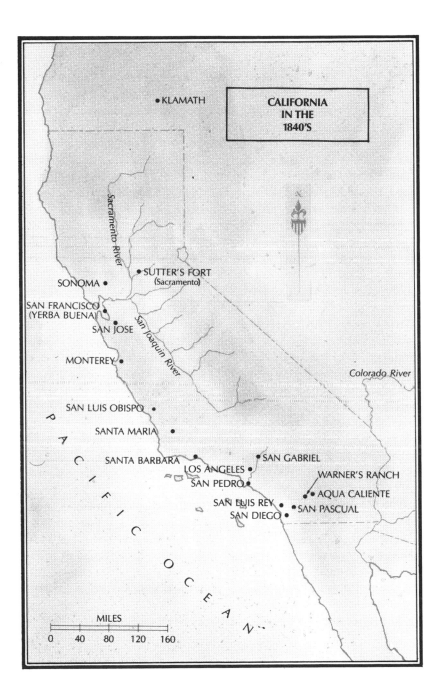

- KLAMATH

**CALIFORNIA
IN THE
1840'S**

Sacramento River

- SUTTER'S FORT
  (Sacramento)

SONOMA •

SAN FRANCISCO
(YERBA BUENA) •

SAN JOSE •

San Joaquin River

MONTEREY •

Colorado River

SAN LUIS OBISPO •

SANTA MARIA •

SANTA BARBARA •   • SAN GABRIEL
          LOS ANGELES •
                    WARNER'S RANCH
          SAN PEDRO •
                    • AQUA CALIENTE
     SAN LUIS REY •
          SAN DIEGO •   • SAN PASCUAL

P A C I F I C   O C E A N

MILES
0   40   80   120   160

had been by far the most important, for they had become the granaries and the educational, religious and cultural centers for all the Indians who lived in areas surrounding them. Several cities, such as San Luis Obispo, Sonoma, San Juan Batista, and San Juan Capistrano, had grown up around them. The missions performed social functions that the soldiers of the presidios had viewed with disdain. Thus, when the Goméz Farías secularization deprived the missions of their lay functions, the Indian populations around them declined from thirty thousand to ten thousand in just ten years.[15]

As of early 1846, by dint of four separate rebellions in a single decade (the latest in 1844), California had achieved the status of a semiautonomous province of Mexico. Theoretically it was administered by a civil governor named Pío Pico, in Los Angeles. But Pico's power was limited by the great distances that lay between settlements and by the lack of means at his disposal to enforce the laws. As a result, one General José María Castro, a man described as "utterly deficient in strength and steadiness of purpose," held sway in the north. At Monterey he gathered a group of followers unacquainted with "discipline, sobriety, and order."[16] Ordinarily, Castro and Pico might have gotten along in their two separate fiefdoms were it not for the fact that Monterey was the only California port that traded with the outside world. All of the revenue from duties was collected there at Monterey, and Castro simply pocketed most of the eighty thousand to one hundred thousand dollars that came in yearly. Pico, four hundred miles away, was powerless to bring Castro to terms.[17] To the outside world, California was virtually ungoverned, the "derelict on the Pacific."

The Californios, as a group, exhibited the Mexican proclivity to be easygoing, fun-loving, and extraordinarily hospitable.* It was said that, along with the all-night fandango, the California man loved his horse above all else, and he was, truly, an unparalleled horseman. But being such an individualist, the Californio was not a good civic participant. He was not overly concerned as to who ruled him, so long as his own rights and religion were not disturbed.

---

*"Though a quasi-war exists [in California], all the amenities of life, and liberty, are preserved; your person, life, and liberty, are as sacred at the hearth of a Californian as they would be at your own fireside. He will never betray you; the rights of hospitality, in his generous judgment, require him to peril his own life in defence of yours. He may fight you on the field, but in his family, you may dance with his daughters, and he himself will make the waltzing string." Walter Colton, *Three Years in California*, pp. 17–18.

The result was that the native Californios, though they represented the largest single group of people in the state, were not the most conspicuous. By 1846 about twelve hundred "foreigners" had arrived on the scene, representing nearly every nation.* And of these the largest group was the Americans. Most of these Yankees, some eight hundred, were concentrated in the Sacramento Valley, as that was the region first reached by the new settlers after crossing the mountains from the east. The Sacramento Valley was dominated by an outpost named Sutter's Fort, owned by a Swiss immigrant of that name. John A. Sutter enjoyed a privileged but precarious position: he was host to the new American settlers but at the same time he was beholden to the Californio government for his continued possession of fifty thousand acres on the Sacramento River. In public Sutter held an official governmental position with, as he boasted, "the power of life and death over everyone in his district."[18] He survived in this balancing act by playing up to both sides. When settlers arrived, he provided for their needs—for a price, of course—and then reported their activities to Castro.[19] On that basis, Sutter's Fort prospered, and by 1844 it boasted fifteen-foot walls and a dozen cannon.[20]

With an estimated 350 new American settlers arriving at Sutter's Fort per year—and with the disaffection of the local people from Mexico City—it was only natural that most Americans, in California and Washington alike, expected the region to gravitate into the Union without the need for bloodshed. Prominent among this group was Thomas O. Larkin. This New Englander, of limited education, had come to this "jumping off place of the world" in 1832 to seek his fortune.[21] He had done well, and in a short time he had become a leading trader in Monterey and had married a prominent local girl. A figure in the community, Larkin had served as an interpreter and mediator when Commodore H. Catesby Jones had precipitately—and mistakenly—seized Monterey in 1842. That incident had raised Larkin's stature in the eyes of the State Department in Washington, and in 1843 he was appointed United States consul in Monterey. As consul, Larkin was a keen and articulate observer, and his reports were the most

---

*One astute observer saw them as "the reckless Californian, the half-wild Indian, the roving trapper of the West, the lawless Mexican, the licentious Spaniard, the scolding Englishman, the absconding Frenchman, the luckless Irishman, the plodding German, the adventurous Mormon." He added that all had come "with the expectation of finding but little work and less law." Colton, p. 19.

reliable sources of information that Washington had available.* He was personally generous, and his hospitality was described as "munificent."[22] So influential was he that when a responsible scholar later wrote of the competition between France, Britain, and the United States, he noted, "In this contest, the United States had two weighty advantages: Larkin, its resourceful consul at Monterey, and the preponderance of its citizens among the foreigners in the territory."[23]

Larkin's status as United States consul did nothing to interfere with his activities as a merchant; in fact, the two activities supplemented each other. And politically he found no conflict between his affection for California and his desire to see that region affiliated with the United States.

Of like mind was a prominent Californio merchant and dispenser of credit in Sonoma, General Mariano Guadalupe Vallejo. Vallejo, once nearly as powerful a figure as Castro, had withdrawn from public life, but as a Californio patriot he had independently concluded that California's future interests lay not with Mexico but with the United States, and he had become known as America's best friend in the region.[24] Vallejo and Larkin, together with Sutter, were therefore convinced that everyone's best interest—theirs and California's—would be served if the United States would allow California to gravitate peacefully into the Union.

"The pear," Larkin wrote, "is near ripe for falling."[25]

*Bernard DeVoto, *The Year of Decision*, p. 20. In early 1846, for example, Larkin sent to Polk a remarkable 3,000-word extremely thorough assessment of the situation in California dealing with the past history of the region, its present condition, and even the prices of every commodity from gold to land to bullock hides.

OCCUPATION
OF THE
WEST

JUNE–OCTOBER 1846

The pear may have been ripe for falling in California, but President James Polk had no intention of merely sitting aside, waiting for it to fall of its own accord. The force he was sending westward under Stephen Kearny was strong—the 1st Dragoons, of three hundred men, the 1st Missouri Mounted Infantry, of one thousand men, and later the 2d Missouri under Colonel Sterling Price. As it turned out, the country west of Santa Fe could sustain only a small fraction of that number.

Kearny was the obvious choice for the mission assigned him. A veteran of the War of 1812, he had spent over thirty years on the western frontier, the last ten of it commanding the elite 1st Dragoons.* At age fifty-two he cut a fine military figure and was known for being "efficient, effective, courteous, quiet, and tough." He was a martinet, with nothing of the politician about him, a Regular through and through.

Kearny was well acquainted with much of the country he was about to cross. During the previous year he had led part of his command on a 2,200-mile "demonstration of force" beyond Fort Laramie to South

---

*Some of the companies of the 1st Dragoons had gone with Wool to join Taylor.

Pass, Wyoming, returning down the eastern edge of the Rockies to Bent's Fort on the Arkansas. Along the way he had held parleys with the Sioux, Cheyennes, and the Arapahos. His task, to discourage the Indians from attacking emigrant trains, had apparently been successful.[1]

Kearny's chief subordinate for this campaign was in his own way as remarkable a man as he was. Colonel Alexander W. Doniphan, a lawyer from Liberty, Missouri, had easily won election to command the 1st Missouri Volunteers despite the fact that the regiment included men more experienced in military matters. Doniphan's election was based entirely on his personal standing with his men, who followed him because he was the biggest and toughest one among them. He had no bluster in his makeup, and he preferred to administer discipline through consensus rather than domination, but despite his informal way of doing things, his authority over his men was unquestioned. Under his leadership they would be reliable.

The men Doniphan brought with him were frontiersmen, alien to the stern discipline of the 1st Dragoons. By and large they were boisterous, good-natured civilian soldiers, who had signed up to seek adventure. Somehow they developed a quick admiration and respect for the austere Kearny, and because they also regarded him as something of a curiosity, many of them followed him aimlessly about Fort Leavenworth for no good reason. Kearny, knowing he would have to depend on these men, readily reciprocated the good feeling.*

With this unconventional force, Kearny set about organizing for his expedition. He knew from his long experience that time was short if he was to make it to California before the snows. Further, since grass and water would be in short supply along the way, he planned to send his army by detachments, dispatching each unit as it became available. The Santa Fe trail had been frequented by traders regularly since 1825, but it had never carried a force even approaching sixteen hundred men at one time.†

---

*One day, perhaps seeking rest, Kearny boarded a steamboat in private. Some volunteers rushed the sentry and boarded. A couple of them slapped Kearny on the back and cried gaily, "You don't git off from us, old hoss! for by Injin we'll go plum through fire and thunder with you. What'll you drink, General?" Before he was through, Kearny had been treated to a generous portion of corn juice. Bernard DeVoto, *The Year of Decision*, p. 232.

　†Kearney's 1st Dragoons:　　　300 men
　　1st Reg, Missouri Vol:　　　860 men
　　Artillery, Major ML Clark:　　250 men

From his trip the year before, Kearny was familiar with Bent's Fort, and he quickly decided on that outpost as the place for resting, refitting, and concentrating his army. He had little choice in his selection because Bent's Fort was the only such established oasis along the Santa Fe Trail. Sticking to that trail ruled out taking the easier and shorter Cimarron Cutoff, and taking the Bent's Fort route would force him later to cross the dangerous Raton Pass, but those matters were secondary; a stop at Bent's Fort was necessary.

Throughout June Kearny sent out the echelons of his army, but he did not depart Fort Leavenworth personally until the last day of the month, two days after Doniphan. Generally he would be following the broad, well-marked Santa Fe Trail. Four weeks after leaving Council Grove, the last outpost of pacified country, his troops reached a grassy meadow nine miles from Bent's Fort. Kearny arrived on the last day of July 1846. His army, except for one squadron of dragoons, was all together.[2]

The trip had not been easy. Kearny's concern regarding the limited resources in grass and water turned out to be well founded. Men had been forced to drink water that horses refused, many becoming sick by doing so. Mosquitoes and buffalo gnats abounded. Faces had been scorched, tongues swollen. Apathy had overcome some men; blind fury had seized others. Sixty horses out of an original hundred in one artillery battery had died.[3] And yet Kearny had driven them on, most units averaging about twenty miles a day, about 650 miles.

Kearny had heard that the people of New Mexico were discontented living under Manuel Armijo as governor, so he believed he could take Santa Fe without fighting. To do so, however, he must persuade the New Mexicans of his peaceful intentions while also convincing them that he could crush them should they try to resist. To accomplish that end, Kearny issued his first proclamation, directed toward the people of New Mexico:

Others: 190 men
Total: 1,600 men
Also 460 horses, 3,700 draft mules, 15,000 cattle and oxen, twelve six-pounders, and four twelve-pounders. Justin Smith, *The War with Mexico*, vol. I, p. 286; David Nevin, *The Mexican War*, p. 109.

The undersigned enters New Mexico with a large military force for the purpose of seeking union with, and ameliorating the condition of the inhabitants. He does this under instructions from his government, and with the assurance that he will be amply sustained in the accomplishment of the object. It is enjoined on the citizens of New Mexico to . . . pursue uninterruptedly their peaceful avocations. So long as they continue in such pursuits they . . . will be respected in their rights, both civil and religious.[4]

In order to ensure that this proclamation would reach the people of Santa Fe, Kearny played shrewdly on human nature. He spared the lives of three captured Mexican spies, who by custom would normally have been shot, and showed them around his camp. He then freed them, well supplied with copies of his proclamation. One of the spies left happily in the company of a long-missing wife, who had been abducted by Indians years before.[*]

To make contact with Armijo, Kearny called on James Magoffin, a prominent Santa Fe trader who happened to be at Bent's Fort at the time. Magoffin was willing to undertake the mission, and he left Bent's Fort on August 1 with an escort. Within a few days he had secured a. personal audience with the governor. When they met, however, Armijo stalled; he was awaiting reinforcements from Chihuahua, he insisted, and for the moment, at least, he would resist the invaders.

A few days later Kearny's army resumed its advance, now traveling at the foot of the Rockies—Pike's Peak was visible for a time—then ascending to the Raton Pass, altitude 7,754 feet. They approached Santa Fe by way of a circuitous route to the east to pass around the base of the Truchas Peak.[†] Forage was still a problem, and for a while, it appeared as though the command would lose more of their mounts. On August 10 Kearny received an unconfirmed report that Armijo, in a meeting, had favored surrender to the Americans but had been overruled.[‡]

Along the way Kearny made it a point to repeat the text of his Bent's

---

*She seemed content with her new surroundings and had remained, bearing a child (voluntarily) by one of Bent's men. The Mexican still wanted her back. Kearny, having ascertained that she was willing, returned her. W. H. Emory, *Notes of a Military Reconnaissance*, pp. 66–67.

†The route of the Santa Fe Trail is essentially unchanged. Today it is covered by Interstate 25, which follows the route almost exactly.

‡H. S. Turner, *The Original Journals*, p. 70. The debate among the New Mexicans apparently was hot. The chief advocate of resistance, Diego Archuleta, went into local politics under the U.S. flag after the war.

Fort proclamation at every town. At Las Vegas, Tecolote, and San Miguel he stood up in the town square and read it out to the assembled citizenry.[5] Somewhere along the line, however, he began to go a step further. He now went so far as to promise United States citizenship to all New Mexicans and prevailed upon the local alcaldes to take the oath of allegiance. Kearny was "unmindful," it was later said, "of the argument that might be brought against his proceedings, in violation of the strict letter of legality, at home."[6]

Two weeks and 250 miles from Bent's Fort, Kearny's men approached Santa Fe from the southwest through the last possible defensive position, Apache Canyon. Kearny had been warned that Armijo would defend here with twelve thousand men, but as it turned out, Armijo had no stomach to fight the Americans, even with the numerical superiority he held. He left the city in the charge of a subordinate and fled to Albuquerque.[7]

As the Americans rode into Santa Fe they found the population in a fairly receptive mood. The alcalde invited Kearny to partake of refreshments in the long one-story Governor's Palace on the Plaza, and the Stars and Stripes was duly hoisted out in front while the Americans fired a salute of thirteen guns. Though the bulk of his troops camped out in the hills, Kearny himself took quarters in the Governor's Palace.

During the next few days the American presence was consolidated. Alcaldes of the nearby towns came in to offer allegiance. On Sunday, August 23, Kearny and his staff attended services at the local church. Four days later he gave a ball for five hundred people, American and Mexican. The evening was reported "harmonious," though the cigar smoke was so strong that Kearny, sick from the fumes, was forced to excuse himself.[8]

There was also business to be done. On August 19, the day after entering the city, Kearny detailed two of his topographical engineers to select the site of a fort to be built above the town. In short order Fort Marcy dominated Santa Fe on a nose only six hundred yards above the Plaza, a potent reminder to New Mexicans and Indians alike of United States authority.

And since his fiat had now made the people of New Mexico U.S. citizens, Kearny decided to create a constitution for the new province. Doniphan, as a lawyer, drafted it. The result was the Kearny Code, which was duly sent back to Washington for approval. And in order to familiarize himself with the countryside down the Rio Grande—and to be seen doing so—Kearny took part of his force on an exploratory expedition. On his return he was ready to move on to California. He had annexed the territory known as New Mexico without firing a shot.

Word of Kearny's success reached President Polk on Friday, October 2, 1846. "General Kearny," he recorded in his diary with characteristic detachment, "has thus far performed his duties well."[9]

Brevet Captain John C. Frémont, Topographical Engineers, U.S. Army, was no run-of-the-mill junior officer. A capable, meticulous engineer, he was, at age thirty-two, respected in the world of scientific exploration, famed among the public as the Pathfinder. More important in the game of power politics, he was the son-in-law of Thomas Hart Benton. Brave and decisive, he was also overweeningly ambitious, headstrong, devious, and a master at publicizing his own exploits and at taking advantage of his connections. He operated nearly as a law unto himself. Up to 1845 Frémont's independence had harmed nobody. His military superiors realized full well that the Corps of Topographical Engineers benefited from the prestige Frémont brought to it. So they winked at his foibles and even cooperated as he planned his own expeditions.

Frémont had begun his career in 1837 as a protégé of Secretary of War Joel Poinsett. After serving as a subordinate in one exploring mission he had become a disciple of Benton the next year, enthusiastically espousing Benton's vision of Manifest Destiny. Benton had been irate when Frémont eloped with his young daughter Jessie, but once the union had been established, Frémont had recovered Benton's full backing.[10] And with that backing, he had become famous, his name a household word.

Actually, Fremont now turned out to be as useful to Benton as the senator was to him. Benton, in his efforts to encourage Western expansion to Oregon, needed someone to keep the Oregon territory in the consciousness of the public. In particular he needed someone to demonstrate that the journey to Oregon was feasible and reasonably safe for settlers. Fremont's two expeditions (1842 and 1843–44) had met that requirement. Thus Benton and Frémont were a team, each providing what the other needed.

By June 1845 Frémont was ready to leave on his third expedition. As usual, he had planned the route himself, and Benton's role had been to suggest it for automatic approval by Colonel John J. Abert, chief of the Topographical Engineers, who complied.

Frémont's prestige had now attracted renowned mountain men to serve him, Kit Carson, Tom ("Broken-Hand") Fitzpatrick, Joseph Walker, Alexis Godey among them. On this trip Frémont's party included, besides these men, twelve Delaware Indians. And though his men carried no military rank, they were veteran fighters, lean and hard-bitten. They all carried twenty-six-pound muskets and long knives.* Frémont, the only military man in the party, seemed to show little or no interest in the impending war. But now, as he neared California, his contingent of sixty armed fighters constituted the most powerful single fighting force in the region. And Frémont, to whom the men were fanatically loyal, was at best a loose cannon on the deck.

Frémont and his party arrived at Sutter's Fort in December 1845, just as the mission of John C. Slidell was being rejected in Mexico. His men were exhausted and starved. Since leaving Fort Leavenworth on June 20, 1845, they had stopped at Bent's Fort and crossed the Sierra Nevada along the path Frémont had discovered the year before. Sutter's Fort would have been an ideal spot to provide the rest and refitting Frémont needed, but he preferred to be on his own. To that end he made a trip to Monterey, where he explained to a suspicious General Castro that his mission was peaceful, that he intended to march northward to find a route to Oregon, and that he would make no trouble. Castro finally granted permission for Frémont's party to stay in California but specified that they must remain in the Sacramento Valley.

In March 1846 Frémont disregarded Castro's conditions and moved from San Jose to a position only about twenty-five miles from Monterey. When Castro ordered Frémont to leave, he refused; instead, he raised the American flag and began to prepare a defense. But Castro had artillery, and when Frémont heard that the Californio was prepar-

*Apparently Frémont intended to conduct his operations in the manner of a military venture. One day out of Fort Leavenworth, by one account, he read the provisions of the Articles of War to his band. Thirteen men hastily turned back for home. Thomas Salathiel Martin, quoted in William H. Goetzmann, *Army Exploration in the American West*, p. 118.

ing a siege, he slipped off in a rage on March 9, under cover of darkness northward toward Oregon. Castro had not heard the last of him.

On February 11, 1846, three weeks before Frémont left Sutter's Fort for Monterey, Lieutenant Archibald Gillespie, U.S.M.C., arrived at Mazatlán, on the west coast of Mexico. There he met with Commodore John D. Sloat, commanding the United States Pacific Squadron, and reported his progress in one of his many long, ingratiating letters to the secretary of the navy. Since his departure from New York the previous November, Gillespie had landed at Veracruz and, in the guise of a merchant, had traveled across Mexico. In obedience to the orders Gillespie carried, Sloat had designated the sloop of war *Cyane* to carry him to Monterey.

British cruisers, however, were closely watching Sloat's movements, and Gillespie feared that their agents might have learned of his mission. If such were the case, any confirmation that Gillespie was carrying dispatches to Monterey might provoke the British naval squadron to move in and raise the Union Jack over Monterey before Sloat could take action. Gillespie and Sloat therefore agreed that the *Cyane* should follow a roundabout route to Monterey, all the way to the Sandwich Islands (Hawaii). Preparations for this long trip delayed the *Cyane* until February 22.[11]

Gillespie arrived at Monterey in mid-April, 1846, and immediately called on Larkin. Gillespie liked Larkin but rejected out of hand the consul's critical attitude toward Frémont's recent conduct.[12] He soon set out in search of Frémont.

Like Frémont, Gillespie headed north by way of Sutter's Fort, which he reached on April 28. Sutter was not impressed with his visitor: "He asked me for horses and a guide to Frémont," he later wrote. "I allowed him to take my favorite mule, he returned it wind-broken."[13] Two weeks after Gillespie's departure, Sutter reported the visit to Castro.

After an arduous and dangerous journey, Gillespie and his small party overtook Frémont in early May on the shores of Upper Klamath Lake, just north of the California-Oregon border. In a dramatic incident, Frémont had been forced to rescue Gillespie from Indians as Gillespie was nearing camp. A raid that night, which nearly wiped out Frémont's camp, probably accounts for the sketchy notes the two men made of the meeting itself.* Thus bound by a common danger, Frémont and Gillespie became allies instantly. And the combination was a natural, as they obviously found themselves compatible—both being energetic, ambitious, impetuous, and contemptuous of the Californios.[14]

Even before Gillespie reached him, Frémont had slowed his pace, delayed by formidable snows. It is likely, therefore, that he was happy to find reason not to continue northward. In any case, once he received the letters that Gillespie had brought from Benton, Frémont turned back to Sutter's Fort. For Frémont the California experience had only begun.

Meanwhile, the earlier confrontation between Frémont and Castro was still sending shock waves between Sacramento and Monterey, for Castro's new belligerence, provoked by Frémont, included threats that frightened all the other American settlers. Seeing themselves as Castro's next targets, a band from Sutter's Fort took matters into their own hands, surprising a group of Californios in mid-June and stealing 150 horses. Soon another group of forty men descended on Sonoma, taking some eighteen Californio prisoners, eight pieces of cannon, 250 stand of arms, and 250 horses.

The commandant at Sonoma, ironically, was Manuel Vallejo, Larkin's friend and co-worker in the effort to bring California peaceably into the Union. When the rowdies from Sutter's Fort beat on the door that morning, Vallejo unwisely invited them in and offered them hospitality. The Americans soon got drunk, and Vallejo, along with three others, eventually found himself riding as a prisoner to Sutter's Fort. By now Frémont had returned from Klamath Lake in time to prevail on Sutter to incarcerate the Californios. Despite Frémont's displeasure, Sutter treated Vallejo and the three other prisoners with the greatest of consideration.[15]

The American settlers in Sonoma then declared themselves independent of Californio rule and established the short-lived California Republic, with William B. Ide, a settler from Vermont, as

*For an exhaustive account of the Indian raids, see Benton, *Thirty Years' View*, vol. II, pp. 690–91.

commander-in-chief. The rebels scratched out a flag, as a symbol of their new "republic," that featured a single star and a crude grizzly bear. The rabble at Sonoma were now known as the Bear Flag Republic.

By the standards of California at that time, the Bear Flaggers constituted a potent force. Only ten days after they had established themselves, they easily repulsed a fifty-man expedition sent by Castro, without a rebel receiving a scratch.[16]

At this point Frémont decided to reveal himself as the instigator of the Bear Flag movement.[17] He sent a message to Washington resigning his commission in the U.S. Army and organized a group that he called the California Battalion. He designated himself as its commander and his new friend Gillespie as adjutant. This battalion included Frémont's original party plus some 190 settlers, including all of Sutter's workmen and all his best Indians.*

On July 4, 1846, at a National Day celebration at Sonoma, Frémont declared that he would conquer all of California. This pronouncement was remarkable because it was made at a time when Frémont had no knowledge of whether or not Mexico and the United States were at war. Larkin, for one, was distressed at the potential violence and bloodshed; to him Frémont's acts were unseemly. "The Bear," he wrote ruefully the next day, "goes beyond all animals in these parts."[18]

At Mazatlán, Commodore John Sloat, aged sixty-five, infirm, and awaiting retirement, remained cautious despite the impetuous acts of his countrymen in the Sacramento Valley. Gillespie had brought instructions to be implemented in case the United States and Mexico went to war, but Sloat was not sure that hostilities existed. Through Mexican sources he had learned, by mid-May 1846, of the Thornton ambush at Matamoros, but that was not enough to cause him to take action. Sloat's hesitancy however, was dispelled by rumors that British Admiral Sir John Seymour was ready to occupy Monterey in the name of the King. To prevent that move, Sloat set sail for California in early June, a worried man.[19]

Sloat arrived with his squadron of five ships at Monterey on July 2,

---

*Oscar Lewis, *Sutter's Fort*, p. 127. Gillespie later denied that he had participated before the United States was known to be at war with Mexico.

1846, and he immediately went ashore to pay his usual courtesy call on the Californio authorities. He then consulted Larkin, who still hoped for peace. Swayed by Larkin's arguments for moving slowly, Sloat still hesitated, haunted by memories of the disgrace that had fallen on Commodore Catesby Jones in 1842 for seizing Monterey without authority.

But Sloat was also concerned that the British fleet would land and occupy Monterey. Allowing such a development would be worse than perpetrating another premature seizure. Then, when he learned that the Bear Flag Republic had been declared, Sloat hastily concluded that Gillespie and Frémont had done so with authority from Washington, and he now felt free to demand that Castro surrender Monterey.

Castro vowed enmity, and Sloat debarked a detachment of 250 sailors and marines. Monterey surrendered without resistance, and at a ceremony in the plaza, the captain of the *Savannah*, William Mervine, read a proclamation assuming United States possession of Upper California. In conciliatory language, Sloat's message promised to protect the rights of the Californio citizens. Sloat's next move was to send Mervine to occupy Yerba Buena.[20]

At this point, the Bear Flag Republic ceased to exist, as Fremont and Gillespie, at the head of 160 horsemen, rode into Monterey on July 19 to be mustered into United States service. But Sloat was in for one final shock: Frémont now admitted that he had orchestrated the Bear Flag movement with no authority from Washington. Three days later Sloat happily turned over his command to the newly arrived Commodore Robert F. Stockton.

Stockton, veteran naval officer and politician, sometime commander of the USS *Princeton*, superpatriot, and conspirator in Texas, was Sloat's diametric opposite in attitude, and on his arrival he determined at once to occupy all of California by force of arms.

Stockton's resources for such military action were spread thin, however. He had only four vessels on hand, which he allocated by sending one to Yerba Buena, one to Monterey, and taking two, the *Congress* and the *Cyane*, to attack Los Angeles.[21] (The fifth vessel was still at Mazatlán.)

The village of Los Angeles was located a few miles inland from its port of San Pedro, and to attack it Stockton needed a land force.

Frémont's California Battalion met his needs, and he forthwith en-
rolled the entire unit into the naval service of the United States.[22]
According to Stockton's plan, the California Battalion would sail in the
Cyane for San Diego in order to cut the line between Los Angeles and
the Mexican state of Sonoma to the south. The *Congress* would raise
the flag at Santa Barbara and then proceed to San Pedro, where some
three hundred sailors and marines would land and march on Los Angeles.[23]

Castro had long since left Monterey and now joined Pico at Los
Angeles. Together they tried to play Britain off against the United
States by asking the British consul if the British could neutralize the
Americans on the sea.[24] But the Englishman, lacking authority, could
promise nothing. Larkin then appeared on the scene and tried to solve
the local situation in a friendly manner. Putting to the test his well-
earned rapport with the Californios, he persuaded Castro and Pico to
ask Stockton to stop and recognize California as an independent republic under American protection. This they did.

Stockton, however, refused any solution other than military conquest. And he had the force. Castro and Pico therefore fled on August
10, and Larkin rode into Los Angeles two days later, almost alone. On
August 13, 1846, Stockton and Frémont, accompanied by a brass band,
marched the eighteen miles from San Pedro.

Four days later, on August 17, a ship arrived at Los Angeles bearing
dispatches that war between the United States and Mexico had finally
been declared. Stockton therefore issued a proclamation that California
belonged to the United States. Law and order were restored, and life
began to return to normal. Soon a newspaper and schoolhouse appeared, and municipal elections were scheduled for September. Stockton established a set of laws and sent them to Washington for approval.
Some acts, such as the capture of certain horse thieves and the return
of the stolen property to their owners, caused a wave of approval among
the Californios.

California was to remain quietly under the United States flag—or so
it seemed.

CHAOS IN CALIFORNIA

〜〜〜 〜〜〜

OCTOBER 1846–JUNE 1847

Despite surface appearances, the pacification of California in August 1846 turned out to be illusory. Though the forces of Castro and Pío Pico had been dispersed, the Californios had no feeling that they had been conquered; they were only awaiting an opportune moment for rebellion. The area of greatest unrest was Los Angeles, where Arnold Gillespie, installed by Frémont as alcalde, was less than a howling success. His harsh measures were burdensome, and his superior attitude was insulting. Because those orderly citizens whose goodwill was so necessary to hold the chronic malcontents in check were the ones most deeply offended, Gillespie had no allies among the people when the disorders began.

A major uprising came to a head within six weeks after Gillespie took office, and it continued to grow until, in late September 1846, Gillespie was forced to surrender his forty-eight-man garrison. Captain José María Flores, a paroled Californio officer, accepted Gillespie's capitulation and granted generous terms of surrender. Gillespie and his men were allowed to march out of the city to San Pedro, and on October 4, 1846, they sailed for Monterey aboard a merchant ship. The Californios under Flores—some three hundred in all—soon subdued the American garrisons in both San Diego and Santa Barbara. Stockton, at

Monterey, was especially frustrated by this disorder because it meant postponing his departure for Mazatlán. He was back where he had been the previous August.

Stockton then set out to restore United States rule. First of all he ordered Frémont, whose California Battalion had remained in the Sacramento Valley, to march to Monterey, and to depart from there by water for San Pedro. Frémont, however, had no fondness for water transportation, and, besides, he had other designs. He therefore found excuses to remain in Sacramento. He would march overland at his own convenience.

Stockton apparently had Frémont sized up by this time and realized that he could not count on him. He therefore set out to retake Los Angeles with the naval forces he had available. The *Savannah* was on hand at Monterey with 225 men, and he could supplement that force with Gillespie's men, who had left Los Angeles with him. Stockton could scrape together a makeshift landing force of about four hundred, all told, which he placed under the command of Captain Mervine. The move, admittedly, was a gamble, for Mervine lacked artillery, horses, and any means of resupply, but Stockton hoped that the Los Angeles garrison was weak enough that Mervine could brush it aside without much of a fight.

The gamble failed. On October 8, 1846, Mervine landed at San Pedro, only to be met by Flores on the plain between that port and Los Angeles. Almost playfully the Californios frustrated the Americans from the outset. Exhibiting their expert horsemanship, the Californios pranced around just out of range of Mervine's small arms and systematically blasted away with their single artillery piece; then, when the dismounted Americans would surge forward too close to the piece, the horsemen would simply tow it away by a rope around the muzzle. Then, at a safe distance, they would fire it again. Mervine finally gave up in frustration; he had lost only four men killed and ten wounded, but he could see that he lacked the force to overcome the resistance that Flores would inevitably put up. He had accomplished nothing.

The failure of the effort meant that the Americans were not likely to retake Los Angeles in the near future, especially because Flores had managed to evacuate all horses and livestock from the surrounding region. The Californios' strategy of keeping the Americans confined to San Pedro and the ports to the north had so far been successful.

In late October, three weeks after the San Pedro fiasco, Commodore

Stockton decided to adopt a new tactic: he would change his base of advance against Los Angeles from San Pedro to San Diego. This he could do, he realized, because Flores, having seized that village, knew he could not retain his hold on it and had left. San Diego would provide Stockton with a good base from which to operate, and the flat terrain around the harbor would permit his naval guns to control the surrounding land area. Furthermore, it was far enough from Flores's cavalry base to promise hope of accumulating supplies and horses from Lower California.

Flores, actually, had his own problems, and they were even greater than those of Stockton. The Californios were halfhearted revolutionaries, and men of fighting age were noticeably absent when the recruiters came searching for them. All supplies, including ammunition, were low, and he had little money on hand with which to pay his troops. To cope with his problems, Flores had decentralized his force, sending Castro to San Luis Obispo with one hundred men, and Andreas Pico (brother of former governor Pío Pico) with another hundred to San Diego to watch Stockton. As he was now elected provisional governor and comandante general by a grateful Californio legislature, Flores remained personally at Los Angeles with two hundred men,[1] and waited for the American reaction.

At about the time that Los Angeles was falling to the Californios, Brigadier General Stephen W. Kearny was winding up his activities in Santa Fe. The area seemed to be pacified, and the people were apparently content. So in preparation for his own move to California, Kearny had appointed a civilian governor, Charles Bent, in his stead. Bent seemed to be an ideal man for the position, and Kearny was confident that he was safe in leaving the administration of New Mexico in his hands.

Kearny was aware that the most difficult part of his transcontinental journey still lay ahead of him. Between Fort Leavenworth and Santa Fe he had been following the well-established Santa Fe Trail, but now he would be following a route known only to a few mountain men, the Gila River route explored by two trappers, Sylvester Pattie and his son James, in 1828.[2] Even Kearny's veteran guide, Tom Fitzpatrick, had never crossed it. So Kearny and his three hundred dragoons were prepared for the worst as they rode down the Rio Grande toward a

point some seventy miles south of Socorro and about 230 miles from
Santa Fe. There he would turn westward through the mountains.

As Kearny approached Socorro on the morning of October 6, 1846,
he met a surprise. Nine wild-looking horsemen descended on his column, whooping like Indians out of sheer exuberance. Their leader
turned out to be none other than Kit Carson, who had left Frémont
in California in order to bear good tidings to Washington. Unaware of
the upheavals that had ousted the Americans from Los Angeles and
Santa Barbara since his departure from California, Carson reported the
situation as it had existed the previous August. The occupation of the
West, Carson disclosed, had been accomplished.

This news brought mixed emotions to Kearny and his men. Tidings
of any victory were, of course, welcome. But the dragoons had come
a long way across mountains and deserts, suffering loneliness and depri-
vations, and up to this time they had not fired a shot. Some were hoping
that this tedium might have been relieved by some action, at least a
"little kick-up" with the enemy.[3]

To Kearny himself, however, this news meant first and foremost a
change in his mission. Up to now his mind had been focused on a
military conquest of California with his three hundred dragoons, but
this turn of events rendered taking such a force through the mountains
unnecessary. An escort sufficient to ensure his own safety was all he
needed, and a smaller party could better survive the shortage of water
and forage along the Gila River. So Kearny sent most of his dragoons
back to Santa Fe. With two companies—one hundred men—he would
continue on to cross the mountains.

At the same time, Kearny prevailed on a disappointed Carson to
hand his dispatches over to Fitzpatrick and personally guide his Army
of the West back to California. Fitzpatrick would carry the news of
victory to a grateful nation; Carson would expose himself once again
to danger and discomfort. Admittedly, Kearny was laying a harsh demand on Carson, a demand he had no formal authority to insist on.
But Carson could see the right in Kearny's position, and he accepted
the change in his lot with only a mild protest.

Kearny's one hundred dragoons left the Rio Grande on October 15,
striking out into the mountains past their first checkpoint, the old
Santa Rita de Cobre Copper Mines, worked by the Patties nearly
twenty years earlier but now a ghost town occupied by an Apache
chief.[4] Five days later Kearny encountered a group of about thirty

Apache warriors. In a peaceful meeting the Apaches swore "eternal friendship" to the whites and a corresponding hatred for the Mexicans. Carson was suspicious, but Kearny's only choice was to pretend to believe them.* The meeting ended with a hearty trading session at the camp, with apparent amity.

On October 20 Kearny reached the Gila River. The trail along the gorge of the river was difficult. Water was plentiful, of course, but the horsemen were forced to cross the stream every half mile or so, as the walls of the gorge jutted down to the very edge of the water. That scene of water and mountain was picturesque, but the roads were bad and did not improve. In the arid climate the dust assailed eyes and noses, and worst of all, the area provided no food. Carson remarked at one point that he had never seen a party on the Gila that did not leave it starving.[5]

On November 22, ten miles short of the point where the Gila empties into the Colorado, Kearny's advance guard came upon a trail of hoofprints that could easily have been made by the mounts of a thousand men. Perhaps Castro was bringing an army from Sonora back to California. Kearny paused briefly to consider his plight. If such a Mexican force was actually in the vicinity, his only hope would be to find it and attack it. Such a bluff, an accepted frontier tactic, might hide the weakness of his force from a large enemy. So Kearny followed the trail of the hoofprints, only to discover that they had been made by a herd of some five hundred horses, escorted by only four men.[6]

The next day, at the junction of the Gila and the Colorado, one of Kearny's officers picked up a suspicious-looking Mexican. The man turned out to be an important messenger from California carrying letters confirming that a counterrevolution had "thrown off the detestable Anglo-Yankee yoke" from Los Angeles, Santa Barbara, and other places. They also described the defeat of Mervine's force at the hands of Flores at San Pedro.

Kearny was sobered. He could dismiss the pompous language in the letters as "Mexican braggadocio," but he could not overlook the con-

*W. H. Emory, *Notes of a Military Reconnaissance,* p. 60. The Apaches could have been partly sincere. The Patties had been allowed to work the mines only because they were not Mexican (William H. Goetzmann, *Army Exploration in the American West,* pp. 46–47). Kearny had three fine reporters along with him: Lt. William Emory, of the Topographical Engineers, Henry S. Turner, his second in command, and Dr. John S. Griffin. With their differing viewpoints, they together provided a balanced picture.

sistency of the reports. On the other hand the information was old—dated October 15—and it might have been overtaken by subsequent events.[7] So Kearny decided to press on, despite the weakness of his tiny force. He crossed the Sandy Desert and, on December 2, reached Warner's Ranch, nearly a thousand miles from Santa Fe.[8]

Warner's Ranch, also known as Agua Caliente, was a hospitable place, like Sutter's Fort, protected and worked by Indians. It was also a clearinghouse for rumor, and Kearny was easily able to confirm all the reports of the Californio revolt. Because of this new information Kearny changed his destination from Los Angeles to San Diego, but he realized that he could easily be intercepted along the way. Fortunately, an Englishman who was leaving for San Diego the next morning volunteered to carry a message from Kearny to Stockton. Kearny quickly wrote a message asking for reinforcements.

The much abbreviated Army of the West left Warner's Ranch on the morning of December 4, 1846. On the other side of a range of rugged hills lay the small valley of San Pascual.

The Battle of San Pascual

Kearny made his way into the Valley of San Pascual carefully, expecting to be confronted by Andreas Pico at every turn of the trail. By now his horses were gone; his mules were worn out; and his men, despite their efforts, could not shield their gunpowder from the downpour that beset them. Under these conditions he covered only thirteen miles that first day, to the Ranchería San Isabel.

On the next day the situation improved, for riding down to meet him was Arnold Gillespie at the head of thirty-five sailors and marines. Stockton had received Kearny's message and responded immediately. Gillespie's men had made the forty miles from San Diego in good time, but he reported that a force under Andrés Pico was waiting to intercept him at the small Indian village of San Pascual, only about nine miles away from Kearny's destination for the evening.

Kearny's men reached their planned campsite, the Rancho Santa María that evening, but they found the area unsuitable for camp. Kearny, impatient, pushed his men forward in the blackness of the early morning. After only a couple of miles he halted and sent Lieutenant Thomas C. Hammond forward to reconnoiter. Hammond found some

Californios, but was discovered and nearly ambushed. Surprise was now lost, and Hammond had not been able to estimate the strength of the enemy in the dark.

Once more, as at the Colorado River, Kearny decided to employ the standard tactic of the time: he ordered an attack. Though his men and animals were exhausted—and he was probably outnumbered—he had nothing to gain by delaying. Besides, Carson and Gillespie, the two men most familiar with the Californios, had assured him that the enemy would run. At 2 A.M., December 6, 1846, Kearny ordered the call to horse.[9]

The village of San Pascual lay at the near (east) end of the broad, flat valley that bore its name. Since Kearny was entering the valley from a narrow ravine, he deployed his men in a column. They continued in the dark behind a twelve-man advance guard commanded by his aide, Captain Abraham R. Johnston. He himself followed next, accompanying the main body, fifty dragoons under Captain Benjamin D. Moore. Gillespie's twenty volunteers and sailors followed, towing the two howitzers of the command.

Kearny's tactic of headlong attack was a desperation move, and one that had worked countless times against Indians. But Andrés Pico was a first-class cavalryman, who, instead of fleeing, was setting an ambush; his horsemen were already in the saddle as Kearny's men stumbled in the dark. The two sides clashed. Then some—but not all—of Pico's horsemen scurried off. Kearny, fooled by the fleeing Californios, saw victory in sight.[10] Behind Johnston's advance guard, Moore spurred the main body, Kearny right behind them, in hot pursuit. On the dragoons went, exhibiting "more courage than conduct."*

All of a sudden the fleeing Californios stopped. Turning on their heels, all 160 horsemen charged the strung-out, panting, disorganized Americans. The dragoons were helpless. Their gunpowder was still wet, and rifle butts were no match for the expert Californio lances. In fifteen minutes the lancers killed eighteen Americans and then, as quickly as they had appeared, they broke off. The main action of the Battle of San Pascual was over.

Stunned, the Americans counted their losses. The eighteen dead included three key officers: Johnston, Moore, and Hammond. Thirteen

---

*John S. Griffin, *A Doctor Comes to California*, p. 47. He loyally blamed Moore, not Kearny, for the miscalculation.

men were wounded, some badly. Kearny had received a lance in the groin that forced him to turn over command to his deputy, Captain Henry S. Turner. Gillespie, also, had received an ugly face wound. The Army of the West had been granted its "little kick-up"; in the process it had lost a third of its strength. And as an added insult, it had lost one of its two howitzers. Stampeding mules had dragged it off in the confusion, and it was last seen arriving into the welcoming ranks of the Californios.

But the Battle of San Pascual now became the long, excruciating siege of San Pascual. Pico did not attack again; instead his horsemen simply hovered, just out of rifle range. Surrounded and burdened with wounded who could be neither moved nor abandoned, Kearny's force would be wiped out unless it received further help from Stockton. So Turner, as commander, sent Alexis Godey and two others early the next morning to San Diego. But as help would be long in arriving, Turner set up camp, collecting the dead. That night Kearny's men buried the eighteen comrades who had marched two thousand miles with them through hardships, dangers, and privations. Turner did everything possible to conceal the graves. The Californios, he knew, would exhume the bodies for plunder; the Indians, for mutilation.[11]

That night Kearny's men were denied even periodic rest. Their position, on a rocky hill, afforded no room to stretch out, and the night was cold and wet. The next morning the "most tattered and ill-fed detachment of men that ever the United States mustered under her colors" set out again, Kearny once more assuming command. Eventually, with enemy horsemen watching every move, his men reached a ranch that provided some chickens and a few cattle. They fed the chickens to the wounded and decided to herd the cattle before them.[12]

The ranch was a welcome respite, but the surrounding area lacked grass and water. So Kearny moved on until confronted once again by a body of Pico's men, this time defending from a position on a hill. With powder now dry, Kearny's advance guard of eight men drove off this outpost, inflicting at least five Californio casualties without loss to themselves. On that hill Kearny had finally found a truly defensible position.[13]

Kearny's men, weak and hungry, would remain on that hill awaiting help. During the first night Lieutenant William Emory took special care of the frail old Mexican, a gentleman of Santa Fe, who served as Kearny's interpreter. Thanks to Emory's solicitude, the old man lived through the night, and when morning came, the New Mexican, attributing his survival to Emory, gave his benefactor his most prized possession, a small cake made of brown flour, "almost black with dirt." On breaking a piece, Emory discovered the bodies of "several of the most loathsome insects." But he ate the cake anyway—and liked it.[14]

The siege now became a waiting game. At one point Pico proposed an exchange of prisoners. Each side had taken only one, so Kearny readily agreed. From the one American prisoner freed from captivity Kearny learned that the Godey party had made it to San Diego but had been captured on return. Stockton had received Kearny's plea for help, but so far as the prisoner knew had taken no steps to respond.[15] That being the case, Kearny decided to send another party that night, December 9, to San Diego. This time he sent three men: Carson, Lieutenant Edward Beale, USN, and an Indian. The Californios now knew that Carson was on the hill, and to stop the famous mountain man from getting through their position, they had posted special sentries.

Carson and his two companions spent the night sliding down the hill on their bellies, their shoes discarded. By morning they had wriggled their way through the ring of enemy sentries. They realized that they had a murderous trip before them, so by prior agreement they went by separate routes, thirty-five miles across jagged rocks to San Diego without shoes. Miraculously, all three survived the ordeal, but Beale's health would be impaired for two years, and even the redoubtable Carson was crippled for several days. Upon arrival, the three messengers learned their miseries had been unnecessary: Stockton had already, before their arrival, sent 180 men to Kearny's rescue.[16]

Back at San Pascual, Kearny remained in a standoff with Pico. On December 10 Kearny decided that he could remain no longer. With no assurance that help was on the way, he decided he would have to shoot his way out the next morning. But as his haggard men awaited daybreak, the sound of voices, talking in English, reached the ears of the outposts. A few minutes later came the tramp of a column and the hail of a sentinel. The detachment of one hundred sailors and eighty marines had arrived, having left San Diego on the night of the ninth, hidden during the day of the tenth, and continued marching that night.

On the appearance of these fresh fighting men, Pico's Californios vanished. And, in Emory's grateful words, "These gallant fellows busied themselves till day distributing their provisions and clothes to the naked and hungry."[17]

The next day Kearny and the remnants of his force staggered into San Diego, their journey finished. They had fought the only real battle of the California campaign, a supreme test of individual and collective courage, shared by dragoons, sailors, and marines alike. In his report Kearny described the action at San Pascual as a "victory." In the commonly accepted definition of the term, it was, for his men had survived and had wound up in possession of the field. But one more such "victory" and the Army of the West would cease to exist.*

At San Diego Kearny's dragoons were greeted with warm hospitality by their navy brethren, who did everything possible to provide for their comfort. Kearny, however, was in low spirits, let down from his exertions of the past two months and still suffering somewhat from his wound. Further, he was a general without an army, as the vast bulk of the forces on hand were members of Stockton's command. But Kearny perked up quickly when he and Stockton began preparing to move northward to take Los Angeles.†

The issue of command, a delicate matter, was taken care of with goodwill. Kearny, as a brigadier general, was the higher ranking officer —Stockton's official rank was captain—but nearly all the troops to be employed were Stockton's sailors and marines. Moreover, Kearny was the newcomer to the region, and he had not completely recovered physically. Kearny therefore volunteered to act as Stockton's "executive

---

*It was presumed at first that Pico had suffered almost no losses, and Kearny's detractors have dubbed the battle a Californio victory. Evidence later turned up that Pico had lost about as many men as Kearny. At the Mission of San Juan de Capistrano, on January 5, 1847, Kearny's surgeon found a house where four Californios were nursing wounds from the battle. Shortly thereafter he raised the estimate by two. Gillespie said later that Pico had suffered twenty-seven dead and wounded. Griffin, pp. 57, 76.

†Emory, p. 114. On p. 115 he lists these troops (officers and men):

Dragoons (Turner)	57
Sailors as artillery (Lt. W.B. Renshaw, USN)	47
Sailors and marines as infantry (Lt. J. Zeilen, USMC)	407
Volunteers (Gillespie)	54
Total:	565

officer" for the operation against Los Angeles.* Presumably Kearny would exercise the field command.

Kearny immediately set out to prepare Stockton's sailors for combat. Stockton had already begun this process, and Kearny agreed with his approach completely. Since infantry drill was complicated in those days, the scheme adopted was to teach the sailors and marines to form up in a hollow square, a fine defensive formation against any attacker. That formation was to be assumed whenever the force was within sight of the enemy. In the attack the square itself would move forward, and supplies would be protected in its center. Fortunately, physical conditioning was no problem because the active life aboard a sailing ship had kept the Jack-tars and marines in tip-top shape. And they were extremely well disciplined; they adapted quickly to their new environment and quickly won high praise from Kearny's staff.[18]

On December 29, 1846, the makeshift command set out for Los Angeles, about 140 miles distant. Since the sand was deep and the sailors were wearing homemade canvas shoes, the pace was slow. The expedition covered only thirty miles in the first three days.

At the Mission of San Luis Rey on January 4, 1847, Stockton received a message from Governor Flores proposing that the two sides suspend hostilities until a treaty of peace between the United States and Mexico decided California's future status. Flores himself would of course remain in office. He was, after all, a Californio.

The message from Flores enraged Stockton, who not only rejected the proposal outright but in the process addressed Flores's messengers in such terms that the Californio's lifelong enmity was assured.†

With all hopes of negotiation gone, Flores was now forced to defend Los Angeles—or, more accurately, to defend his honor by going through the motions of defending Los Angeles. To do so he had about 450 badly armed and poorly motivated men, four artillery pieces, and

---

*"At the request of Com. R.F. Stockton," he later reported, "I consented to take command of an expedition against [Los Angeles] . . . Commodore Stockton accompanied us." Kearny to TAG, January 12, 1847, Exec. Doc. November 1, pp. 516–17.

†Emory, p. 117. Flores had signed himself as "Governor and Commander in Chief." Stockton, on the other hand, considered Flores to be a rebel. Stockton "would shoot him if he, the Commodore, could lay his hands on him" (Griffin, pp. 58–9).

inadequate powder for a prolonged fight. He had expected Frémont's
California Battalion to be the greatest threat against him, but Stockton
had arrived first. So Flores placed his troops on a ridge six hundred
yards behind the San Gabriel River, about twelve miles from the village
of Los Angeles.[19]

On January 8, 1847, Stockton's force arrived on the San Gabriel
River and headed for the Bartolo Ford. Kearny, once more in high
spirits, paid personal visits to each of the units in the force. This date,
he announced happily, was the anniversary of Andrew Jackson's victory
at New Orleans in 1815, a fact he mystically assumed would bestow
on his men unusual fighting prowess.

In early afternoon the hollow square began fording the river to face
a band of mounted Californios, supported by artillery, on the low
escarpment ahead.[20]

The Battle of San Gabriel was simple and quick. Most of the problems lay in getting the wagons across the river, even though the river,
some fifty to a hundred yards wide, was nowhere more than knee-
deep.[21] Flores's cavalry attacks were hopelessly ineffective against the
hollow square, and the Californio artillery was totally useless. American
artillery was taking its toll, and Stockton, apparently needing to participate personally in some way, played the part of a gunner and sighted
one of the pieces personally. In ninety minutes Stockton's force had
taken the ridge north of the San Gabriel River.

The Americans camped on the heights during the night of the eighth,
and the next morning, with the enemy out of sight, they moved out
across the wide mesa leading to the San Fernando River. Except for
sporadic enemy artillery fire, which was quickly silenced, the Americans
were unopposed until they neared Los Angeles itself, at which time
some Californio cavalry charged halfheartedly down a hillock against
the side of the hollow square. A round of grape sufficed to disperse
them. The Battle of Mesa was over except for an evening alarm that
turned out to be false.[22] The Americans camped for the night just
outside the city.

Thus ended the skirmishes known as the battles of San Gabriel and
La Mesa. American losses: one man killed, thirteen wounded, including
Gillespie and one other officer. Since the Californios carried off their

casualties, Kearny had no way of estimating the number. He reported only that "it must have been considerable."[23]

The next morning, January 10, 1847, a deputation from Los Angeles approached Stockton's camp. Flores, they said, would evacuate the city if Californio property and persons would be respected. Stockton agreed to those terms, but Kearny, as a precaution, disposed the troops for battle. It was well that he did, for the streets turned out to be full of hostile citizens, some of them drunk, who "brandished their arms and saluted [the Americans] with every form of reproach." The dragoons had difficulty restraining themselves when they noticed a Californio wearing a dragoon's coat stolen from the disinterred body of one of their comrades killed at San Pascual.[24]

By this time most of the Californio army had dispersed, and Flores fled south to Sonora, leaving Andrés Pico with only about a hundred men to command.[25]

During both battles, San Pascual and San Gabriel, Frémont's California Battalion had been conspicuously absent. Around midnight of January 14, 1847, however, Frémont and his men rode casually into the American camp, near Los Angeles, hauling several pieces of artillery, one of which, to the annoyance of Kearny's men, was the howitzer they had lost at San Pascual.[26] But more important than the howitzer was the document that Frémont carried in his hands: the "treaty" of Cahuenga, signed between Frémont and Andrés Pico. Its existence came as a surprise to everyone.

Frémont had stayed at Sacramento for about a month after deciding not to move south in October. In late November he had begun the four-hundred-mile journey overland.[27] Though not dangerous, his march was arduous and uncomfortable. At San Luis Obispo, Frémont had found a great bonanza when he captured Jesús Pico, a cousin of Andrés Pico. Like Andrés, Jesús was a parole violator, and for that crime he expected to be shot. When Frémont spared his life, it was not surprising that he became one of Frémont's devoted followers, and that he quickly arranged for Frémont to meet with his cousin. The remnants of Pico's army were straggling northward from Los Angeles, but Jesús Pico succeeded in locating him. Andrés then presented a peace proposal to Frémont, who took it upon himself to sign it on behalf of the United States. Never mind that he was subordinate to both Stockton and Kearny and that they were both within communicating distance.

The Treaty of Cahuenga granted everything that the Californios could wish for, including provisions that Stockton had previously refused. It called for the Californios to lay down their arms and retire to their occupations, in return for which parole violators would be forgiven. All Californios would be granted the rights of American citizens without being required to take an oath of allegiance. The agreement was more generous than necessary, considering that the Americans now enjoyed an overpowering military advantage.* Nevertheless, Stockton quickly accepted the pact, and the California conflict came to an end. Stockton might not have been able to negotiate even that generous a peace himself, considering the way he had treated Flores's representatives at San Luis Rey.[28]

Unfortunately, the California campaign ended with an internecine quarrel that could have been dangerous had the Californios been inclined to rebel. The impasse was as unnecessary as it was unseemly.

On January 16, 1847, less than a week after the American occupation of Los Angeles, Commodore Stockton arbitrarily reappointed John C. Frémont as governor of California. This he did in the face of the orders from the President that Kearny produced directing him to assume that position. Stockton maintained that Polk's orders had been overtaken by his own consolidation of power in that region.

Kearny protested the next day, but Stockton would have none of his remonstrances. By the "Law of Nations," he contended that he had the right to set policy.

Kearny was thus placed in an impossible situation. Although he had no personal interest in being governor of this barren land, he was determined to carry out Polk's orders. On the other hand, he was in no position to enforce his demands. His surviving dragoons constituted only a small fraction of the forces on hand, and Frémont, who commanded the strongest land force in the region, sided with Stockton for his own selfish purposes.

*Griffin (p. 66) estimates the figures at 1,100 men and several pieces against the 500 infantry that Pico had managed to scrape up after San Gabriel.

On January 18, 1847, the day following his confrontation with Stockton and Frémont, Kearny left Los Angeles with his fifty men, bound for San Diego. There he bided his time pending further word from Washington, even after Lieutenant Colonel Philip St. George Cooke arrived with the Mormon Battalion to support him. Meanwhile Stockton went ahead with his plans.*

The issue was settled two weeks later by the arrival of Stockton's successor, Commodore Branford Shubrick, whose appearance in early February was greeted with joy by soldiers, sailors, and Californios alike.† Shubrick, a sensible man, quickly lifted martial law and dispatched the *Cyane* to San Diego to bring Kearny to Monterey for a conference. When the two met, Shubrick quickly recognized Kearny's authority but persuaded him to delay assuming authority pending the arrival of Colonel Richard B. Mason, 1st Dragoons, who was expected in a couple of days.

Mason arrived as expected, carrying orders from the President to take over the governorship himself whenever Kearny should determine that the territory was "pacified." So Kearny assumed authority, with Shubrick's assent, and set about "regularizing" Fremont's California Battalion.

Frémont, frustrated, resisted violently, threatening a revolt and challenging Mason to a duel.[29] But Frémont's luck had run out; the members of the California Battalion, having accomplished what they had set out to do, soon melted into the countryside of the Sacramento. Even Stockton, shorn of his command, soon traveled overland to the East with Gillespie. In June 1847 Kearny and Frémont departed also. Frémont would stand court-martial for insubordination, charges preferred by his onetime friend Stephen Kearny.‡

*The issue was a sore one with Kearny's men. All agreed that Frémont deserved court-martial, and most, such as Griffin (p. 71) agreed that Kearny was powerless. But Henry Turner (*The Original Journals*, pp. 155–56) put it uncharitably: "The secret of the whole matter is, [Kearny] is afraid of giving offense to Benton. He says that he will prefer charges against Frémont . . . but I do not believe it. I think he will do nothing calculated to give displeasure to Col. Benton."

†"Commodore Stockton's conduct out here has been extraordinary. . . . He is a low, trifling, truckling politician, regarded with as much contempt by the officers of the Navy, as by those of the Army . . . Commodore Shubrick's arrival is a cause of great rejoicing; both [Stockton] and Fremont have become the most unimportant people in the Territory. . . . Turner, pp. 156–57.

‡For a full treatment of this subject, see Bernard DeVoto, *The Year of Decision*, pp. 456–67, who comes foursquare on the side of Kearny. He describes Stockton as a "fool" and Frémont as "a blunderer on a truly dangerous scale." He is lavish in his praise for Kearny. Others, while critical of Stockton and Frémont, are less laudatory regarding Kearny. See Justin Smith, *The War with Mexico*, vol. II, p. 454.

.   .   .

Thus ended the California episode which, with all its blunders and pettiness, consolidated American control of California for the duration of the Mexican-American conflict. Could it have been done better? Possibly so, although the object was achieved largely by the threat of force rather than by violence on the battlefield. Certainly a great deal of effort and recrimination—not to mention some bloodshed—could have been avoided had the peaceful counsel of Larkin, Sutter, and Vallejo prevailed.

TERROR
IN TAOS

DECEMBER 1846–APRIL 1847

Colonel Alexander Doniphan's 1st Missouri Regiment, originally intended to accompany Kearny to California, had remained behind at Santa Fe on Kearny's orders. Kearny had visualized that Doniphan, upon the arrival of Sterling Price's 2d Regiment, should then set out southward to Chihuahua, where he would report to General John E. Wool. Wool was expected to arrive any day.

Seventy-five miles down the Rio Grande from Santa Fe, however, Kearny had come upon a gruesome sight. The Apaches had just raided the Mexican town of Pulvidera, killing the men and taking the horses and women. The Americans shuddered to contemplate the women's fate. They would be taken to wife by their captors but treated as slaves, even beaten, by the other wives.* As the United States had assumed responsibility for the area, Kearny now directed Doniphan to suspend his march southward and take the local Indians to task. Once satisfied that the Indians would make no more trouble, Doniphan could then, and only then, set out.

Doniphan received this change of orders in early October 1846, and

---

*"The most unfortunate thing which can befall a captive woman is to be claimed by two persons. In this case, she is either shot or delivered up for indiscriminate violence." W. H. Emory, *Notes of a Military Reconnaissance*, p. 50.

at about the same time Sterling Price arrived with seventeen hundred men—twelve hundred from his own 2d Missouri Mounted Infantry plus five hundred of the Mormon Battalion. It was now urgent for Doniphan to leave Santa Fe; that town of three thousand souls could never support so many occupying troops, even after the Mormons had left for California.

Doniphan therefore left Santa Fe and began the arduous task of subduing the Apaches.* Because of the snows, it took him seven weeks to ferret them out of the mountains. Eventually, however, Doniphan brought them to the point where they were willing to sign a peace treaty. He then sped up his plans to leave when he learned that caravans of civilians, bound for Chihuahua, were holding up at Valverde, pending his ability to escort them.

To save time, Doniphan split his small army into two sections, and on December 16, 1846, he personally led his 850 mounted riflemen south from Valverde, leaving the second section to follow. Along with the first section Doniphan took those civilians who had been waiting for an escort.

Donipan's first destination was El Paso, about two hundred miles away, and to get there he was forced to cross over ninety miles of the deadly Jornada del Muerto (Journey of Death), altitude seven thousand feet.

On Christmas afternoon, 1846, Doniphan's vanguard arrived at a level spot about thirty miles north of El Paso where the Brazito River flows into the Rio Grande. Proceeding with as little regard for security as they had for discipline, Doniphan's disorderly volunteers were suddenly surprised to discover a Mexican battalion of about twelve hundred men (by Doniphan's estimate) drawn up in front of them. Fortunately for Doniphan, their Mexican commander, Colonel Ponce de León, sent a formal demand for Doniphan to surrender—a demand that provided a welcome delay. Doniphan had time to assemble his men in some sort of order.

The ensuing skirmish was finished in forty minutes. De León's poorly motivated cavalry attacked Doniphan's sharpshooters with grim results: one hundred Mexicans killed or wounded, no Americans dead. After this so-called Battle of the Brazito, Doniphan's men moved in and occupied El Paso, a town full of traders who heartily welcomed the

*The tribes were Eutaws and Navajos, branches of the Apache nation.

arrival of the Americans. Doniphan then concentrated the two sections of his force and refitted for the long march ahead.[1]

Back in Santa Fe, however, all was not going well. The American volunteers, bored in the dismal, dirty little town, were conducting themselves badly. Riots and drunkenness were common. Moreover, the proud New Mexicans, like the citizens of California, were feeling the humiliation of former Governor Manuel Armijo's abject surrender the previous August. Plots against the Americans began to brew. Two men, Tomás Ortiz and Diego Archuleta, began a conspiracy to assassinate both Price and Governor Charles Bent, and the circle of plotters soon expanded to include several members of the Armijo family and several clergy. But word of the plot leaked, and some of the conspirators were arrested. The leaders escaped, but the ease with which the plot had been detected gave the occupation force an added degree of complacency.[2] Thus, on December 26 Governor Bent was writing to Secretary of State Buchanan in a soothing tone: "So far as I am informed, this conspiracy is confined to the four northern counties of the Territory, and the men considered as leaders in the affair can not be said to be men of much standing.[3]

Bent felt completely at home in Santa Fe. Though he had come from St. Louis in 1826, he had lived in this region ever since, a partner with his brother William in the Bent's Fort enterprise. Through the years William Bent had tended to mind the store back at the fort while Charles promoted family enterprises in Santa Fe, Taos, and Chihuahua. The trade was lucrative, and Bent was well known and respected in New Mexico. He spent much time in Santa Fe but kept his retiring Mexican wife and children at his home in the trading center of Taos. He considered himself one of the people despite his "Anglo" birth.*

But Bent underestimated the state of discontent among the people and overestimated the personal esteem in which he was held. He knew he had enemies, the influential Archbishop Martinez, in Taos, among them. But Bent did not believe that hostility would ever result in

---

*Taos, the modern-day art center eighty miles north of Santa Fe, was at that time the third largest town in New Mexico, with a population of over three thousand. The home of Kit Carson since 1825, it was a truly neutral trading post. Both Indians and whites forswore border warfare in its vicinity.

violence. Ignoring the advice of some of his friends to stay under guard in Santa Fe, Bent left Santa Fe for Taos on January 14, 1847, to spend a short vacation with his family.

As Bent reached the edge of Taos he was met by a mob of Indians from the nearby pueblo. They claimed that two of their friends had been unjustly jailed for theft and demanded that Bent release them. Calmly, Bent explained that such action would have to come from the proper authorities; he had no such power. The mob, apparently pacified, dispersed, and Bent continued on and reached his home. On hand were some houseguests, one of whom was Josefa Jaramillo Carson, Kit Carson's beautiful seventeen-year-old wife, Bent's sister-in-law. Though the Carson house was only a block away from Bent's, Josefa customarily sought the security of the governor's home while her husband was off with Frémont in California.

At about six in the morning of January 19, 1847, Governor Bent was awakened by a rap on the door. It turned out to be a messenger, who warned of a mob heading toward his house. The local Indians, headed by Pablo Montoyo and Tomás Romero, had gathered the previous night and in a frenzy had descended upon the jail and killed the town prefecto and the sheriff. Shortly after the messenger left, a mob began pounding at the door. When Bent asked them what they wanted, they said, "We want your head, gringo, we do not want for any of you gringos to govern us, as we have come to kill you."[4]

Bent was taken aback but not yet alarmed; he still had time to escape out the back way and flee by horseback. But his pride deterred him. He was, after all, governor, and he had his family in the house. Further, his powers of persuasion had calmed the people before.

"What wrong have I done you?" he pleaded. "I have always helped you, I have cured you when you were sick and I have never charged you."

"Yes," one of the Indians answered, "but you have to die now so that no American is going to govern us." At that the mob—some were drunk—began shooting wildly with arrows and guns. Bent was hit but not instantly killed. He stalled for time while the women of the household frantically beat the soft adobe wall of the front hall to make an escape hole through which they hoped to reach the house next door.

But flight was impossible for Bent. He had taken several arrows in his body, been thrown to the floor and scalped alive before he could

shake himself loose. Meanwhile the women scurried through the hole.
Bent tried to follow them, but he was forced to pause to remove a
painful arrow.*

The exact circumstances of Bent's final moments are unclear. But
somewhere, in the foyer or in the next house, Bent was decapitated.
The mob paused, uncertain whether to kill the women. But because
they were Mexican, the ruffians spared them. Mrs. Bent and Josefa
Carson, of course, hastily hid their light-skinned children.

Finally the Indians calmed down and remorse set in. Many were
sorry, and one cried that they had been fools; they should have kept
the governor hostage.[5]

The killing and plunder spread all over the Taos region. Simeon
Turley and six others were murdered at nearby Arroyo Hondo, where
Turley for years had been distilling strong liquor, some of which may
have set off the mob violence. At the town of Mora, also, another eight
Americans were killed.[6] Many of the American residents were away for
a time, a fact that probably saved their lives. But one of them was Kit
Carson. Had he been there, who knows what he could have done?

Colonel Sterling Price received news of the Taos massacre the next day.
At the same time he learned that the rebels were on the march south
from Taos to Santa Fe, picking up new recruits at every town. Such
a situation called for a speedy response. But since Price could not
denude Santa Fe of American troops, he sent for a battalion from
Albuquerque, and, with five companies of his 2d Missouri, plus Angney's infantry battalion and a company of New Mexico volunteers, set
out for Taos on January 23. His force at this time totaled 353 men, with
four mountain howitzers. Except for the New Mexico volunteers, all
of Price's men were dismounted.†

At a small town called Canada, one day out of Santa Fe, Price's force
met a sizable band of New Mexicans, fifteen hundred men. Price
quickly succeeded in brushing this force out of its entrenchments,
killing an estimated thirty-six. Soon thereafter Price was joined by a
company of the 1st Dragoons, under the command of Captain J.H.K.

---

*Michael McNierney, ed., *Taos 1847*, p. 14.
†Price to TAG, February 15, 1847, Exec. Doc. No. 1, p. 521. The commander of the volunteers
was Captain Ceran St. Vrain, a former partner of Bent's.

Burgwin, and another company of the 2d Missouri volunteers. His force had now grown to a respectable 479 men.*

Price's march was far from easy, taking him over high mountains, through areas where the snow was two feet deep. And it was resisted; at Embudo Pass he was met again, with results similar to those at Canada. Nevertheless, his force arrived intact at Taos on February 2, 1847. North of the town, in the renowned Pueblo of Taos, the rebels were preparing to make their stand.

The centuries-old Pueblo of Taos consisted of two large pyramidal apartment houses, each about 125 yards long and seven stories high, facing each other, their long axes running east to west. A stream flowed between them. Each of the large apartment buildings could hold about five or six hundred men, and together they formed a square enclosure, about 250 yards on each side, surrounded by a wall. Inside the northwest corner of this enclosure stood an adobe mission church, whose formidable walls made it a natural fortress. The church faced north, with a corral to the south.[7]

Price's reconnaissance indicated that the bulk of the rebels had assembled inside the courtyard north of the stream, and the church seemed to hold the heaviest concentration. Price therefore decided to attack that position, but since an infantry assault would be costly, he spent the whole of Wednesday, February 3, pounding the thick earthen wall with his light artillery. At the end of the day, with his troops weary and his ammunition low, Price retired back into Taos to allow his men a good night's rest.

The next day Price was back in place, determined to bring the affair to a decision. To ensure that no rebel could escape, Price placed St. Vrain's and Slack's mounted men in a copse to the east of the enclosure. Angney's battalion would attack the northern face of the church while Burgwin's dragoons and another company would assault the western. At 11 A.M. all forces jumped the wall together. Swiftly they crossed the open space to the cover of the church wall, where they began to knock down the adobe. Burgwin's men brought up a ladder, and someone was able to set the roof on fire. Burgwin, with some of his men, crossed to the south of the church and attempted to break

---

*Ibid., pp. 521–22. It will be recalled that Kearny had sent back two hundred of his original three hundred dragoons.

in from the corral. The effort failed, and Burgwin was mortally wounded.

In the meantime, however, Price's artillery had blasted a hole in the western wall of the church; Price ordered his six-pounder brought around to that side, and it began pumping shells through the openings. By 3 P.M. the six-pounder was hauled to a point fifty yards from the wall; after a few rounds it was brought up within ten, where it could spray its fire more effectively inside. By now the church was full of smoke and the rebels had gone. The storming party entered without opposition.

Having abandoned the church, the New Mexican rebels fled to the two apartment houses; fifty who tried to escape the enclosure by climbing over the wall were slaughtered. When nightfall came, Price's men remained in place, prepared to finish off the rest the next morning.

But there would be no fight the next day. The rebels, seeing that their situation was hopeless, gave up. Price believed that the ferocity of the battle had taught the rebels a lesson and accepted the truce on the condition that Romero and Montoyo, the main instigators of Bent's death, be surrendered for trial. That agreed to, the battle was over. Rebel losses were estimated at about 150 killed. American losses came to seven killed (including Burgwin) at first count, though some of the forty-five wounded later died.*

The rebels dispersed. Of the leaders, only Romero and Montoyo were taken alive. Romero was later murdered by a bereaved relative of a victim while awaiting trial in jail. Montoyo was tried in the home of Padre Martinez,† with Mrs. Bent on hand to point a finger at him. Of the two judges, one had been a close friend of Bent's; the other was the father of a man brutally murdered the same night as Bent. The jury was composed of friends and relatives of the various murder victims. Under these circumstances it is not surprising that Montoyo, together with six others, was found guilty and sentenced to death. He was

---

*Ibid., pp. 522–25. The pueblo still stands as it did in 1847, its mud walls unaffected by the events a century and a half earlier. The church, however, has remained in ruins. The pueblo prospers. Inside Taos, about five miles away, Governor Bent's house still has the hole in the front foyer where it is claimed that he and his family attempted their escape.

†Martinez was suspected of being behind the rebellion in Taos, but the accusation has never been proven.

hanged in the Plaza of Taos in April 1847. Five more New Mexicans and four Indians later met the same fate.[8]

The territory then settled down to peaceful pursuits. Though conditions remained as bad as before—none of the causes of the rebellion had been eliminated—the New Mexicans sullenly tolerated American rule pending the outcome of the war.

MISSOURI
XENOPHON

◁◁◎◎ ◎◎▷▷

JANUARY–MAY 1847

On May 21, 1847, the advance guard of Colonel Alexander Doniphan's 1st Missouri Mounted Infantry pitched camp at San Juan, fifteen miles from Brigadier General John E. Wool's headquarters at Buena Vista. Doniphan's men had just trekked across 3,500 miles of barren wasteland, having left Missouri in June 1846 as part of Stephen Kearny's force. From Santa Fe they had ridden independently through El Paso, Chihuahua, and Parras. They had withstood all the hazards and discomforts of frontier travel—ice, sleet, heat, lack of water—for long stretches.

Though Doniphan's men had endured much, their feat was not, in itself, unique in the Mexican War. But "Doniphan's March" was destined to become famous in history for several reasons. For one, Doniphan's force consisted entirely of a single volunteer regiment, operating under a volunteer colonel. And timing was fortuitous; the regiment returned home just before the rest of the one-year volunteer units. But most of all, the march was to become famous by the personality of the extraordinary man who led them.

Not only morally but physically Alexander Doniphan was a big man, described by an awed admirer as towering nearly six and a half feet, and weighing over 240 pounds. His fingers were said to be nine inches long, and he had feet to match. His sandy red hair stuck out "like porcupine quills," and his men claimed that he was "not afraid of the Devil or the God that made him."[1] And yet Doniphan was a man possessed of a certain sense of humor and habitually wore a smile; he unabashedly lavished a manly tenderness on the troops who had unanimously elected him to his position, and he made them feel that they shared in his decisions. His leadership was of the frontier variety, not that assiduously taught at West Point.

Doniphan had been a famous trial lawyer in Missouri, one of the best, and had commanded several militia regiments before the war. Though respectful to his military superiors as a rule, he once proved his moral fiber by his open defiance of an order directing him to execute a group of Mormons condemned for treason and had made his defiance stick.* Only such a man as Doniphan could have led an unlikely group of volunteers to perform as his did.

After the Battle of the Brazito at Christmas, 1846, Doniphan's force settled into El Paso for a rest. While there Doniphan received word that Wool, whom he was supposed to join at Chihuahua, had now been sent to Saltillo rather than to Chihuahua as originally planned. Santa Anna, Doniphan learned, was posing a threat to Taylor in the latter's stretched-out position, and Wool was going to Saltillo to reinforce him.

While the prospect of action excited Doniphan, Wool's absence at Chihuahua created a problem. Doniphan was stranded, alone, at El Paso, contributing nothing to the prosecution of the war. He had the choice, therefore, of either retracing his steps to Santa Fe or of continuing on to Chihuahua, where, he had heard, a large Mexican force was collecting. The march forward would be much the bolder course.

Doniphan had his own way of making such a decision: he put it to a vote among his men. The men, undoubtedly influenced by Doniphan's own preference, voted to push on to Chihuahua. So Doniphan

---

*The order in question was Governor Lillburn W. Boggs's "Extermination Order" of October 1838. "I will not obey your order," Doniphan wrote his military superior. "My brigade shall march for Liberty tomorrow morning, and if you execute these men I will hold you responsible before an earthly tribunal, so help me God." Bernard DeVoto, *The Year of Decision*, pp. 83–84.

determined to do just that, but only after Major Merriwether Lewis Clark, commander of the Missouri artillery, could join him. Without that artillery, an expedition to Chihuahua would be not merely bold but suicidal.

When Clark and Captain Richard H. Weightman arrived at El Paso with six pieces of artillery in early February, Doniphan was ready to head out. Along with the 924 men of his formal command, he took with him the train of traders and teamsters he had picked up at Ververde, organizing them into an irregular fighting unit. The civilians in his party made up a train of 315 wagons over and above those belonging to the companies and commissary.[2] The expedition thus took on the aspect of a migration as well as of a military force.

Nor was there anything "military" about the conduct of the Missourians. Their camp was no showpiece. One civilian, an Englishman, remarked that, aside from a rough alignment of the tents, all uniformity in bivouac ceased. The camp, he noted, was "strewn with the bones and offal of the cattle slaughtered for its supply, and not the slightest attention was paid to keeping it clear from other accumulations of filth." The men were "unwashed and unshaven, ragged and dirty." Even sensible military precautions were ignored, as the men had, by vote, decreed that posting of lookouts at night was unnecessary. As a result, " one fine day three Navajo Indians ran off with a flock of eight hundred sheep belonging to the camp, killing the two volunteers in charge of them." Mules and horses strayed over the country. "In fact," the Englishman concluded, with a touch of superiority, "the most total want of discipline was apparent in everything."[3]

But disciplined or not, Doniphan's rabble survived extremes of climate and terrain in the course of the three-hundred-mile march to Chihuahua. They crossed two vast deserts, one of them sixty miles wide. Water was scarce, and so was game, but the area was rich in rattlesnakes, copperheads, tarantulas, and Mexican spies. The snakes and tarantulas could not be made to talk, but captured spies could. From them Doniphan learned that about seven hundred Mexican cavalry waited in his path. That seemed plausible, but for a long time no Mexican cavalry appeared as the Missourians marched southward.

As Doniphan approached, Mexican authorities in Chihuahua were facing a torn population. The people held the deep-seated hatred for the gringos that pervaded other parts of Mexico, but their hostility was mitigated by the very profitable trade that flourished between Chihuahua, Santa Fe, and thence eastward to Missouri. That trade did, indeed, provide much of the population's livelihood, and the former governor of Chihuahua had been inclined to friendship with the Americans before the government in Mexico City had recalled him in August 1846.

The current governor was an active, ambitious man named Angel Trias, who rallied the population to resistance. For a while Trias made progress toward establishing a respectable defense, casting artillery pieces from local resources and training infantrymen to use them. However, as at Tampico, Santa Anna stepped in and began denuding the Zacatecas-Chihuahua region of regular troops in order to build the army for his expedition to Buena Vista. In spite of that, Trias believed that sufficient national guardsmen remained on hand at Chihuahua to repel any force of fewer than a thousand Americans.

With Doniphan's approach in late February 1847, General García Condé arrived from Mexico City to take command of Chihuahua. By now Condé had accumulated about 1,500 infantry (some of them regulars), 1,200 cavalry, and 119 artillerymen manning ten brass cannon and nine musketoons. This force of nearly three thousand* bolstered Mexican confidence to the point that Condé actually filled a whole wagon with lariats, intending to tie the Missourians to their saddles after he had taken them prisoner.[4]

The Battle of Sacramento, February 28, 1847

For all his bravado, García Condé realized that his troops were untrained, so he prudently elected to defend against the inferior American force rather than attack it. He selected a position about fifteen miles north of Chihuahua, just forward of the Sacramento River, on a plateau that lay between the river and a dry arroyo. Pushing out ahead

*Justin Smith, *The War with Mexico*, vol. I, p. 306. Doniphan, in his report (Exec. Doc. No. 1, p. 501), saw the Mexican force a little differently, at 1,200 cavalry, 1,200 infantry, 300 artillerymen, and 1,420 rancheros. However, Smith's figures come from Mexican sources. The counts of artillery pieces are consistent all around. These figures do not include the 1000 rancheros on hand.

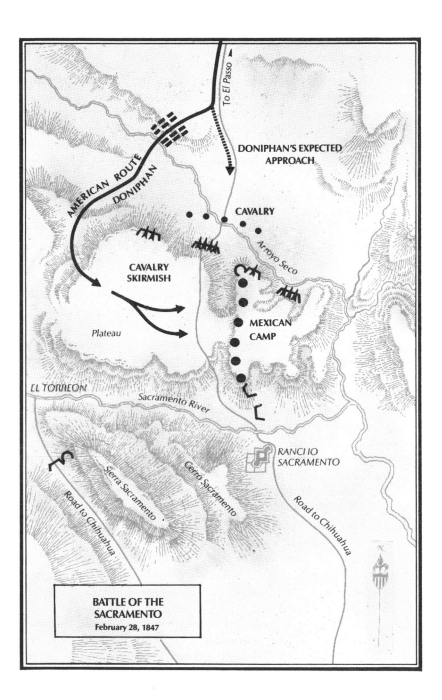

To El Passo

DONIPHAN'S EXPECTED
APPROACH

AMERICAN ROUTE

DONIPHAN

CAVALRY

Arroyo Seco

CAVALRY
SKIRMISH

MEXICAN
CAMP

Plateau

EL TORREON

Sacramento River

RANCHO
SACRAMENTO

Sierra Sacramento

Cerro Sacramento

Road to Chihuahua

Road to Chihuahua

N

BATTLE OF THE
SACRAMENTO
February 28, 1847

of the river was an unconventional move, but the plateau provided a stronger defensive line than did the fordable river. The position lay in a gap only a mile and a half wide between two mountains, and the northern rim of the plateau, facing in Doniphan's direction, presented a formidable sixty-foot wall, broken only by a single road. That wall was sufficiently precipitous, Condé believed, to force the Americans to keep their cumbersome wagons on the main road. Since the road ran right below an easily defended cut, Condé reasoned that Doniphan would be forced to reduce the strong position overlooking that cut—at unacceptable cost. Along that position, therefore, he placed three batteries, one behind another, all facing northwest to cover the anticipated American route.

Condé's dispositions made excellent sense—so long as the Missourians stuck to the road. So certain was Condé that the Americans would not move across the tundra to the west that he left it undefended.

But Doniphan did not do as Condé expected. His force moved out at sunrise of Sunday, February 28, and soon scouts had discovered that the escarpment could be climbed even by wagons at a newly discovered point to the west. So as Doniphan's force approached the arroyo he sent his cavalry screen in that direction, to mount the escarpment far beyond range of Condé's guns. The rest of the command followed. Behind the cavalry the three hundred wagons were drawn up in four columns, with the bulk of the artillery and infantry concealed between the wagons. All depended on the ability of Doniphan's men to haul the wagons from the gulch of the arroyo to the mesa above.*

By early afternoon, after several hours of struggle and cursing, Doniphan's men finally dragged all the wagons and artillery across the bottom of the arroyo and up the cliff. Then at 3 P.M. Condé's cavalry (eight hundred men) detected the wagons on the plain and attacked. Clark's and Weightman's artillery quickly drove them back, and Doniphan advanced southeastward, to the rear corner of the Mexican position. His wagons retained formation, his artillery and infantry remained between the the wagons, and his cavalry led the way.

On came Doniphan's four columns, bypassing the Mexican positions on his left. As he pulled within range, Doniphan trained his artillery on the rear corner of the Mexican position and concentrated fire on

---

*The four-abreast formation was common in the West. It avoided permitting one accident to hold up the entire column; it formed up easily for defense; and it reduced the number of drivers eating the others' dust.

the decisive point while avoiding the bulk of the Mexican fire. Once that corner of the Mexican position was reduced, he turned northward and began picking off, one by one, the other positions in front of it.

Throughout the battle Doniphan's tactics were unconventional, for he sent Weightman's artillery forward, supported by his three companies of cavalry instead of the infantry. Coordination was admittedly ragged, but eventually the three artillery companies were successful in reducing the redoubts.* The fighting was severe, hand to hand. Gun butts did their grisly work of bashing out brains. Many horses were shot, but miraculously only one American was killed outright,† and the Mexican position collapsed.

Doniphan, in his report, claimed that the enemy lost "his entire artillery, 10 wagons, masses of beans and pinola, and [apparently as an afterthought] three hundred killed and about the same number wounded." Losses among the Missourians: one killed, one mortally wounded, seven "so wounded as to recover without the loss of any limbs." And he added proudly, "Much had been said, and justly said, of the gallantry of our artillery, unlimbering within 250 yards of the enemy at Palo Alto; but how much more daring was the charge of Captain Weightman, when he unlimbered within fifty yards of the redoubts of the enemy."⁵

Doniphan took formal possession of Chihuahua on March 1, 1847. As in camp, however, the American occupation was no spit-and-polish operation. In fact, since most of the townspeople had fled, Doniphan's men simply moved into their houses and used them as they wished. Susan Magoffin, wife of the James Magoffin of Bent's Fort, expressed shock in her celebrated diary as she described the scene. It was filled with Missouri volunteers "who though good to fight are not careful at all how much they soil the property of a friend much less an enemy." She tended to take the side of "the good citizens of Chi" who, she lamented, had never dreamed that "their loved homes would be turned into quarters for common soldiers, their fine houses turned into stables,

---

*Doniphan to TAG, April 4, 1847, Exec. Doc. No. 1, p. 500. Captain Hudson "anticipated" Doniphan's command and attacked on his own; Parsons specifically asked permission to charge.

†Either suffering from a death wish or remarkably poor judgment, Major Samuel C. Owens, one of the wagon irregulars, charged on horseback far out ahead of the rest, and he was cut down immediately.

their public drinking fountain used as a bathing trough." But the good Mrs. Magoffin was no democrat when it came to her own comforts. Though the Mexican homes were too good for the common soldiers, her party "took a comfortable house a square off from the plaza, as none could be had in it, and spent three weeks in it as pleasantly as we could under the circumstances."[6]

Once ensconced in Chihuahua, Doniphan had to decide his next move. He had attained his prize but he could never, with a thousand men, subdue the country around it. Furthermore, as he was alone, without Wool's force, he expected his position to become daily more dangerous. So he sent a side expedition to Durango to see if danger was threatening from the south, and waited.

The scouting expedition soon returned with reassurances that no Mexican force was threatening Chihuahua for the moment, but Doniphan was still impatient to leave Chihuahua. On March 20, therefore, he sent a message to Wool, whom he still considered his immediate commander. In the message he described his position as "exceedingly embarrassing." Most of his men, he pleaded, had been in the service since the first of June 1846, during which time they had not received one cent of pay. They had now marched more than two thousand miles and, with their term of service nearly up, they were restless to return to Moclova and join Wool's command.

Doniphan added that he could not leave Chihuahua safely for some days, and the American merchants, having several hundred thousand dollars at stake, were violently opposed to his leaving. Doniphan protested that he was "anxious and willing" to protect the merchants as far as he could, but he objected to remaining "as a mere wagon guard." Always courteous, Doniphan assured his superior that he would obey any orders cheerfully, but (not yet having heard of Taylor's victory at Buena Vista) feared that "there is ample use for us with you." Above all, he wanted to join Wool before his regiment's term of service expired.[7]

On receiving Doniphan's letter, Wool sent it on to Taylor at Monterrey. Taylor, in turn, sent a copy on to Washington on April 4, advising that he was ordering Doniphan to join Wool. He confirmed that the traders with Doniphan would "have their election to remain in Chihuahua, or come under the protection of the column to Saltillo."[8]

Doniphan, meanwhile, was doing all he could to ensure the safety of the civilians who would be staying behind. He made overtures to the Mexicans, proposing to "neutralize" Chihuahua if the merchants would be protected. He would commit the United States to evacuate the city and agree not to return, provided that the State of Chihuahua remained neutral.[9] The Mexicans refused this offer, so when Taylor's order reached him on April 25, Doniphan gave the merchants the choice Taylor had ordered. They could travel with Doniphan to Saltillo or they could remain. Many chose to go with him, but some remained behind at Chihuahua. Doniphan then called in the Mexican authorities and demanded a promise that they would treat the American residents of Chihuahua decently, threatening to return if they did not. The Mexicans were willing to promise informally, so Doniphan felt he had done everything possible.

Three days later Doniphan's caravan began the march to Saltillo. On May 11 they reached Parras, where Wool had camped some months before. There Doniphan's advance guard skirmished with a band of Lipan Indians, who had robbed a local ranch, carrying off women, children, and livestock. One of Doniphan's companies ambushed the Indians and liberated the captives and the property. Doniphan thus repaid, in a way, the people of Parras for their earlier friendliness to Wool and their care of the sick that Wool had been forced to leave behind.*

Upon making contact with Wool's outposts at Buena Vista, Reid's men awaited the arrival of the rest of Doniphan's column. When it arrived, Doniphan agreed to put on a military review for their immediate commander. To make his men look like conventional soldiers was impossible, but they were conscious that they were heroes, and they were proud. A military pedant would have scoffed at the review itself, but in the light of the accomplishments of this 1st Missouri, nobody dared. The ceremony was repeated a few days later back at Monterrey, this time for Zachary Taylor.

---

*Reid Report, May 21, 1847, Exec. Doc. No. 60, p. 1144. The episode had a bizarre sequel. Adolph Wislizenus, a German "medical practitioner" freed by Doniphan at Chihuahua, came to the scene two days after the fight. Among the fifteen Indian corpses was a handsome medicine man. As the bodies were being left to the wolves, Wislizenus took home with him the skull of the medicine man. His journal made no mention of how he rendered the flesh of the medicine man's face from his skull. Adolph Wislizenus, *Memoir of a Tour to Northern Mexico*, pp. 70–72.

According to the law of May 1846, Doniphan's men could have been retained at Monterrey until the end of their enlistments, the last day of May 1847. But they could be of no use; no enemy was anywhere near, and the men were eager to return home. So Taylor sent them back immediately, to be discharged and paid in New Orleans and sent home to warm welcomes.

Doniphan's men were no unsung heroes. They were, in fact, feted extravagantly. Senator Thomas Hart Benton made a special journey from Washington to greet them with a speech of congratulations; sheet music was dedicated to them—the front cover picturing Doniphan in dashing full-dress uniform. William Cullen Bryant would compare Doniphan to Xenophon, whose ten thousand Greeks had made a similar excursion through Asia Minor in the fourth century B.C.

"Those two men," wrote the editor of the New York *Post,* were "two military commanders who have made the most extraordinary marches known in the annals of warfare of their times."[10]

WINFIELD
SCOTT'S
WAR

THE SIEGE OF
VERACRUZ
~~~~~

NOVEMBER 1846–MARCH 1847

On March 12, 1847, Major General Winfield Scott penned an
exultant report from a beach south of Veracruz:

> Sir,—The colors of the United States were triumphantly planted
> ashore, in full view of the city and its castle, and under the constant fire
> of both, in the afternoon of the 9th instant. . . . The whole army reached
> shore in fine style, and without direct opposition, accident, or loss.[1]

That message marked the end of the first step of a long, hard, bloody
campaign. But though only a beginning, the landing was a feat in itself,
worthy of a moment's gloating.

Planning for the landing at Veracruz had begun months before, in
October 1846, when Scott had begun his campaign with Polk and
Marcy to secure approval of the operation—with Scott himself as
commander. The three memos that Scott had written to encourage
approval had been so complete in themselves that they had formed the
basis for planning and procurement.

Scott's general concept never changed: (a) that Mexico City must
be approached from Veracruz rather than from Taylor's position at
Monterrey;[2] (b) that speed was necessary because of the seasonal on-

slaught of the dreaded *vómito* (yellow fever) in the vicinity of Veracruz; (c) that the need for speed precluded the use of any port other than Veracruz; (d) that Fort San Juan de Ulúa, guarding Veracruz from the sea, could not be assaulted directly; (e) that the city could be taken by landing an army some distance away and then reducing its defenses by assault or siege; and (f) that special boats, or scows, should be constructed to land his force outside the range of the enemy's guns.

Scott's memos varied in details, however—or, rather, became progressively more refined. At first he estimated that ten thousand or so men would suffice; the first wave would consist of twenty-five hundred men, plus two light artillery batteries; the cavalry and artillery horses would come ashore in subsequent waves. At first he hoped that the expedition could be fitted out by New Year's Day, 1847, and that reinforcements would eventually bring his total to twenty thousand men.*

A little over two weeks later, a more confident Scott had trimmed his requirements a bit, in anticipation of help from Conner's blockading Home Squadron, specifically—drawing some twelve hundred men for the purpose of the landing itself. And to meet his estimate of twenty thousand men total, he proposed to take the bulk of the necessary troops from Taylor. Scott estimated Taylor's total strength, including Wool's troops, at twenty thousand men, so he could take nine thousand and still leave Taylor eleven thousand. Scott urged that sea transport be gathered at once, and that construction of landing craft begin soon.[3]

Scott's final memo, four days later, added a significant assumption: that nine additional volunteer regiments, a total of 6,750 men, would be inducted into United States service. And he specified his shipping requirements: 50 ships of 500 to 750 tons each and 140 flatboats, enough to carry five thousand men in the first wave.[4]

Scott's campaign to secure the Veracruz command for himself reached its emotional climax three days later in his memorable meeting with Polk. When Scott hastily departed Washington on November 26, he was then hoping to have his entire force afloat on January 15, or, at the latest, February 1, 1847.[5]

·   ·   ·

*Scott to Marcy, October 27, 1847, Exec. Doc. No. 59. The ten thousand would be broken down into two thousand cavalry, six hundred artillery, and the rest infantry. All the artillery and half the cavalry would be regular troops.

Scott had proposed the largest amphibious invasion yet attempted in history. He had the men and supplies he needed, but success in collecting adequate sea transport, that bugaboo of amphibious operations,* would always hang in the balance. The fifty sea transports, fortunately, already existed, as the standard merchant sailing vessels of the time would suffice. Only a portion of the necessary transports belonged to the government, however; the rest were still at sea plying the merchant trade, and arrangements for chartering them had to be made in person at the various ports, as no telegraph was yet in place between ports. Fortunately for Scott, the man responsible, Quartermaster General Thomas S. Jesup, was an independent and resourceful man, and he approached his challenge with confidence. In order to begin chartering vessels in time, Jesup left Washington for New Orleans even before Scott. Since the seagoing vessels were going to be needed at the Brazos and Tampico in two months, both Jesup and Scott would suffer much suspense during the next few weeks.

The matter of flatboats, the craft that would deliver men from the decks of the transports, was easier, in a way, because they were to be constructed in the ports under the direct control of Jesup's own men. The instructions for their design were exacting,† a fact that may have accounted for the eventual shortfall in production. Of the 141 landing craft ordered, only sixty-five would arrive in time for use.

Though Scott's army would travel on its own chartered ships and land in craft belonging to the War Department, Scott had always counted on the assistance of the U.S. Navy. From New Orleans he wrote Commodore David E. Conner, who was blockading Veracruz, requesting help and advice.‡ He was not disappointed in his request, for Conner, though aging and sick, was determined to assist Scott in any way he could. In answering Scott's letter, Conner initially advised

---

*Nearly a century later, planning for the cross-Channel invasion of France (Overlord) would encounter the same difficulties, the shortage of landing ships (LSTs).

†There were to be three types of boats, one size forty feet long, another forty feet nine inches, and a third thirty-five feet nine inches. The breadth of each boat was specified exactly, as were the depth (four feet four and a half inches for the largest), the number and size of oars, and the weight of the anchor (150 pounds). Each large boat was to weigh 6,280 pounds, the materials for each part being specified in detail. One hundred forty-one of these boats were ordered. The price, considered exorbitant, was $795 per boat, though the price was to be reduced by $10 for every day each boat was late. Temple, WG, pp. 60–62.

‡This move seems obvious. It is mentioned because Conner's son, Philip Conner, had the impression that Scott had originally planned to ignore the Navy in conducting his expedition. See P.S.P. Conner, *The Home Squadron Under Commodore Conner in the War with Mexico.*

that five thousand men could bring about a bloodless surrender of
Veracruz in a siege of ten days. He would be there to help, and in order
to facilitate coordination he recommended that Scott direct his flotilla
toward his own headquarters at Anton Lizardo, near Veracruz. On
Scott's arrival, Conner could point out the sites he considered feasible
for the landing. And, most important, Conner urged speed. "The
present would be the most favorable time for the contemplated
attack. . . ."[6]

But the attack could not be mounted at the time recommended by
Conner—or even close to that time. Scott's first transports would not
even reach the Brazos before the middle of February, almost a month
after Conner had penned his letter.

By now Scott was no longer euphoric about his relationship with the
President. As he was about to leave New Orleans for the Brazos, a
stranger sidled up to him with word that Polk had requested Congress to institute a new military rank, the supergrade of lieutenant
general.[7] If Congress should authorize such a position, everyone in
Washington supposed that it would be filled by Senator Benton.
Scott at first refused to believe such a thing, preferring to assume that
any such new rank would be created for himself. He therefore continued to maintain a friendly as well as an official correspondence
with Marcy. As time passed, however, Scott came to realize that his
earlier predictions were coming to pass: he was indeed being fired
upon from his rear.*

Scott's army was assembling in two places; troops coming directly from
the United States were assembling at the Brazos and the units being
transferred to his command from Taylor were arriving at Tampico. The

---

*Winfield Scott Memoirs, vol. I, pp. 399–400. Scott's suspicions of Polk—reciprocated, of
course—were confirmed by the case of Colonel William S. Harney, commander of the 2d
Dragoons. Harney had been headstrong and insubordinate as part of Wool's command, and had
caused losses and embarrassment. And when Scott ordered him to return to Monterrey, Harney
refused to leave. Worth, in temporary command, placed him under court-martial. Scott then
remitted the sentence and restored Harney to command, but not before Polk had concluded that
Harney's only fault lay in his being a Democrat. The incident was damaging to mutual trust
between president and general. Justin Smith, The War with Mexico, vol. I, pp. 268–69, 364–65;
James K. Polk, Diary, February 20, 1847, p. 198.

two bodies of troops needed to be united before moving on Veracruz. But how? A rendezvous at sea would involve too many imponderables, and the harbor at Tampico was too small to accommodate the whole fleet.

Scott therefore decided to stage his army on the sandy coral harbor of Lobos Island, located about sixty miles south of Tampico. Scott went personally to Tampico, and then, accompanied by the bulk of his troops, he sailed on to Lobos, arriving in mid-February 1847.

At Lobos Scott found that some of the volunteer regiments and some of the requisitioned ships had already arrived, but the landing craft had not appeared. He therefore spent two tense weeks drilling his troops and organizing his command structure on the hundred-acre island. Time passed slowly for the troops on that diminutive coral reef.

By March 2, 1847, adequate numbers of Scott's landing craft had finally arrived and he had completed the organization of his twelve thousand men. Therefore, on that day, he issued orders for them to move.* Scott loved pageantry, and he made a point of standing bare-headed on the deck of the steamer *Massachusetts* as it took its place at the head of the sailing fleet. Scott's own blue flag advertised his presence—as if that had been necessary—and "peal after peal of cheers resounded from ship to ship. . . . The sailors broke into their hearty songs; the sails filled gracefully; and the fleet stood away."[8]

. . .

*Organization as follows (noted in Emory Upton, *The Military Policy of the United States,* p. 211)

Worth's Division
  Artillery: 9 companies, 2d Art.; 4 companies, 3d Art.
  Infantry: 4th, 5th, 6th, and 8th infantries.
Twiggs' Division
  Artillery: 12 companies, 1st Art.; 6 companies, 4th Art.
  Infantry: 2d, 3d, and 7th infantries
  Regiment of Mounted Rifles
Patterson's Division
  Infantry: 3d Illinois, 4th Illinois, New York
  Regiment, 1st Tennessee, 2d Tennessee, Kentucky
  Regiment, 1st Pennsylvania, 2d Pennsylvania,
  South Carolina Regiment, Mounted Tennessee
  Volunteers
Army troops: 1st and 2d dragoons (6 companies), Engr Co.,
  Ordnance Co.

For two days the pace was slow, but for the last part of the trip a norther* pushed the fleet on. By March 5 Scott's men beheld the spires of Ciudad Veracruz—City of the True Cross—with the formidable fortress of San Juan de Ulúa guarding it from the sea. On the horizon, about fifty miles inland but visible in the clear air, stood the 15,000-foot peak of Oriziba. Just off the Isla Verde, five miles seaward of the city, the *Massachusetts* was greeted by the sloops *Albany* and *John Adams*, whose pilots were to guide Scott's ships into the lagoon of Anton Lizardo. Scott's fleet of transports anchored between Anton Lizardo and the island of Salmadia, some twelve miles from Veracruz.

For the next two days, officers from Conner's Home Squadron assisted Scott's men in launching, inspecting, and arranging the flatboats in accordance with Scott's organization plan.[9] By now Conner had narrowed down his choices for Scott's landing beaches to two. Conner personally favored the smooth beach called the Collada, as it was near the city and sheltered from northers by the nearby Sacrificios Island, but that site was too small to handle Scott's transports. Conner had therefore devised a plan to deal with that deficiency: if Scott would agree, Conner could land the army from his naval vessels, whose great size would reduce the number of ships necessary to enter that small area. Scott tentatively accepted Conner's offer at once. If the beach appeared satisfactory, the Navy would put the Army ashore.[10]

To afford Scott the chance to examine the beaches for himself, Conner arranged for Scott and his staff to accompany him aboard a small ship. On March 7 Scott, satisfied with the site, concurred in Conner's plan. The outing would have been unremarkable had the ship not ventured too close to the Fort of San Juan de Ulúa and drawn several Mexican shells. The Mexican gunners scored no hits, but a few shots splashed close by. A lucky round might have sunk the vessel and the United States would have lost not only Scott and Conner but all of Scott's general officers, plus critical members of his staff. George Meade, one of the members, wrote home disapprovingly that "one shot, hitting the vessel . . . might have been the means of breaking up the expedition."[11] And nobody could have foreseen the effect of such a mishap on the

*A "norther" is a very strong wind from the north. It is usually not accompanied by any precipitation, but its effect on the water and on the sandy beaches is dramatic.

American Civil War, still years in the future. The two men destined to command the Union and Confederate armies at Gettysburg were aboard, Meade and Robert E. Lee, along with Joseph E. Johnston and P.G.T. Beauregard.

The landing at Collada had been planned for the next day, March 8, but in the previous evening a norther hit and disrupted all activity that day, deferring the landing until March 9. The maneuver itself was involved, as it required all of Scott's troops to be transferred from their own ships to Conner's naval vessels and then transferred again to the flatboats. The first stage was performed during the morning, near Anton Lizardo; then the fleet sailed behind Sacrificios Island in the afternoon, and the troops clambered into the flatboats. Each boat, commanded by a naval officer, carried seventy soldiers; sailors manned the oars.

Near sunset of a picture-perfect day, Scott's men cheered as they passed him, still on the steamer *Massachusetts*. With his brigade leading the army, William J. Worth was the first man on the beach. Fire from the city and San Juan was negligible, and to Scott's surprise, only a few ineffective skirmishers greeted the first wave of 5,500 men as they splashed ashore. By evening the rest of Scott's nearly twelve thousand men had been landed. It was a remarkable operation, both for its size and for the efficiency with which it was carried out.*

Veracruz was a crowded city. Although home to fifteen thousand people, it occupied very little land. Essentially it was shaped like a half-moon, its straight "diameter" running southeast to northwest along only a mile of beach. The city was surrounded by a wall, along which stood Fort Santiago on the southeast corner and Fort Concepción on the northwest, with others in between.

Scott had already decided to reduce the city by siege rather than by assault despite protests from Worth and other impatient officers. To keep his troops at a safe distance from the Mexican artillery, he selected a trench line running along a ridge of low sand hills about two miles

*Scott, pp. 419–20. P.H.P. Conner (p. 36) claims that two ships, the *Raritan* and the *Potomac*, carried over five thousand men between Anton Lizardo and Sacrificios Island, where they met the flatboats.

from the city. To hammer the city with his artillery, he planned to place four batteries far out in front of his infantry—with infantry protection, of course. The line of dunes was long, about eight miles, and merely to occupy and organize it would require a great deal of effort. Two weeks would pass before Scott could begin active operations.[12]

Without tents, Scott's men spent an uncomfortable first night ashore; and the next morning Worth began pushing inland to occupy all of his preplanned positions. Though no Mexicans stood in his way, he was hampered by the nature of the terrain. The soft sand dunes were covered with thorny mimosa and prickly pears, forming a nearly impassable chaparral, which the soldiers had to cut with axes. Between the dunes lay stands of water to be forded or detoured. Nevertheless, Worth's men pushed on vigorously.[13]

Scott planned to position his troops by "skinning the cat." Worth's division, in the lead, was to hack its way only about a third of the distance and then stop. Patterson's volunteers would pass through to occupy the center. Twiggs's division would then continue to fill the gap from Patterson to the northwest anchor at a town called Vergara. Twiggs's task would have been easier, of course, had he landed somewhere near Vergara, but no beaches existed at that end of the line. In any case, the onerous task of cutting the chaparral was distributed as evenly as possible, and the whole position was occupied at the end of the third day.

Scott retained his headquarters near Collada at the southeast end of the line, where he could supervise the flow of supply from the beaches and remain in contact with Conner.

Another norther hit on March 13, forcing the naval vessels to seek safety in open waters, and communications between Scott's army and Conner's squadron were cut off. But some work continued on land, despite the wind-driven sand that filled holes almost as soon as they were dug. Only when the gale abated were the sailors able to begin landing the first of the mortars, artillery, and horses. The animals were particularly welcome to Twiggs's men up at Vergara, whose supplies were delivered a long distance overland.[14]

Scott now turned his attention to emplacing his artillery. He had two possible firing areas to consider. One possibility was on the water in Worth's sector, called Point Horno. This position, though exposed to

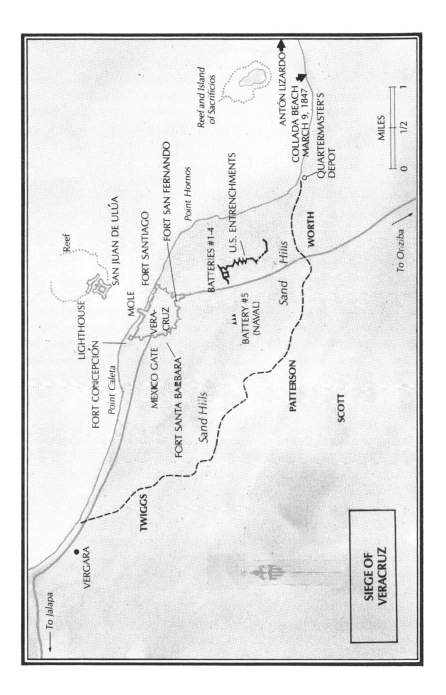

To Jalapa

VERGARA

TWIGGS

Sand Hills

FORT SANTA BARBARA

MEXICO GATE

FORT CONCEPCIÓN

Point Caleta

LIGHTHOUSE

MOLE

VERA-CRUZ

FORT SANTIAGO

FORT SAN FERNANDO

SAN JUAN DE ULÚA

Reef

BATTERIES #1-4

U.S. ENTRENCHMENTS

Point Hornos

Reef and Island of Sacrificios

ANTÓN LIZARDO

COLLADA BEACH
MARCH 9, 1847

QUARTERMASTER'S
DEPOT

BATTERY #5
(NAVAL)

Sand Hills

WORTH

To Orizaba

PATTERSON

SCOTT

Sand Hills

MILES

0   1/2   1

SIEGE OF
VERACRUZ

Mexican fire, was close in and fairly well sheltered by the ground. Scott's engineer,[15] however, soon found another that seemed preferable because it was safer and could still bring fire on the city. Scott's men began preparing this position for occupation by his ten mortars (organized into Batteries 1, 2, and 3) and later for his four twenty-four-pounder howitzers (Battery 4).

By March 18, however, Scott was becoming distraught because his heavy mortars had not arrived as he had expected. There was nothing he could do, of course, except to write Marcy in a bitter tone, pointing out that it had been "stipulated and agreed" the previous November that all his mortars would arrive at the Brazos by mid-January. "My disappointment and chagrin," he concluded, "may be imagined."* Scott was depending on those heavy mortars to pound the city into surrender.

Conner now made another offer: he could supply some heavy guns from his ships to reinforce Scott's fire on land. Scott, however, stalled on that proposition, partly because of pride, no doubt, but more because of the work necessary to move the guns ashore. Scott hoped that this expedient would not be necessary.[16] On the evening of March 19, with his artillery in place, Scott notified Conner that firing might begin the next day, in which case he would inform the commodore so that his ships could join in.[17] But again Scott delayed a couple of days, and finally, on March 21, he decided to accept Conner's offer of naval guns to join in the bombardment from the land.

Scott's reluctant request for artillery help reached Conner just as the commodore was about to turn over command of the Home Squadron to Commodore Matthew C. Perry, in accordance with orders from the Navy Department.† Scott's officers were disturbed by the change because of the high degree of mutual regard and cooperation that had been developed between Scott and Conner. Every one of Scott's officers who could be spared from pressing duties paid a call on Conner, and those who could not sent notes.

Fortunately, Commodore Perry continued Conner's policy of close cooperation and support, and his immediate response, on receiving Scott's request for heavy guns was to assent, provided the artillery was

---

*Scott to Marcy, March 18, 1847, Exec. Doc. No. 60, p. 222. He wrote Jesup an even sterner letter the next day (see Exec. Doc. No. 60, p. 913).

†The timing was regrettable in that it implied some dissatisfaction with Conner. Actually, his tour had been extended, based on the premise that the siege would occur in February.

manned by his own gunners. That arrangement being quite acceptable to Scott, the engineer troops began dragging the six monstrous guns across the sands and chaparral to their selected position. Captain Robert E. Lee, who had nearly met death at the hands of a careless sentry the night before, directed their emplacement. So well was the movement concealed behind the dunes that the Mexicans were completely unaware of it.*

Scott did not wait for the naval guns, however. On March 22 he issued an ultimatum to Mexican General Juan Morales to surrender both the city and the fort. Morales answered defiantly, and even the foreigners in the city chose to ignore Scott's warning. Scott therefore cut all communication between the city and the various neutral ships observing from the Gulf. That evening he opened fire with his mortars and howitzers.

By the next evening, March 23, the naval battery opened fire under the personal command of Captain J. H. Aulick, second in command of the Home Squadron. But the Mexicans were adept at handling heavy coast artillery, and once they recovered from their surprise, they responded. The American seamen, who had spent months of boredom blockading a country that had no navy, were delighted with the idea of fighting. They were undaunted even when a shell killed four of their number, and Commodore Perry rotated the crew daily so as to give more than one group a chance to share in "the glories."[18]

By March 25 Scott's 24-pounders were also brought into action. Thus, as of March 25, ten 10-inch mortars, four 24-pounders, two 8-inch siege howitzers, three 32-pounders, and three long 8-inch Paixhans were pounding Veracruz and its walls.

Civilians bore the brunt of the suffering in the city. Day and night the mortars, howitzers, and Paixhans bombarded the town, supplemented by broadsides from the small naval vessels. So many shells hit the Cathedral of San Agustín and the powder magazine that the Mexi-

---

*Raphael Semmes, *Service Afloat and Ashore during the Mexican War*, p. 134. These guns, claimed to be the heaviest "ever before mounted in siege," would greatly augment the fire that Scott could bring to bear on the city. Three of these 6,300-pound monsters fired solid shot of 32 pounds each, sufficient to soften the walls of the forts around the city; and the other three, called Paixhans, fired 62-pound explosive shells with exceedingly heavy casings that allowed considerable penetration before explosion.

cans accused the Americans of concentrating on these targets. The batteries at Forts Santiago, San José, San Fernando, and Santa Barbara returned the fire, as did those of San Juan de Ulúa. Mexican observers reported, however, that the Americans were able to keep four to six shells continually in the air.[19]

The effect of the bombardment was decisive. That same afternoon, March 25, the consuls of England, France, and Prussia sent a message to Scott, asking him to suspend the bombardment while the foreigners, as well as the Mexican women and children, left the city. Pointedly recalling his warning of the twenty-second, Scott refused,[20] at the same time happy that he had earlier decided to forgo an infantry assault in favor of a siege.* The sneers of Worth and others had turned out to be empty.

The foreign consuls in Veracruz had had enough. On receiving Scott's refusal of their request, they immediately cornered General Morales, asking him to surrender. Morales feigned sickness—a traditional ploy to avoid unpleasantness—and turned over command to his deputy, General J. J. Landero. Landero, who knew what was expected of him, sent Scott a message proposing that both sides appoint commissioners to arrange a "convention." Scott ordered his batteries to cease fire, and the representatives† met for the first time on the afternoon of the twenty-sixth.

The ensuing negotiations sounded like a dreary repetition of the commissioners' haggling at Monterrey, but they were shorter. At first the

---

*"We, of course, gentlemen, must take the city and castle before the return of the *vomito*—if not by headwork, the slow scientific process, by storming—and then escape, by pushing the conquest into the healthy interior. I am strongly inclined to attempt the former unless you can convince me that the other is preferable. Since our thorough reconnoissance, I think the suggestion practicable with a very moderate loss on our part.

"The second method would, no doubt, be equally successful, but at the cost of an immense slaughter to both sides, including non-combatants—Mexican men, women, and children—because assaults must be made in the dark, and the assailants dare not lose time in taking and guarding prisoners without incurring the uncertainty of becoming captives themselves, till all the strongholds of the city are occupied. The horrors of such slaughter, with the usual terrible accompaniments, are most revolting. Besides these objections, it is necessary to take into account the probable loss of some two thousand, perhaps three thousand, of our best men in the assault, and I have received but half the numbers promised me. How then could we hope to penetrate the interior?" Scott, vol. II, pp. 423–24. Scott was writing this, it must be remembered, nearly twenty years after the fact.

†R. S. Ripley, *The War with Mexico*, pp. 40–41. Americans: Worth, Pillow, and Totten. Mexicans: Colonels Herrera, Villaneuva, and Robles.

Mexicans demanded that their garrison of three thousand men be allowed to march out, without parole, carrying arms and accoutrements. That refused, they met again the next day with new instructions. The snag now lay in the fact that Morales, as Scott had suspected, had not given Landero authority to surrender Fort San Juan. But Scott's patience was running out, and when it became obvious that Scott was about to recommence the bombardment, the Mexicans signed the agreement. It was 9 P.M., March 27, 1847.

Considering the relative positions of the two sides, the terms granted the Mexican garrison were generous to the Mexican garrison. Both the city and Fort San Juan de Ulúa were to be surrendered with all arms and officers, but men were to be paroled until regularly exchanged. The garrison could march with full honors to the field where arms would be turned over. The rights of the people of Veracruz, both religious and civil, were to be respected.*

On receiving the news of the signing, an exultant Winfield Scott nearly tore the messenger from his horse to give him a hearty embrace.

---

*In the last phase, Captain Aulick, representing Commodore Perry, signed as a fourth commissioner.

U.S. Congress, Exec. Doc. No. 1, p. 237. The five thousand Mexican soldiers in the city and fort were commanded by five generals, eighteen colonels, thirty-seven lieutenant colonels, five majors, ninety captains, and 180 lieutenants. Of these Scott "as an act of grace and policy," released one general, two colonels, four lieutenant colonels, one major, ten captains, and twenty lieutenants. He sent them to Mexico City "to use a peace influence, if they will." Hitchcock, p. 247.

CERRO GORDO

APRIL 1847

Winfield Scott's objective in Mexico, consistent with Polk's, was of necessity to "conquer a peace," for a few thousand bayonets could never subjugate a unified nation of seven million people. His only hope, therefore, was to win the acceptance, if not the warm friendship, of the Mexican population.

He began this campaign by granting generous terms of surrender at Veracruz. But conciliation required that the American command comport itself well in its dealings with Mexican citizens. Enforcing discipline on the troops was difficult, as confinement and hardships they had undergone pushed them toward excesses. Scott's General Order No. 20 proclaiming martial law was directed as much toward his troops as it was toward the civilian population. And since a general order, in itself, could never deter boisterous troops from committing depradations, Scott issued a follow-up order with the plaintive comment, "Cruel have been the disappointments of the general-in-chief, and all the good officers and soldiers of this army." In that order the general restricted his troops to the city and specifically forbade any killing of domestic animals.[1] Scott meant what he said, and any disorder was dealt with severely. During the second week of April, Hitchcock witnessed the hanging of an American soldier for rape.[2]

Scott also set out to court the Roman Catholic Church in an attempt to convince the clergy that an American victory would work to their advantage. To that end he ordered American soldiers to salute priests on the streets and he personally requested permission of the clergy to conduct religious services for his troops in two of the local churches. The Mexican priests agreed to this rather startling request, provided that they could officiate themselves.

But Scott, the showman, went even further. On Sunday, April 4, he and his staff donned resplendent full-dress uniforms and joined the new city governor in attending services at the Veracruz cathedral. The priests entered into the spirit of the occasion, and an unwary General Scott was pressed into joining a procession around the church carrying a large lighted candle. The sight of the rather pompous general-in-chief thus submitting to the directions of the priests caused much suppressed amusement among Scott's staff, but at least the general had done his best. His political partisans pointed to his gesture in attending Catholic mass as proof that he was placing his military mission above his presidential aspirations at home. Word of it would inevitably cause pain among Scott's "Native American" political supporters.[3]

Veracruz, while an important city and port, was only a base from which to advance on Mexico City. The hazards of such an expedition to the center of the country were enormous, yet Scott never entertained thoughts of any lesser goal. All energies were directed toward that end.

A major decision had to be made: Which route should Scott's army follow? Assuming he would start from Veracruz,* Scott had two choices: the National Road, taken by Cortez in 1519, or the Orizaba Road.† Either one would take Scott's men out of the unhealthy lowlands quickly, but because the National Highway, by way of Jalapa, Perote, and Puebla, was in better condition at that time, Scott selected that route.

---

*Scott rejected a hypocritical letter from Marcy, obviously written for political consumption, suggesting a supply line from Tampico rather than from Veracruz, because Tampico was reputed to be less afflicted with the *vómito* during the warm months. Marcy supposedly wished to make Scott "acquainted with the views of the President in regard to preserving the health of the troops." Marcy to Scott, March 13, 1847, Exec. Doc. No. 60, p. 905.

†The French would use the other road past Orizaba in their campaign to install Maximillian in 1863 (Matthew Steele, *American Campaigns*, p. 107). The main road today follows the Orizaba Road rather than the National Highway of 1847.

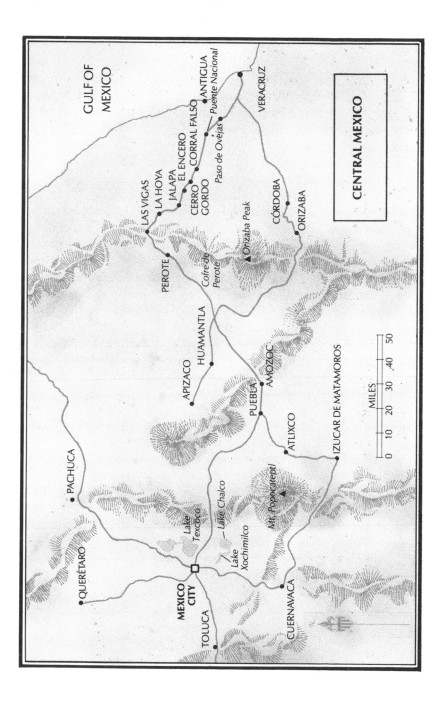

GULF OF MEXICO

ANTIGUA
Puente Nacional
VERACRUZ
CORRAL FALSO
EL ENCERO
JALAPA
LA HOYA
LAS VIGAS
CERRO GORDO
Paso de Ovejas
CÓRDOBA
ORIZABA
▲ *Orizaba Peak*
PEROTE
Cofre de Perote
HUAMANTLA
APIZACO
AMOZOC
PUEBLA
ATLIXCO
IZUCAR DE MATAMOROS
PACHUCA
QUERÉTARO
Lake Texcoco
— *Lake Chalco*
Lake Xochimilco
▲ *Mt. Popocatepl*
MEXICO CITY
TOLUCA
CUERNAVACA

CENTRAL MEXICO

MILES
0 10 20 30 40 50

Scott's main problem lay in the shortage of transportation. Ample food and ammunition were on hand, but Scott lacked the means of carrying them. Wagons would have to come from home and Scott had not the least hope that any would arrive. Therefore he placed his hopes on procuring mules from the Mexican countryside. To that end he sent a brigade under Brigadier General John Quitman to Alvarado, south of Veracruz, but few animals were obtained.[4] Another expedition, to Antigua, was partially successful. After these two efforts, Scott still had only about a quarter of the eight thousand animals he needed,[5] so he decided to send only a portion of his army ahead; the rest of his troops would be forced to wait at Veracruz until he could obtain more transport.[*]

In planning his march from Veracruz inland, Scott this time selected Twiggs rather than Worth to command the advance division. The choice was probably based on the fact that Twiggs's division, on the northward sector of the Veracruz siege perimeter, was closest to the National Highway. The vainglorious Worth, however, refused to recognize this logic and protested. When Scott replied that the other generals were also entitled to the "position of honor," Worth considered this a personal rejection. After all, he had been Scott's close friend ever since serving as his aide during the War of 1812, and had even named his son Winfield Scott Worth. With this clash, the long friendship between Scott and Worth began to unravel.

Antonio López de Santa Anna arrived back at San Luis Potosí from the battlefield of Buena Vista on March 9, 1847, the same day that Scott was landing at Veracruz. The return journey had been frightful, far more devastating than either the march northward or even the battle. His army had struggled along for sixteen days—exposed, starving, parched. In all, including the losses suffered in the battle and the two marches, some 10,500 Mexican troops had perished, well over half the number that had proudly set out from San Luis Potosí a month before.[†]

Santa Anna himself would not stay long at San Luis Potosí, for a new

*Scott never solved the problem. In the subsequent campaign he moved his army a portion at a time until he later abandoned efforts to supply from Veracruz.

†The length of time is not certain. Alcaraz, the source of this information, counts the month of February as containing thirty days. The estimate of sixteen days takes that into consideration.

revolution had broken out in Mexico City,* centered on the person of Gómez Farías, in whose lap Santa Anna had left his political troubles when he himself had found it advisable to take the field three months before.†

Gómez Farías, the idealist, had apparently changed little since his previous stint as Santa Anna's stand-in back in 1833. He was now recognized as the leader of the radical wing of the Federalist party, and had set out once again to abolish the traditional privileges of the Church and the army. In this objective, the war was his ally; not only did it keep the generals out of Mexico City; but it also created a great need for revenue, which could be provided only from the coffers of the Church. He pushed through two laws, one on January 11, 1847, and another on February 4, 1847, that called for excessive levies. The Church, alarmed, mustered enough pressure that even the followers of Gómez Farías turned against him. But he would not give up; he remained in office and put up a strong fight for both political and physical survival.

On February 27, as Santa Anna's army was staggering back from Agua Nueva, General Peña y Barragán revolted in the capital with the support of the Church. Gómez Farías showed strength, however, and the rebellion soon needed an estimated additional forty thousand dollars to continue for another week. At that point, an American agent, Moses Y. Beach, stepped in. Beach, the editor of the New York *Sun*, was in Mexico City on supposedly private business, but he had actually been sent by Polk and Buchanan to work for peace behind the scenes. Expecting that Peña and the Church would be more amenable to that end than Gómez Farías, Beach encouraged the rebels to continue. Gómez Farías arrested his political opponents, including the moderate and respected Gómez Pedraza.[6]

In early March, Peña y Barragán wrote to Santa Anna, urging him to return and "take possession of the Presidential chair." Santa Anna, on receipt of the letter, decided to take two of his fittest corps and head

---

*That upheaval had nothing to do with the Battle of Buena Vista, for that battle was viewed, for the moment, as a victory.

†In the election of December 1846, it will be recalled, Santa Anna's margin in the presidential vote was a squeaking 11 to 9. Considering his personal position to be safer in the field, he had left in haste, leaving with Gómez Farías, the elected vice president, to serve as acting president.

for Mexico City. At that point he was still not certain whether he would support Gómez Farías or Peña y Barragan; and even when he learned that the clergy would pay him two million pesos to bring about the repeal of the two objectionable laws, he still refused to commit himself.[7]

Fortune now smiled once again on Santa Anna: word arrived that Scott had landed near Veracruz, and once more the people turned to the Napoleon of the West and national unity became the watchword. On the day that Santa Anna entered the suburb of Guadalupe Hidalgo (March 21, 1847) all fighting among the factions ceased, and his prestige and power again stood supreme. He displayed captured American flags and artillery, which the people took as evidence that he had won a great victory at Buena Vista. He would win more, he promised. Most important, his arrival at Mexico City had averted bloodshed in the streets.*

Santa Anna's political future, as he well realized, depended on his defeating Scott on the battlefield. Such a feat would enable Mexico to negotiate a favorable peace with the United States and permanently establish Santa Anna as Mexican dictator. But to achieve it meant rebuilding his army quickly, and Congress was cooperative only up to a point. It authorized Santa Anna to extract twenty million pesos from the Church authorities in exchange for repeal of the two anticlerical laws,[8] and it elected his henchman Pedro María Anaya as provisional president. But it was chary with Santa Anna's requests for military funds, and with an eye to the future it even rejected some of Santa Anna's recommendations for army promotions. No matter; in public Santa Anna loudly proclaimed: "My duty is to sacrifice myself, and I will know how to fulfill it! Perhaps the American hosts may proudly tread the imperial capital of Azteca. I will never witness such opprobrium, for I am decided first to die fighting!"[9] And the people loved it.

As Scott had occupied Veracruz before Santa Anna could consolidate power in Mexico City, Santa Anna had to find a point at which to set up a defense of the capital. He calculated that Scott, after taking

---

*"The happy termination of this insurrection was owing to General Santa Anna; he saved a multitude of people, whose death would have filled Mexico with mourning." Ramón Alcaraz, *The Other Side,* p. 166.

Veracruz, would probably advance along the National Highway, so he sent three infantry brigades along that road to meet him, following up with a cavalry brigade and two thousand National Guardsmen from Perote. All were to be under the temporary command of General Valentín Canalizo, a strange, headstrong little man, recently an interim president, and a Santa Anna loyalist. Specifically Canalizo was directed to seize the National Bridge, a critical point on the highway between Cerro Gordo and Veracruz.[10]

News of the fall of Veracruz reached Santa Anna on March 30, 1847, and he realized that he must take personal command of the force in the field at once. He left Mexico City four days later, through streets crammed with screaming crowds, and soon reached his ranch, El Encero, located just beyond Jalapa. At a pass near the small town of Cerro Gordo and a hill of the same name he planned to make his stand. From the comfort of his own hacienda Santa Anna could direct preparations.

Santa Anna selected a strong position, a pass where the Highway was dominated on either side by hills, and where his right flank was protected by the Rio del Plan, a substantial stream. The key feature of the region was the hill of Cerro Gordo (Fat Mountain), also known as El Telégrafo, a broad elevation about a thousand feet high, which stood just to the left (from Santa Anna's viewpoint) of the Highway. Right of the Highway, across the road from Cerro Gordo, steep cliffs overlooked the Rio del Plan less than a half mile away.

Santa Anna's position also had depth. At about a mile in front of Cerro Gordo, between the Highway and the Rio del Plan, the ground dropped off suddenly to the front, presenting any advancing army with three steep cliffs. Together the cliffs constituted more than an outpost; they formed a defensive position of their own.

His front and right flank thus protected, Santa Anna had only to look at his left, or northern, flank. The ground north of the Highway (which ran roughly east to west at Cerro Gordo) seemed impassable. A deep ravine on the north converged with the Highway four miles ahead at Plan del Rio. About a half mile northeast of Cerro Gordo stood a flat-topped hill named La Atalaya, slightly lower and at some distance from the Highway. Between the ravine and La Atalaya the land was solid chaparral, cut up by gullies and hills, and Santa Anna decided that he need fear no attack from that direction. Scott would be forced to approach along the National Highway.

To defend this position Santa Anna had succeeded, by mid-April, in

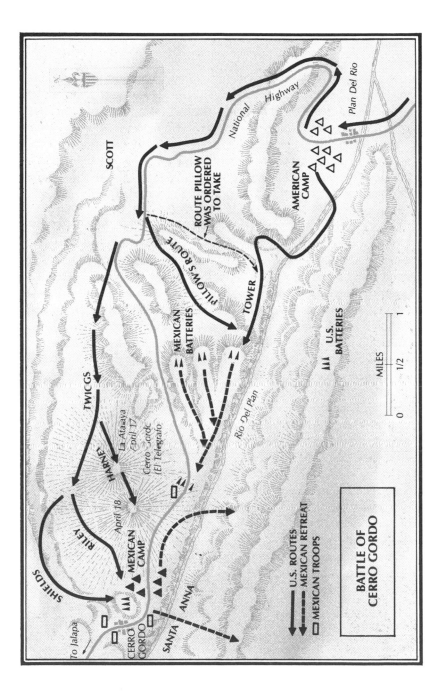

BATTLE OF
CERRO GORDO

U.S. ROUTES
MEXICAN RETREAT
MEXICAN TROOPS

MILES
0   1/2   1

Plan Del Rio

National Highway

SCOTT

AMERICAN CAMP

ROUTE PILLOW WAS ORDERED TO TAKE

PILLOW'S ROUTE

TOWER

MEXICAN BATTERIES

U.S. BATTERIES

Rio Del Plan

TWIGGS

La Atalaya
April 17

Cerro Gordo
(El Telegrafo)

HARNEY

April 18

RILEY

SHIELDS

MEXICAN CAMP

SANTA ANNA

CERRO GORDO

To Jalapa

scraping up about twelve thousand troops, supported by forty-three pieces of artillery.[11] It was a larger force than Scott's, but it was unreliable, as many of the troops, parolees from Veracruz, had been garnered only in the previous few days. Santa Anna could use these troops only in a fixed defense. He placed most of them on Cerro Gordo, but he also placed a battery of artillery on each of the three cliffs up ahead on the right. The rest he kept in reserve back at the town of Cerro Gordo. He placed only an outpost on La Atalaya. Thus disposed, he waited.

Brigadier General David E. Twiggs was exercising independent command for the first time since bringing the 2d Dragoons overland to Corpus Christi. In personality he presented a striking contrast to his competitor Worth. Twiggs was not handsome or dashing; sixty years old, of medium height, broad-shouldered and bullnecked, he was a stout and robust man, his features heavy under his "exuberant mass of tow-white hair, with beard and whiskers of the same color." His gruff appearance was consistent with his demeanor. Still, he was a favorite among his men, although one observer believed that his popularity was based on "his brusqueness and coarseness of manner, and a singular habit of swearing most vehemently . . . on the most trifling of occasions."* In his own way, Twiggs was the kind of commander that many soldiers enjoy.

On the morning of April 8 Twiggs rode at the head of his column along the National Highway toward the hills. Jalapa lay far beyond. His force consisted of 2,600 infantry, two light field batteries, six twenty-four-pounders, two eight-inch howitzers, four ten-inch mortars, and a squadron of dragoons.[12]

The march did not begin auspiciously. The first thirteen miles were slow and painful, as the men had to march through loose sand

*George Ballantine, *An English Soldier in the U.S. Army*, p. 163. At a halt along a march, some of Twiggs's men found some brandy in an apartment in the same building that Twiggs was occupying. The owner reported the looting, and Twiggs took matters into his own hands. "The anger of General Twiggs as he rushed to the scene, and the celerity with which the marauders 'vamosed the ranch,' as they heard the ominous alarm of 'here's old Davy,' transcend description. Two or three of the unlucky wights, however, he met on the threshold of the door, on their way out; these he seized by the collar and swung round till he had an opportunity of administering a sound kick to their posteriors. None of them, however, stayed to remonstrate on these rather unpleasant demonstrations of the old General's love of justice. . . ." Ballantine, pp. 168–69.

that was ankle-deep. In addition, Twiggs made the strange error of allowing the head of his column to march too fast, causing many men in the rear to fall out, risking murder by Mexican rancheros. A full third of the command dropped out; the bulk of the missing men soon caught up, but some were in no hurry, taking time to shoot cattle and plunder the houses of the Mexicans. By stages they would rejoin their units.[13]

The next day's march was easier, over level land and at a slower pace. For eight miles the column passed through cool woods. On the third day Twiggs roused the men early and took the road before sunrise. By 11 A.M. the head of the column spied the famed National Bridge, which crossed the Rio Antigua. The scenery was breathtaking here, and the few soldiers of Scottish origin found the banks of the river, with their tufts of flowering shrubs, "exceedingly like the section of a Scotch river glen."[14] The troops enjoyed the sparkling waters and paid little attention to the flimsy huts of the nearby village; they also failed to notice traces of fortifications recently constructed and demolished by General Canalizo, whose men, having heard of the fall of Veracruz, had shortly before departed panic-stricken.[15]

Twiggs's command moved forward early the next day, but the march became fatiguing as the country became hilly. By noon Twiggs entered the village of Plan del Rio, the site of a sturdy bridge over a river called the Rio del Plan. His dragoons flushed out a troop of Mexican lancers, who fled after firing a few random shots. The dragoons did not pursue; their horses were too tired.[16]

At this point Twiggs learned that Santa Anna was gathering a strong force at a pass about four miles up the National Highway. He ordered a halt, posting local security and beginning a reconnaissance of the field that would later be known as Cerro Gordo. It was the evening of April 11, 1847.

Twiggs's division was followed by that of Robert Patterson, which arrived the next day. Patterson was to automatically assume command of the sector when the forces were joined, since he carried the rank of major general. But Patterson was ill, and he consented uncomfortably to leaving the command to Twiggs, whose fighting blood was up. Twiggs began planning an assault on the Mexican position, to be launched early on April 14.

First Lieutenant Pierre G. T. Beauregard, the engineer assigned to Patterson's division, had been placed in charge of the engineers reconnoitering Twiggs's front. The work had already been started by Lieutenants Zealous B. Tower,* Joseph E. Johnston, and W.H.T. Brooks, Twiggs's aide. On the morning of April 13, Brooks conducted Beauregard along a small path he had discovered around to the right (Santa Anna's left) that promised an opportunity to flank the seemingly impregnable Mexican position along the National Highway. Undetected by Mexican outposts, Beauregard climbed to the top of La Ayatala, in sight of the crest of Cerro Gordo. Satisfied, he returned and reported to General Twiggs. Tower had meanwhile taken General Pillow, from Patterson's division, to reconnoiter the Mexican right, where Santa Anna had placed his three artillery batteries. Pillow had been designated to attack in that area.

That evening Twiggs issued his attack orders. His maneuver scheme concentrated on Pillow's assault, whose volunteers had been ordered to attack enemy batteries at bayonet point. Regimental and company commanders involved passed the word as cheerfully as possible, but none was happy. Sensing Twiggs's limitations and aware that the whole army was not present, they feared that they were "in danger of a defeat, or a victory purchased by a lavish and useless expenditure of life."[17]

Later that evening Beauregard returned to his tent at Patterson's headquarters. Patterson called to him from his sickbed and asked the lieutenant's opinion of Twiggs's plan. The plan would work, Beauregard answered, but it entailed unnecessary risks. It would be better, he thought, to concentrate the entire army against the Cerro Gordo position and conduct only a demonstration against the three batteries. Concerned, Patterson sent Beauregard to present his viewpoint to Twiggs.

Aware of the general's volatile nature, Beauregard was uncomfortable as he approached Twiggs's tent. But Twiggs was alone, in a quiet mood, and when Beauregard asked if he could express some opinions regarding the attack, he willingly assented.

Beauregard knew that Patterson and Twiggs bore no love for each other, and therefore, despite his modest rank, Beauregard decided to take responsibility for his mission upon his own shoulders. He outlined

---

*Zealous Bates Tower, first in the West Point Class of 1841. (Beauregard was second in the Class of 1838.) Tower later became a major general, U.S. Volunteers, and briefly superintendent of West Point. Johnston became a general, CSA.

his views, emphasizing the advantages of concentrating all available forces against Cerro Gordo itself.

Twiggs paused and reflected. "You may be right, sir," he said. "But it is already late, I have given my orders, and to change them now might occasion too much confusion and uncertainty. Don't you think we will succeed anyhow?"

"Certainly, sir, but I think we ought to throw all the chances in our favor."

The conversation turned out to be academic. Patterson, becoming more worried with each passing hour, took himself off sick report and assumed command that evening.* At about 11:00 P.M., as officers and soldiers alike sat despondent around their campfires, news arrived that Patterson had postponed the attack. Countenances instantly brightened, and "all retired to sleep, carrying the news that the attack was deferred until Scott came up."[18]

Scott arrived at Plan del Rio at noon on April 14, and was cheered loudly by his troops.† Without waiting for rest or refreshment, he plunged immediately into his plans to attack the Mexican position, although there was no need for quick action. His army was now clear of the *vómito* region, and he had time to make a thorough study of Santa Anna's position. Scott hoped that the route around the Mexican left would render a frontal attack unnecessary, and he assigned Captain Robert E. Lee, who had come with him from Veracruz, to direct the scouting; Beauregard, who had taken sick, was relegated to limited duties with the staff.

Lee began his reconnaissance the morning after his arrival, following Beauregard's route and confirming its feasibility—so far as it went. But

---

*Pierre Beauregard, *With Beauregard in Mexico*, pp. 32–38. Twiggs's reaction is unknown, but it could not have been pleasant. Beauregard, who thought well of Twiggs, claimed later to believe that Twiggs would yet have altered his plan to fit Beauregard's.

†Their enthusiasm was heightened by the impressive display of military attire. Grant wrote later, "General Scott . . . always wore all the uniform prescribed or allowed by law when he inspected his lines; word would be sent to all division and brigade commanders in advance, notifying them of the hour when the commanding general might be expected. This was done so that all the army might be under arms to salute their chief as he passed. On these occasions he wore his dress uniform, cocked hat, aiguillets, sabre, and spurs. His staff proper, besides all officers constructively on his staff—engineers, inspectors, quartermasters, etc., that could be spared—followed, also in prescribed uniform and in prescribed order." U.S. Grant, *Personal Memoirs*, vol. I, pp. 138–39.

Lee carried the search further to the Mexican rear, crossing several gullies until he was satisfied he had passed the main flank.* Lee reported his findings, and Scott ordered a road (hereafter called the Trail) constructed along that route. Hacking through the thick woods would be risky as well as arduous work, but the construction parties apparently escaped detection.

By the morning of Saturday, April 17, with Worth's division having arrived from Veracruz, Scott was ready to attack. He sent Twiggs along the newly cut Trail, expecting him to occupy and bivouac at La Atalaya, preparatory to a major attack the next morning on Cerro Gordo and the Jalapa road. Though Scott had only 8,500 effectives against an estimated 12,000 to 18,000 Mexicans, he never doubted success.†

Twiggs's division was at that time organized into two infantry brigades, normally those of Colonels Persifor F. Smith and Bennet Riley. Smith was sick that day, so Scott detached Colonel W. S. Harney to command his brigade. And to give Twiggs the needed strength, Scott attached Shields's brigade of volunteers to him.

"Old Davy" roused his men at 4:30 A.M. and soon moved out along the National Highway. After covering about three miles he turned off to the right, onto the Trail. The Trail was rough, and it took him four hours to cover only four miles to the foot of La Atalaya. In accordance with Scott's "suggestion," Twiggs then sent a company of the 7th Infantry to occupy the hill, expecting to brush aside the Mexican pickets.

It was not to be that easy. Mexican troops appeared from Cerro Gordo and counterattacked up the northwest slope of La Atalaya. Twiggs thereupon committed Harney's brigade on the other side with the order "First Artillery and Rifles fall into line, and charge up the hill!" The hill was taken, but someone asked Twiggs how far to push. Twiggs, in the heat of battle, shouted "Charge'em to hell!" His troops took his order too literally and continued pursuit halfway to Cerro Gordo, much too far. The small force was soon pinned down by thou-

---

*Freeman (R.E. Lee, vol. I, pp. 238–241) gives a dramatic account of Lee's being trapped at a spring, where the Mexicans came to draw water. Lee was forced to spend much of a day hidden behind a log only feet from where the soldiers came periodically to rest. Freeman does not, however, pinpoint the exact location of the spring.

†Justin Smith, The War with Mexico, vol. II, p. 50. Scott's orders to Twiggs were verbal. Thus Smith, through his extensive research, has determined these orders by the memories of witnesses.

sands of Mexican infantry and a crossfire of artillery. To retreat was impossible, so those in the advance simply bided their time, hiding behind rocks and trees, sending back occasional shots against desultory Mexican fire until sunset made it safe to retreat to La Atalaya. Toward the end of the afternoon the Mexicans seemed to form up in preparation for a charge, but one mountain howitzer, loaded with grape, threw them into confusion with a single shot.[19]

Thus ended a day that was supposed to have seen only an approach march. Several units were employed to extricate the forces that had gone too far, and U.S. losses were heavy. Twiggs's force camped that night on Atalaya. Santa Anna, believing the attack to have been Scott's main effort, exulted in his "victory."*

Earlier that afternoon Scott had issued General Order No. 111, assigning specific missions for the next day's attack. Twiggs was to continue through the woods, beyond the end of the Trail, to seize ground controlling the National Highway as it wandered westward from the Mexican rear. This would be difficult; the woods were thick, and none of the scouting missions had actually reached the extension of that road. Shields was to remain attached to Twiggs, and Worth was to follow Shields.

As a secondary attack, Pillow was to march in the early morning "along the route he has carefully reconnoitred" and, upon hearing the "report of arms on our right," was to "pierce the enemy's line," the three batteries between the Highway and the river, ahead of Cerro Gordo. He was to attack, "the nearer to the river the better—as he may select." Pillow was then to turn "right or left, or both," to attack the batteries in the rear or, if they were abandoned, to pursue.[20]

So confident was Scott that he added: "This pursuit may be continued many miles, until stopped by darkness or enemy fortifications, toward Jalapa."[21]

.   .   .

*Justin Smith, *The War with Mexico*, vol. II, pp. 50–52. Scott, in his report of April 23, 1847, was typically generous. Twiggs, he wrote, "was, of necessity, drawn into action in taking up the ground for its bivouack and the opposing height for our artillery. It will be seen that many of our officers and men were killed or wounded in this sharp combat—handsomely commenced by a company of the 7th infantry. . . ." Scott to Marcy, April 23, 1847, Exec. Doc. No. 1, pp. 261–62.

The attack of April 18 began with an assault on Cerro Gordo from La Atalaya, atop which the Americans had laboriously hauled a twenty-four-pounder the previous night. Harney remained in command of the lead brigade, consisting of the 3d and 7th infantries, and C. F. Smith's dismounted "red-leg infantry." Harney's own 1st Dragoons would cover his left.

The attack was fierce but decisive. In the taciturn language of an official report, Scott stated that "Twiggs's division, storming the strong and vital point of Cerro Gordo, pierced the centre, gained command of all the entrenchments, and cut them off from support."[22]

In the more poetic words of a dramatic historian, Harney more than justified his earlier retention of command: "Superbly tall, his athletic figure needed no plume; the sword in his long arm waved them on; like the keen edge of a billow rushing upon the shore his calm, shrill voice rode the tumult."[23]

The Mexicans, of course, saw the attack differently. The Americans, they conceded, charged "with firmness, deploying as skirmishers, covering themselves among the bushes and briers." The din of musketry equaled the excitement of the fight. They saw "death, flapping her wings over that bloody field," fire and thick smoke, thousands of men "crimsoned with the contest." Mexicans and Americans alike "fell in heaps in the midst of the confusion," and were "instantly replaced by others." They saw "the gallant General Vasquez" fall, in all his energies, "with a glorious death, amidst the tumult of battle." They were overwhelmed by the superior numbers of the Americans, who first gained the lower works of the position and, "without losing an instant," quickly assaulted the crest.

Mexican reinforcements charged in eagerly, bayonets fixed, only to find themselves fighting hand to hand with a superior enemy. Surrounded on all sides, the defenders panicked and fell into disorder, literally rolling together, "borne along by the multitude, which poured onward like a torrent from the height."[24]

Cerro Gordo had fallen to Scott.

Scott's intense desire to avoid offending his masters in Washington was reflected in his preliminary report to Secretary Marcy: "Brigadier General Pillow and his brigade twice assaulted with great daring the enemy's line of batteries on our left; and though without success, they contributed much to distract and dismay their immediate opponents."[25] These judicious words glossed over the failure of Pillow's secondary attack on the three Mexican batteries between the Highway and the Rio del Plan.

The failure of that attack did not have a catastrophic effect on the battle as a whole; success at Cerro Gordo and the Mexican rear made it of little consequence. But many lives were needlessly lost, and relations between Scott and Pillow began to deteriorate.

The employment of Pillow's brigade of two Tennessee and two Pennsylvania regiments against those three formidable batteries was a questionable mission, to be sure. Beauregard, for one, had recommended only a demonstration, not an attack. Perhaps Scott expected Pillow to confine his activities to a demonstration, but Pillow's orders read otherwise. Certainly that was the way Pillow saw it.

Though an aggressive debater, Pillow was no shock trooper on the battlefield. So when he received his orders, he protested, calling his mission a "desperate undertaking." Scott tried to reassure him: Pillow was not to attack until he heard firing from the Cerro Gordo, at which time the entire Mexican line should collapse, he said. But Pillow was not to be calmed. In a burst of histrionics, he declared that as a soldier he would follow Scott's orders even if—as he expected—"he left his bones there." In his agitation he would not budge from the meeting until Scott subtly mentioned the word "discipline," at which point Pillow stalked out.[26]

Pillow's mission was open to question, but his execution of it caused chaos. He began by quarreling with Lieutenant Tower, who was intimately familiar with the ground, over the best approach route to the attack position, insisting on following a trail that would continually expose his flank to fire from the three batteries.* He then became exasperated with his commanders. One outburst, directed at Colonel Wyncoop, of the 1st Pennsylvania, was loud enough to alert the Mexican batteries, who began pouring grape into the 2d Tennessee. Its commander, Colonel William T. Haskell, then decided on his own to attack, at which time seven or eight pieces of new Mexican artillery appeared. Haskell's men fell back in confusion.[27]

---

*George McClellan, *The Mexican War Diary*, pp. 81–82, believed that Tower should have been more forceful. But McClellan was the worst kind of military pedant. That morning he had bade farewell to his friends as if not expecting to see them again, as he had been designated to die with the volunteers.

Pillow then lost control of himself, engaging Haskell in a shouting match and soon disappearing from the field after receiving a minor wound in the arm.*

The Mexican position on Cerro Gordo had collapsed by 10 A.M., however, and white flags soon appeared on the Mexican lines in front of Pillow. Disappointed, Colonel Wyncoop was determined to attack with his 1st Pennsylvania anyway. "Tell General Pillow," Wyncoop warned, "that if I don't get an order to charge in half an hour, I'll be damned if I don't charge anyhow."[28] But he relented before causing more carnage.

Though Twiggs's main attack was made on Cerro Gordo, Scott's original plan had actually called for the main effort to cut the National Highway in the Mexican rear. Twiggs, however, had become preoccupied with the fight between La Atalaya and Cerro Gordo and he sent Shields's brigade, which consisted of the 3d Illinois, 4th Illinois, and the New York Regiment, to cut the road alone. By the morning of the eighteenth Shields was ready to head north of the main position and descend on the five-gun Mexican battery at the village of Cerro Gordo.

Shields's route, now well beyond the ground previously monitored, was extremely difficult, even though the distance was only two miles. His men broke out of the woods at about the same time that Cerro Gordo came under final attack. But Shields commanded only three hundred raw volunteer infantry against two thousand Mexican cavalry and a five-gun battery. His men were repulsed and Shields himself was seriously wounded in the head.† But the Mexicans had no idea of knowing how many Americans were following Shields through the woods. "The Yankees! They have come out to the road! Every one for himself!" Cries like these went up and down the line. Combined with

---

*McClellan, p. 84. The most damning accusation came from a Pennsylvania volunteer: "By this time, Brig.-Gen. Gideon Johnston Pillow . . . was seen going down the hill in our rear, and was no more seen or heard from until the whole engagement was over. . . . Our regiment, in fact the whole division, began to get impatient and excited in not getting orders from our generals to charge. . . . The question now is asked, where was Gens. Patterson and Pillow during this heavy firing? They were not where they promised to be, nor could the three messengers sent by Col. Wyncoop to find them. So where was Gens. Patterson and Pillow? Echo answers, Where?" J. Jacob Oswandel, *Notes on the Mexican War*, pp. 127–28.

†The first reports reaching Scott were that Shields had been mortally wounded. Scott liked Shields, and the grief he expressed in his initial report was sincere.

an attack by Riley's brigade on Shields's left, the Mexican defense collapsed.[29]

During the battle, Santa Anna had first taken station along the National Highway with his three forward batteries. Later, when the action switched to the hill of Cerro Gordo, he had gone there. But once Shields cut the highway behind him, Santa Anna had realized that the battle was lost, so he had assembled a small party and tried to escape toward Jalapa. But it was too late; Shields had cut the road. Santa Anna's personal carriage was riddled with shot, his six mules killed. Worst of all, he lost six thousand dollars, with which he purportedly intended to pay his army. Santa Anna fled the field on foot, starting toward the American camp and then cutting through small pathways across the Rio del Plan, toward Orizaba and temporary safety. Thousands of Mexican troops ran in the same direction, every tie of command and obedience broken, "safety alone being the object, and all being involved in a frightful whirl." The desperate men left a track of blood on the road, and all military distinction and respect disappeared. Badges of rank became "marks for sarcasms, that were only meted out according to their grade and humiliation."[30]

The Battle of Cerro Gordo had resulted in a victory far more complete than even Scott had expected. Indeed, the three thousand prisoners created an "embarrassment." Scott was probably relieved that over a thousand escaped.[31]

In the words of one Mexican reporter: Cerro Gordo was lost! Mexico was open to the iniquity of the invader.[32]

"MR. POLK'S WAR"

❧ ❧

A s the year 1846 faded into 1847, the mood of the American people toward the war with Mexico began to sour. The disenchantment had begun earlier—protest had, in fact, always existed—but now, some eight months since Polk's first call for volunteers, disaffection was growing to the point where it might hinder the war effort.

The outburst of patriotism in response to Taylor's perceived danger on the Rio Grande had lasted throughout the summer of 1846. The War Bill, which provided generously for the prosecution of the war, had passed overwhelmingly in both houses of Congress despite the refusal of John Quincy Adams and thirteen other die-hard abolitionist congressmen to make the vote unanimous. The Immortal Fourteen, as their admirers dubbed them, were generally regarded as irresponsible, and only Adams's prestige as a former president saved him from being tarred with the same brush.

Though doubts about the war respected no geographical boundaries, serious protest was concentrated in New England. True, one of the leading abolitionist Whigs, second only to Adams, was Congressman Joshua Giddings, of Ohio. But the real hotbed was Massachusetts, the traditional spawning ground of radicalism from the days of the Boston

Tea Party. There abolitionist literary figures resisted the war from the outset. One of them, a twenty-seven-year-old poet and literary critic named James Russell Lowell, wrote the first of his celebrated "Biglow Papers" when the ink was hardly dry on the War Bill.* And Henry David Thoreau, enraged over the Massachusetts governor's call for volunteers, voluntarily went to jail for refusing to pay his state taxes. (He was bailed out by friends after one night.)

But these early protests were ineffective. The conservatives, the dominant wing of the Whig party, reasoned that their predecessors, the Federalists, had become extinct because of their refusal to support the War of 1812. Thus while Whig conservatives, such as Daniel Webster, roundly criticized Polk's manipulative actions in bringing on the conflict, they still voted the means to support it. Whigs, as a whole, regarded Lowell as extreme; and even Ralph Waldo Emerson, despite his personal disapproval of the war, viewed Thoreau's gesture as empty. After all, none of the taxes Thoreau refused to pay would have contributed, even indirectly, to financing the armies in Mexico.

The American people retained the patriotic fervor that had engulfed them in spring, 1846. Zachary Taylor's early victories at Palo Alto and Resaca de la Palma, after all, had been fought by regular troops from "somewhere else." For some time the optimism prevalent in nearly all of the U.S. conflicts remained. The people believed that the war would be won quickly and cheaply.

As the summer of 1846 dragged on, however, impatience began to set in. After the first heady victories nothing more happened. Volunteers returned home without having seen battle; some died of disease and their bereaved loved ones were denied the satisfaction of knowing that they had met a heroic death. As discontent grew, some of the

---

*Lowell's first protest poem was published as early as June 17, 1846, in the Boston *Courier*. It was written in Yankee dialect, the first of a series later published as the Biglow Papers. After condemning war as murder, the poem labeled the war as a scheme of "them nigger-driven States":

> They may talk o' Freedom's airy
>   Tell they's pupple in the face,—
> It's a grand gret cemetary
>   For the barthrights of our race;
> They jest want this Californy
>   So's to lug new slave-states in
> To abuse ye, an' to scorn ye,
>   And to plunder ye like sin.

James Russell Lowell, *The Biglow Papers*, Boston, 1848. Quoted in John H. Schroeder, *Mr. Polk's War*, which has a complete treatment of dissent during the Mexican War.

criticism was directed toward even Taylor himself, the public's favorite.*

While the public was waiting for signs of action on the Rio Grande in the late summer of 1846 the link between the war with Mexico and the expansion of slavery came to the forefront in the Congress. Polk unwittingly triggered this development.

In early August, just as Congress was nearing adjournment, the President asked for an appropriation of $2 million, to be kept on hand for payment to any Mexican government that would sign a treaty. Such a payment Polk regarded as a sort of "earnest money," an advance against whatever sum would be paid later for territorial concessions.

Polk's thought, reasonable enough, was that such an amount of ready cash would ensure that the signatory Mexican government would survive long enough to allow for Senate ratification. But the request had far-reaching consequences, for it confirmed what many had suspected all along: that Polk intended to annex territory as a result of the war. In turn it directed the attention of Congress to the possible consequences of territorial expansion. Sectionalism was thus introduced as an issue in the Mexican War, and the two political parties were now, for the first time, broken into four: proslave and abolitionist Whigs; and proslave and abolitionist Democrats.

As this $2 million bill was being debated in Congress, a radical Democratic congressman from Pennsylvania introduced a critical amendment. David Wilmot, following the lead of New York representative Hugh White, introduced the famous Wilmot Proviso, which placed as a condition for approval of the $2 million bill a stipulation "that, as an express and fundamental condition to the acquisition of any territory from the Republic of Mexico by the United States . . . neither slavery nor involuntary servitude shall ever exist in any part of said territory."[1] The amendment, actually, was not a device to help secure passage of the bill: rather, it had the effect of defining the Whig opposition to it. So while the $2 million bill as amended passed the House by a narrow margin, it fell victim to a filibuster in the Senate. Polk received word of the outcome on August 10, 1846, and expressed

*The resulting pressure made Taylor move prematurely to Monterrey.

disgust with both the rejection of the appropriation bill and the amendment—"mischievous" in his eyes—that had defeated it.[2]

On October 2, 1846, word reached Washington of Kearny's capture
of Santa Fe. Stockton's occupation of California and Taylor's victory
at Monterrey became known soon thereafter. To most people these
were good tidings, but to those who feared expansionism the actions
of both Kearny and Stockton in proclaiming U.S. annexation of these
territories were illegal. Polk astutely sidestepped these protests by passing the blame to the commanders themselves, and since Congress was
in recess, the repercussions were minimal. But with the fall of Monterrey came the first substantial casualty lists. And worse, the public was
now coming to realize that Santa Anna, whom Polk had permitted to
run the blockade off Veracruz, had no intention of making peace.

   Thus, by the third week of October 1846, while Polk and his cabinet
were secretly discussing a campaign to bring the war to Veracruz,[3] the
public was becoming conscious that the war would be long and that
more volunteers would have to be called up. This distressing situation
was attributed almost universally to the "mendaciousness" of Polk. In
the words of the Boston *Atlas,* the conflict had become "Mr. Polk's
War."[4]

   The growing mistrust of Polk was caused partly by the circumstances
of his nomination and election, enhanced by outrage at his deft maneu-
vering the previous May. The airing of Polk's orders to Kearny and
Stockton added fuel to the fire. But the mistrust was directed basically
toward the personality of Polk himself. He was viewed as a small-time
Tennessee politician, a "cold, narrow, methodical, dogged, plodding,
obstinate partisan, deeply convinced of his importance and responsibility, very wanting in humor, very wanting in ideality, very wanting
in soulfulness, inclined to be sly, and quite incapable of seeing things
in a great way."[5] But of all these faults, his lack of humor may have
been his worst shortcoming, for without that weapon against calumny,
he was vulnerable to the most unfair of the accusations that were
brought against him.

   Those accusations reached out to include his cabinet as well as
himself. As the Washington correspondent of the Boston *Atlas* commented, they were the "little fellows," and "were they all thrown in

a bag together, it would make little difference which came out first."[6] Such attacks were important not for their truth, such as it was, but for the effect they had on people's attitudes.

Polk responded to criticism of himself in the humorless manner that might be expected. He made no effort to develop himself into a more appealing, more effective politician. Instead he struck back, condemning his detractors. In his second State of the Union Message, delivered on December 8, 1846, he spent about eight thousand words dwelling on the rightness of every United States position vis-à-vis Mexico beginning as far back as 1819. Then, even in the face of the $2 million bill and his secret orders to Kearny and Stockton, he stuck to his claim that territorial gains were not the object of the war:

> The war has not been waged with a view to conquest, but, having been commenced by Mexico, it has been carried into the enemy's country and will be vigorously prosecuted there with a view to obtain an honorable peace, and thereby secure ample indemnity. . . ."[7]

And then he went on to condemn anyone who disagreed with him. The terms "unjust, unnecessary, and aggression," he declaimed, were devised to "encourage the enemy and to protract the war." Advocating and adhering to the Mexican cause would "give them 'aid and comfort.' "[8] In effect he declared it unpatriotic to criticize the justness of the war.

The second session of the Twenty-ninth Congress, which met in the late summer of 1846, would be responsible for the continued prosecution of the war. By the end of the session, the following March, the terms of service for the first volunteers would be nearly up, and more manpower would have to be raised and more funds appropriated. Fortunately, the peak of dissent had not yet been reached. Had Congress been faced with the same decisions only six months later, the outcome of the Mexican War might have been quite different. As it was, the fear of appearing unpatriotic still prevailed, and the President received most—if not all—of the support he requested.

In his State of the Union Message, Polk had asked for authority to float a $23 million twenty-year loan to cover rising governmental costs, a figure that could be reduced if he were given the authority to impose an additional revenue duty on certain articles, and if he could offer more attractive terms for sales of public lands. He also revived his request for a $2 million down payment for lands to be purchased from Mexico, which figure was soon raised to $3 million. This request, of course, had been frustrated the previous August.[9] So much for the finances; he also needed troops.

Marcy's report of December 5, 1846, had recommended the raising and organizing of ten new regiments of regulars (one of dragoons and nine of infantry). And while a request for this augmentation was not included in the President's message, it was introduced in the House later that month. The authorization bill passed the House quickly, on January 11, 1847, prompted primarily by concern over Worth's position at Saltillo, which was reportedly precarious.[10] So far so good. But Polk stirred up the rancor of the Congress by pursuing his quixotic request to establish the new rank of lieutenant general in the army, still intending to bestow it on Senator Benton.[11] Not only did this measure stand no chance, but it provided a rallying point on which Whigs and Calhoun Democrats (as well as those concerned with military competence) could agree.* It soon became apparent that Calhoun, controlling the votes of four loyal senators, held the balance of power between the thin Democratic majority and the united Whigs.

Calhoun, like the conservative Whigs, was disposed to be cautious when it came to obstructing measures needed to supply the armies; nevertheless he seemed to enjoy exercising his ability to make Polk worry. Using his voting bloc, he managed to delay passage of the Ten-Regiment Bill in the Senate; in fact, on the evening of Monday, February 8, Senator Lewis Cass came by the White House to tell Polk that the Senate had killed a compromise version between the two houses that would have provided those troops. Polk accurately blamed Calhoun. But the measure was not really dead. Two days later another

---

*Benton's hope to take command of the army in Mexico died hard. Even after the creation of a lieutenant generalcy was rejected in Congress, Benton and Senator Allen called on Polk in late January, Benton declaring that he would accept the command in Mexico at any rank, major general or lieutenant colonel. Later, in early March 1847, Polk actually commissioned Benton as a major general, but upon learning that Polk could not place him in command in Mexico without replacing Scott, Taylor, Butler, and Patterson, Benton declined. It is noteworthy that Sam Houston felt that the promotions should have been tendered to him rather than to Benton. Polk, *Diary*, January 23, 1847, pp. 190–91; March 3, 1847, p. 200; March 10, 1847, p. 202.

compromise was found and the two houses passed it.[12] And both the loan bill and the military appropriations bill passed with whopping majorities.*

On Saturday, April 10, 1847, President Polk made one of the truly important decisions of the war when he selected Nicholas P. Trist as emissary to negotiate a peace with Mexico. The decision was made quickly.

On that spring day a fast ship pulled into Baltimore harbor from Pensacola bringing the welcome news that Veracruz had surrendered to General Scott on March 27. The message was addressed to the Baltimore *Sun,* whose editors placed the happy tidings on the telegraph to Washington only after making use of it first. On receiving the word, though unofficially, Polk for once allowed himself to exult; "This was joyful news," he wrote in his diary. Two hours later a detailed report arrived from Baltimore by train.[13]

Immediately Polk assembled his cabinet. The fall of Veracruz, he announced, called urgently for a commissioner vested with plenipotentiary powers. Such a man should be on hand at General Scott's headquarters, "ready to take advantage of circumstances as they might arise to negotiate for peace."[14]

The cabinet readily agreed to this principle, but the problem of selecting such a commissioner was not so easy; the prestige to be gained by negotiating a peace treaty would be an incalculable asset to any politician harboring presidential ambitions for 1848. And giving such a plum to one man would stir up sufficient jealousy among other Democratic senators as to jeopardize ratification of any treaty, regardless of its provisions.

Polk, in the final analysis, desired instinctively to keep control of the process himself. That consideration would point toward sending his own man, the secretary of state. Buchanan agreed, but argued, quite rightly, that he personally could not leave his position in Washington to cool his heels indefinitely at Scott's headquarters in Mexico. However, he had been thinking about this problem, and he came up with

---

*The loan bill passed the House 165 to 22; the Senate 43 to 2. The appropriations bill passed the House by 152 to 28; the Senate, by roll call. Journal of the House of Representatives, 29th Cong., 2d Sess.; Senate Journal, 29th Cong., 2d Sess. Quoted in John H. Schroeder, *Mr. Polk's War,* p. 72.

a ready solution: to deputize the Chief Clerk of the State Department, Nicholas P. Trist, to go in his stead.

Trist possessed many qualifications for this responsibility. In the hierarchy of the time, he was the highest ranking professional officer in the State Department. He carried impressive credentials: he had studied law under Thomas Jefferson (to whom he was related by marriage), he had been a cadet at West Point, and he had been Andrew Jackson's private secretary. He was fluent in Spanish and well acquainted with the ways of Latin Americans, having been the United States consul at Havana. He was dignified, intelligent, personable, and energetic. Trist seemed ideal, and Polk was taken with the idea of sending him.

Polk interviewed Trist that same afternoon, and without hesitation the latter agreed to sail immediately for Veracruz. During the conversation, Polk warned his new representative that the instructions to be issued him would be sealed, their contents highly secret and not to be divulged even to Scott. In fact, Polk even balked for a moment at allowing another State Department member to assist in preparing the instructions.

Trist understood; he would carry with him the draft of a treaty of peace—and the hope that the Mexican government would accept it.[15]

"I BEG
TO BE RECALLED"

APRIL–JUNE 1847

Once more in his roller-coaster career Santa Anna was fleeing for his life. He sat silent as his horse picked its way into the steep valley of the Rio del Plan and as he and his fellow refugees forded the river and ascended the other side. Parties of Americans, he knew, were probably somewhere about, but no gringos materialized, and as Santa Anna, Ampudia, and others rode along, they gradually gathered up a small detachment. Once across the river, they turned abruptly westward toward Jalapa, hoping to reach Santa Anna's ranch, El Encero. As they rode along, gunfire heard across the Rio del Plan told them that the Americans were still mopping up the remnants of Santa Anna's army.

On approaching El Encero, Santa Anna's party spotted American cavalry in the distance. The Americans saw them also and fired. Santa Anna quickly changed plans; he gave up hope of reaching his ranch and turned his party southward toward Orizaba.[1]

Santa Anna was despondent. A few hours earlier he had sat proud in the saddle, "possessed of power and of hopes of the brightest glory"; he was now "humbled and confused, seeking among the wretched a refuge to flee to." Those "wretched," however, were far from subservient. At one point Santa Anna asked a nearby curate to exchange horses,

as his own was worn out. The clergyman refused. Santa Anna's followers secretly applauded the priest's defiance, but they stayed on with
Santa Anna.

Early the next morning the party came upon a comfortable hacienda
whose owner was hospitable, and Santa Anna decided to stay awhile.
But that night the worried overseer warned that an American party was
approaching. Santa Anna called for his comfortable litter, but his
orderlies managed to make it "unready for his use," so he once again
left on horseback. Cold and exhaustion began to take their toll, but
Santa Anna's party finally reached the town of Orizaba two days later.
There they were met by the dignitaries of the town, along with some
generals who had arrived earlier.

At Orizaba the atmosphere was also hostile, but along the way Santa
Anna had received a touch of encouragement. At the small but prosper-
ous town of Huatusco the ayuntamiento had treated him with such
sincere respect as to restore the dictator's hope of once more regaining
power. But Santa Anna showed his rising spirits in his own peculiar
way, by pouring out his anger at a group of fleeing soldiers, "uttering
a thousand unbecoming expressions, and cruelly chastising them with
his whip." So at Orizaba a hopeful Santa Anna, ignoring the prevailing
sullenness, set about reassembling what troops he could. Soon he had
organized a personal escort of four thousand men.[2]

The immediate reaction of the Americans after Cerro Gordo was one
of relief—collective relief that the battle had been won so easily and
personal relief at having survived. The troops of Twiggs's division were
shaking hands and congratulating one another, eyes glistening and
voices trembling, when they spied General Scott approaching. The
men crowded about as he spoke:

> Brother soldiers, I am proud to call you brothers, and your country
> will be proud to hear of your conduct this day. Our victory has cost us
> the lives of a number of brave men, but they died fighting for the honour
> of their country. Soldiers, you have a claim on my gratitude for your
> conduct this day, which I will never forget.[3]

Stilted, perhaps—a pompous version of Henry V—but sincere. The
general spoke with hat in hand, though still mounted, and he was "very

much affected, and tears rolled over the furrowed cheeks of the majestic old hero." And "many a rough and weather-beaten countenance" shed "sympathetic drops." Scott rode off, bowing and waving his hat.[4]

But little time could be wasted on exultation. Much remained to be done, the most immediate of which was the inevitable burying of the dead. Scott employed Mexican prisoners as well as American troops for the purpose. As always, it was a grisly task, but it was also a pathetic one. A large number of young women lay strewn among the corpses, women who had followed their husbands and lovers when Santa Anna had scraped up his makeshift civilian army. They, as well as the men, had paid the price.*

The scene of carnage also had its humanitarian side. Mexican surgeons remaining on the field not only aided their own countrymen but also treated Americans. General Shields reportedly survived his head wound only through the efforts of a Mexican surgeon. One cynic had a theory for the doctor's competence: he "came from a land unmatched for the practice it provided in curing wounds of all the shooting and stabbing varieties." And there was an occasional chuckle. One woman, shot in the leg, at first refused to allow the surgeon to examine the wound, although such modesty was considered "extremely rare among the women of the lower classes in Mexico."[5]

Once the dead were buried and the wounded cared for, Scott turned his attention to the future. Almost immediately he decided, over the objections of many, to release the Mexican prisoners he had taken, placing them on parole.† He had not the means, he explained, to feed them.

But while part of the army was cleaning up, the Americans' pursuit of the fragmented Mexican army continued toward Jalapa, only four miles away. By now General Patterson had recovered from his sickness sufficiently to command this pursuit, and he did it with gusto. One of

*"Among these we observed the body of a young and handsome though coarsely attired female, apparently not more than eighteen years of age. She had been the wife of one of the soldiers, and had stayed with him during the action. Perhaps they were newly married, and had been spending their honeymoon amid the horrid din of war. One could scarcely help wondering which among that group of ghastly corpses had been her husband. For among them he must be; it would be impossible to picture him flying on the road to Jalapa, and leaving behind the bleeding corpse of his young and beautiful bride." George Ballantine, *An English Soldier in the U.S. Army*, pp. 199–200.

†Hitchcock, inspector general, estimated 199 officers and 2,837 men were paroled. Another 1,000 had escaped. K. Jack Bauer, *The Mexican War*, p. 168. Scott reported American losses at 63 killed, 367 wounded (Exec. Doc. No. 1, p. 974).

his units, the 4th Illinois, took time out to loot Santa Anna's former campsite, where they picked up a wooden leg, undoubtedly one that had belonged to the president himself. Some of the jealous regulars questioned the authenticity of the leg's previous ownership, but the ornate limb provided a grand prize to send to the United States. For years thereafter it was proudly displayed in the Illinois State Capitol.[6]

Jalapa was a pretty town, a welcome relief to troops who had spent months of discomfort on the water, in the trenches around Veracruz, and on the road to Cerro Gordo. Kirby Smith, the melancholy captain of the 3d Infantry, found the mountain village the "prettiest town I have seen, surrounded by the finest country with the most delicious climate in the world, the thermometer never rising above eighty degrees or falling much below sixty." In the town was a chapel originally built by Cortez, now joined with a Franciscan monastery.

And yet Smith's delight was tempered with foreboding. Even the decisive battle of Cerro Gordo, he predicted, would not terminate the war. The Americans would have to take every town and fortress in the nation. "What a stupid people they are!" he fumed. "They can do nothing and their continued defeats should convince them of it. They have lost six great battles; we have captured six hundred and eighty cannon, nearly one hundred thousand stand of arms, made twenty thousand prisoners, have the greatest portion of their country and are fast advancing on their Capital which must soon be ours,—yet they refuse to treat! 'Those the gods wish to destroy, they first make mad'!"[7]

Kirby Smith's conclusions were wisely taken. Indeed the victory at Cerro Gordo was so complete that Scott had gloated in a letter to Taylor that "Mexico no longer has an army."[8] But Santa Anna's forte remained his ability to restore decimated armies. And the newly released prisoners, to whom the word "parole" meant nothing, could be reassembled. Santa Anna could soon fight again.

But far more serious, from the American point of view, was the decimation of Scott's army, not from battle but from the consequences of the War Bill that had been passed in haste in May of 1846. Now three thousand of his volunteers—nearly all of them—had served the year they had signed up for. Legally they were authorized, if they wished, to remain in service for the duration of the war, but a canvass of the ranks indicated that few would sign up—they had experienced enough. Therefore, on May 3, barely two weeks after Cerro Gordo, Scott published General Order No. 135:

> The general-in-chief regrets to learn . . . that, in all probability, not one man in ten of those regiments will be inclined to volunteer for the war. This pre-determination offers, in his opinion, no ground for reproach, considering the long, arduous, faithful, and gallant services of these corps. . . .*

The order pointed out that the departure of the volunteers would delay the end of the war, but admitted sadly that the general-in-chief could not, in good faith, hold these troops longer. Scott would not "throw upon them the necessity of returning to embark at Vera Cruz, at the season known to be, at that place, the most fatal to life."[9]

Accordingly, the seven regiments marched out of Jalapa on May 6, 1846, under the command of General Patterson. The seriously wounded, much to their sorrow, would have to wait. Since Mexican guerrillas had made the road to Veracruz impassable for all but the most heavily armed escorts, most of those left behind would be held for a whole month longer.[10]

During that month of May the troops became bored, then unruly. The wounded were dying daily. Just before leaving, the last of the volunteers were subjected to the spectacle of five soldiers being punished in public. "It chills one's blood," wrote one, "to see free Americans tied up and whipped like dogs, in a market yard in a foreign land."[11]

Scott was now left with only a little over seven thousand men.[12] Nevertheless, he was confident of the prowess of his troops. On May 6, therefore, as the volunteers were departing, he sent part of his army, under Worth, to Puebla. As Worth's force wound their way past the Fortress of Perote, one regiment was to stop off as a garrison. With Worth's departure, Scott had only about three thousand men with him at Jalapa.[13]

Puebla was about sixty miles from Jalapa, and Worth's force was no

---

*U.S. Congress, Exec. Doc. No. 60, p. 956. The regiments referred to were the Tennessee cavalry, the 3d and 4th Illinois infantry, the 1st and 2d Tennessee infantry, the Georgia infantry, and the Alabama infantry.

larger than Scott's. But the split was not so rash as it might seem. Santa Anna was not yet ready to fight again, and Scott was counting heavily on a great ally at Puebla: the Roman Catholic Church. Scott's courting of the bishops at Veracruz might have been helpful, and Santa Anna was their primary enemy. Ever since his return the previous summer Santa Anna had been drawing on Church resources without qualm.

At first the clergy, like the Mexican liberals, had supported continuation of the war in hopes that Santa Anna would be destroyed in battle. But the dictator had proved indestructible, and Moses Y. Beach, in Mexico City, had now convinced the priests that they would be fairly treated by the Americans if they would work for peace. He had met with success: the bishop of Puebla had arranged for the removal of the town governor, who was hostile to Scott, and substituted was a man more "dedicated to the cause of peace."[14] Thus, although the municipal officialdom at Puebla received Worth's arrival coldly, the people, influenced by the priests, were friendly.[15]

A circular that Scott had prepared, with the assistance of a priest from Puebla, helped a great deal to keep order in the city. It promised, among other things, that the army of the United States would always respect the private property of every class, as well as the property of the Mexican Church: "Wo [sic] to him who does not—where we are." It ended the promise with a threat: "I shall march with this army upon Puebla and Mexico. I do not conceal this from you.[16]

On May 19, four days after his arrival at Puebla, Worth sent back an optimistic report. He estimated that some six hundred to eight hundred "beggarly cavalry" might be infesting the area between the two points —no force that could stand up to a hundred disciplined Americans. He could get along until Scott arrived with the rest of the army, he added, and waxed enthusiastic about Scott's circular, asserting that he had had a third edition struck off. "It . . . has produced more decided effects than all the blows from Palo Alto to Cerro Gordo."[17]

Soon Scott decided to move forward. He left a small garrison at Jalapa and arrived in Puebla on May 28, 1847.

Scott's force had been reduced to a fraction of the strength he needed. But his greatest practical problem was the maintenance of his commu-

nications with the coast. Mexican guerrillas along the National Highway were making it too dangerous to dispatch convoys without substantial escorts. After the train had left for Veracruz in early May, escorted
by three thousand "old" volunteers, Scott did not expect those six
hundred wagons to return for many months, for he could not spare
enough men to convoy them. With two thousand men sick and
wounded distributed among Veracruz, Jalapa and Perote, Scott calculated that providing garrisons for those three places had reduced his
active army at Puebla to an alarming 5,820 men. So those garrisons
would have to be brought up to Puebla. On June 4, 1847, Scott
abandoned all stations between Veracruz and Puebla, effectively cutting his army off from the coast. With no supply line, he would live
off the land.[18]

Learning of Scott's desperate move, the aged Duke of Wellington,
who had been marking every one of Scott's movements on a map, now
concluded that his old acquaintance had overreached himself. "Scott
is lost!" he declared. "He has been carried away by successes! He can't
take the city, and he can't fall back on his bases."[19]

Winfield Scott could amass armies, land them on foreign shores, invest
cities, decimate foes, even cut his small force loose in hostile country
and still keep his aplomb. But whenever he encountered a real or
imagined slight from Marcy and Polk—which was often—he became
nearly unhinged. Thus he interpreted the arrival of Nicholas Trist,
bearing a confidential message for the Mexican government, only as
another effort on Polk's part to humiliate him. The possibility that a
civilian might properly negotiate a peace with Mexico seems not to
have crossed his mind.

Trist's conduct, however, contributed mightily to Scott's rage.
While still in Washington, Trist had been indoctrinated with Polk's
and Marcy's distaste for Scott, which they had made plain. When Trist
arrived at Scott's headquarters, Polk had advised, he should place his
trust in that Cincinnatus, that Scipio Africanus, Gideon Johnson Pillow. Trist's job would be to "perform a Great National Act and inciden-
tally to put Winfield Scott where he belonged."[20]

To all this Trist had been receptive, for despite his impressive credentials and all his surface amiability, Trist suffered from delusions of
grandeur. Polk had played on that weakness by hinting that he, Trist,

might find himself considered as the 1848 Democratic nominee for the presidency if he handled Scott and the Mexicans well. During the necessary wait, while the State and War departments were preparing his credentials and secret messages,* Trist had been afforded time to think about the wonderful possibilities of his situation.

Trist arrived at Veracruz from New Orleans on May 6, 1847. Unfortunately for the relations between him and Scott, he became violently ill upon landing and was unable to travel. From his sickbed he sent Scott certain documents to be forwarded to Mexico City—sealed, via courier. He pointedly did not intend that Scott should see any of them, including the set of instructions that Buchanan had issued him. Even though he had been "authorized" to give Scott a copy of the draft treaty he did not do so. Instead Trist penned his own letter, which must have been tactless in the extreme.†

Had Trist himself been able to deliver the documents to Scott, his personal charm might have lessened the general's distress; as it was, his letter was so upsetting that Scott apparently neglected to study the letter of explanation that Marcy had sent directly to him. At first glance Marcy's words appeared to confirm Scott's suspicions that he was being insulted:

Mr. Trist is clothed with such diplomatic powers as will authorize him to enter into arrangements with the government of Mexico for the suspension of hostilities. Should he make known to you, in writing, that the contingency has occurred, in consequence of which the President is willing that further active military operations should cease, you will regard such notice as a direction from the President. . . ."

Scott apparently overlooked the caveats that came later in the letter and quickly concluded that Trist was authorized to decide on his own when Scott should cease fighting. This was bitter to a commander in dire jeopardy, his force down to six thousand men, with no reinforcements known to be coming, and cut off from his base of supply!

To make matters even worse, Scott was already annoyed by the

---

*His letter of introduction to the Mexican government, the draft treaty (sealed), the formal commission from the president, a letter of credence from the secretary of state, and authority to draw on the Treasury for $3 million, to be advanced upon the ratification of the treaty, and also an informal letter from Marcy to Scott. Bauer, p. 282.

†Justin Smith, *The War with Mexico*, vol. II, p. 128. Trist's letter has been lost, but Smith logically concludes that it was "top-lofty" and "high-strung."

presence of Lieutenant Raphael Semmes, USN, who had been sent by Commodore Perry to seek escort to Mexico City in order to intercede on behalf of a midshipman who was unjustly being held there as a spy. Scott learned of Semmes's futile mission only from the credentials the lieutenant carried. He had received no direct word from Perry or anyone else.

The combination of these two outside demands was too much for Winfield Scott. He answered Trist's letter directly, expressing his regret that the base commander at Veracruz had diverted troops to bring Trist's letter—and Semmes—to Puebla. The core of his message was contained in a short paragraph: ". . . I see that the Secretary of War proposes to degrade me, by requiring that I, as the commander of this army, shall defer to you, the chief clerk of the Department of State, the question of continuing or discontinuing hostilities."

That Scott would not tolerate. He finished by demanding that Trist refer any overtures regarding a suspension of hostilities to himself because "the safety of this army demands no less, and I am responsible for that safety. . . ."[21]

Scott did not write Marcy at length other than to pen a curt cover letter and enclose a copy of his own tirade to Trist. Marcy replied with some restraint at the end of May, promising replacements for Scott's departed volunteers but reproving Scott for his liberality in releasing prisoners. Then, turning to Scott's letter to Trist, Marcy regretted that Scott had written a letter of such an "extraordinary character" to Trist, concluding that "it will be no less regretted by yourself on more reflection and information."

Marcy's letter then went on to conjecture, very wisely, that if Trist could have been present (and willing to show all the dispatches), Scott would not have had "any just ground of complaint." He explained that Trist had been "the bearer of that despatch to yourself—not to the Mexican government—and when he delivered it into your hands his agency had ceased."[22] That was not the way it had appeared at Jalapa, nor was it the impression Trist had given.

Trist was by this time as furious as Scott, and when he finally arrived at Jalapa on May 14, he refused to pay a courtesy call. Scott likewise refused to call on Trist, choosing instead to write further insulting letters. Even after the army had arrived at Puebla, Scott called Trist's latest missive a "farrago of insolence, conceit, and arrogance," and referred to the author as "the personification of Danton, Marat, and

St. Just," promising to throw back any further insults with "the contempt and scorn which you merit at my hands."[23]

Scott did, however, provide for Trist's physical comfort—at Persifor Smith's mess, not his own. When word of the childish proceedings reached the War Department, Marcy, who knew both men, groaned. "I fear Scott and Trist have got to writing. If so, all is lost![24]

Marcy had read Scott accurately. On June 4, 1847, Scott wrote, "Considering the many cruel disappointments and mortifications I have been made to feel since I left Washington . . . I beg to be recalled from this army the moment that it may be safe for any person to embark at Vera Cruz. . . ."[25]

THAT SPLENDID
CITY!

JULY–AUGUST 1847

Scott remained at Puebla for three months, far longer than he had ever intended to. His original plans had been based on the assumption that he would receive reinforcements to replace the troops he had lost in early May, but the new regiments he had expected had been diverted by Polk and Marcy to Taylor during that period (March 1847) in which Taylor was presumed to be in peril at Saltillo. Though Taylor was safe after the battle of Buena Vista, those volunteer regiments were now too far away to do Scott any good. Scott would have to await the next contingent of volunteers and "new" regulars.

But Scott, a survivor, spent the time constructively. While occupying Puebla he established order and confidence, effected a reconciliation with Trist, developed a system of local supply and intelligence, and did his best to make peace with Santa Anna. Though this last enterprise came to naught, the effort was worthwhile.

Scott's first task, that of restoring his authority over the troops and the civilian populace, was distasteful, especially since any action he took would reflect on Worth. But Scott could not avoid the issue. Worth, on approaching Puebla in mid-May, had apparently been carried away by the friendly reception he had received, and had responded by granting extremely liberal terms for the surrender of the city. In particular he had granted the Mexican courts the right to try the cases of civilians accused of murdering American soldiers. The Mexicans had quickly abused that concession, and the morale of Worth's troops had suffered accordingly. And Worth's continual and unnecessary alerts, triggered by fears of nonexistent enemy threats, had become so frequent that the beating of the drums had become known in his command as "Worth's scarecrows."[1] Little wonder that the troops welcomed Scott's arrival and assumption of command nearly as heartily as they had in April, just before Cerro Gordo.

Scott attempted to restore order in Puebla with the least possible public display. To reverse Worth's concession regarding the power of Mexican courts, he simply dusted off General Order No. 20, originally issued at Veracruz, in which he had established martial law.[2] And to stop the needless calls to arms, he reversed the policy of taking off in hot pursuit anytime the enemy molested one of his outposts. But even after Scott arrived, Worth issued an unfounded warning to his division that a plot was afoot to poison the drinking water, and the Mexican population was insulted. When Scott requested Worth to withdraw the offending circular, Worth became so incensed that he demanded a court of inquiry. The court, consisting of Quitman, Twiggs, and Persifor Smith, found Worth at fault and recommended a rebuke. Scott limited the distribution of the court's findings to the division commanders, but from that day on all semblance of friendship between Worth and Scott was gone.[3]

Despite these difficulties, which were more attributable to American mismanagement than to Mexican hostility, relations between the two nationalities were not bad. Puebla was a center of religious culture, and its streets abounded with priests and nuns. And since the Catholic Church was tilted against Santa Anna, its discipline kept the atmosphere quiet. And an indication that not all Mexicans were hostile was that Hitchcock was able to recruit a band of irregulars as a spy company. The company was composed largely of outlaws, and its members were despised by the Mexican populace, but whatever its virtues and shortcomings, this group provided Scott with valuable information.[4]

In July 1847, Scott began to receive some reinforcements at Puebla. The first contingent, commanded by Gideon Pillow, now a major general, arrived on July 8.* Pillow's total party, nearly 4,500 men, was actually composed of three detachments that had left Veracruz beginning in early June. The first of these had been under Colonel J. S. McIntosh and the second had been under Brigadier General George Cadwalader. The first two, which had early consolidated as protection against further guerrilla attacks, had been held up at Perote by order of Pillow, who was the third in line. No harm had resulted from the pause at Perote except that the delay had temporarily deprived Scott of the much needed $200,000 in specie that McIntosh had been carrying.

After Pillow and Cadwalader, no more reinforcements reached Scott for over three weeks. The next one marched in on August 6, 1847, under the command of Brigadier General Franklin Pierce, a New England politician who six months earlier had refused the post of attorney general of the United States in order to enlist as a volunteer. Though Pierce's force was strong—about 2,400 men—Scott was sufficiently concerned for his safety that he sent Persifor Smith's brigade back to Perote to escort Pierce in. The difficulties were such that Pierce had found it necessary to leave many sick and some wounded at Perote.[5]

In the meantime, happily for the Americans cause, Scott and Trist had patched up their feud; in fact, the two men had now become warm friends. Trist had remained a member of Quitman's mess for some time without even meeting with the general-in-chief. This interlude gave the two men time to reconsider their respective positions, neither one of which was too secure, and to realize that they had work to do together.†
On June 24, 1847, Trist received encouraging news from the Mexican

*Ripley, The War with Mexico, vol. II, pp. 130–39; Justin Smith, the War with Mexico, vol. II, pp. 76–77. The two accounts vary slightly on the dates. These come from Smith, who wrote the later, more accurate account. Pillow marched his men so hard that six of them died of exhaustion along the way. Niles Register, July 10, 1847, quoted in Charlie W. Elliott, Winfield Scott, p. 489.

†Buchanan, on June 14, 1847, wrote to Trist. Agreeing that Scott's letter had been "extraordinary" and "well calculated to wound your feelings and excite your indignation," he implied that much of the fault lay with Trist's secretiveness: "This letter surely never would have been written, had he awaited your arrival at his head-quarters and read the instructions and the project of a treaty with Mexico, which you were authorized to communicate to him confidentially. The perusal of these documents must have put to flight the unfounded suspicions, in regard to your mission, which seem to have pre-occupied his mind and influenced his conduct." It then went

government through the British minister, Charles Bankhead, and Bankhead's representative, Edward Thornton. Santa Anna, it advised, viewed negotiations favorably, provided some lubricant in the form of gold was applied to his palm. Trist pondered this and decided that it was worth the gamble, but he needed Scott's cooperation if only because Scott held the necessary money in his possession. Trist therefore wrote Scott a civil letter explaining the situation, together with a copy of his authority to act as a commissioner.[6] Scott quickly responded to Trist's overture with a cordial note, and then, as Trist was still ailing, sent a box of guava marmalade to him by way of Persifor Smith:

My dear sir:

Looking over my stores, I find a box of Guava marmalade which, perhaps, the physician may not consider improper to make part of the diet of your sick companion.

Yours very truly
Winfield Scott[7]

These gestures provided the rationale for the two men to meet personally, and when they did, they discovered that they liked each other. So by late July Trist was writing to Buchanan of Scott's "purest public spirit," and a "fidelity and devotion which could not be surpassed . . . in regard to the restoration of peace."[8] And Scott, not to be outdone, was writing to Marcy asking that his former letters describing Trist as "the personification of Danton, Marat, and St. Just all in one" be disregarded. Scott now directed that Trist be treated as the American Minister, not as a mere clerk. All the guards in the headquarters were to be turned out upon Trist's approach, and he was to be tendered appropriate honors on all occasions.[9]

But the issue that had brought Scott and Trist together, Santa Anna's not-so-indirect demand for a bribe, was a touchy one. Indulging in bribery, even for the loftiest of causes, was recognized as dangerous

---

on to remind Trist that he had been instructed to exercise "no further agency" after Buchanan's letter to the Mexican foreign minister had been "placed in the hands of General Scott." Buchanan to Trist, Jun 14, 1847, Exec. Doc. No. 60, pp. 826–27.

business. The two men conferred on the subject several times, and they finally decided that the potential benefit of acceding to Santa Anna's demand was worth the risk. As a result, in mid-July Trist was summarizing their thoughts by writing, "We are both convinced that the only way in which the indefinite protraction of this war can possibly be prevented . . . is by the secret expenditure of money in Mexico." Ten thousand dollars' down payment would be required, to be followed by another million when a treaty was ratified.

Scott, though he agreed, was uncomfortable. He rationalized the bribe on the basis that Santa Anna, in requesting it, had put the onus upon himself. And precedent existed; the United States government had sanctioned the secret expenditure of $500,000 in the negotiations over the northeastern boundary with Canada; furthermore, contrary to popular American belief, the United States had habitually given tribute to the Barbary pirates at the beginning of the century.[10] Thus reassured, Scott proposed that Trist request the needed million dollars from him, and he would in turn sign a draft on the Treasury in Washington to come out of the funds of the army.[11] The initial ten thousand Scott was able to provide on the spot out of his fund for secret expenses.

Nevertheless, Scott deemed it advisable to secure the support of his generals, of whom at least Pillow, Shields, and Quitman were influential Democrats. The support of Pillow was particularly desirable, so when he arrived from Veracruz, he was soon brought in on the matter. Pillow was at first reticent, but as the discussion proceeded he began to withdraw his objections. Quitman doubted that the move would sit well at home. Shields, as a former supreme court justice of Illinois, had misgivings but refused to commit himself. He would, he said, leave the matter completely in Trist's hands. But out of friendship for Scott, Shields hoped that the general could be disassociated with the decision, confining his role to that of Trist's agent for procuring the money.[12]

By now the troops who had been at Puebla the entire three months were rested and drilled, and those who had just arrived had at least been introduced to hardship. And since the negotiations with Santa Anna were too indefinite to affect Scott's plans to move on to Mexico City, he went about organizing his army for its final campaign against Mexico City.

The army now comprised some 14,000 men, of whom 2,500 were

sick and 600 more convalescing.[13] He organized his force into four divisions: the 1st Division (Brevet Major General Worth), the 2d Division (Brigadier General Twiggs), Major General Pillow's Division, and Brigadier General Quitman's Division. Three of these were considered "regular," as Pillow's two brigades (Cadwalader and Pierce) consisted of recruits who had recently signed up for the duration of the war. They were, however, officered mostly by volunteers.*

With this force Scott was ready to combat a Mexican army estimated at that time to be 36,000 men and one hundred cannon.[14]

The deal that Santa Anna had proposed to the United States government—to sign a favorable peace in exchange for a million dollar bribe —was never consummated. At some convenient point Santa Anna "discovered" the Mexican law of April 20, 1847, that declared it high treason for any official to treat with the enemy. So he simply pocketed the $10,000 advance.

Perhaps Santa Anna was influenced in the withdrawal of his offer by the increasing evidence of Scott's difficulties in maintaining any sort of communication with the coast. So with his usual optimism, Santa Anna again set about to destroy the hated invader.†

---

*1st Division (Worth)
   Garland's brigade: 2d Art., 3d Art., 4th Inf.
   Clarke's brigade: 3d, 6th, 8th infs., Co A, 2d Art.,
      Light Art. Bn.
2d Division (Twiggs)
   P. F. Smith's brigade: 1st Art., 3d Inf., Rifle Regt.
   Riley's brigade: 4th Art., 2d and 7th infs, Engr. Co.,
      Ord. Co, Light Co. K, 1st Art.
Pillow's Division
   Pierce's brigade: 9th, 12th, 15th infs.
   Cadawaler's brigade: Voltiguers, 11th and 14th infs,
      Light Co. I, 1st Art.
Quitman's Division
   Shield's brigade: New York Regt., South Carolina Regt.,
      Marine detachment.
   Watson's brigade: 2d Pennsylvania Regt.; H Co., 3d Art.;
      C Co., 3d Dragoons.
   Harney's brigade: 1st Bn., Cavalry; 2d Bn., Cavalry.
The above list appears in Emory Upton, *The Military Policy of the United States*, p. 214.
†Charles W. Elliott, *Winfield Scott*, p. 500. Scott (*Memoirs*, p. 466) described Santa Anna thus: "His vigilance and energy were unquestionable, and his powers of creating and organizing worthy of admiration. He was also great in administrative ability, and though not deficient in personal courage, he, on the field of battle, failed in quickness of perception and rapidity of combination. Hence his defeats."

Rallying the people, however, was not easy, for they had been bewildered after the rout at Cerro Gordo. But once Santa Anna had occupied Mexico City with troops, he could count on Mexican pride to support its defense. According to the Mexicans, ". . . it was much more glorious to submit fighting, than to leave the gates of Mexico City open, without firing a gun at the North Americans."[15] So the people pitched in. Bells and old ordnance from the Castle of Chapultepec were melted down to cast new cannon; new muskets, sold by foreigners at Mexican ports or through Guatemala, were produced; other small arms were shaken down from the closets of the populace. Mortars, bayonets, and projectiles were feverishly produced. And always behind the effort was the mind and will of Santa Anna.[16]

The building blocks for reorganizing a respectable army were also in being. To begin with, some four thousand veterans of Buena Vista had remained at San Luis Potosí under the command of General Gabriel Valencia. Valencia was an unreliable subordinate, but so long as "the new patriotism" burned, he would probably behave himself. So on Santa Anna's order Valencia arrived at Guadalupe Hidalgo on July 27.[17]

Valencia's backbone of regular troops would be supplemented, of course, by nearly 10,000 men from the National Guard. In addition, Santa Anna had brought 3,500 men back from Puebla, and some 10,000 troops were already in Mexico City. Juan Alvarez's Army of the South provided 2,500, and Canalizo still had a few thousand. All together, Santa Anna could total up a force of some 25,000 men, possibly 30,000.[18]

Despite his advantage in numbers, however, Santa Anna's strategy still called for remaining on the defensive. Some criticized him for timidity, but he was realistic. His army lacked cohesion and discipline, and it would find offensive maneuvers difficult. But far more important, the Valley of Mexico was so marshy that large-scale, cross-country movement for any army, even Scott's would be impossible. Though seven thousand feet above sea level, Mexico City lay at the lowest point of a flat tableland, the ground always soggy but now worse because the Mexicans had flooded it. The soil could not carry artillery and horses. Any movement in the valley would be questionable, and approaches to the city itself were limited to the several built-up causeways. Numbers of men could not maneuver between them. So with those restrictions on maneuver, Santa Anna would be unable to take full advantage of his numerical superiority. On the other hand, he could afford enough troops to garrison each causeway. Each causeway force could defend like Horatius at the bridge.

As Santa Anna began planning his defense he preferred, of course, to meet Scott as far from the gates of Mexico City as possible, taking advantage of the limited road net, broken up by lakes, for distances of many miles. Since only one road crossed the mountains from Puebla to Mexico City, Santa Anna knew where Scott would be coming—up to Buena Vista, a town about thirty miles east of Mexico City. Once Scott reached that town from the east, he would have the choice of continuing westward over any one of three smaller ones, one of which led directly to Mexico City while the other two followed more circuitous routes.

These three branches were each canalized by three large lakes to the east of the city. The largest, Lake Texcoco, stood east and northeast, extending so far north that nearly everyone, certainly Santa Anna, considered the road around its far shore infeasible. The other two lakes, Xochimilco and Chalco, were lined up east to west, both of them south of Texcoco. Of these, Xochimilco was closer to the city; indeed, one nose, at Mexicaltzingo, extended to a point only about five miles from the San Antonio gate. East of Xochimilco, of course, was Lake Chalco, a corner of which reached almost to Buena Vista. Between Lakes Xochimilco and Chalco was a narrow isthmus with another road, making it possible for Scott to go between the lakes to approach the city from the south.

Of the three approaches, Santa Anna's eyes were fixed on the direct one, the National Highway from Puebla, which ran from Buena Vista to the San Lazaro gate, just south of Lake Texcoco. Santa Anna decided to block that road at El Peñón, a conical hill about ten miles from the city. As the defense at El Peñón would represent the "post of honor," Santa Anna placed his National Guard troops on that position. Obviously he was playing politics: favoring those troops most identified with the people was calculated to fan their ardor. Thus the toughest fighting, should Scott attack from that direction, would fall to the troops least trained for combat.

To make the most of this gesture, Santa Anna established El Peñón amid great pageantry. On August 10, 1847, the first brigade, that of

General Anaya, marched through the streets of Mexico City, with the Grand Plaza filled with people, the balconies and roofs of the city crowded with citizens. Band music of the 11th infantry "filled the air with its inspiring martial sounds; a thousand *vivas* answered it, and the National Guard marched, bearing with them the good wishes of all."

The brigades had impressive names: the Victoria, the Hidalgo, the Independencia and the Bravos. Each unit represented its own walk of life, and each had its enthusiastic partisans amid the cheers. Military utility was subordinated to the show. Anaya's brigade, for example, "entered the Palace: then twice displayed through the central streets of the city; and the ladies ran to the balconies at the sound of that musical strain which converted the polka into a hymn of the Guard." But emotions were mixed; enthusiasm, grief, tenderness, solicitude, each found its place.

Later that morning, Santa Anna rode out to El Penon, accompanied by a large staff and brilliant escort. "They saluted him with the musical beats of honor and with enthusiastic *vivas*. A crowd then collected and began building grocery stands, eating-houses, stores, and liquor shops, and at once a portable city sprang from the earth. Enterprising souls soon converted the ditches at the side of the road into canals to bring furniture, war materials, and curiosities of all kinds by canoe. All made their way easily along, by keeping time with favorite songs. . . ."[19]

Thus the Mexicans set about to defend their capital.

Scott's leading division, Twiggs's, marched out of Puebla on Saturday, August 7, 1847. Pierce's men had arrived only the day before, but they would have a few days' rest, as Scott was sending his army out one division at a time. To keep each segment within reasonable reach of one another, he directed that one division would leave each morning but each would make only a half day's march daily. Thus no unit would ever be more than a half day's march from support, from both the division ahead of it and the one behind. To his regret, Scott was forced to leave his sick and wounded behind at Puebla. The army itself would advance, "with naked blade in hand."*

.   .   .

*Scott, *Memoirs*, vol. II, p. 466. Sequence was Twiggs, Quitman, Worth, and Pillow.

Above: Taylor at Buena Vista. Though the figures are made more visible than they would be in an actual battle, this painting gives a true picture of the terrain and a reasonable version of how Taylor might have looked, except for the proper uniform that Taylor never wore. *Library of Congress. Below:* A sketch of the Battle of Buena Vista. A very accurate impression of the terrain. *Library of Congress*

Andrés Pico. Pico was universally respected among Californios and Americans alike. He remained prominent in California after the war. This likeness shows him in his later years. *Seaver Center for Western History Research, Natural History Museum, Los Angeles County*

Brigadier General Stephen Watts Kearny. An excellent photograph, much better than the formal portraits, which shows a rugged, tough, relatively unpretentious frontier officer. *Kit Carson Foundation, Taos*

Above: Two unknown sailors. Though the U.S. Navy sustained only minimal loses in the Mexican War, the task of blockading the Mexican coastlines on two oceans was onerous and thankless. But these two jaunty tars seem undaunted. *Michael Bremer Collection. Below:* Two Californio gentlemen. *Michael Bremer Collection*

Below left: Unknown infantry major. One of the tough young men who made Taylor's and Scott's armies so formidable. *Michael Bremer Collection. Below right:* Colonel Alexander W. Doniphan, 1st Missouri Volunteers. *Courtesy Colonel Doniphan Carter*

Veracruz landing. *Library of Congress. Inset:* Commodore David E. Conner. As Conner was past retirement age when the war with Mexico broke out, this likeness must have been painted either from memory or at some time earlier. *Official US Navy photograph*

One of Doniphan's Volunteers. The Missourians were even less "military" than the rest of the volunteers. They were, however, exceedingly courageous and resourceful fighters. *Library of Congress*

J. D. Tisdell.

GROSVENOR

Above: Train of pack mules. *Library of Congress. Below:* Assault on Cerro Gordo. The Battle of Cerro Gordo, which was fought on mountainous terrain, is difficult to depict graphically. Nevertheless, the hand-to-hand fighting was severe, as this picture shows. *Library of Congress*

Captain Robert E. Lee. Taken just before the Civil War, this photo shows Lee much as he appeared during the Mexican War, without the beard he is usually associated with. *Library of Congress*

Brigadier General John A. Quitman. *Michael Bremer Collection*

Brigadier General Persifor F. Smith.

Archibald Yell. *Courtesy William W. Hughes*

The Battle of Contreras (Padierna). An excellent painting, it shows Twiggs's (later Pillow's) position, with Magruder's battery on the left. It was from this spot that the various units—Riley, Cadwalader, Shields, Persifor Smith, and others—headed down to the right to envelop Valencia's force in the center background. *Defense Audio Visual Agency, Washington, D.C.*

Above: Storming the San Mateo Convent, Churubusco. *Library of Congress. Below:* The San Mateo Convent at Churubusco. The convent was nearly but not quite as formidable as this painting portrays it. To storm it required highly motivated troops. The Mexican defenders, though demoralized, had their will to resist bolstered by the desperation of the San Patricio Battalion of American deserters, who knew what their fate would be if captured by the Americans. *Defense Audio Visual Agency, Washington, D.C.*

The Castle of Chapultepec from the Molino del Rey. This etching shows the relative position of the Molino to the Castle of Chapultepec. It explains to some degree why Scott considered it advisable to take the Molino. He ordered Worth to take it under the erroneous assumption that the walls were lightly held. *Library of Congress*

Above: The Castle of Chapultepec. A formidable sight from the bottom of the hill. This scene is viewed from the approximate position of today's monument to the Niños Perdidos. Though the hill is high, the actual walls of the castle are less imposing than they appear in this picture. *Library of Congress. Below:* Hanging of the San Patricio deserters. Scott would have spared the lives of deserters had it not been for the example such action would have set for those who still had to fight. As it was, he restricted execution to those soldiers who deserted after the war began. This painting was done from the fertile imagination of Sam Chamberlain, who was not there. *West Point Museum, United States Military Academy*

Storming the Castle of Chapultepec. An excellent artist's reconstruction. *Library of Congress*

Death of the Niños. Though Mexican cadets were among the defenders of Chapultepec—and though some were killed—the legend of the Niños Perdidos has been much embellished in Mexican accounts of the battle. Even the names of the "lost children"—for that is what they were—are historically questionable. However, as with the scene of Washington crossing the Delaware, the Niños legend is important to Mexican folklore. *Charles M. Tyson*

General Gabriel Valencia. This photo is completely consistent with the common view of Valencia—handsome, aristocratic, and headstrong. *Alcatrax*

Winfield Scott enters Mexico City in triumph. The great plaza, shown in this painting, is virtually unchanged today. *Library of Congress*

Peña y Peña. *Benson Collection, University of Texas, Austin*

Nicholas Trist in later life. Cartoons of the time show Trist as clean-shaven, which he undoubtedly was during the Mexican War. Beards became fashionable much later.
Library of Congress

This march into the Valley of Mexico was risky. As was observed from over the seas, the difficulty of capturing Mexico City would be exceeded only by the almost unthinkable alternative of marching back to Veracruz. But for the first five days, at least, Scott encountered little resistance, though he had halfway expected Santa Anna to defend at the Rio Frio, just to the west of Puebla. Thus the most memorable feature of this arduous march was the scenery. The climax for each soldier occurred on the third day, when each unit would reach the crest of the high ridge that lay at the base of Popocatépetl (Smoking Mountain). There before them spread the Valley of Mexico.

Witnesses vied in describing the view, certainly one of the most magnificent in Mexico. At an altitude of ten thousand feet—three thousand feet above the flat valley—the viewer could take in the entire plain, spread before him like a map. The valley was hemmed in by "a circle of stupendous, rugged, and dark mountains, forming a most perfect combination of the sublime and the beautiful." The circumference of the basin itself was estimated as 120 miles long, and in the clear air all was visible to the glance.

The towers of Mexico City, twenty-five miles away, stood out clearly. The large green plain was almost devoid of trees except around the city itself, "dotted with white churches, spires, and haciendas." The three great lakes—Texcoco, Chalco, and Xochimilco—appeared as great sheets of water; the soldiers understood that once upon a time they covered the entire basin. Pocopocatépetl and its brother giant, Iztaccíhuatl, lay twenty miles away, though the clear air made the distance appear to be only two or three miles.[20]

Winfield Scott, never one to play down the drama of a situation, described it years later as "the object of all our dreams and hopes—toils and dangers;—once the gorgeous seat of the Montezumas." Filled With "religious awe," Scott exulted: *"That splendid city soon shall be ours!"*

BLOODY
FRIDAY

AUGUST 19–20, 1847

O n August 12, 1847, Brigadier General David E. Twiggs's advance guard passed the crossroads at Buena Vista and pushed on a couple of miles to the small town of Ayotla. Ahead loomed the fortified position of El Peñón, and just behind it lay Mexico City itself, the shining objective of the whole campaign. Twiggs's arrival at this point meant that the moment of decision had come for Winfield Scott, who was at a crossroads both literally and figuratively. For now Scott must decide once and for all whether to continue the last twenty miles on the National Highway—assaulting the formidable El Peñón along the way—or turn south of Lake Chalco and approach Mexico City indirectly.

Scott had been anticipating this moment of decision a long time. Back at Puebla, he had assigned two officers, Major William Turnbull* and Captain R. E. Lee, to study his various options. In a fatherly way Scott had supervised them, at first pitting them against each other and then allowing them to pool their efforts. By combining their respective intelligence sources, Turnbull and Lee had garnered a great deal of

*Chief topographical engineer.

information on the situation around Mexico City, particularly the defenses of El Peñón and the road net around the lakes. Basing his plans on their work, Scott had tentatively decided to leave the main highway and to take one of the roads south of Lake Chalco instead.[1]

But a map study conducted from seventy-five miles away had its limitations; studying the ground in person was also necessary. Scott could not perform his reconnaissance himself, but he had come to trust Lee, and on Lee's shoulders he placed the responsibility of checking the various routes in person. Lee set out at once.

Lee decided that his first requirement would be to confirm the intelligence he and Turnbull had gathered about the Mexican position at El Peñón. Making full use of the whole engineer detachment, he soon concluded that his earlier information had indeed been true: El Peñón was the principal Mexican defense, defended by about seven thousand men and thirty cannon. So he began the search to find another way, one that would encounter lighter resistance. First he considered a small road that branched off to the left of the National Highway a couple of miles short of El Peñón and led to the small village of Mexicalcingo. But that road was too restricted,[2] so Lee turned to another, which had heretofore been unreported, that led around the south of Lake Chalco and was "quite good, although narrow and rough."[3] If passable, that road would eventually join the Acapulco Road at San Agustín, directly south of Mexico City. The Acapulco Road would provide the new axis for Scott's advance.

Lee reported these preliminary findings to Scott, who in turn ordered Worth, now located at the town of Chalco, to reconnoiter the San Agustín route that Lee had suggested. Lee accordingly sent all the information he had to James Mason, Worth's division engineer.[4]

Worth apparently preferred to depend on his own people rather than on Scott's engineers, so he gave the reconnaissance task to James Duncan, now a brevet lieutenant colonel. Duncan found the road to be excellent, "not easily obstructed or defended." He so reported to Worth that same evening.[5]

That was enough for Scott. The next morning he moved Worth's division south and then west toward San Agustín, followed by Pillow's and Quitman's divisions, leaving Twiggs at Ayotla to threaten El Peñón for one more day. As Twiggs was marching off he was attacked by a cavalry force of twice his numbers, but he beat it off without much difficulty. The Mexican unit was Alvarez's cavalry, part of Valencia's force, which was on its way down from Valencia's previous station north of Mexico City to a new position.*

On August 18, Scott's army, after a march of twenty-five miles through the mud, closed in on San Agustín. The Acapulco road would be Scott's new axis of advance toward Mexico City, from the south rather than from the east.

As early as August 14 Santa Anna had been aware that Scott was considering a movement to the south. Scouts had discovered and reported the American reconnaissance parties along the Chalco route. Further, his spies had picked up rumors of such a move. But these indications could not be counted on as conclusive, and Santa Anna did not want to believe them. Reluctant to evacuate El Peñón, he remained there, confining his actions to harassing Twiggs and to laying plans for his eventual defense to the south. His lethargy made Scott's march easier; the few small raids the Americans encountered along the way were quickly brushed off.[6]

By the seventeenth of August, however, Santa Anna was forced to acknowledge that Scott had moved south and that he would have to remove his force from El Peñón and assume positions south of Mexico City. He executed the move amid the grief of a population that had cheered Peñón's occupation a few days earlier. And many were more than "mournful"; they were frightened. Hordes left the city, leaving their doors and balconies closed: "The sight alone of the deserted city inspired sorrow and a shudder. It resembled beauty without life, and the naked bones of a skull where lovely eyes had sparkled."[7]

But Santa Anna, always looking to the future, energetically went about setting up his new defense line. The terrain was favorable for defense: the Churubusco River, running southwestward from Mexicalcinco, provided a reasonable obstacle between the town of Churubusco and Lake Xochimilco, and Santa Anna placed his forces behind it. To the southwest, however, he ran his line a bit forward, assigning Valencia (with 5,500 men) a position at San Angel; Francisco Pérez (with

---

*Scott report, August 19, 1847, Exec. Doc. No. 1, pp. 303–4. Alcaraz, *The Other Side*, p. 266, says that the attack was made by Alvarez, the cavalryman attached to Valencia: ". . . at dawn on the [16th], General Alvarez was on the rear-guard of the enemy, who discharged a few cannon without any result."

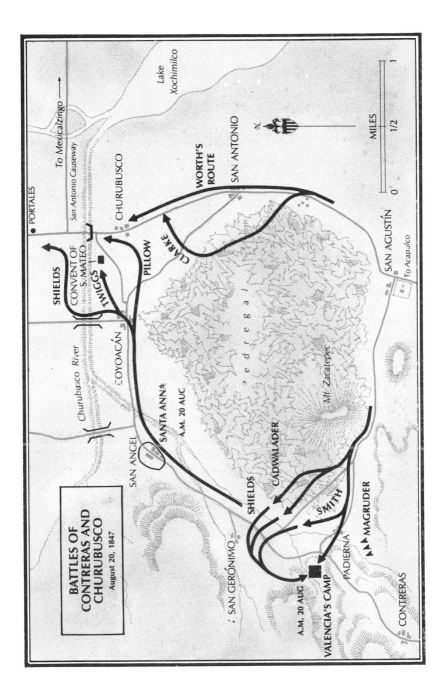

BATTLES OF CONTRERAS AND CHURUBUSCO
August 20, 1847

PORTALES

To Mexicalzingo →

Lake Xochimilco

SAN ANTONIO

WORTH'S ROUTE

CHURUBUSCO

San Antonio Causeway

CLARKE

PILLOW

SHIELDS

CONVENT OF S. MATEO

TWIGGS

COYOACÁN

Churubusco River

SAN AGUSTÍN

To Acapulco

SANTA ANNA
A.M. 20 AUG

SAN ANGEL

Pedregal

Mt Zacatepec

SHIELDS

CADWALADER

SMITH

MAGRUDER

SAN GERÓNIMO

PADIERNA

A.M. 20 AUG

VALENCIA'S CAMP

CONTRERAS

MILES

0   1/2   1

3,500) at Coyoacán two miles east; and Nicolas Bravo at Churubusco three miles to the east of Pérez. These units, only five miles from end to end, could reinforce one another readily. And unwilling to abandon El Peñón entirely, Santa Anna left General Manuel Rincón on that hill as a reserve. He established his own headquarters with that of Bravo at Churubusco.

Santa Anna's defending force was counted at twenty thousand, twice that of Scott.[8]

On August 18, 1847, Scott sent Worth's division northward from San Agustín toward Mexico City. Harney's dragoons, in the lead, ran into heavy cannon fire from a strong position at San Antonio, some three miles south of Churubusco. The first round from Santa Anna's cannon killed the luckless Seth Thornton, whose capture at Matamoros sixteen months earlier had precipitated the war. In the face of heavy hostile fire, Worth paused and sent the engineers out to evaluate the position. They returned quickly, advising that San Antonio could not be out-flanked because a formidable lava field called the Pedregal lay to the west and to the east the water was too deep. Rather than attacking up the San Antonio causeway, therefore, Scott ordered Worth to halt, threaten the position, and wait.[9]

Scott's situation was now decidedly uncomfortable. The horses lacked forage; rations were short and growing musty. When Scott inspected his troops, waiting in the ditches beside their wagons and horses, his face looked grim. It was now morning of August 19, 1847, and the time had come for the general-in-chief to act decisively.

Padierna/Contreras

General Gabriel Valencia, commander of the Army of the North, was not the kind of subordinate that Santa Anna would have selected if given a free choice. The two men were so hostile toward each other that Santa Anna habitually kept Valencia as far from Mexico City as possible. He also tried to keep Valencia from gaining too much in the way of military laurels. Sometimes the result of this effort had been expensive, as at the battle of Cerro Gordo, which Santa Anna had fought with Valencia sitting inactive at San Luis Potosí. Valencia was more than a difficult commander for Santa Anna to cope with; he was also Santa Anna's political rival. Back in 1841 Valencia had been an ally of sorts when he had joined with Lombardini and others to help Santa Anna oust President Bustamante. But Valencia, with Alvarez, had later been among the officers who had deposed Santa Anna in late 1844. Valencia's latest political activity had been to assist Paredes in overthrowing Herrera during the winter of 1845.

Valencia was heavyset, bullnecked, and blue-eyed. Further, he has been described as a "conspirator, a drunkard, a dolt, and a volcano."[10] But Valencia possessed a certain panache, and his division, the elite of the army, followed him willingly. Now, with the population only tolerating Santa Anna, Valencia saw his opportunity approaching. So confident was he of overthrowing the president that he carried with him the names of men he would appoint to his cabinet when he came to power.[11]

In an army consisting of allied warlords, Santa Anna could not replace Valencia, but neither could he enforce his orders on Valencia. As soon as Valencia arrived at San Angel, on the right (west) of Santa Anna's new defensive line, he immediately scorned that inconspicuous position and pushed forward to a hill about five miles down the road, near the town of Contreras. There Valencia could fight his own, independent battle. This move, if successful, just might give him such recognition as to catapult him into power, displacing the discredited Santa Anna. So when he received Santa Anna's orders instructing him to remain at San Angel, he ignored them and, instead, moved his four thousand veterans on to a position between the Indian village of Padierna and Contreras.[12]

When Santa Anna learned of the move, he immediately sent orders to Valencia on the morning of August 18 to withdraw back to San Angel.* Valencia answered in a deferential tone but did not comply. His arguments were persuasive, at least to him: his position was "auxiliary"; if the Americans should attack in force at San Antonio, he could attack their rear. But if the Americans should attack him, then Santa Anna could hit their rear at San Antonio. Eventually, Santa Anna gave up. He would, he declared, "leave Valencia to act on his own responsibility."[13]

---

*Actually, Valencia was ordered to take his infantry back to Coyoacán and send his artillery to Churubusco. Alcaraz, p. 270; R.S. Ripley, *The War with Mexico*, vol. II, quoting official Mexican correspondence, p. 208.

Valencia, out on a limb, had given Scott the chance to rescue his waning fortunes.

The battles of Contreras and Churubusco, both fought on Friday, August 20, 1847, were actually two parts of one battle. The towns were only seven miles apart; they were fought within a few hours of each other; and most of the troops involved at Churubusco had participated in some way at Contreras.

The key to the two battles was the great, supposedly impassable lava bed called the Pedregal. This forbidding obstacle was oval-shaped, with its longer axis running east to west about five miles across, its shorter about three miles from south to north. Santa Anna's base, Churubusco, lay on the northern rim of the oval; Scott's San Agustín, on the southern rim. Both towns were a little east of the oval's north–south axis. The most direct route between Churubusco and San Agustín, therefore, was the generally north–south road that bent around to the east of the Pedregal, running through San Antonio. But that position was strongly defended, and the only possible alternative way for Scott to reach Churubusco would be to encircle the western edge of the Pedregal, provided sufficient roads existed.

Since the San Antonio position would be expensive to reduce, Scott now began to give serious thought to following the roundabout route to the west. So to determine the feasibility of the roads in that direction, Scott turned once more to Lee, and on the eighteenth Lee took an infantry regiment and two companies of dragoons to check it. Essentially, the trail followed the southern edge of the Pedregal, and though rough, it was feasible for infantry. With some work, it could be made to carry artillery. After three miles Lee and his men reached the top of Mount Zacatepec, where they encountered Mexican guerrillas. That meeting was enough to convince Lee of the route's feasibility: if the Mexicans could reach this point from the west, the Americans could follow the path they had taken. Lee and his men returned to San Agustín.[14]

That evening Scott held a council of war. As was his custom, he listened carefully to the various reports without committing himself. Mason, the engineer who had scouted the road to San Antonio, recommended assaulting that position; Lee believed that casualties could be minimized by crossing to the west. Both presentations were impressive, and Scott deferred his decision. By morning, however, he had decided to take the road that Lee had scouted across the Pedregal. He would envelop Churubusco and San Antonio from the west.

Scott was unaware at this time that Valencia had set up a substantial position in his path, and he expected little or no resistance. He therefore remained back at San Agustín. Five hundred men, he ordered, all from Pillow's division, would constitute a work party to make the Pedregal road fit to carry artillery. Twiggs's division would protect the road builders[15] and "brush the enemy away" should they become "impertinent." But then, if any action should become serious—which Scott did not expect—Pillow was to join in the fight with his whole command, and at the same time assume the command.[16] Scott would, in that case, be soon on the ground.

Twiggs was unhappy to be subordinated to the unpopular Pillow, nearly thirty years his junior, but he set out on the morning of August 19. Since Worth's division at San Antonio was earmarked to follow the route blazed by Twiggs and Pillow, Scott had committed three of his four divisions to the movement around the Pedregal. Only a disappointed Quitman was left in reserve at San Agustín.

Under Lee's supervision, Pillow's men worked hard all morning and into the early afternoon. Gradually they hacked across the "raging sea of molten rock"[17] until they had fashioned an acceptable road past Mount Zacatepec to a point overlooking the small towns of Padierna in front, San Geronimo to the right, and Contreras to the left.* Because of a strange shape of the ground, Scott could actually see San Geronimo from the roof of his house in San Agustín.

In early afternoon, after the road was nearly completed, Twiggs's lead units came under fire as they descended the forward slopes of Zacatepec. Perhaps hoping to destroy the opposition without having to call on Pillow, Twiggs instantly sent two batteries of artillery forward to unlimber and begin firing. For a while the artillerists, under Captain John Magruder, held their own against twenty-two heavy Mexican guns, but eventually, outgunned, they were forced to withdraw. At that moment Pillow arrived to take command.

Pillow apparently intended to run this battle without sending for Scott, for he sent word to Colonel Riley, in the lead, to proceed down

---

*The towns are regularly confused. Scott's map (Exec. Doc. No. 1, p. 304) mistakenly calls San Geronimo Contreras. Hence the erroneous name for the battle. The real Contreras never saw an American soldier, at least not until later.

the banks of the river, cross over, and seize San Geronimo on the other side, thereby cutting this Mexican position off from its lifeline, the San Angel road. Riley, a suspicious old soldier, first asked if his own commander, Twiggs, had been made aware of this order. Pillow assured Riley, correctly, that he had, and a staff officer from Twiggs rode up and confirmed his word. Riley then dismounted and at the head of his men struggled down the rugged banks, across the river to Padierna, to the Ansaldo orchard,[18] and finally to San Geronimo, which he found deserted. On the way, he was threatened at times by lancers, by Torre-jón's cavalry, and finally by artillery fire from Valencia's position. He was not, however, attacked by infantry, as Valencia was preoccupied with the duel that was raging between his artillery and Magruder's battery to the east.

Soon Pillow realized that Riley, isolated at San Geronimo, was in danger. Accordingly he sent Cadwalader and then the 15th Infantry under Colonel George W. Morgan, both from his own division.[19] Later in the day, having been reinforced, Riley began scouting the rear (western) side of Valencia's position. Valencia did nothing to stop him, his eyes still on the artillery duel. At the end of the day, with Magruder's guns withdrawn, Valencia believed he had repulsed a major American attack. He happily declared victory and began to celebrate by boasting, promoting all his officers, and getting drunk.[20]

But Riley, Cadwalader, and Morgan were in a precarious spot, for now they were able to detect a major Mexican force coming down the San Angel road. The 3,500 Americans, isolated between Valencia and what would turn out to be Santa Anna's main body, were ripe for slaughter. But Pillow did nothing to extricate them other than issuing and then rescinding an order for Riley to retire.[21]

Enter Persifor F. Smith, the Princeton lawyer from New Orleans, veteran of the Florida war and hero of Monterrey. This unassuming man, who lacked the flamboyance, the ego, and the pretensions of Pillow, Scott, Worth, and others, was destined in the next twenty-four hours to rescue the doubtful fortunes of Scott's army.

Smith's brigade had been in the vanguard of Twiggs's division when the first rounds had come in from Valencia's position, and when Magruder's batteries were placed into position to return the fire, Smith's brigade had been put in place so as to give them infantry protection.

Smith had been kept in that position, as Riley, Cadwalader, and Morgan had been committed. Now Smith's was the only brigade on hand that had not been in the fight.

From his position supporting Magruder, Smith could see the plight of the three units across the stream and saw that he should go to their assistance. But Valencia's position was straight across the stream from him, its heavy artillery still pointed in his direction. Smith quickly concluded, therefore, that a frontal attack would be expensive; furthermore, an attack to the left toward Contreras (Valencia's right) would do nothing to cut Valencia off from the reinforcing army. Therefore, on his own, with no orders from Pillow, Twiggs, or Scott, Smith determined to move out to the right, along the general route followed by the others. After making an effort to find some senior to confirm his course of action, he called his battalion commanders together, told them what he planned, and ordered Magruder to recommence firing to cover him. He then led his men off by the right flank.[22]

Smith debouched from the Pedregal at the rear of Morgan's 15th Infantry at about an hour before sunset. There he could see the considerable Mexican force drawn up between him and San Angel. Taking command of Cadwalader's and Morgan's units—Riley was out of contact—Smith set up a defensive position. Soon, however, he received word that Riley had been located beyond the village, and he began preparing to attack northward. Cadwalader, however, was finding difficulty with the terrain to his front and seemed unable to understand his orders. With these complications, and with darkness coming on, Smith canceled his assault. He still had no inkling at the time that the force between him and San Angel was commanded by Santa Anna in person.[23]

Santa Anna, on his part, was remarkably lethargic. It was late in the day, and before him lay a difficult ravine. So he failed to attack the Americans between him and Valencia—a missed opportunity. No explanation for this failure is completely satisfactory. Possibly his pique against Valencia was the reason. Santa Anna, of course, had personal and political differences with most of his generals, and those differences were generally forgotten on the battlefield. But Valencia's case was special, for even if Santa Anna crushed the Americans under those circumstances, Valencia could claim credit, with some reason, for having chosen the site of victory.* On the other hand, Santa Anna was never very quick or perceptive on the battlefield, and his failure may have stemmed simply from that failing. Whatever the reasons, he brought disaster upon himself.

After Persifor Smith had canceled his late-afternoon attack, he began pondering his next move. Riley, who had now been located up ahead, volunteered that his engineers had discovered a way around to the rear of Valencia's position. Smith, without seeing the ground, seized on the opportunity to surround Valencia on three sides and attack the position at daybreak. Scott was too far away to give his permission, but Smith wanted Scott informed. But how? Lee quickly solved the problem by volunteering to make the hazardous trip back to Scott, who was last heard of at Zacatepec. Smith accepted Lee's offer and added an additional message: his command would move out to attack Valencia at 3 A.M. with or without orders, but to support him he requested Scott to order a diversionary action on Valencia's front.

Lee made his way, with a few men, through the blackness of the night over the desolate Pedregal. The night was becoming stormy, and he was forced to depend on his own acute sense of direction, guided by occasional bursts of lightning, to find his way. On reaching Zacatepec, however, Lee discovered to his disappointment that Scott had returned to San Agustín for the night. So the weary engineer continued the remaining three miles, arriving at Scott's headquarters by 11 P.M., to find Scott calmly writing his report of the day's operations, confident but glad to receive news.[24]

Scott had been concerned about Smith's situation, so concerned that he had sent seven officers out to find Smith; all of them had returned unsuccessful. On receiving Lee's news, therefore, Scott was relieved, and he sent Twiggs and Lee out to scrape up troops for the morning

*Justin Smith (*The War with Mexico*, vol. II, p. 106) seems to have had no doubt. "Santa Anna, devoured by passions and perplexities, now" ordered Valencia "to retreat at once. Not long afterwards two of Valencia's aides reached San Angel, bringing news that, instead of being exterminated, thousands of Americans were established in the San Geronimo woods. Don't talk to me, Santa Anna cried to the aides, who endeavored to excuse the situation; Valencia is an ambitious, insubordinate sot; he deserves to have his brains blown out, and I will not expose my men to the storm for him; let him spike his guns, make the ammunition useless, and retreat." It should be noted that the incident Smith reports occurred at the end of the day, after the opportunity had been missed.

demonstration. Before long they located Franklin Pierce's brigade, temporarily commanded by Colonel T. B. Ransom, of the 9th Infantry.*

At Padierna, Smith was preparing to attack Valencia at daybreak. Riley's brigade moved out shortly before 3 A.M., and Cadwalader's brigade, following, was split, with two of his regiments going with Riley and the other two staying to face Santa Anna's force. Morgan's 15th Infantry was to follow Riley but be prepared to face Santa Anna if necessary. Shields, who had joined him the previous night, was to remain in San Geronimo.† Riley's path was difficult, and it was broad daylight, three hours later, before he and Cadwalader's regiments were in position. Two imponderables had assisted them: (1) the cold storms during the night had caused the Mexican pickets around Valencia to retreat to shelter, and (2) Santa Anna had withdrawn northward from his advanced position to San Angel. Smith need not worry about his rear.[25]

Valencia's men, shivering and cold, sat up all night expecting Santa Anna to reinforce them. When dawn came, they looked toward San Angel and saw that Santa Anna had retired. In a panic, some of the men began to desert; the rest were disheartened.[26] Then the Americans hit.

The assault lasted only seventeen minutes. Valencia's men broke and ran, many intercepted by Shields as they attempted to escape toward San Angel. Santa Anna could see the rout from the distance but, instead of coming to Valencia's rescue, continued retiring toward

*Douglas Freeman, *R. E. Lee*, pp. 264–65. Pierce had been injured in a fall from his horse the previous day. All in all, his Mexican War career was unimpressive. However, U. S. Grant, in his *Memoirs*, vol. I, p. 147, wrote, "The next day, when Pierce's brigade . . . was ordered against the flank and rear of the enemy . . . General Pierce attempted to accompany them. He was not sufficiently recovered to do so, and he fainted. This circumstance gave rise to exceedingly unfair and unjust criticisms of him when he became a candidate for the Presidency. Whatever General Pierce's qualifications may have been for the Presidency, he was a gentleman and a man of courage."

†Ibid., pp. 100–101. Smith, though junior to Shields, retained command of the forces. Perhaps neither man was aware of his dates or rank; perhaps, in view of Smith's far greater familiarity with the terrain, Shields chose to ignore it. But Smith later expressed appreciation of Shields's magnanimity, and in any case it was a wise arrangement.

Churubusco. Valencia himself escaped the American trap and made his way northward alone, giving San Angel a wide berth after learning that Santa Anna had issued an order for him to be shot.

The Americans showed no mercy, pursuing to the best of their capacities all the way to San Angel amid the confusion. Just as they were entering the town Persifor Smith encountered Pillow,[27] who had arrived just after the battle to assume command.

So much for Padierna/Contreras, a battle that Scott had never expected to fight. Scott had committed 4,500 men against 7,000, "with 12,000 more hovering in sight." Of these, Scott claimed to have killed 700, with 813 prisoners, including four generals.* Santa Anna had missed a great opportunity to deliver a devastating blow against an enemy who could not afford a defeat, but at least most of his army was still intact.

But not for long. Scott, who received word of the victory as he was halfway between San Agustín and Padierna, took immediate action to pursue. Perceiving correctly that the collapse of Valencia's position would signal a Mexican retreat all along the line, he halted the movement of Worth's and Quitman's divisions toward San Angel and ordered them back. Worth, he directed, should wait until Pillow's division, converging upon Churubusco from San Angel, cut the Churubusco–San Antonio road from the rear. Then Worth was to pursue as the enemy retreated. Scott himself continued to the San Angel road. When he reached Cayoacán, a few miles beyond San Angel, he caught up with Pillow and Smith. There, amid the cheers of his troops, he resumed direct control of his army.[28]

Worth, however, did not wait for Pillow to come to his support. Instead he sent Clarke's brigade westward through the Pedregal to the rear of San Antonio, and that threat caused the garrison on his front to flee in panic. Worth pursued them up the road toward Churubusco. Both main roads to the Rio Churubusco, from San Angel and San Antonio, were now open, both the scenes of hot pursuit.

*Scott report, August 28, 1847, Exec. Doc. No. 1, p. 308. Being written so close to the event, the report can be accepted only as approximate. Great rejoicing accompanied the recapture of two artillery pieces from the 4th Artillery, taken by Santa Anna at Buena Vista.

. . .

Santa Anna, meanwhile, had regained his composure somewhat and decided to bring what troops could be saved back within the walls of Mexico City. To do so, however, he knew that he must keep the Churubusco bridge across the river open for his fleeing troops.

The bridge at Churubusco, over the river of the same name, was protected by two main defenses. One was the formidable *tête de pont* protecting the main bridge itself, and the other was the massive and heavily defended San Mateo Convent, about five hundred yards to the southwest. Santa Anna ordered these two positions held at all costs. To some the order seemed superfluous. In both the *tête de pont* and the convent were artillerymen who had deserted the U.S. Army as far back as Matamoros. The men of the infamous San Patricio Battalion, aware that capture would mean the gallows, would form the backbone of any defense.

Unfortunately for his men, Winfield Scott acted hastily. Unaware of the strength of the two positions at Churubusco, and for once careless of the need for reconnaissance, he ordered all-out attack upon both positions. He was aware of two other bridges across the Rio Churubusco, one of which crossed between the road hub of Coyoacán and the rear of Churubusco. Across that bridge he sent Shields, reinforced by Pierce, toward the town of Portales, north of Churubusco. Had Scott known of the strength and determination with which the convent and the *tête de pont* would be held, he probably would have bypassed them, sending the bulk of his forces behind Shields. As it was, he pursued—as any other commander would have—headlong.

Churubusco

The Battle of Churubusco, which began around noon of Friday, August 20, 1847, really consisted of three independent actions: (1) the main attack (Worth and Pillow) on the Churubusco bridge, (2) the attack on the Convent (Twiggs), and (3) the turning movement to Portales, north of the Churubusco bridge (Shields and Pierce). In so allocating his forces, Scott had committed all his brigades, and his power to affect the battle was limited. Thus, when Lee reported to him that Shields and Pierce were in trouble at Portales, Scott was forced to raid Twiggs's reserve, sending the Mounted Rifles and one company of dragoons to their aid. It was a small reinforcement, but it arrived in time to turn the tide for the left wing.[29]

The first position to give way under American attack was the *tête de pont* at Churubusco, turned from the east. Clarke's brigade (5th, 6th, and 8th infantries) and Cadwalader's brigade (11th and 14th infantries), supported by Duncan's artillery battalion (2,600 total), converged on this position of between seven thousand and nine thousand of the enemy. When the works were carried, by the bayonet, even the professional Worth felt his mind "filled with wonder," and his heart "filled with gratitude."[30] The feat on the part of officers and men had been spectacular.

Once the *tête de pont* was reduced, Worth was able to turn his fire on the Convent, and its fate was doomed. Captain Edmund B. Alexander, commanding the 3d Infantry, was the first over the rampart, and once more the bayonet was the final, decisive weapon. Twenty minutes later, after a battle of two and a half hours, the Convent of San Mateo fell.[31] What was left of the San Patricio Battalion was captured.

On the north, at Portales, Shields had been faced with heavy odds. His final triumph was muted, for just as the enemy was breaking and scattering, Worth's triumphant men came charging up the road from Churubusco. The pursuit began again but was ineffective, by and large, because of the restriction to the causeways. The pursuing cavalry was unable to envelop the fugitives.

One small episode remained. It would probably have gone unnoticed by history except for the future prominence of the two dragoons involved. Not hearing Harney's order to halt, Captain Philip Kearny and Lieutenant Richard S. Ewell continued the chase all the way to a gate of Mexico City. Here they dashed into heavy Mexican musket fire, Kearny suffering a mangled left arm that had to be amputated. Almost exactly fifteen years later, the two comrades would both be casualties near Bull Run, Virginia. Kearny would be killed fighting for the Union; Ewell seriously wounded fighting for the Confederacy.*

---

*Ewell, with Jackson, lost his leg at Groveton, August 29, 1862. Kearny was actually killed at Chantilly, just after the Second Battle of Bull Run, September 1, 1862.

. . .

Santa Anna was devastated. In a single day, he had lost an estimated four thousand killed or wounded. Among the three thousand captured were eight generals (two of them former presidents of Mexico). And none of his organizations survived as entities.

But Scott had suffered also. By his own admission, he lost 1,053 officers and men that day, of whom 139 were killed.[32] He could have taken the city.

But he did not.

THE
HALLS OF
MONTEZUMA

AUGUST–SEPTEMBER 14, 1847

Santa Anna arrived back at the Palace of the Montezumas in Mexico City early on the afternoon of August 20, "possessed of a black depair from the unfortunate events of the war."[1] All around him, confusion and disillusionment enveloped the population of the city. Less than ten days earlier, their National Guard had occupied El Penon amid flowery speeches and stirring martial music. Even the day before, the people had felt secure in the belief that the hated Scott, overextended, was doomed. Now, in the course of less than twenty-four hours, their world had been shattered.

But Santa Anna's usual resilience made itself felt again. Even as the gringos were mopping up the convent at Churubusco, Santa Anna was assembling his ministers of government to decide what to do next. He had an answer: a truce. With some respite, he hoped, he might still reorganize his troops and present an effective defense of the city. Some of the more realistic ministers urged immediate surrender, but Santa Anna was finally able to form a consensus: a truce should be negotiated through either the Spanish minister, Bermudez de Castro, or the English consul general, Edward Mackintosh.

De Castro, on being approached, quickly refused, but Mackintosh accepted, and by the evening of the same day Mackintosh and Edward

Thornton were on their way to San Agustín to visit Scott. Their purported reason for the visit was to ask for a safeguard for British subjects to leave the city, but the real reason, the Americans suspected, was to "prepare the way for peace."*

Scott paid little heed to that visit, and the next morning he moved his headquarters forward to Coyoacán, preparing for an assault on the vulnerable city. Before the attack could be launched, however, General Ignacio Mora y Villamil, the Mexican chief of engineers, arrived with a sealed packet for Trist containing a note from the Mexican foreign minister, J. R. Pacheco, to Buchanan—an answer to the note Trist had delivered several months earlier. Pacheco's note haughtily declared that he was now ready to "receive" Trist, and that he would consider whether Buchanan's proposals were consistent with Mexican "honor." The note also proposed a year's truce, to be observed while a permanent peace was being negotiated.[2]

Pacheco's note was, of course, an exercise in futility, but Mora, an astute individual, advised Scott informally that Santa Anna would happily settle for a short truce, to take place immediately. Scott and Trist consulted. Certainly, a truce seemed desirable. Scott believed that he could seize the city forthwith; but if he did so, he might "scatter the elements of peace, excite a spirit of national desperation, and thus indefinitely postpone the hope of accommodation." He therefore set aside his summons for Santa Anna to surrender the city, and substituted a conciliatory note proposing a truce. The army, he reported to Marcy, "very cheerfully sacrificed . . . the *eclat* that would have followed an entrance—sword in hand—into a great capital."[3]

Winfield Scott was a great soldier—one of the greatest—but as a letter writer, he had not learned from his previous mistakes. Living as he did in a world of Walter Scott's *Ivanhoe*, he seemed unable to predict the way his lofty wording would be received by lesser mortals. That fault had nearly confined him to Washington the previous May and had delayed the development of his friendship with Trist. In this case, Scott's effort to be conciliatory ruffled some feathers by his first

---

*Ramón Alcaraz, *The Other Side*, p. 301. Santa Anna's selection of the British consul general rather than the minister is interesting. Perhaps he desired to picture the negotiation as a local affair, and therefore turned to the consul, who was accredited to the city. But perhaps it was because Mackintosh, being a large property owner in Mexico, had an extra incentive to promote peace. When Mackintosh was spied in the party conferring with Scott, a reporter from the New Orlean *Picayune*, who knew Mackintosh, reportedly exclaimed, "It's no use, we're humbugged —Mackintosh is among them!" Charles Dufour, *The Mexican War*, pp. 257–58.

sentence: "Sir: Too much blood has already been shed in this unnatural war between the two great republics of this continent."[4] The problem lay in the two words, "unnatural war." The Spanish translation of the harmless term was inexact, and to some of the Mexicans it was indelicate;* to more practical men, such as Santa Anna, the tone of the whole letter, including the questionable phrase, indicated weakness. But regardless of the wording, Santa Anna had what he wanted, a truce, and he accepted it immediately. At the same time he kept his troops under arms and frantically placed them in advantageous defensive positions, positions that they could occupy during the truce.†

On Sunday, August 22, commissioners from both sides met at Mackintosh's home in Tacubaya. Generals Mora and Benito Quijano sat for the Mexicans; Quitman, Persifor Smith, and Pierce for the Americans.‡ After a long discussion they reached a truce. It was a remarkable document by modern standards, for it provided for a great deal of normal intercourse between the two belligerents. It forbade either side from indulging in any military activity, such as the building of fortifications within a range of ninety miles of Mexico City, and it prohibited the Americans from interfering with normal traffic in and out of the city. In return, Americans were allowed to draw supplies from Mexico City itself. Prisoners were to be exchanged and the wounded cared for. The civil rights of the Mexicans in occupied territories would be respected. The truce could be terminated by either side with forty-eight hours' notice.[5]

The truce was probably a wise effort, based on what Scott understood of the Mexican situation. Wise or not, proposing it was certainly well motivated on Scott's part, and, according to his friend Hitchcock, Scott had always considered stopping short of the city itself as a means of securing peace without completely humiliating the Mexicans.§ But

---

*Alcaraz, p. 301n, writes, "The original English says 'of nature'... Now, to Spanish delicacy, a war against nature is a perfect novelty, not only disgusting, but a deadly insult.... adding a new species to what was punished in the sodomites of scripture...."

†Alcaraz (p. 302) says that Santa Anna personally ordered one unit into the garita of Candelaria at 2 A.M. on the twenty-first.

‡Scott was cautious in his selection of representatives; all were lawyers and all were Democrats.

§"Just before he left Puebla . . . General Scott wrote a memorandum, one of the most remarkable ever penned by any commander in any campaign on record. . . . [He] stated that he would advance upon the capital, and *would either defeat the enemy in view of the city, if they would give him battle, or he would take a strong position from the enemy, and then, if he could restrain the enthusiasm of his troops, he would halt outside of the city and take measures to give those in the city an opportunity to save the capital by making a peace."* Hitchcock, letter, January 23, 1848, in Exec. Doc. No. 65, Pillow court-martial, p. 524. Italics in the original.

Scott was deluding himself if he believed, as he had reported, that his men were cheerful about stopping short of the city. They were not. The "eclat" of occupying a major capital was not what they wanted— soldiers rarely worry much about such things—and they knew that Santa Anna, if given time, could fortify the capital, making its capture far more costly in lives. Kirby Smith, the articulate pessimist, was writing for many: "We are in a strange situation—a conquering army on a hill overlooking an enemy's capital, which is perfectly at our mercy, yet not permitted to enter it, and compelled to submit to all manner of insults from its corrupt inhabitants."[6]

But wise or not, the truce failed. On the very first day an American supply train was turned back at a garita of Mexico City. Santa Anna apologized quickly, but similar incidents followed. On the morning of August 27 a train of a hundred wagons entered the city to draw provisions in accordance with the convention. Mobs shouting "Let the Yankees die" threw stones. Then, when the lancers appeared to restore order, the people called their own troops "cowards" and exhorted the Almighty to visit instant death not only upon the Americans but even more on Santa Anna, who had made such arrangements.[7] Far more serious were the military violations. Santa Anna, not surprisingly, made full use of the time to rebuild his force, as he had always planned. And though his activities were hidden as well as possible, the Americans knew. Beauregard, Kirby Smith, and Hitchcock, among many others, were outraged at the fact that Scott was observing the truce whereas Santa Anna was not. Smith even reported evidence in writing to Scott, who declared Smith's informant a "liar."[8]

What finally brought the truce to an end, however, was the failure of the peace negotiations. For over a week, until September 2, Trist and Scott still held some hope for success in the talks between Trist and the Mexican commissioners. But on that day, with no progress concerning future boundaries in prospect, Trist presented them with an ultimatum and both sides agreed to adjourn until the sixth. By the time the sixth arrived Scott had learned that Santa Anna, in grand council, had decided, on receiving Trist's notice, to recommence overt fortification of the city. Consequently, Scott sent a note accusing Santa Anna of violating the 3d Article of the convention—the article forbidding military activity.[9] He further gave notice that if he had not received "full satisfaction" on these matters by noon of the next day, he would consider the armistice at an end. Scott was not concerned with the forty-eight-hour restriction on terminating the truce; Santa Anna, in Scott's mind, had terminated it three days earlier.

The same day, Santa Anna answered that he would "repel force by force, with the decision and energy which my high obligations place upon me."*

Hostilities had now officially recommenced, and Scott, with his usual thoroughness, began a study of the approaches to Mexico City before attacking it. As always, the burden of the scouting fell on the shoulders of Scott's engineers, now headed by Lee during the sickness of his senior, Major Smith. In a sense the problem was simple. The fields between the causeways—some marsh, some inundated—were impassable, certainly for artillery, so Scott's decision was limited to simply selecting which of the causeways to use. Confinement to these elevated roadbeds made Scott's problems difficult because they were narrow, and if defended by determined troops could be very strong, as they could not be outflanked. However, the defending troops bunched up on a causeway would be vulnerable to American artillery. The problem, therefore, was far from insoluble.†

On the south and west of Mexico City—the only approaches under consideration—six of these causeways led up to the garitas, solid square buildings that ordinarily served as tollgates. Two led from the west: the San Cosme and the Belen. Both of these, however, originated under the strong castle of Chapultepec, so Scott first considered the four to the south, which were, left to right, (a) the Piedad causeway, which joined the Belen causeway at the Belen garita, (b) the Niño Perdido causeway, that led from the Niño Perdido garita southwest to San Angel, (c) the San Antonio causeway, which ran also from the San

---

*Exec. Doc. No. 1, pp. 355, 361. Santa Anna made an eloquent case for the breakdown: " . . . I cannot be blind to the truth, that the true cause of the threats of renewing hostilities, contained in the note of your excellency, is that I have not been willing to sign a treaty which would lessen considerably not only the territory of the republic, but that dignity and integrity which all nations defend to the last extremity. And if these considerations do not have the same weight in the mind of your excellency, the responsibility before the world, who can easily distinguish on whose side is moderation and justice, will fall upon you.

†"Each of these routes (an elevated causeway) presents a double roadway on the sides of an aqueduct of strong masonry, and great height, resting on open arches and massive pillars, which, together, afford fine points for attack and defense. The sideways of both aqueducts are, moreover, defended by many strong breastworks at the gates, and before reaching them. As we had expected, we found the four tracks unusually dry and solid for the season." Scott report, September 18, 1847, Exec. Doc. No. 1, p. 381.

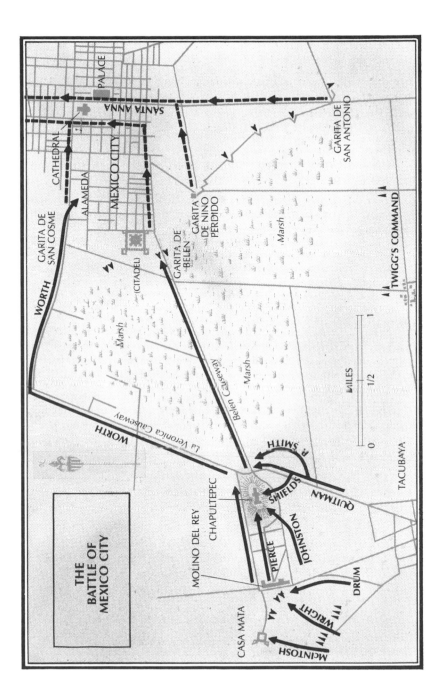

THE BATTLE OF MEXICO CITY

Antonio garita due south to Churubusco, and finally (d) the Paseo de la Viga, to the east. The main Mexican fortifications outside the city were the Castle of Chapultepec, the Molino del Rey (King's Mill) a mile to the southwest of Chapultepec, and the Casa de la Mata, beyond Molino del Rey.

As of September 7, when the truce ended, Scott was with Worth's division, at Tacubaya, only about a mile from Chapultepec; Twiggs was at San Angel, Pillow at Mixcoac, and Quitman still back at San Agustín.[10] Scott and his engineers were examining the three direct approaches to the city from the south.

Molina del Rey

On the afternoon of September 7, 1847, word came to Scott that a large body of Mexican troops had been detected in the vicinity of Molino del Rey, "within a mile and a third" of Scott's headquarters at Tacubaya. Molino del Rey was a "huge pile of stone buildings, 200 yards long," which housed a flour mill and, in former times, a cannon foundry.[11] The report went on to say that large deposits of powder were located nearby and that many church bells were being sent out to the Molino for casting as guns. Scott therefore paused. Since his main force would not be ready to assault the city for a couple of days, he now believed that a minor action to take the Molino would be a sensible move. As the action seemed to require only one reinforced division, Scott selected the one nearest, Worth's, located at Tacubaya.* To give added strength, Scott attached Cadwalader's brigade from Pillow's division and 270 dragoons under Major E. V. Sumner.[12]

Worth moved out the morning of September 8 with his 3,500 men, guided by James Mason and James Duncan, who together had previously scouted the area. He saw before him a well-defended position,

*Not everyone considered the forthcoming operation "minor." Captain E. Kirby Smith wrote home that evening, "I have just learned that the plan of attack is arranged. A forlorn hope of five hundred men commanded by Major G. Wright is to carry the foundry and blow it up. At the same time an attack from our artillery, the rest of the first division and Cadwalader's brigade is to be made upon their line and Chapultepec, our battalion forming the reserve. This operation is to commence at three in the morning. Tomorrow will be a day of slaughter. I firmly trust and pray that victory may crown our efforts though the odds are immense. I am thankful that you do not know the peril we are in. Good night." Kirby Smith, *To Mexico with Scott*, p. 217. Those were the last words that Smith ever wrote.

with two strong points, the Molino on the right and the Casa Mata about six hundred yards to the left. Though the Mexican artillery was located between them, the two strongpoints presented the main problem.

Worth employed his division admirably. In the center he placed Duncan's battery to neutralize the enemy artillery and pound the Molino. Then, on his right, he sent Garland's brigade, with Huger's battery, to cut off possible reinforcements from Chapultepec and attack the Molino from the east. Clarke's brigade he sent to reduce the potent Casa Mata, and Sumner's 270 dragoons to hold off any cavalry raids from the west. To assault the Molino, he organized a storming party, under Major George Wright, of five hundred men picked from the various regiments.[13] These assault troops, though selected soldiers, had no personal loyalty to the makeshift unit; they were strangers to their teammates.*

The plan deserved better results. As it was, Santa Anna had become aware of Scott's order to Worth, and he was ready. He placed five brigades, supported by artillery, in the Molino, and stationed four thousand cavalry, under Alvarez at Los Morales, to Worth's west, in position to charge and destroy his rear and flank.[14] Strangely, he put nobody in overall charge of the defense; each unit fought on its own. But the result was a major battle, not the skirmish that Scott and Worth had expected.

At the start the spotlight was on Wright's storming party. Huger's guns raked the Molino in support as Wright's men went forward under heavy Mexican artillery and musket fire. Outside the Molino Wright overran the Mexican infantry and artillery at the point of the bayonet, turning the guns on the fugitives. But soon the fleeing Mexicans discovered that Wright was leading only a small party. They thereupon turned around and counterattacked, bringing him again under withering fire. Eleven out of Wright's fourteen officers were struck down, Wright among them. The rest of the Americans broke, but were rescued by the success of Garland's brigade and Huger's battery as they surged into the Molino from the west. Wright's men dispersed, released to find their own regiments. Back with their units, they uniformly performed well for the rest of the battle.[15]

---

*Such storming parties were not uncommon. They had a wry nickname, the "forlorn hope."

Garland had taken the Molino, and Worth could now concentrate on the Casa Mata. Duncan's and Huger's batteries were turned in that direction while Clarke's 2d Brigade, under the command of McIntosh, soon discovered that the position was a stone fortress, not the mere earthen revetment previously supposed. Though the Americans surrounded the old Spanish position, they were repulsed by the heavy fire. As they paused they could see defenders come out of the Casa and murder their wounded comrades. It was an expensive crime; the Americans would remember.

At this point, Worth detected large Mexican reinforcements—Alvarez's cavalry and infantry—beyond a ravine to the west. Duncan's battery arrived on that flank, however, and its fire dissuaded Alvarez from attacking. In the meantime the intrepid Sumner, with his handful of dragoons, crossed the ravine and defied Alcaraz in his own territory. No cavalry engagement took place; Sumner's losses came from the Casa Mata.

The Mexicans in the Casa Mata were in a hopeless position, without artillery and with walls crumbling. They might have surrendered if they had only been pounded a little longer. But the impetuous Worth ordered McIntosh to assault. McIntosh obeyed—and quickly fell, as did his second and third in command. The brigade dropped back, and only some time later, under the shells of Duncan's artillery, did the garrison of the Casa Mata flee, leaving it in Worth's hands.[16]

The entire battle of Molino del Rey took only two hours.[17] But fighting had been fierce, and Worth, though successful, could have been destroyed. As it was, the cost to his division was frightful: 116 dead, among them Lieutenant Colonel Scott, commanding the 5th Infantry (which lost 38 percent of its effective strength),[18] and Captain Kirby Smith, temporarily in command of the light infantry. Among the 671 wounded, many of them severely, were not only Colonel McIntosh but also Major Waite, commanding the 8th Infantry.* These casualties exceeded those of Taylor at Monterrey—and they came from a force half of Taylor's size.

Ironically, Worth found no evidence of a foundry at Molino del Rey. His bloody attack had accomplished nothing more than to deliver a blow against an already low Mexican morale.

*Douglas Freeman, *R. E. Lee*, p. 117; Worth report, September 10, 1847, Exec. Doc. No. 1, pp. 362–64. Total Mexican losses were estimated at 700 captured, 2,000 killed and wounded, 2,000 deserters. Justin Smith, *The War with Mexico*, vol. II, p. 147.

. . .

Scott observed the capture of Molino del Rey on September 8, though he allowed Worth to conduct the battle without interference. The next day, again ready to concentrate on the approaches to the city, he took Lee with him to the Niño Perdido road. There they could look to the east at the San Antonio garita, which was vulnerable because it stuck out far to the south of the other gates. Meanwhile, Beauregard, Tower, and I. I. Stevens went to the right, up the Paseo de la Viga, where they could scrutinize the same San Antonio garita from twelve hundred yards to the east. From what they could see, both the San Antonio and the La Viga approaches were rapidly being built up. They estimated that each gate held eleven artillery pieces but could hold many more.[19] Obviously, there was no time to lose in attacking.

Scott, nevertheless, spent two more days checking the ground. Then, late on September 11, he called a council of war in the little church at La Piedad. Present, as usual, were his general officers and his staff, the most visible of whom were his engineers. By now he had reduced his problem to a single decision: Should he secure the fortress of Chapultepec before attacking the city, or should he bypass it, concentrating on the San Antonio garita? He lacked the resources to sustain a failure; therefore this decision would be crucial.

Scott's procedure was unusual. He began by stating his own preference, to seize the hill of Chapultepec. He had been advised, he said, that Chapultepec was not really so strong as it appeared; perhaps it could be demolished by a one-day bombardment. And with its fall the Mexican government was likely to come to terms without an assault on the city itself. Having thus stated his views, Scott then—and only then—requested the views of his staff.

Fortunately, despite his pompous ways, Scott did not intimidate his officers, and they spoke their pieces freely. First came Lee, acting senior engineer, who recommended approaching the city from the south, taking the San Antonio garita first. Three other engineers, as well as four of the generals, agreed with him. But one engineer had not been heard from. Scott, pointing to the corner, asked a previously silent Beauregard his opinion. Beauregard sprang to his feet and presented a long, technical argument in favor of the Chapultepec attack. Rather than feint from the west and attack from the south, he reasoned, the army could probably convince Santa Anna that the attack would come at the San Antonio garita—and then attack Chapultepec. So persuasive was Beauregard that Franklin Pierce, one of the conferees, changed his vote. Only one vote counted, however, and that was Scott's. He chose to reduce Chapultepec.

"Gentlemen," he said impressively. "We will attack by the western gates. The general officers present here will remain for further orders —the meeting is dissolved."*

Chapultepec

Santa Anna had far more troops on his rolls than did Scott, but since he was uncertain about Scott's plans, he decided to distribute nearly all his men among the garitas. To encourage Santa Anna's uncertainty, Scott organized a feint to be executed in the area of the San Antonio causeway. To do this, he ordered Quitman to move up from his present position at Coyoacán and join Pillow at La Piedad. The march was to be made in daylight in hopes that Mexican scouts would observe them heading in that direction. Then, after dark, both divisions were to withdraw to Tacubaya. Pillow would then move up to Molino del Rey, from which he would attack Chapultepec from the west while Quitman would prepare to attack the southeast corner from Tacubaya. The two regular divisions—worn out—were to follow up. Twiggs was to demonstrate with Riley's brigade at Piedad; P. F. Smith's brigade would start out in reserve at San Angel. Worth was to follow Pillow, support him, and pass through to Mexico City once Pillow had seized Chapultepec.[20]

But Scott still hoped to reduce Chapultepec by artillery fire alone, even hoping that the city might surrender without the suffering and bloodshed of an assault. Accordingly, Scott placed one battery (Drum) at the Hacienda Condesa, along the road from Tacubaya to the city; the second (Hagner) near the road from the Molino, facing the southwest corner; and two others (Brooks and Anderson) in a third position just south of the Molino itself. Recent captures had trebled the power of his siege pieces: available in place were sixteen-pound siege guns, eight-inch howitzers, a ten-inch mortar and a twenty-four pounder.[21]

---

*Justin Smith, *The War with Mexico*, vol. II, p. 149. The author cannot help wondering how much this decision was affected by a desire to justify the blunder of the attack on Molino del Rey by utilizing that route.

The batteries opened up at 5 A.M., September 12. The fire was light at first. Then the walls of the castle began to be pierced, and the roof was partly destroyed. Even while the bombardment was going on, however, Mexican engineers were attempting to make repairs. At about noon Santa Anna visited Chapultepec and found old Nicholas Bravo, hero of the 1821 Mexican revolution, calmly eating his breakfast, "the balls and bombs crashing about him." During the day the bombardment grew heavier. The Americans were now keeping a projectile in the air at all times. "In the corridor, converted into a surgical hospital, were found mixed up the putrid bodies, the wounded breathing mournful groans and the young boys of the College," of whom fifty were remaining. Medical supplies were gone. Too late Santa Anna and Bravo realized that they could have placed most of their infantry troops at the bottom of the hill, thus preventing many needless deaths. Bravo, with no intention of giving up hope, still requested reinforcements, but Santa Anna refused to send any until the attack should begin.[22]

The die was cast: the assault would come the next morning.

The morning of September 13, 1847, promised to be a beautiful day, the skies a deep blue, as one might expect at an altitude of a mile and a half in the days before industrial smog. The air would be warm. But for Scott's troops it was a day of foreboding. The victories they had won had been dear—the Molino, in particular. The army was greatly reduced, opposing an enemy of overwhelming numbers. There was gloom among the officers as well. As they left the final meeting the night before, even Worth had said privately, "We shall be defeated." And Scott himself had said to Hitchcock, "I have my misgivings."[23]

Chapultepec, with its enclosure, was a position about three-quarters of a mile long and about a quarter mile wide, the length running roughly east to west. The north and east sides were too precipitous to be scaled; of the other two, by far the gentler slope would be on the west, the direction of the Molino, though the approach led through a cypress swamp. Pillow's division, assembling at the Molino, would make the main assault with Pierce's brigade leading. Pierce's men would scale the walls of the extensive gardens, advance past the ancient cypresses, and slosh through the half mile of mud to attack the castle.

Quitman, on Pillow's right, would follow the causeway that led from Tacubaya to the southeast corner. There he would scale the walls of the gardens and seize control of the steep, winding pathway that led upward to the base of the walls. Once Chapultepec was taken, Quitman's men would be able to continue on the Belem Causeway eastward to Mexico City.

To assault the walls, Scott had organized scaling parties similar to that used previously at the Molino. A party of 265 selected officers and men (another "forlorn hope") had been provided by Twiggs to lead Quitman's division; a similar party, provided by Worth, was to lead Pillow's.[24] The assaulting troops, including a detachment of forty marines, would all be regulars.

Chapultepec was actually not so formidable as it appeared. Though it stood nearly two hundred feet above the level of the marsh, that height included the hill leading up. And since the walls were precipitous, its defenders were unable to deliver aimed fire at their base. The building could hold only 260 Mexican troops, including the group of young Military College cadets who, at their own insistence, had been allowed to remain. Santa Anna stationed another six hundred troops outside the castle to defend the walls around the courtyard, some of them sharpshooters in the trees.

The bombardment began at dawn, as planned, pouring shot and shell into the castle until 7:30 A.M., at which time muzzles were lowered to rake the defenders of the walls surrounding the grounds. After thirty minutes the firing stopped; the time for the attack had come. Pierce's brigade poured out of the Molino del Rey, went over the walls, and, meeting little resistance at first, waded through the cypress marsh. But soon resistance stiffened and Pierce's men took casualties. Colonel T. B. Ransom, commanding the 9th Infantry, received a rifle bullet through the forehead. Pillow was taken out of action early with a wound in the ankle. In pain but conscious, Pillow called for Worth, exhorting him to "make great haste."[25] Meanwhile the artillery and mortar fire concentrated once more on the walls of the castle.

Quitman's advance party, on the Tacubaya causeway to the south, was held up.* But one regiment, Joseph E. Johnston's gray-coated

---

*Quitman's "forlorn hope," under Captain Silas Casey, was supplemented by a detachment of forty marines under Captain John G. Reynolds, USMC, and 120 volunteers under Major Levi Twiggs, USMC. Both Casey and Twiggs were killed.

Voltiguers, struggled over the south wall and fell in on Pillow's (Pierce's) right. Persifor Smith's brigade was sent by Twiggs to help Quitman.

Smith made an unsuccessful effort to turn the Mexicans in Quitman's area, whereupon Quitman sent the New York and Pennsylvania volunteers off the causeway, across the ditches, and around the redan in the garden wall. An opening was made, and the South Carolina Palmetto Regiment followed, along with Clarke's brigade (Worth) that had also been sent to Quitman's assistance. Lieutenant James Longstreet, of the 8th Infantry, was wounded; George Pickett, of the same regiment, seized the colors Longstreet had been carrying.[26] Soon troops from Quitman's, Pillow's, and Worth's divisions were intermingled at the foot of the Chapultepec wall.

There the advance halted; the scaling ladders had not yet come up. For a long fifteen minutes Pierce's and Johnston's infantrymen crouched at the castle's base, below an exchange of blazing fire, in temporary safety. Sharpshooters kept Mexican heads down. Then a few ladders came. The first in place were toppled, the daring assault troops with them. But soon enough ladders arrived to allow fifty men to climb simultaneously. They moved swiftly, and the defenders at the walls fell back.

By 9:30 A.M., only two hours since the beginning of the action, the flag of Johnston's Voltiguer Regiment flew above the east walls of Chapultepec, and the hand-to-hand slaughter throughout the castle began. The Americans, thirsting to avenge the cruel and needless slaughter of their wounded comrades at Molino del Rey, killed Mexicans unmercifully. General Bravo survived to surrender his bejeweled sword, but not six of the young cadets who chose to die rather than surrender. One of these young boys met his doom by plunging off the wall with the Mexican flag clutched in his arms.*

On a small hillock below Chapultepec thirty doomed men stood on mule carts, nooses around their necks. These members of the San Patricio Battalion of deserters, captured at the Convent of Churu-

---

*The six would be immortalized in Mexico as Los Niños Heroicos (heroic children). They are memorialized by an impressive monument at the foot of Chapultepec today.

busco, had since been tried and condemned. When the American flag appeared above the walls of Chapultepec, the mules would be whipped, and the deserters would dangle in the air.

Scott would have preferred to show mercy. Indeed, of the sixty-nine captured, those who had deserted before hostilities began on April 26, 1846, had been spared, though lashed, imprisoned, and sometimes branded. Had the war been over, Scott said privately that he would have granted mercy to all of them. But the failure of negotiations during the truce had sealed the prisoners' fate. Scott could not allow a precedence of clemency in an army bound to suffer severe casualties in the fighting ahead.[27]

The deserters, rough men in a rough age, accepted their lot with a sardonic humor. One of their number had lost his legs in the fighting at Churubusco. His fellows found it amusing that he would be able to dance in the air as well as the rest of them. The flag went up, whips snapped, and the mules lurched forward.

Chapultepec had fallen. All in all, Santa Anna lost 1,800 men that morning. Scott lost one-quarter as many. Hardly had the mopping up been completed—Scott had just arrived—than two commanders, Quitman and Worth, ordered their forces to rush down the causeways toward Mexico City itself. They encountered resistance, but by the end of the day Worth (who had passed through Pillow) was in possession of the San Cosme garita on the northwest corner of the city; Quitman had the Belen garita on the southwest corner.

During the night Santa Anna decided to evacuate the city and allow his army to rest. Sporadic fighting would go on the next morning but by midday, September 14, 1847, General Scott himself rode triumphantly through the City Square amid the deafening cheers of what was left of his army.

NICHOLAS
TRIST'S
WAR

OCCUPATION

AUTUMN IN MEXICO CITY, 1847

The people of Mexico City did not roll over and play dead merely because Scott entered its gates in triumph. Quite the contrary. Santa Anna, to be sure, had retreated to Guadelupe Hildago, outside town, to await developments, but the crowds in the streets were not so docile.

Even as Scott was taking possession of the Grand Plaza, leperos (beggars) had already sacked the unguarded palace. Now they clustered around the plaza and, supposedly provoked by the "haughtiness" of the Americans, became unruly. The crowds were dispersed for the moment, but as the Americans began to march off to quarters an unidentified Mexican fired a shot. Others followed; one intended for Worth hit Garland in the leg. Convicts, whom Santa Anna had released from jail, joined the mobs. The situation was becoming serious. For a while it appeared that Scott's veterans would have to fight another battle, but quick action, the reflex of men accustomed to combat, saved the day. The units formed ranks to fire, loaded their artillery pieces with canister, and began raking the streets. Lookouts spotted buildings from which shots had been fired. Solid shot blasted holes in the walls and angry soldiers poured through to kill and pillage. Since most of the civilians were fighting only with stones, resistance in any one place melted away quickly.

By noon Scott's men held all the critical points of the city, and mob violence subsided.* Mobs roamed the streets of the unlighted city that cold night, and dead bodies littered the cobblestones. Patrols kept the mobs under control, however, though most of the people spent the night watching in fear. With the dawn a semblance of order prevailed at first, but a little later some of the violence resumed. At about the same time a few Mexican cavalry appeared at the gates of the city, but when they were dispersed, all hopes for the return of Santa Anna dissipated. And now the people, realizing that the resistance had come principally from the lower and not the privileged classes, refused to join in the fighting. The violence became sporadic, with probably more civilians killed than soldiers.[1]

Scott, an old hand at occupation, went about his task methodically. On the day he entered Mexico City he issued General Order No. 284, warning his troops that the war was not over, and urging them to be "sober, orderly, and merciful." Meanwhile he confirmed his appointment of John Quitman as governor of the city.[2] On September 17, 1847, he republished his former general order establishing martial law, which applied to soldiers and civilians alike. The next day he assigned specific occupation responsibilities for each of his major units.†

Under Scott's watchful direction the city gradually calmed down. By mid-October it could be considered pacified.

Scott made efforts, as an adjunct to his disciplinary measures, to create a somewhat civilized atmosphere in which soldiers and civilians could get along. One means of communication with the troops was afforded by the newspaper, *The American Star,* that had first been circulated back at Jalapa. Now the *Star* was joined by a rival, the *North American.* The latter never attained the stature of the *Star,* however,

---

*At noon the president of the Ayuntamiento issued this notice to the people of the city: "The general in charge of the American forces which have occupied the city this morning has informed the Ayuntamiento that if within three hours, counted from the time this notice is posted, there is not an entire cessation of the acts of hostility now being committed . . . he will proceed with all rigor against the guilty, permitting their goods and property to be sacked and razing the block in which are situated the houses from which the American troops are fired upon." Quoted in Justin Smith, *The War with Mexico,* vol. II, p. 420.

†Exec. Doc. No. 1, p. 387. Example: "2. The first division on, or near, the direct route from the gate of San Cosme towards the cathedral, and extending a little beyond the east end of the Alameda. This division will keep a competent guard, with two guns of medium calibre, at that gate."

because it was apparent that it had been established with an ulterior motive: to instill in the minds of Yankees and Mexicans alike the advantages of annexing the whole of Mexico to the United States. Mexican papers in the city also flourished, including the *Eco del Comercio*, favoring peace with the United States, and *El Conrejo*, a scandal sheet that even the Mexicans admitted "occasionally contained some wit."[3]

The American officers soon formed an exclusive club, the descendant of which exists to this day. It was called the Aztec Club, and membership was extended to all officers who had served in the campaign from Vercruz on. Needless to say, membership carried much prestige not only in Mexico but also at home.

Santa Anna, at Guadalupe, had heard of the first uprisings in Mexico City and had sent the marauding parties that had approached its gates. But by September 15 he realized that the disturbances had been quelled. Accordingly, he resigned from the presidency of Mexico in favor of Manuel de la Peña y Peña, president of the Supreme Court of Justice. Then, with a small army of volunteers, he set out for Puebla, where the American sick and wounded of Cerro Gordo were still recuperating. If he could take that city, cutting Scott's communications with the coast, Santa Anna might still force Scott to fight his way back; he then might turn defeat into victory.

But Santa Anna's men had little heart for the enterprise because their leader no longer represented glory and grandeur. Therefore, when Santa Anna sent a futile ultimatum to Colonel C. F. Childs, who was in command of the American garrison at Puebla, his men refused to assault. Santa Anna had to settle for laying down a half-hearted siege.*

Meanwhile, guerrilla operations continued around the countryside as the Mexicans harassed Scott's line of communications. The more determined Mexicans still placed some hope in these guerrilla activities, recalling the effectiveness of such operations against Napoleon in Spain, and even more recently by the Mexicans against the Spaniards in the years leading up to independence in 1821. The main weakness

---

*Justin Smith (vol. II, pp. 174–75) estimates Santa Anna's force at 2,000 cavalry, 2,500 National Guard, 600 cavalry under Alvarez, and 600 irregulars under J. Rea.

in the 1847 version of the heroic guerrilla war lay in the lack of spirit among the guerrillas themselves. When they found the Americans alert, they often took the easier course and looted their own countrymen. Even Mexican women and children were not exempt from abuse. Such atrocities, of course, cost them the support of the people, so necessary to successful guerrilla operations.

Meanwhile, Scott's reinforcements kept coming. On August 6, 1847, about three weeks after Pierce had left Veracruz, Major F. T. Lally, 9th Infantry, set out with a force of a thousand men, consisting of eleven companies of new regular army replacements and two companies of volunteer cavalry. Opposing Lally's advance was a force of some two thousand Mexicans under Juan Soto, governor of the State of Veracruz.

Lally followed the National Highway, and his expedition seemed almost like a replay of Scott's campaign during the previous April. He was opposed at the National Bridge, at Cerro Gordo (where he attacked along the route employed by Pillow during the earlier battle), and at Jalapa itself. He arrived at Jalapa on August 19, the day of Contreras and Churubusco, his men worn out and disorganized. Of his original force, two hundred—one out of five—were wounded or sick, and his animals were completely exhausted. He would need a long time to reorganize and refit his command, so his force settled in among the friendly inhabitants of Jalapa.[4]

On September 20, 1847, a month after Lally arrived at Jalapa, a stronger force, under Brigadier General Joseph Lane, departed Veracruz along the same route. Lane, a veteran of Buena Vista, had been detached from Taylor's army when all hopes of operations against San Luis Potosí from Saltillo had been given up. All of Lane's men were volunteers: one regiment from Indiana, one from Ohio, two battalions of recruits, and five companies of volunteer infantry. Altogether his force came to a respectable 2,500 men.[5]

Lane encountered only minor harassment before reaching Jalapa and joining up with Lally. When he learned of Child's predicament at Puebla, he decided to push on ahead without pausing. Lally went with him, and Jalapa was once more without a garrison.

Santa Anna, still besieging Puebla, learned of Lane's approach and decided not to resist at the pass of El Pinal, but rather to hide out at Huamantla, a town that lay just to the north of the National Highway, in hopes that Lane might pass on without noticing him. After Lane had gone by, Santa Anna hoped he could strike the rear of Lane's column. Lane, however, learned of Santa Anna's whereabouts, and on October 8 decided to attack him where he was.

Lane's advance guard was led by Captain Sam Walker, the Texan who had joined Zachary Taylor back at Point Isabel. Walker surprised Santa Anna's outposts and pursued them into town. At the main plaza, however, Walker's men found themselves facing five hundred Mexican lancers, supported by two pieces of artillery.

Walker's force was shattered. Walker himself was killed, and the grief of his comrades was great. It was ironical that Walker should have come through so many tight spots during the war, from Palo Alto and Monterrey on, only to fall in an insignificant town after the fall of Mexico City.

The rest of the American force was saved from a worse fate only by the arrival of Lane's main body of infantry. Lane attacked with a regiment and battalion abreast, and captured the two guns that Walker had attacked, along with a large quantity of ammunition. But they had paid a heavy price. Lane continued on his way, evacuating Huamantla after remaining there for only one night.[6]

By now Santa Anna's luck had again run out. Just after the battle at Huamantla he received a message from President Peña y Peña courteously directing him to turn over his command to an old rival Manuel Rincón, and to retire to a place of his choosing. There Santa Anna would await a court martial, appointed to evaluate his conduct of the war.[7]

By December 14, 1847, Scott's force in Mexico City numbered only about eight thousand effectives, barely enough to keep the city itself pacified.[8] Scott did, however, realize the wisdom of sending expeditions to other parts of the country—to San Luis Potosí, for example, or to Mazatlán, as Commodore Shubrick had asked him to do.* But such

---

*"General— . . . I am sure I need not urge upon you the importance of holding this place [Mazatlán], and how desirable it is that the ships should be able to withdraw their men, and cruise. We can then hermetically seal the coast of Mexico on this side. . . . Let me hear from you.

expeditions would have to await further reinforcements. Scott estimated that expeditions to Zacatecas and San Luis Potosí would require five thousand men each—or seven thousand to the latter alone. And assuming that he kept seven thousand in Mexico City, he needed many more men than he had, even as of early January 1848.[9]

Eventually the reinforcements began to arrive. Aside from Lane's brigade, which remained at Puebla, Major General Robert Patterson, who had returned to Mexico, departed Veracruz with 3,000 men on November 1, 1847. After leaving a regiment at National Bridge, he continued on, arriving at Jalapa on the eighth with 2,600 men. He was followed by a column of 4,000 men under Major General William O. Butler, who had recovered from his wound at Monterrey, and another 1,300 under the ubiquitous Colonel Joseph E. Johnston. By the time all these reinforcements arrived at Mexico City Scott had at his disposal nearly 15,000 troops.[10]

But Scott did not send large forces to other parts of Mexico. At one point, in mid-December, he issued a hopeful order indicating that the army was about "to spread itself over, and to occupy, the republic of Mexico,[11] But only ten days later Scott informed Marcy that the "intolerable work" of bringing the new recruits to "respectable degrees of discipline, instruction, and conduct" must be continued in Mexico City. And with his fondness for hyperbole, added: "My daily distresses under this head weigh me to the earth."*

Scott received a good deal of criticism for failing to occupy key outlying areas, particularly because of the effect of idleness on the many troops crowded up in Mexico City. "There is nothing more demoralizing to a large body of men than the idle occupation of a large and luxurious capital," wrote one officer, admittedly an avowed enemy of Scott's. For a while, he continued, "the outrages and robberies were trifling and unimportant, and in comparison with those common among the Mexicans themselves, they sunk into utter significance."[12] But soon gam-

---

... PS—I had the honor to receive this morning your letter of the 2d, and learn with deep regret that it does not enter into your plans to send forces to this coast *at once*." Shubrick to Scott, December 17, 18, 1847, Exec. Doc. No. 60, pp. 1084–85.

*Scott to Marcy, December 25, 1847, Exec. Doc. No. 60, p. 1048. He did, in fact, send expeditions to the great mines at Real del Monte and to Toluca, the capital of the Province of Mexico.

blers of all kinds had come to the city, and licenses for gambling "hells" were being issued freely. Officers and soldiers habitually caroused in these places, "which varied in degree as much as the talents and capitals of their keepers."[13]

The Mexicans saw the same thing:

> In the lower apartments there was gambling, on the second floor drinking saloons, billiards and halls for dancing, and those above were chiefly devoted to purposes which propriety will not permit us to mention. From nine o'clock in the evening until two or three in the morning, their orgies continued, which had never before been seen in Mexico. The Mexican fair sex were more abundant than could have been wished, consisting chiefly of wicked, and sometimes allured girls, or obliged by want to exchange their honor for a piece of bread for their families.[14]

It is difficult to visualize how the presence of six thousand men could reduce the population of Mexico City to poverty, but the reports were doubtless correct in essence. On the whole, the occupation of Mexico City was relatively calm and orderly, as far as such occupations go. But in no way does the lax atmosphere of occupation duty explain the disgraceful controversy that erupted among the senior officers of the army. Some of the sorry mess can be attributed to the frazzled nerves of those who had carried heavy combat responsibilities. And without a doubt some of Scott's decisions were worthy of criticism, but this cabal was unique in U.S. military annals. Although others were involved, the main troublemaker was Gideon J. Pillow.

Pillow had much to gain from the glories of the battlefield, inept though he was in actual combat. He had joined up with fame and glory in mind. Through sheer favoritism he had been promoted to the position of second ranking officer of Scott's army. Therefore, before the arrival of Patterson in mid-December, Scott's removal could have placed him in command. It had even been intimated that if he occupied such a prominent position, Pillow could find himself being nominated for president in 1848. But it is doubtful that Pillow was that calculating. Writing years later, Scott rather generously described him as "an anomaly,—without the least malignity in his nature—amiable, and possessed of some acuteness, but . . . wholly indifferent in the choice between truth and falsehood, honesty and dishonesty;—ever as ready to attain an end by the one as the other, and habitually boastful of acts of cleverness at the total sacrifice of moral character."[15]

Pillow's first brush with Scott occurred immediately after the army entered Mexico City. Pillow, or an aide of Pillow's, had removed one of the two howitzers that had been taken at Chapultepec, and had placed it in Pillow's baggage wagon, presumably as a souvenir. Such an appropriation was in violation of the accepted premise that such booty was government property. There someone, a disenchanted subordinate no doubt, had discovered it, and before Pillow could get rid of the evidence, court-martial charges had been filed against him. Pillow's efforts to throw the blame on two young lieutenants failed, and on October 27, 1847, a court reprimanded him. It conceded that Pillow had returned the howitzer but held to the "strong impression" that he had done so only when caught.[16] Nothing came of the incident for the moment.

The real uproar began with the submission of Pillow's report of the battles of Contreras, Churubusco, and Chapultepec. In that report, dated August 24, 1847, he assumed credit for exercising command of the whole army during the battle of Contreras, hardly mentioning Scott. Later, he took credit for ordering the army's assault on Chapultepec, and as a final whopper he claimed to have ordered Quitman and Worth to attack the causeways to the city after the fall of Chapultepec.*

Scott was inclined to be tactful for once, and pointed out these discrepancies in a courteous letter to Pillow, dated October 2. Among the items Scott wished corrected was a portion bestowing the gratuitous praise that Pillow had lavished on himself, a technical impropriety in that Scott was Pillow's senior. Pillow answered from his bedside, nursing his minor but painful ankle wound. His letter was astonishingly obsequious, protesting, for example, that "For your uniform kindness and friendship I shall ever feel, and, I trust, manifest, a proper sense of *gratitude.* † In conclusion, however, Pillow requested Scott to "favor me with a few minutes' call, as I am unable to call upon you."[17]

Perhaps Scott could have reduced the virulence of later recrimina-

---

*Scott to Pillow, October 2, 1847, Exec. Doc. No. 60, pp. 1015–16. Also Pillow's report, August 24, 1847, Exec. Doc. No. 1, pp. 333–341. Some of these discrepancies cannot be found in Pillow's report as published, as Pillow later made some changes.

†Pillow to Scott, October 3, 1847, Exec. Doc. No. 60, p. 1017. Italics in original. Pillow had the habit of underlining nearly every fifth word.

tions had he magnanimously visited Pillow, using as an excuse Pillow's incapacity. Such a generous gesture might have defused the matter. Scott, however, was overly conscious of his own position as general-in-chief, and he demurred, along with a long explanation involving the other burdens he was carrying. Pillow answered with another long letter by return courier, and the next day Scott wrote that he regretted that Pillow had made any changes at all in his original report, advising that he would forward all reports to the War Department as written.[18]

There the matter might have ended, but it was actually just beginning, for at about that time two inflammatory newspaper articles reached Mexico City. One of them, published in the New Orleans *Delta* on September 10, was written by an anonymous person who signed himself "Leonidas." It contained some startling claims:

> [Pillow's] plan of battle [at Contreras] and the disposition of his forces, were most judicious and successful. He evinced in this, as he has done on other occasions, that masterly military genius and profound knowledge of the science of war, which has astonished so much the mere martinets of the profession. His plan was very similar to that by which Napoleon effected the reduction of the fortress of Ulm. . . . During this great battle, which lasted two days, General Pillow was in command of all the forces engaged, except General Worth's division, and this was not engaged. . . . General Scott gave but one order and that was to reinforce General Cadwalader's brigade."[19]

The article had been reprinted in the *Picayune* with some embellishments that were probably intended to show how ridiculous Pillow's claims had been,* and it soon reappeared in the *American Star*, the local newspaper of the American army in Mexico City.

As might be expected, the Leonidas article caused both mirth and fury depending on individual dispositions, among the other participants in the battles. And Pillow, on the basis of circumstances, was indisputably identified as the author of the piece. The correspondent for the *Delta*, James L. Freaner, discovered that the Leonidas article was nearly identical with one that Pillow had asked him to send in over his own signature. Recognizing it as highly inaccurate, Freaner had

---

*New Orleans *Delta*, September 10, 1847, reprinted in Exec. Doc. No. 65, pp. 385–89. The *Picayune* edition added this: "[A Mexican] made one terrible charge at our General with his lance, which the latter evaded with great promptitude and avidity, using his sword, tossed the weapon of the Mexican high in the air and then quietly blew his brains out with his revolver."

refused to file it, and he now concluded that someone had surreptitiously inserted it in his dispatch case.* Caught red-handed, Pillow now became subdued for a while.

There again the episode might have ended, but on October 23 the *Star* reprinted another article, this one originating in the Pittsburgh *Post* and subsequently reproduced by the Washington *Union* and a sheet in Tampico. This article did not involve Pillow; instead, it claimed that Worth and Duncan had rescued Scott from his own errors by persuading him to adopt the Chalco route on August 15 rather than assaulting El Peñón frontally. The piece was followed in late October by another from Mexico City—this time eulogizing Pillow again—under the pen name of "Veritas."[20]

Scott had reached the end of his patience. Up to this time he had tended to defer to Pillow, but now, on November 12, he hit back. In a remarkable document, he first cited a twenty-year-old army regulation, still legally in effect, that forbade the publication of "any private letters, or reports, relative to military marches and operations," as they "are frequently mischievous in design, and always disgraceful to the army." Further, any officer found guilty of "making such report for publication without special permission . . . shall be dismissed from the service."[21] This regulation Scott used as the legal basis for General Order No. 349, in which he strongly castigated the writers of the "Leonidas" and "Veritas" letters. Petulantly he observed that the only "echoes from home of the brilliant operations of our arms in this basin" had come from newspapers in New Orleans and Tampico, which identified the writers of the reports as the "principal heroes of the scandalous letters." Then, with a surge of righteous indignation, he added:

> False credit can, no doubt, be obtained at home, by such despicable self-puffings and malignant exclusion of others; but at the expense of the just esteem and consideration of all honorable officers, who love their country, their profession, and the truth of history.[22]

This outburst in official communications now involved Worth for the first time. Technically, Worth was innocent of Scott's accusation; Duncan, not he, had written a letter to a Pittsburgh friend that had

---

*Freaner often allowed various officers to send letters in his case because of the speed with which it reached New Orleans.

provided the basis for the greatly exaggerated Tampico letter. But Worth, rankling under real or imagined slights from Scott, now informed Scott by letter that the "prevailing opinion in this army" assumed that Scott's words, referring to "scandalous" behavior and invoking "the indignation of the great number" applied to himself. Worth demanded to know whether the general-in-chief meant the epithet to apply to him.[23]

Essentially, Scott's answer was that he would have court-martialed the culprits if he could identify them. As to any personal implications, if the shoe fit, so be it. That brush-off neither satisfied nor cowed Worth, and two days later he appealed directly to the President through Marcy, his friend and fellow New Yorker. He accused Scott of "arbitrary and illegal conduct, [of] malicious and gross injustice." In accordance with military propriety, he provided Scott with a copy.[24]

Duncan now entered the fray, declaring himself (only partially accurately) as the writer of the "Veritas" letter. Then when Scott learned that Pillow was asking Polk to disapprove the court-martial findings in the howitzer matter, he arrested all three—Worth, Duncan, and Pillow —and placed them under court-martial charges for insubordination. Until a reaction could be received from Washington, there the matter stood as of mid-November 1847.

The unpleasantness between Scott and three of his foremost subordinates failed to dampen the spirits of Old Fuss and Feathers. He had won too many victories during his lifetime and suffered too many defeats. He had been a general officer during the War of 1812, when Pillow was a baby; as for Worth, he would always, in Scott's mind, be his former aide who had succeeded largely through his own kindnesses. So Scott went about his business as usual.

On November 5, 1847, Scott received a communication from Juan Manual, archbishop of Mexico, protesting the prolonged retention of Mexican soldiers as prisoners. Scott responded politely five days later, explaining that he had granted paroles after the capture of Veracruz and after Cerro Gordo only to discover that the parolees had taken up arms again. He needed the archbishop's assistance in this matter before he could parole any of the prisoners he held.

The archbishop complied by becoming involved in the parole process. The new parole form required the parolee to swear "before God our Lord and on this Holy Cross" that he would not take up arms during the war unless duly exchanged. The consequences would be that God would reward compliance and punish noncompliance. The procedure took six weeks to complete, and the prisoners were duly released in late December.[25]

Scott had other concerns, one of which was the requirement that Mexico pay an indemnity. The war was becoming increasingly unpopular in the United States, and the target of the resentment was the President himself. So Polk was insistent that the occupation pay for itself. Accordingly, when Scott first entered Mexico City on September 14, he had levied an assessment of $150,000, and had set about learning the amount of tax that each state of Mexico had paid to the Mexican federal government in 1843—he would levy the same amount as payment to the United States government.* By the end of the year Scott had finished his study and published General Orders No. 395, levying an annual assessment of $3,046,498, distributed proportionally, upon the nineteen states of Mexico. The State of Mexico, including the city, was to pay $668,332.[26]

On December 8, 1847, Scott gave a dinner in honor of Brigadier General David E. Twiggs, who was departing to take command at Veracruz. The extensive guest list included Trist and selected generals, Patterson, Cadwalader, Pierce, Caleb Cushing, and Persifor Smith among them. Also present were such brigade and regimental commanders as Withers, Wyncoop, Bonham, Lally, and Hitchcock.

The evening was particularly memorable to Hitchcock for the toast that Scott gave to the United States Military Academy. The group present included only three former cadets: Trist, Hitchcock, and With-

*Scott to Marcy, December 25, 1847, Exec. Doc. No. 60, p. 1048. Winfield Scott (Memoirs, pp. 582–83) mentions, besides the $150,000, $50,000 produced by sale of Mexican government tobacco and "two or three smaller sums for licenses, etc.,—making a total of about $220,000." These funds he spent on $60,000 for extra blankets and shoes; an amount of $10 each to wounded men; and "about $118,000 remitted to Washington to constitute a basis for an Army Asylum —for disabled men, not officers." The rest he later turned over to his successor, General Butler. The Army Asylum, still in existence, is now called the Old Soldiers Home.

ers—the academy graduates actually being toasted were not, in general, high-enough ranking to be present.

After telling the three to "consider themselves under the table, Scott went on to declare that but for the "science of the Military Academy, . . . this army, multiplied by four, could not have entered the capital of Mexico."[27]

PEACE

❧ ❧

AUTUMN 1847–JUNE 1848

While Winfield Scott was pacifying Mexico City, James K. Polk was running out of patience in Washington. For nearly three weeks the President had been fretting about the armistice that Scott had signed with Santa Anna at the gates of the city, and now, on October 4, 1847, he decided to take action. He would recall Trist and direct Scott to begin making sure that the Mexicans paid for the support of his army.*

The next day Polk explained his line of reasoning to his cabinet. He was not, as yet, particularly dissatisfied with Trist himself, but he feared that Trist's continued presence would probably encourage the Mexican government in the belief "that the United States was so anxious for peace that they would ultimately conclude one upon the Mexican terms."[1] So Polk directed Buchanan to send a letter of recall to Trist; at the same time Marcy was to transmit Polk's wishes to Scott in regard to levies on the Mexican people. Marcy accordingly directed Scott to throw the burden of sustaining American forces "to the utmost extent" upon the people of Mexico.[2]

---

*Polk, *Diary*, October 4, 1847, p. 267. As noted above, Scott had already begun making levies to that end.

Two weeks later, Polk's attitude toward Trist suddenly changed from indifference to anger. On October 21, 1847, the Southern mail brought a recent message from Trist outlining the terms he had been proposing to the Mexicans. One of them sent Polk into a rage: this was Trist's offer to grant the territory between the Nueces River and the Rio Grande to Mexico. Whereas Polk had reacted indifferently the day before, on learning of Scott's occupation of Mexico City, he now wrote, "[Trist] had no right to depart from his instructions, and I disapprove his conduct in doing so."

These were not good days for Polk. His critics were becoming more and more vindictive, and support for the war, damaged by the heavy casualty lists, was waning. And to add to his ill humor, Senator Benton called the next day and backed the President into a corner in defense of Benton's son-in-law, John C. Frémont, whose court-martial for insubordination in California was about to begin in Washington. Polk had approved Kearny's actions in preferring those charges against Frémont, but he held his tongue—and his ground—as the powerful senator blustered. But the ordeal apparently took its toll, for Polk vented pent-up fury when he berated Trist's actions before the cabinet the next day: "Mr. Trist has managed the negotiation very bunglingly and with no ability. . . . I expressed in strong and decided terms my disapprobation of his conduct. . . ."*

In Mexico City, Nicholas Trist was, of course, unaware that he had been recalled, and he dealt with the Mexicans patiently. On October 20, the day before Polk's explosion, he reopened peace negotiations with the Peña government. Thing went slowly. Trist had to wait for two weeks to learn that Peña would appoint commissioners "in a few days."

Peña, of course, knew in general what terms Trist would propose, and he, personally, was favorably disposed to accept them, as his goal was peace. But Peña was a Moderato, and others felt differently. The radical Puros, his main political opposition, desired the war to continue until the Americans had completely destroyed the vestiges of the old Mexican army and had discredited the Church; with these two institu-

---

*Polk Diary, October 21, 23, 1847, pp. 271-72. The conjecture regarding the link between the Benton episode and Polk's disposition the next day is the author's.

tions out of the way, they could bring about the social reforms they advocated. Other Mexican politicians, less idealistic, were reluctant to advocate peace for fear of being accused of bribery. And some still clung to the hope that American Whigs would force Polk to sign easy peace terms in order to bring the troops home. But since Peña's Moderatos represented the bulk of the influential Mexican people, it appeared that peace would come about, albeit slowly.[3]

The Mexican governmental structure also had delay built into it. Peña himself, even though he was the leading statesman at the time, was legally only a caretaker president pending the election of an official "interim president." The election, held on November 11, 1847, turned out favorably for the Moderatos with the decisive election of Pedro María Anaya, and a week later a meeting of seven states supported a movement for peace.* Progress toward peace, though steady, was time-consuming.

On November 16, 1847, Polk's order recalling Trist arrived at Mexico City. Trist accepted his recall philosophically at first, thinking that the government in Washington might benefit from a firsthand account of the situation in Mexico. And he had plenty of time to prepare for his departure, as Scott could not provide him escort to Veracruz before December 4. The interim gave Trist a couple of weeks to think his situation over.

To his surprise, Trist discovered that many influential men in Mexico were considering his recall to be a very grave mistake. Edward Thornton, of the British legation, was one, and he soon began to adopt the role of "honest broker" between Trist and the Mexicans. As Trist and Thornton were on cordial terms, Trist asked Thornton, who happened to be leaving for Querétaro, to deliver the news of his relief informally to Peña and to ask if he could provide some proposal for Trist to take back. Peña, now foreign minister, took the news hard. With Trist gone, he reasoned, Mexico could attain peace only by sending a request for negotiations to Washington—an action so humiliating to Mexico that no Mexican government could afford to take it.

*Justin Smith, The War with Mexico, vol. II, p. 236. Only San Luis Potosí, with its belligerent governor, objected.

So Peña asked Thornton to notify Trist, on his return to Mexico City, that his commissioners were ready to talk at once, that the governors approved the "principle" of peace, and that the British government would not interfere.

Trist was now in a difficult situation. He could no longer continue negotiations legally; even the ugly word "traitorous" occasionally cropped up in his mind.[4] On the other hand, Trist saw that abandoning his negotiations, so delicately launched, could be disastrous. He agreed with Peña that the Mexicans would never go to Washington with hat in hand; the alternative would be years of American occupation, at great expense, with unforeseen results.

Many respected voices were now urging Trist to remain in Mexico —those of Peña, Thornton, Scott, and even the correspondent James Freaner. But even this expression of confidence among his associates could never have been persuasive had Trist not been convinced himself. So on December 4, 1847, Trist decided that he would stay. At least the time it took for the mails to make a round trip would give him another few weeks.

But though Peña had given assurances of speed, the Mexicans continued to delay. At this time the point at issue in the negotiations was the boundary between the two nations. The commissioners were prepared to accept Trist's official proposal (which did not conform to his own views) that it follow the Rio Grande until it reached 32 degrees north, and thence west. But they had no power—they had not been confirmed by the Senate. So Trist, having defied his notice of recall, was forced to wait.

The Mexicans were receiving mixed messages from the outside world, the most important of which was the rumor that the Whigs in the United States would force easier terms than those Trist was offering. Trist tried to combat that hope by citing another school of thought in the United States, one that favored occupying and annexing all of Mexico. And the much honored "right of conquest" could justify a lesser evil: retaining control of Chihuahua, Veracruz, and other points occupied by American forces. One potential complication, fortunately, was dispelled—that of British interference. Britain would provide "good offices" but nothing more. She would not take sides with Mexico.

The talks, though hampered by foot dragging among the various factions of Mexico, were cordial. Trist remained on friendly terms with the Mexican negotiators, especially the head, J. B. Couto.* And the British representatives, while remaining neutral, continued to assist.

By this time Scott had openly assumed a supporting role to Trist. His pecuniary assessments on the Mexican states, for example, were useful in demonstrating to Mexico that the American occupation could sustain itself for a long time. And his confining his occupation to Mexico City (and a few critical points outside) had political as well as military motivations. Thus his sudden discovery of his inability to occupy either Zacatecas or San Luis Potosí, despite his previous announcement,[5] made Trist's peace negotiations with the Mexicans much easier.

On January 6, 1848, Scott told Hitchcock that he expected a treaty within three days.[6] But still the suspense continued, always under the threat of stern reaction from Washington. On January 8, 1848, Anaya's one-month term as interim president expired, and Peña once more took office. Talks continued amid domestic confusion,† until, at the end of January, the Mexicans were ready to sign a treaty. They accepted Trist's terms but demanded $30 million in payment. That amount of money Trist could not grant, so he declared the negotiations ended.[7]

But the atmosphere still remained cordial. On January 30 Scott was invited by the ayuntamiento of Mexico City to visit the ruins of a Carmelite convent about fifteen miles outside the city. He accepted with pleasure, but he was cautious: while the city fathers and prominent Mexicans went by carriage, Scott and his staff, with Generals Butler and P. F. Smith, went on horseback. At 8 A.M. they left the city, accompanied by an infantry regiment for the first five miles. Thereafter they proceeded under the guard of two companies of dragoons.

At the festive dinner Scott sat with the alcalde, and was entertained by a fine band of musicians. Toasts generally ran to sentiments of peace, though some of the Mexicans were open in hoping the war might be continued until all the clergy and the army were destroyed. In early

---

*Couto said of Trist, after the signing of the treaty, "Of him there remain in Mexico none but grateful and honoring recollections." Justin Smith, vol. II, p. 323.

†An insurrection in San Luis Potosí, though put down, threatened disintegration of the entire country.

afternoon Scott and his staff started back for Mexico City, warmed by the hospitality of a onetime enemy, and more convinced than ever that peace was at hand.[8]

Two days later Freaner, who had now attained the status of a quasi staff officer, passed the word that Trist was joining the Mexican commissioners at the sacred shrine of Guadalupe Hidalgo for the purpose of signing a peace agreement. By that evening, copies of an agreed-upon text were shown to members of Scott's staff.

On Wednesday morning, February 2, 1848, Trist and the Mexican commissioners met at Guadalupe Hidalgo, and there they signed the treaty of that name. The boundary between the two countries would run along the Rio Grande to the southern boundary of New Mexico —close to Trist's earlier proposal—thence west along the Gila River to the Gulf of California. From there it would run westward along a line just south of San Diego to the Pacific Ocean. The United States would assume Mexico's debts to its citizens and pay $15 million for the territory it gained. Scott, at Trist's behest, "pledged his word" that he would suspend hostilities.[9]

But the internecine fighting among the victors themselves had not ended. On February 9, 1848, one week after the signing of the Treaty of Cuadalupe Hidalgo, Winfield Scott penned an angry letter to the secretary of war that contained these lines:

> Slips from newspapers and letters from Washington have come to interested parties here, representing, I learn, that the President has determined to place me before a court . . . and that I am to be superseded by Major-General Butler. My poor services with this most gallant army are at length to be requited as I have long been led to expect they would be.*

And so they were. On February 18, 1848, Scott received a legalistic letter from Marcy that began: "In view of the present state of things in the army under your immediate command, and in compliance with the assurance contained in my reply to your letter of the 4th of June,

---

*Scott to Marcy, February 9, 1848, Winfield Scott *Memoirs*, vol. II, 572–73. One of the sources of information was an article in the American *Star*, published in Mexico City, on February 7, 1848.

wherein you asked to be recalled, the President has determined to relieve you from further duty as commanding general in Mexico." The letter went on to designate Butler as Scott's successor and to instruct Scott to appear before a court of inquiry, appointed to investigate the charges Scott had leveled against Pillow and Duncan as well as the charges presented against him by Worth. The general-in-chief was therefore to be a defendant as well as an accuser in the forthcoming court of inquiry.

Scott had been through this type of thing before, and although he blustered in a long letter to Marcy,[11] he turned over the army to Butler with goodwill and attended the first session of the court of inquiry, which convened in late February. In late April 1848, with the court suspended, he left for home, refusing all ceremonies and honors.

Scott had seemed reconciled to his situation, but Scott's army was not. Robert E. Lee, for one, mourned that Scott, having performed his task, had been turned out as an "old horse to die."[12] Less restrained were others. One lieutenant described Scott's departure:

> Grey haired officers and rugged soldiers wept when they parted from their General, and a host of officers followed him to the Penon, to obtain word from, or exchange one look with their hero and their idol.[13]

However, many officers and men had been critical of Scott's decisions during the fighting. Polk's action in peace now cemented the army—and much of the public—behind him.

One last incident, small but significant, closes the Winfield Scott story. Shortly after his relief from command, Scott received a remarkable offer from certain prominent figures in Mexico who favored annexation of Mexico to the United States. They proposed that Scott resign from the United States Army—which he was legally free to do—and issue a pronunciamento declaring himself dictator of Mexico for a term of six years.

The proposition was not so chimerical as it might appear. Scott observed that 70 percent of his men would be discharged in place when the peace was ratified. With a generous offer, such as a pay raise of 10 to 20 percent, he believed he could maintain a force in Mexico of some 15,000 men. He was already in control of the principal ports, arsenals, forts, and even the mines of Mexico. But Scott did not, despite his disappointments, contemplate this offer seriously, though he seemed to enjoy toying with it. He rejected it, he later claimed, because he feared the consequences to the United States of assimilating Mexico as being "perilous to the free institutions of his country." And he made a nod to "the wishes of the Polk administration."[14] Public reasons aside, Scott was too much of an American soldier to participate in such a questionable scheme.

President Polk saw that he had no choice but to accept the Treaty of Guadalupe Hidalgo and submit it to the Senate. Such a prospect infuriated him. The fact that Nicholas Trist had negotiated the treaty without portfolio rankled him. But Polk himself had provided a prece-dent for honoring such an informal treaty, as he had been prepared to accept a treaty nearly a year earlier if it could have been negotiated secretly by Moses Y. Beach.* What infuriated Polk the most was the attitude of the man who had signed the treaty. For Trist, once he had crossed the Rubicon of staying without authority, had become progres-sively more secure in his own rightness and more contemptuous of Polk and Buchanan—becoming, in fact, far more anti-Polk than his friend Scott. Trist's whole attitude was now one of defiance: he would no longer serve in the government; he referred to Gideon Pillow as a "reptile"; and he wrote of Polk, "His mind is too corrupt or too imbecile. . . . I say the same of every man capable of retaining a seat in his cabinet during the last 3,4, or 5 months."[15] Fortunately, Trist's most defiant letter did not, at this time, come to light. In it he asserted

---

*When Beach was in Mexico, Polk had recorded in his diary: "Wednesday, 14th April, 1847. —After night Mr. Buchanan called and read me a letter which he had received this evening from Moses Beach of the New York Sun. . . . Mr. Beach describes the revolutionary condition of Mexico, but expresses the opinion that a treaty may be made which would be satisfactory to the United States, and leaves the inference that he make such a treaty. . . . Mr. Buchanan [the previous November] informed him confidentially of the terms on which we would treat, and it was deemed advisable to constitute him a secret agent to Mexico. He was so constituted . . . but was not clothed with any diplomatic powers. He may miscontrue his authority and it may be possible that he may induce the Mexican authorities . . . to make a treaty with him. Should he do so, and it is a good one, I will waive his authority to make it, and submit it to the Senate for ratification. It will be a good joke if he will assume the authority and take the whole country by surprise and make a treaty." Polk, *Diary*, pp. 217–18.

that the land between the Nueces and the Rio Grande was as much a part of Tamaulipas as the counties of Accomac and Northampton were part of Virginia.[16]

Nevertheless, Polk rose above his anger. Exercising his customary "excellent judgment as to what was and what was not attainable,"[17] he decided to accept the treaty. It had given him all he had sought, and to repudiate it would play into the hands of those who described him as "Polk the Mendacious." So on receipt of the treaty (delivered at the hands of Freaner) he once again, as he had at the beginning of the war, called his cabinet into session on a Sunday. On Monday they met again, and though Buchanan and Walker opposed it initially,* Marcy, Mason, Johnson, and Attorney General Nathan Clifford favored it. As this treaty demanded no territory not already occupied by the United States, it had the best possible chance of ratification by Mexico.

On Tuesday, February 22, the anniversary of the first day of Buena Vista, President Polk submitted the Treaty of Guadalupe Hidalgo to the United States Senate. Its ratification was by no means a foregone conclusion. Whig opponents, led by Daniel Webster, opposed it on the grounds that they disapproved of any territorial acquisition. More numerous were those who demanded more, not fewer, concessions from Mexico. Some, such as Houston and Jefferson Davis, claimed to object on the basis that the treaty had been negotiated by a private citizen. And by now Benton was opposed to anything Polk requested because of his anger over the Frémont affair.

The debate was reaching a white heat, and ratification appeared dubious.

Congressman John Quincy Adams, former president of the United States, had served his country well. He performed his last civic contribution in a strange way—by dying. On the evening of February 22, the same day that the treaty was submitted, Adams died. As a representative, Adams would not have been able to vote on the treaty, but his influence, as one of the Immortal Fourteen, was great. However, it was

---

*Buchanan, formerly the man of peace, now complained that the treaty did not cede enough territory to the United States.

his stature as a former president, and the recess that the proper ceremonies necessitated, that made the difference. For while Congress was in recess, tempers had time to cool. When the Senate resumed debate on Monday, February 28, members returned to their task with a noticeably improved sense of responsibility.

But ratification was still questionable. The very evening it was submitted, Polk learned that four members (out of five) of the Senate Foreign Affairs Committee had voted against it on the basis that Trist had negotiated without authority. They intended to recommend that Polk send a new commission, with proper powers, to Mexico.

Polk retaliated strongly. After properly berating Trist as "insolent and insubordinate," he pointed out that the issue at stake was not Trist himself but the treaty. If the Senate insisted upon a new commission, he continued, he hoped they would advise him what terms they would accept. And, finally, he summed up his whole position:

> If the treaty in its present form is ratified, there will be added to the United States an immense empire, the value of which twenty years hence it would be difficult to calculate.[18]

For several more days the fate of the treaty hung in the balance. About a dozen Democrats, it was estimated, would vote against it because it demanded too little territory. The Senate went into executive session, in which Webster demanded a new commission; Houston still refused to recognize Trist's authority; Houston and Davis now wanted more territory; and Baldwin, of New England, wanted a provision prohibiting slavery in the acquired territory.[19] But finally the Senate settled for certain modifications. And on March 10, a year and a day after the Veracruz landing, it ratified a modified version of Guadalupe Hidalgo by a vote of 38 to 14, four senators abstaining.* Polk sent a commission consisting of Attorney General Nathan Clifford and Senator Ambrose Sevier to carry the treaty to Mexico City.

The war was now almost over. Much time elapsed between the arrival of the senatorial party and ratification by the Mexican Senate on May 25, 1848. But the final approval was inevitable, as the Mexicans

---

*Polk gave credit to Magnum, who, "though a Whig, is a gentleman." Exec. Doc. No. 52, quoted in Eugene McCormac, *James K. Polk*, p. 548.

had no other choice: all the territory ceded was in American hands. In the words of Bernardo Cuoto, one of the negotiators,

> The present treaty does not merely prevent an increase of our losses by a continuance of the war; but it serves to recover the better part of that which was already under the control of the conquering army of the United States; it is more exactly an agreement of recovery than an agreement of cession.[20]

On June 12, 1848, Clifford sent home a thrilling message: "The flag of the United States was taken down from the national palace in this city and that of the Mexican republic was hoisted."

Peace had arrived almost exactly nine months from the day that Scott had occupied Mexico City.

EPILOGUE

And so it was over, a two-year war between two neighbors on the North American continent. It had been a costly war by any standard. The loss of lives had been appalling on both sides. The Americans, for their part, suffered 13,780 dead, and thousands more wounded beyond recovery. The cost in treasure was estimated at about $100 million.* The cost to Mexico had been even greater.

The Treaty of Guadalupe Hidalgo provided that the United States should pay Mexico a sum of $15 million in compensation for the territories she ceded. In addition, the United States assumed responsibility for some $3 million owed by Mexico to American citizens before the war. Together these payments came close to the $25 million that

---

*Emory Upton, *The Military Policy of the United States*, pp. 216–18. The number of men in service were 31,024 regulars (old and new establishments and including 548 marines) and 73,532 volunteers. Of these 944 regulars (including nine marines) were killed or died of wounds; 607 volunteers met the same fate. Disease and accidents killed 5821 regulars (including three marines) and 6408 volunteers. In the field, the volunteer losses from disease far exceeded the rate for regulars, but the regulars had the job of garrisoning Veracruz and other unhealthy places. Only about one death in eight came from enemy action.

John Slidell, in late 1845, had been authorized to offer,* and the boundaries that resulted from the treaty closely resembled those that Slidell had been instructed to seek.

By all logic, then, both nations would have been better served if those boundary changes could have been effected by a purchase, negotiated without fighting. But even though she had virtually lost all control over New Mexico and California, Mexico could never have relinquished territory without a fight. For such a transfer would not have been the result of a voluntary agreement like the Louisiana Purchase of 1803; it would have resembled the Eighteenth-Century partitions of Poland or the consequence of the notorious Munich agreement of 1938. Few peoples, certainly not the proud Mexicans, would ever entertain offers to purchase parts of their countries; though it cost Mexico dearly to resist, it is to her credit that she did.

As to the strong sense of guilt felt by many Americans over their government's seizure of New Mexico and California, let me add one more point, that the "right of conquest" was more respected in the nineteenth century that it is today, and that right was cited by some to justify annexation of Tamaulipas, Nuevo León, and even Veracruz. Even the idea of annexing all of Mexico, outlandish as it may seem today, received strong support in some quarters on both sides of the Rio Grande. The Treaty of Guadalupe Hidalgo, in fact, was castigated in the Senate more for its leniency than for its acquisition of Mexican territory.

It was a dirty war, its costly nature due more to disease and hardship than to enemy action. The sufferings of the individual soldiers—American and Mexican alike—exceeded today's imagination. Taylor's trek from Corpus Christi to Matamoros, Santa Anna's march from San Luis Potosí to Agua Nueva, Wool's march from San Antonio to Parras, Doniphan's and Kearny's marches, the deadly climate of Veracruz— it is doubtful that soldiers on the North American continent have ever

---

*Upton (p. 221) places expenditures during the years 1846–1848 at $74 million for the army, $27 million for the navy. This figure of $101 million exceeded the 1843 expenditure level by about $81 million. But taking into consideration all other expenditures, including $15 million payment to Mexico, Justin Smith estimates the total cost at about $100 million above "normal" expenditures. Justin Smith, vol. II, p. 267.

Mexican records were so poor—or nonexistent—that Justin Smith, the greatest scholar on the Mexican War, does not even address the subject.

withstood anything like them before or since. Discipline was perforce brutal, and desertions were therefore heavy. But heroism and the stoic bearing of physical hardship were more prevalent than human failure. This was no minor episode in our history.

Much has been written about the quality of leadership under which the troops of both sides fought. Mexican leadership, sadly, can be dismissed with an expression of sympathy for the brave Mexican troops who were betrayed by generals motivated primarily by greed and political concerns. It is significant that the flawed Santa Anna was the most capable leader of the Mexicans.

The unbroken string of American victories that culminated in the successful end of the war becloud the fact that the American forces—Taylor's, Scott's, Wool's and Kearny's—were often placed in precarious positions. Taylor operated on a shoestring; Scott, on less than that, which made it impossible for him to maintain a line of communications with Veracruz on the coast. The paucity of support from Washington was a by-product of Polk's parsimony, his suspicions of his generals, and his constant underestimation of the problems they were facing. Anxious to run the war as cheaply as possible to justify his role in bringing it on, he was frustrated, rightly, by an unquestionable lethargy in the War and Navy departments in Washington. The quartermaster, in particular, fell short of meeting the legitimate needs of the armies in the field, though Thomas Jesup deserves sympathy for the gargantuan tasks that were laid before him. It is to his credit that he did as well as he did in contracting for ships, constructing landing craft, and sending thousands of tons of ammunition to two fronts in Mexico, all by wagon or mule.

The American military system had not yet come of age, but on the whole the accomplishments of both the Army and the Navy are worthy of admiration.

This narrative has left many loose ends regarding the fortunes of several of the protagonists. A summary of the later stages in the lives of Polk, Scott, and Pillow, in particular, may be of interest.

The court of inquiry ordered by Polk in January 1848 to investigate Pillow, Worth, Duncan, and Scott was actually conducted in Mexico City. The acrimonious proceedings dragged on through April and then recessed, to be continued later in Frederick, Maryland. Scott, relieved of command, fell ill of the *vómito* on the way home and nearly died. Not completely recovered, he disembarked in New York and was greeted and feted as a hero. Congress, ignoring the cloud under which Polk wanted to keep him, voted Scott its thanks.[1] But the court of inquiry, resuming its dreary proceedings at Frederick, continued until other events diverted the public's attention. Its findings, while critical of Pillow, largely whitewashed him. Pillow was able to celebrate his minor triumph at the White House as a guest of the President.

The controversy had the effect of thwarting Scott's political ambitions in 1848.* While the inquiry was in progress the Whigs met at Philadelphia and, following the lead of Senator John Crittenden, nominated Zachary Taylor for president. Taylor defeated Democratic candidate Senator Lewis Cass in the 1848 election without even bothering to campaign.

Thus the ultimate humiliation was inflicted upon James Polk, the president who had made every effort to politicize the war. The ordeal of riding down Pennsylvania Avenue with Zachary Taylor for the inauguration ceremony must have been more than even his enemies could have wished upon him. Worn out from overwork on details, Polk died in Nashville three months after leaving office, at age fifty-four.

But what of Polk's law partner, Gideon Pillow? That controversial man apparently changed his spots but little in the years following 1848. After going back to civilian life in Tennessee, Pillow returned to uniform in the Civil War. Perhaps fortunately for the Union, the uniform he donned was gray. He was last heard of evacuating his troops at Fort Donelson, on the Cumberland River, in February 1862. The victor in that campaign had been a junior officer in the same army, Ulysses S. Grant.

And the flamboyant William Jenkins Worth? Worth's political ambitions had always been chimerical, and his role in the controversy with Scott did him no good. He remained in the army and died in Texas in 1851. His name is immortalized not by his real heroism in the Mexican War but by a fort he later established on what was then the Texas frontier—Fort Worth.

And the two colorful characters from the West, Stephen W. Kearny and John C. Frémont? On return to the East from California, they

---

*The Whigs nominated Scott in 1852. He was defeated by his former subordinate Franklin Pierce. He remained as general-in-chief, U.S. Army, until late in 1861, retiring with the rank of brevet lieutenant general.

continued their previous conflict throughout Frémont's much publicized court-martial. Throughout this "public circus,"[2] Benton did everything he could to assist his son-in-law, and his main weapon, still, was bombast, "the Thunderer turned demagogue."[3] But the military court defied the senator and found Frémont guilty of insubordination, and sentenced him to dismissal from the army. At the completion of his part in the hearings, in early 1848, Kearny was sent as governor to Veracruz and later to Mexico City. Then, like Scott, he fell victim to the *vómito*, but, unlike Scott, survived only long enough to return to Washington and be honored by promotion to brevet major general. On his deathbed he asked to see Jessie Frémont, "once his friend, daughter of one man and wife of another man who had once been his friends."[4] But Jessie Frémont held Kearny responsible for all that had happened to her menfolk, and Kearny died with his wish to see her unfulfilled.

Frémont, like Pillow, learned no lessons from his tribulations. Polk attempted unsuccessfully to mollify Benton by remitting Frémont's dismissal, but Frémont, in a rage, resigned his Army commission anyway. Still wielding influence, he soon led another expedition to the Rocky Mountains, this time without either Carson or Fitzpatrick, and the result was a disaster. His party became lost in the snows, some of the members resorting to cannibalism before the survivors were rescued.[5] Still immensely popular in California, Frémont was elected as one of its first two senators in 1850, and in 1856 he became the first presidential nominee of the Republican party, losing the election to the aging James Buchanan. Frémont later reentered the service of the United States as a major general of volunteers during the Civil War and ineptly commanded a division during the 1862 Shenandoah Valley campaign. He lived until 1890 but, like Nicholas Trist, died down on his luck.

Santa Anna's roller-coaster career did not end with his removal from office in late 1847. On April 20, 1853, the Napoleon of the West was inaugurated once more as president of the Mexican Republic. That presidency lasted about two and a half years, and in 1855 Santa Anna was exiled again. He visited New York in May 1866 and finished his memoirs in 1874, when he was permitted to return to Mexico as a private citizen. He died unnoticed in Mexico City on June 21, 1876. His career of ups and downs was symbolic of the confusion that gripped Mexico throughout the nineteenth century.

. . .

The Mexican War cast a pall over the relations between the United States and Mexico, a pall that lasts to this day because the Mexicans have never become reconciled to it. Their history since 1848 has not been happy: subjugation to the foreign emperor Maximilian; rebuilding by the celebrated Juarez soon thereafter; a long period of dictatorship under Díaz; revolutions shortly after the turn of the century; a one-party government—all accompanied by chronic poverty and corruption. Throughout their tribulations the Mexicans have found it convenient to blame the Colossus of the North for their misfortunes.

Indeed the United States has hardly been blameless since 1848, and its actions toward Mexico have been marred by such episodes as the Pershing Punitive Expedition (1916) in pursuit of Pancho Villa.

But even though U.S. actions during the last few decades have been generally honorable, resentment continues to smolder, and the war that raged between 1846 and 1848 is often cited as a major cause of Mexican woes: "Alas, poor Mexico! So far from God and so close to the United States!"

APPENDIX 1

Instability. The word is synonymous with the condition of Mexico in 1844—and had been ever since it attained independence from Spain in 1821. Mexico was a society torn by conflicts of loyalty and interests. Part of this stemmed from its fragmented culture, a mixture of the Aztec and the Spanish. In contrast to the United States, where English colonists replaced rather than mixed with the indigenous Indians, Spain superimposed its authority and customs on the natives, thus forming a Mexican society that was a blend of Spanish and Aztec. As the Spaniards had brought few women, Mexicans of undiluted Spanish ancestry were distinctly in the minority. By 1844 two million of Mexico's seven million residents were mestizos (persons of mixed blood) and four million were Indians, which left only about one million Mexicans of purely Spanish lineage.

Race as such, however, was of little importance to Mexican society in this period. Place of origin—whether one was Spanish-born (Gachupine) or Mexican-born (Creole)—was far more important. The "upper-crust" Gachupines and their immediate offspring tended not to dirty their hands, it is fair to say, so real political power had long since drifted away from them. Every Mexican president up to this time had come from a single group: Creole generals.

The Spanish political infrastructure, though it provided stability, had never been fully accepted by the population, and governmental control had always been tenuous, especially among the Indians and the poor. During the years of Spanish rule, which ended in 1821, order had been maintained by the armed might of the viceroy. But the viceroy's military forces were manned and led almost exclusively by Creoles; Spain had ruled Mexico largely by using Mexican mercenaries in the pay of the Crown.

By exercising authority over the masses, it was only logical that the Creole elite should become creatures of privilege. Both the Roman Catholic Church and the army enjoyed the *fuero*, immunity from the authority of the courts. The Church amassed vast wealth, but at the same time it performed services for the people; the great, ornate cathedrals provided the poor with their only glimpse of beauty, and the small humble chapels were centers of community and devotion. Thus it was aptly said that every Mexican had two homes, his hovel and his place of worship. But at the top levels of the Church the hierarchy had succumbed to secular practices, preoccupied with preserving its own status in the chaos that was Mexico.

Though powerful in political affairs, the army was a weak fighting force. Its show troops, especially its spectacular cavalry, were capable of putting on great pageantry in Mexico City, thus giving the population a false sense of security, but most of the fighting in the many small internecine wars had long been conducted by ill-trained conscripts, who fought periodically for one general or another. With no emphasis on professionalism—and with the Army's preoccupation with political power—it is not surprising that the officer class was innocent of technical military matters. And discipline, while severe on the soldiers, was a joke where their leaders were concerned.*

By the beginning of the nineteenth century, inequities between rich and poor, between the privileged and the downtrodden, had become an unbearable burden on the less favored citizens of Mexico. Rebellion against the Gachupines broke out in 1810, when a poor parish priest, Miguel Hidalgo y Costilla, was induced to join a group of revolutionary officers in Querétaro who were plotting against the viceroy. Hidalgo was a man of great personal magnetism, and he soon became its leader. At first successful in his efforts, he proclaimed Mexican independence in September 1810.

But Hidalgo, in common with most visionaries, lacked a sense of political reality; he thought that the Indians would protect the rights and persons of the Creoles while rising against the Gachupines—and this assumption turned out to be a grave error. After seizing Guanajuato, Hidalgo's Indians slaughtered all whites in the city, whether of Mexican or Spanish birth. Hidalgo himself seemed incapable of controlling his followers and began showing signs of instability. The revolution lost support, and his followers deserted. On January 1811 Hidalgo was captured at Chihuahua and was soon executed. His head was displayed on a post in Guanajuato for ten years.

Soon after Hidalgo's death another populist priest, José María Moreles y Pavón, assumed leadership of the rebellion. More capable

---

*In 1840 the Army's rolls carried 24,000 officers and only 20,000 enlisted men.

and realistic than Hidalgo, Moreles denounced Spain, defined his objectives, and managed to last, with many ups and down, until his own capture and execution in 1815.

The revolution finally succeeded, in 1821, not because of the backing of the masses but because of the disenchantment of the favored, who feared that a recent liberalization of the home government in Spain might deprive them of some of their privileges in Mexico. Agustín Iturbide, a Mexican officer in the service of the viceroy, simply changed sides, taking his soldiers with him. In issuing the Plan of Iguala he pronounced three guarantees: (1) the continuation of the Catholic Church, (2) the independence of Mexico from Spain, and (3) the union in Mexico of Gachupines and Creoles. Soon Iturbide was joined by Vicente Guerrero, a true anti-Spanish rebel.

Mexican independence was assured when the United States took the lead in recognizing her as a sovereign country, the first country to do so. However, since the Plan of Iguala had called for a constitutional monarchy, and since Mexico could not find a suitable Spanish nobleman to come and rule, Iturbide declared himself emperor. This last act was his undoing; within a year he was ousted from power and exiled. On his ill-advised return to Mexico in 1824 he was caught and executed.

The revolution—or revolutions—had devastated Mexico. Violence had cost six hundred thousand lives, and Mexico's industry had been destroyed. In addition, with the removal of Spanish authority, virtual anarchy prevailed. Of the presidents of Mexico between 1821 and 1844, only one, Guadalupe Victoria, managed to serve out his full four years.* And even he sustained a revolution during his last days in office —a young Santa Anna was among the instigators—though Victoria was allowed to finish out his term. It was this chronic condition of anarchy that had allowed Santa Anna periodically to seize power.

*That he had done, between 1825 and 1829, by securing a substantial loan from Britain, which had enabled him to pay the Army.

APPENDIX 2

American artillery at the time of the Mexican War was the equal if not the superior of any artillery in the world. Farseeing secretaries of war in the past—John C. Calhoun, Lewis Cass, and Joel Poinsett—had made their contributions. Of these, Joel Poinsett in 1840 had performed the most critical service by sending a board of officers to Europe to study the artillery arm and to bring back cannon from the various nations for the Ordnance Department to study. As a result, a full system of United States artillery appeared in 1841,* just in time for the war with Mexico.

The so-called family of weapons, model 1840, included two light artillery pieces designed for field use, the six-pounder gun and the twelve-pounder howitzer.† Of these, the six-pounder gun, with its range of 1,500 yards and weight of 880 pounds, was the "basic field piece" of the army.‡ For siege purposes, a collection of heavy howitzers was developed. These included eighteen and twenty-four-pounder guns, eight-inch howitzers, and eight- and ten-inch mortars. The siege guns were heavy, some reaching up to 5,600 pounds in weight, and were impracticable for field use.

In 1844 the United States Army had four artillery regiments along with its eight infantry regiments. Each artillery regiment had ten companies of fifty men each. Only one company in each regiment, however, was designated as "light," fit for use with the infantry. Thus when Taylor moved to Corpus Christi and later to Matamoros, there were only four highly trained light, or "flying," artillery companies in the army. Of these he received three, not enough to provide one per infantry regiment.§ The artillery companies of four guns—or sec-

---

*Lester R. Dillon., Jr., *American Artillery in the Mexican War,* p. 10.

†A gun fires a flat trajectory. A howitzer, usually a smaller piece for the same size of shot, fires with a reduced powder charge and with an elevated muzzle. A mortar, usually a heavy piece, fires at a steep angle, usually about forty-five degrees.

‡Dillon, p. 11.

§Co. "A," 2d Art. (James Duncan); Co. "C," 3d Art. (Samuel Ringgold); Co. "E," 3d Art. (Braxton Bragg). Co. "B," 4th Art. (John M. Washington) later joined Taylor as part of General John E. Wool's division.

tions of two—were logically placed at the point of greatest danger. The outcome of a battle, therefore, might well be decided by the performance of a regular lieutenant commanding an artillery company rather than the infantry colonel whose regiment he was supporting.

SEQUENCE OF EVENTS

1844

November 2	James K. Polk elected president of the United States.
December 6	Antonio López de Santa Anna ousted as president of Mexico.

1845

March 1	President John Tyler signs annexation proposal to Texas.
March 4	Polk inaugurated as tenth president of the United States.
July 4	Texas Congress accepts annexation as a state to United States.
July 25	Brig. Gen. Zachary Taylor lands a force near Corpus Cristi, Texas.
November 16	Polk confers with Senator Benton on Oregon and California. As a result, he sends messages via Lieut. Arnold Gillespie to Sloat, Larkin, and Frémont in California.
December 6	Polk's emissary, John Slidell, reaches Mexico City.
December 9	Capt. John C. Frémont arrives at Sutter's Fort, California.

1846

March 8	Taylor leaves Corpus Cristi for Rio Grande.
March 9	Frémont departs vicinity of Monterey for Klamath.
March 28	Taylor arrives on Rio Grande at Matamoros.
April 25	Capt. Seth Thornton's force ambushed, Brownsville, Texas.
May 8	Battle of Palo Alto.
May 9	Battle of the Resaca de la Palma.
May 13	Congress ratifies existence of war, passes War Bill. Polk and Scott confer.
June 15	Oregon treaty signed between United States and Britain.
June 16	Col. Stephen W. Kearney leaves Fort Leavenworth for Santa Fe.

July 4	Bear Flag Republic declared at Sonoma, California.
July 7	Monterey, California, occupied by force under Commodore Sloat.
July 23	Commodore Robert F. Stockton arrives at Monterey, California.
August 13	Los Angeles occupied by force under Stockton.
August 16	Santa Anna returns to Mexico, landing at Veracruz.
August 17	Kearny occupies Santa Fe, New Mexico, without resistance.
September 20–24	Taylor seizes Monterrey, Nuevo León.
September 25	Brig. Gen. Kearny departs Santa Fe for California.
September 29	Gillespie, as governor, surrenders Los Angeles to Flores.
November 19	Polk appoints Scott to command the expedition to Veracruz.
November 23	Maj. Gen. Winfield Scott leaves Washington for Rio Grande.
December 12	Col. Alexander Doniphan departs New Mexico for El Paso.
December 6	Battle of San Pascual, near San Diego, California.
December 12	Kearny arrives in San Diego.

1847

January 3	Scott arrives at Camargo.
January 8	Battle of San Gabriel, Los Angeles.
February 3–4	Col. Sterling Price subdues New Mexican rebels at Taos.
February 22–23	Taylor defeats Santa Anna at Buena Vista.
February 28	Doniphan, after Battle of Sacramento, occupies Chihuahua.
March 2	Scott departs Lobos Island for Veracruz.
March 9	Scott lands at Veracruz.
March 29	Veracruz surrenders.
April 18	Battle of Cerro Gordo, occupation of Jalapa.
May 14	Nicholas Trist, Polk's emissary, arrives at Jalapa.
May 21	Doniphan joins Wool at Buena Vista.
May 28	Scott moves main army to Puebla.
June 3	Scott is cut off from Veracruz.
August 20	Battles of Contreras and Churubusco.
August 24	Truce between Scott and Santa Anna.

September 6	Truce terminated.
September 8	Reduction of the Molino del Rey.
September 13	Assault on Chapultepec.
September 14	Scott occupies Mexico City.
September 17	Polk sends message of recall to Trist (received November 16).
October 9	Sam Walker, Texas Rangers, killed at Huamantla.

1848

February 2	Trist and Peña sign Treaty of Guadalupe Hidalgo.
March 10	Treaty of Guadalupe Hidalgo ratified by U.S. Congress.
May 30	Treaty ratified by Mexican Congress.
July 15	Last U.S. troops, under Worth, leave Veracruz.

NOTES

INTRODUCTION

1. Grant, *Memoirs,* vol. I, p. 53.
2. Justin Smith, *The War with Mexico,* vol. 1, p. 155.
3. DeVoto, p. 510.
4. Upton, pp. 216–18.
5. Ripley, vol. 1, pp. 575–77.
6. Grant, vol. 1, p. 95.

CHAPTER 1
PRELUDE

1. Santa Anna, *The Eagle,* p. 55.
2. Bancroft, *History of Mexico,* vol. 5, p. 277, quoted in Calcott, p. 215.

CHAPTER 2
THE AGE OF SANTA ANNA

1. Calcott, pp. 10–11.
2. Ibid., p. 11.
3. Oakah Jones, p. 60.
4. Calcott, p. 78.
5. Crawford, p. 265.

CHAPTER 3
ANNEXATION

1. Justin Smith, *The Annexation of Texas,* p. 370; Pletcher, p. 177.
2. Donelson to Calhoun, December 26, 1844. Calhoun papers.
3. *Madisonian,* February 21, 1845.
4. Sellers, p. 206.
5. Adams, *Memoirs,* vol. 12, pp. 178–79.
6. McCormac, p. 251.
7. Sellers, p. 235.
8. Jackson to Polk, May 2, 1845. Basset, vol. 6, p. 404.

9. Remini, p. 46.
10. Justin Smith, *The Annexation of Texas,* p. 410.
11. Price, pp. 118, 122.
12. Bancroft to Stockton, June 2, 1845.

CHAPTER 4
OLD ZACK

1. Marcy to Taylor, May 28, 1845. Exec. Doc. No. 60, pp. 79–80.
2. Marcy to Taylor June 15, 1845. Ibid.
3. Hitchcock, p. 193.
4. Ibid., p. 197.
5. Chamberlain, pp. 140–41.
6. Meade, p. 26.
7. Hitchcock, pp. 200–201.
8. E. Kirby Smith, letters, August 28 and September 18, 1845.
9. Hitchcock, p. 203.
10. Ibid., pp. 204–6.
11. Meade, pp. 44–45.

CHAPTER 5
MISSION OF ''PEACE''

1. Sellers, pp. 306–9.
2. Castel, "Winfield Scott."
3. Polk, *Diary,* April 1, 1846, p. 69.
4. Ibid., September 29, 1845, pp. 12–13.
5. Ibid., October 24, 1845, pp. 17–18.
6. Hussey, "The Origin of the Gillespie Mission," p. 46.
7. Ibid., p. 52.
8. Gillespie to Bancroft, November 16, 1845. *California Historical Society Quarterly,* vol. 18(3), 1939.
9. Polk, *Diary,* December 2, 1845, p. 30.
10. Perkins, *The Monroe Doctrine 1826–67.*
11. *The State of the Union Messages of the Presidents,* vol. 1, pp. 634–45.
12. Sellers, p. 339.
13. Polk Diary, December 2, December 5, and December 6, p. 30.
14. Sellers, p. 331.
15. Poinsett to Van Buren, May 26, 1846, in Sellers, p. 265.
16. Sellers, pp. 336–38.

17. Slidell to Peña y Peña, December 1845. In Sellers, p. 399.
18. Polk, *Diary*, December 23, 1845, p. 36.
19. Slidell to Buchanan, December 27, 1845. In Sellers, p. 400.
20. Marcy to Taylor, January 13, 1846, Exec. Doc. No. 60., p. 90.

CHAPTER 6
AMERICAN BLOOD
UPON AMERICAN SOIL

1. Marcy to Scott, January 13, 1846. Exec. Doc. No. 60, 30th Cong., 1st sess., p. 91.
2. Taylor to TAG, February 4, 1846, Exec. Doc. No. 60, p. 116.
3. Ibid., p. 117.
4. Ibid., March 8, 1846; Exec. Doc. No. 60, pp. 118–19.
5. Ibid., March 8, 1846; Exec. Doc. No. 60, pp. 118–19.
6. Ibid., March 12, 1846. Letter, Conner to Taylor from USS *Falmouth* (off Veracruz), March 2, 1846. Proclamation of Canales, February 1846. Exec. Doc. No. 60, pp. 121–23.
7. Kirby Smith, writing to wife. Progressive letter with beginning date of March 17, 1846.
8. Taylor to TAG, March 21, 1846, Exec. Doc. No. 60, p. 124.
9. Ibid., p. 123–25.
10. Smith's letter to wife.
11. Ibid., March 29, 1846.
12. Minutes of an interview between Worth and Vega, on the right bank of the Rio Grande, March 28, 1846. Exec. Doc. No. 60, pp. 134–38.
13. Polk, *Diary*, February 16, 1846, pp. 52, 53.
14. Sellers, p. 402.
15. Polk, *Diary*, March 6 and 8, 1846, pp. 60–61.
16. Ibid., April 22, 1846, pp. 72–73.
17. Ibid., March 28, 1846, pp. 67–68.
18. Ibid., pp. 67–69.
19. Ibid., April 7, 1846, pp. 69–70.
20. Alcaraz, p. 38.
21. Hitchcock, p. 218.
22. Meade, p. 54; Barbour, p. 25. Barbour's favorable impression of the officers was not shared by other observers.
23. Meade, p. 54.
24. Nevin, pp. 27–28.
25. Hitchcock, April 7, 1846.
26. Meade, letter, April 7, 1846, pp. 55–56.

27. Kirby Smith, letter to his wife, April 9, 1846, pp. 35–37.
28. Justin Smith, *The War with Mexico*, vol. 1, p. 117.
29. Alcaraz, p. 39.
30. Ibid. See also Wilcox, p. 42.
31. Ampudia to Taylor, April 12, 1846, Exec. Doc. No. 60, p. 140.
32. Taylor to Ampudia, April 12, 1846, Exec. Doc. No. 60, pp. 139–40.
33. Meade, letter, April 15, 1846, p. 57; Alcaraz, p. 37.
34. Nevin, p. 28.
35. Taylor to TAG, April 26, 1846, Exec. Doc. No. 60, p. 141.
36. Polk, *Diary,* May 8, 1846, p. 81.
37. Ibid.
38. Sellers, p. 408.
39. Polk's message to Congress, May 11, 1846, Exec. Doc. No. 60, p. 8.

CHAPTER 7
''I WAS GLAD I WAS NOT WITH THEM''

1. Ferguson.
2. Alcaraz, pp. 42–44.
3. Ibid.
4. Grant, *Memoirs,* vol. 1, p. 92.
5. Henry, W.S., p. 104.
6. The source of information is an old manuscript owned by Colonel Bruce Aiken of Brownsville.
7. Order No. 58, dated May 7, 1846.
8. Justin Smith, *The War with Mexico*, vol. 1, p. 164.
9. Alcaraz, p. 49.
10. Ibid., p. 50.
11. Resaca de Guerrero. Alcaraz, p. 50*n.*
12. Taylor to TAG, May 9, 12, 1846, Exec. Doc. No. 60, pp. 296, 297; Meade, May 15, p. 83.
13. Dobie, pp. 119, 120.

CHAPTER 8
''A HASTY PLATE OF SOUP''

1. Wilcox, pp. 45–47.
2. Upton., p. 201.
3. Exec. Doc. No. 196, p. 6, quoted in Upton, p. 202.

4. Report of the secretary of war, December 5, 1846, Exec. Doc. No. 4, p. 47.
5. Crittenden, vol. 1, pp. 241–42.
6. Report of the secretary of war, Exec. Doc. No. 4, p. 47.
7. Seward, letter, January 4, 1846, p. 771.
8. William Henry Harrison to Crittenden, November 7, 1839. Crittenden, vol. 1, p. 113.
9. Crittenden to Clay, July 2, 1844. Crittenden, vol. 1, p. 185.
10. Sellers, p. 312.
11. Polk, *Diary*, May 13, 1846, p. 90.
12. Ibid., pp. 90–92.
13. Exec. Doc. No. 60, p. 774.
14. Polk, *Diary*, May 14, 1846, pp. 93–94.
15. Ibid., May 19, 1846, p. 96.
16. Scott to R. P. Letcher, June 5, 1846. Crittenden vol. 1, 245–47.
17. Scott to Marcy, May 21, 1845, *Congressional Globe Appendix*, p. 650.
18. Scott to Archer, February 6, 1846, copy, Polk Papers.
19. Polk, *Diary*, May 21, 1846, p. 99.
20. Ibid., May 23, 1846, p. 103.
21. Ibid., May 25, 1846, p. 651.
22. Ibid., p. 652. Scott to Marcy, May 25, 1846
23. *Congressional Globe*, pp. 903–4.
24. Ibid., p. 904.
25. Ibid., pp. 1025–26.

CHAPTER 9
BUILDUP

1. Grant, *Memoirs*, vol. 1, p. 92.
2. Taylor to TAG, May 18, 1846, Exec. Doc. No. 60, p. 298.
3. Ibid., p. 297.
4. Ibid., pp. 297–98, and Taylor to Wood, May 19, 1846, p. 3. These documents are consistent. However, each contains some facts absent in the other.
5. March to Taylor, July 6, 1845.
6. Order No. 65, Matamoros, May 23, 1846. Exec. Doc. No. 60, p. 490.
7. Taylor, Order No. 62, Headquarters, Army of Occupation, Camp Near Fort Brown, Texas, May 17, 1846. Exec. Doc. No. 60, p. 489.
8. Taylor to TAG, Matamoros, May 20, 1846, Exec. Doc. No. 60, p. 299.
9. By the act of February 28, 1795.
10. Marcy to Taylor, May 28, 1846, Exec. Doc. No. 60, pp. 281–82.

11. Webb, pp. 8, 9.
12. Reid, p. 26.
13. Ibid., pp. 41–42.
14. Taylor to Wood, September 3, 1846, Exec. Doc. No. 60, p. 6.
15. Marcy to Taylor, June 8, 1846, Exec. Doc. No. 60, p. 324.
16. Marcy to Kearny, June 3, 1846, Exec. Doc. No. 60, p. 153.
17. Justin Smith, *The War with Mexico*, vol. 1, p. 267.
18. Marcy to Kearny, June 3, 1846, Exec. Doc. No. 60, p. 154.
19. Taylor to TAG, July 2, 1846. Exec. Doc. No. 60, p. 331.
20. Ibid., May 21, 1846, Exec. Doc. No. 60, p. 300.
21. Reid, pp. 45, 46.
22. Ibid., pp. 46–47.
23. Taylor to Wood, July 25, 1846, Exec. Doc. No. 60, p. 30.
24. Ibid., August 11, 1846, Exec. Doc. No. 60, pp. 31, 39–41.
25. Giddings, pp. 28–31.
26. Ibid., pp. 39, 40.
27. Ibid., p. 49.
28. Ibid., pp. 63–65.
29. Ibid., pp. 70–71.
30. Ibid., pp. 71–72.
31. Ibid., pp. 74–75.
32. Ibid., pp. 79–81.
33. Ibid., pp. 83–84.
34. Nichols, p. 128.
35. Taylor to Wood, August 23, 1846, Exec. Doc. No. 60, pp. 45–46.
36. Pillow to Mary Pillow, August 16, 1846. Stonesifer, p. 55.
37. Exec. Doc. No. 60, p. 418.

CHAPTER 10
THE SOLDIER
OF THE PEOPLE RETURNS

1. Alcaraz, pp. 69–71.
2. Justin Smith, *The War with Mexico*, vol. 1, pp. 214–15.
3. Ibid., pp. 216–17.
4. Conner to Bancroft, August 16, 1846. Exec. Doc. No. 60, p. 776.
5. Calcott, p. 240.
6. See Exec. Doc. No. 60, pp. 777–86, for the full text.
7. Niles *Register*, September 26, 1846, p. 49.

CHAPTER 11
MONTERREY I: APPROACH

1. Kenly, pp. 76–77.
2. Ibid., p. 81.
3. Ibid., p. 83.
4. Giddings, p. 112.
5. Ibid., p. 113.
6. Ibid., pp. 114–15.
7. William Henry, pp. 173–75.
8. Justin Smith, *The War with Mexico*, vol. 1, p. 230.
9. Alcaraz, p. 68.
10. Taylor to Wood, Cerralvo, September 10, 1846, Exec. Doc. No. 60, p. 54.
11. William Henry, September 11, 1846, p. 179.
12. Meade, September 17, 1846, pp. 129–30.
13. Ibid., pp. 91–92.
14. Ibid., p. 92.
15. Ibid., pp. 92–93.
16. William Henry, September 17, 1846, p. 187.
17. Giddings, p. 128.
18. Kenly, pp. 94–95; William Henry, p. 190.
19. Kenly, pp. 93–94.

CHAPTER 12
MONTERREY II:
"THREE GLORIOUS DAYS"

1. Taylor to TAG, Monterey, October 9, 1846, Exec. Doc. No. 60, p. 83; Justin Smith, *The War with Mexico*, vol. 1, p. 239; Wilcox, p. 91.
2. Kenly, p. 98.
3. Bill, p. 129.
4. Taylor to TAG, October 9, 1846, Exec. Doc. No. 60, p. 83. "Report." Reid, p. 152.
5. Meade, letter, September 27, 1846, p. 133.
6. William Henry, p. 193.
7. Reid, p. 157.
8. Taylor report to TAG, October 9, 1846, Exec. Doc. No. 60, p. 83.
9. Worth report, Exec. Doc. No. 60, p. 103.
10. William Henry, p. 193.
11. Worth report, Exec. Doc. No. 60, pp. 103–4.
12. Justin Smith, *The War with Mexico*, vol. 1, pp. 244–45.

13. Reid, p. 163.
14. Ibid., p. 165.
15. Kenly, pp. 105–6.
16. Justin Smith, *The War with Mexico*, vol. 1, p. 249.
17. Giddings, p. 161.
18. Kenly, p. 107.
19. Giddings, p. 164.
20. William Henry, pp. 194–95.
21. Ibid., p. 195.
22. Alcaraz, p. 73.
23. Ibid., pp. 252–53; Kenly, p. 111; Giddings, p. 167.
24. Worth report, Exec. Doc. No. 4, p. 105.
25. Ibid., pp. 104–5.
26. Nichols, p. 154.
27. Taylor report, October 9, 1846, Exec. Doc. No. 4.
28. Ibid.
29. Worth report, September 1846, Exec. Doc. No. 4, p. 105.

CHAPTER 13
MONTERREY III: TRUCE

1. Reid, p. 200.
2. Ibid.
3. Ibid.
4. Giddings, p. 204.
5. Taylor to Wood, October 12, 1846, Exec. Doc. No. 60, p. 60.
6. William Henry, p. 212.
7. Ripley, vol. 1, p. 237. See also Exec. Doc. No. 60, pp. 348–49.
8. Ibid., p. 240.
9. The principal source is Ripley, pp. 241–43. See also Exec. Doc. No. 60, pp. 349–50.
10. Kenly, pp. 131.
11. Ibid., pp. 131–32.
12. Ibid., p. 132.
13. William Henry, pp. 217–18.
14. Alcaraz, pp. 79–80.
15. Ibid., p. 80.
16. Taylor to Wood, Exec. Doc. No. 60, p. 60
17. Polk, *Diary*, October 12, 1846, p. 156.
18. Ibid.
19. Marcy to Taylor, Exec. Doc. No. 60, pp. 355, 356.

20. Meade, pp. 138–39.
21. David to *National Union*, dated January 2, 1847, quoted in Reid, pp. 205–6.

CHAPTER 14
SECOND BEGINNING

1. Ripley, vol. 1, p. 363.
2. Alcaraz, pp. 83–84.
3. Ibid., pp. 88–89.
4. See Calcott, table, p. 249*n*.
5. Alcaraz, p. 92.
6. Ibid., pp. 86–87.
7. William Henry, pp. 231, 234.
8. Polk, *Diary*, May 28, 1846, p. 106.
9. Jones to Wool, June 11, 1846, Exec. Doc. No. 60, p. 328.
10. Chamberlain, pp. 273–74.
11. Taylor to TAG, October 15, 1846, Exec. Doc. No. 60, pp. 351–54; Ripley, vol. 1, p. 313.
12. Justin Smith, *The War with Mexico*, vol. 1, pp. 279–80.
13. Ibid., pp. 281–82.
14. Scott to Taylor, September 26, 1846, in Crittenden, vol. 2, p. 257.
15. Taylor, *Letters*, November 10, 1846, pp. 66–67.
16. Justin Smith, *The War with Mexico*, vol. 1, p. 373.
17. McCormac, p. 560; Benton, vol. 2, p. 693.
18. Elbert Smith, p. 216; Benton, vol. 2, p. 693.
19. Polk, *Diary*, November 10, 1846, p. 163.
20. Elbert Smith, p. 216.
21. Scott to Marcy, September 12, 1846, in Crittenden, vol. 1, p. 250.
22. Marcy to Scott, September 14, 1846, in Crittenden, vol. 1, p. 250.
23. Polk, *Diary*, November 12, 1846, p. 166.
24. Ibid., November 18, 1846, pp. 169–70.
25. Ibid., November 19, 1846, pp. 170–71.

CHAPTER 15
BUENA VISTA I:
"THE GREATEST ANXIETY"

1. Taylor to TAG, July 2, 1846, Exec. Doc. No. 60, p. 331.
2. Ibid., October 15, 1846, Exec. Doc. No. 60, p. 352.

3. Ibid., pp. 352–53.
4. Marcy to Taylor, October 22, 1846, Exec. Doc. No. 60, p. 364.
5. Ibid., p. 265.
6. William Henry, p. 245.
7. Ibid., pp. 245–46.
8. Ibid.
9. Ibid.
10. Polk, *Diary*, November 21, 1846, p. 174.
11. Scott to Taylor, New York, November 25, 1846, Exec. Doc. No. 60, pp. 373–74.
12. Ibid.
13. Taylor to Crittenden, January 26, 1847, in Crittenden, vol. 1, p. 272.
14. Justin Smith, *The War with Mexico*, vol. 1, p. 358.
15. Taylor to TAG, December 22, 1846, Exec. Doc. No. 60, p. 385.
16. Taylor to Scott, December 26, 1846, Exec. Doc. No. 60, p. 848.
17. Taylor to TAG, January 7, 1847. Exec. Doc. No. 60, pp. 387–88.
18. Scott to Butler, January 3, 1847, Exec. Doc. No. 60, p. 852.
19. Scott to Taylor, January 3, 1847, Exec. Doc. No. 60, pp. 849–50.
20. Ripley, vol. 1, p. 345; *West Point Register*, 1980, p. 238.
21. Taylor to Scott, January 15, 1847, Exec. Doc. No. 60, p. 863.
22. Scott to Taylor, January 26, 1847, Exec. Doc. No. 60, p. 864.
23. Taylor to TAG, January 26, 1847, Exec. Doc. No. 60, pp. 1159–60.
24. Ibid., February 7, 1847, Exec. Doc. No. 60, pp. 1162–63.
25. Scott to Marcy, February 4, 1847, Exec. Doc. No. 60, p. 876.
26. Alcaraz, pp. 114–45; Justin Smith, *The War with Mexico*, vol. 1, p. 380.
27. Alcaraz, p. 120.
28. Crittenden to Taylor, undated, in Crittenden, vol. 1, p. 280.
29. Ibid., p. 279.

CHAPTER 16
BUENA VISTA II: "A NEAR RUN THING"

1. Chamberlain, p. 106.
2. Ibid., pp. 106–9.
3. Justin Smith, *The War with Mexico*, vol. 1, p. 382.
4. Alcaraz, p. 122.
5. Taylor to TAG, March 6, 1847, Exec. Doc. No. 60, p. 142.
6. Exec. Doc. No. 60, p. 98.
7. Ibid.
8. Taylor to TAG, March 6, 1847, Exec. Doc. No. 60, p. 134.

9. Justin Smith, *The War with Mexico*, vol. 1, pp. 388–89; Wilcox, p. 217.
10. Wilcox, pp. 221–23.
11. Justin Smith, *The War with Mexico*, vol. 1, p. 391; Ripley, vol. 1, p. 413; Taylor's report, March 6, 1847, Exec. Doc. No. 1, pp. 133–35.
12. Justin Smith, *The War with Mexico*, vol. 1, pp. 391–93.
13. Ibid., p. 396.
14. Ibid., p. 398.
15. Taylor to TAG, March 1, 1847, Exec. Doc. No. 1, p. 99.

CHAPTER 17
"THE PEAR IS
RIPE FOR FALLING"

1. De Voto, p. 115.
2. Ibid., p. 13.
3. Ibid., p. 6.
4. Ibid., p. 17.
5. Rives, pp. 106–7.
6. Ibid., pp. 108–9.
7. Lavender, pp. 57, 62, 117.
8. Ibid., p. 106.
9. Ibid., p. 107.
10. Justin Smith, *The War with Mexico*, vol. 1, p. 286.
11. Lavender, p. 204.
12. Rives, vol. I, pp. 480–484. Justin Smith, *The War with Mexico*, vol. 1, pp. 285–86.
13. DeVoto, p. 20.
14. Ibid., p. 321.
15. Hutchinson, pp. 56, 57, 58, 67.
16. Colton, p. 14.
17. Justin Smith, *The War with Mexico*, vol. 1, p. 320.
18. Lewis, *Sutter's Fort*, p. 117.
19. Ibid., p. 122.
20. Frémont's report, 1843–44, in Goetzmann, p. 98.
21. Harlow, p. 14.
22. See "California in 1846: A Report to the U.S. Government," reprinted from *The Pacific Monthly*, December 1863, in Lewis, *California in 1846*, (San Francisco: Grabhorn Press, 1934); Colton, p. 17.
23. Lewis, *The United States Conquest of California*, p. ix.

24. Hutchinson, p. 99.
25. Larkin to Leidesdorff, April 23, 1846, in Hawgood, p. 55.

CHAPTER 18
OCCUPATION OF THE WEST

1. Goetzmann, pp. 112–13.
2. Turner, p. 66.
3. Justin Smith, *The War with Mexico*, vol. 1, pp. 288–89.
4. Exec. Doc. No. 60, p. 168. See also Exec. Doc. No. 60, pp. 172–75, and account of William H. Emory, Exec. Doc. No. 7, p. 33.
5. Justin Smith, *The War with Mexico*, vol. 1, p. 291.
6. Turner, pp. 71–72; Ripley, vol. 1, p. 284.
7. Turner, p. 72.
8. Ibid., pp. 73–4.
9. Polk, *Diary*, October 2, 1846, p. 153.
10. Goetzmann, p. 68.
11. Gillespie and the Conquest of California," *California Historical Society Quarterly*, Spring 1938, pp. 123–30.
12. Ibid., Gillespie to Bancroft, April 18, 1846, Monterey, p. 136.
13. Lewis, *Sutter's Fort*, pp. 120–22.
14. "Letter from the Farthest West," June 10, 1846, quoted in Lewis, *The United States Conquest of California*, p. 25.
15. Ibid., June 24, 1846, quoted in Lewis, *The United States Conquest of California*, pp. 31–32. See also Nevin, pp. 99, 104.
16. Nevin, p. 105.
17. Lewis, *Sutter's Fort*, p. 125.
18. Larkin to Leidesdorff, July 5, 1846, in Hawgood, pp. 82–83.
19. Justin Smith, *The War with Mexico*, vol. 1, p. 334.
20. Ibid., p. 335.
21. Colton, p. 15.
22. Justin Smith, *The War with Mexico*, vol. 1, p. 336.
23. Colton, p. 20.
24. Los Angeles County Museum of Natural History.

CHAPTER 19
CHAOS IN CALIFORNIA

1. Nevin, p. 115; Justin Smith, *The War with Mexico*, vol. 1, p. 340.
2. Goetzmann, p. 47.

3. Griffin, p. 20.
4. Goetzmann, p. 134.
5. Griffin, pp. 25–26.
6. Emory, pp. 94–95.
7. Ibid., p. 96.
8. Turner, p. 123; Emory, maps, pp. 25 and 35.
9. Emory, p. 108. DeVoto, 357.
10. Kearny to TAG, December 13, 1846, Exec. Doc. No. 1, p. 515.
11. Emory, p. 109.
12. Ibid., pp. 109–10.
13. Kearny to TAG, December 13, 1846, Exec. Doc. No. 1, p. 516.
14. Emory, p. 111.
15. Ibid.
16. DeVoto, p. 358.
17. Emory, p. 112.
18. Griffin, p. 53.
19. Justin Smith, *The War with Mexico*, vol. I, p. 343.
20. Griffin, p. 67; Kearny to TAG January 12, 1847, Exec. Doc. No. 1, p. 517.
21. Emory, p. 119.
22. Ibid., pp. 120–21.
23. Kearny to TAG, January 12, 1847, Exec. Doc. No. 1, p. 517.
24. Emory, p. 121.
25. Justin Smith, *The War with Mexico*, vol. 1, p. 345.
26. Griffin, p. 65.
27. Justin Smith, *The War with Mexico*, vol. 1, p. 345.
28. Griffin, p. 660.
29. DeVoto, p. 459; Bauer, p. 196. Kearny forbade the duel.

CHAPTER 20
TERROR IN TAOS

1. Justin Smith, *The War with Mexico*, vol. 1, pp. 299–302.
2. McNierney, p. 4.
3. Bent to Buchanan, December 26, 1846, in McNierney, pp. 7–8.
4. Unpublished manuscript of Teresina Bent Scheurich, Bent's daughter, a witness.
5. Estergreen, p. 21.
6. Ibid.

7. Ibid., p. 524, with sketch map facing.
8. McNierney, p. 5; Estergreen, p. 23.

CHAPTER 21
MISSOURI XENOPHON

1. Nelson McClanahan to John McClanahan, June 19, 1847, McClanahan-Taylor papers, Southern Historical Collection, North Carolina. Quoted in Smith and Judah, p. 32.
2. Justin Smith, *The War with Mexico*, vol. 2, p. 303.
3. Ruxton, George F., *Adventures in Mexico and the Rock Mountains* (London: John Murray, 1847), quoted in Smith and Judah, pp. 296–97.
4. William H. Richardson, *Journal of William H. Richardson, a Private in Col. Doniphan's Command*, (Baltimore: J. Robinson, 1847), in Smith and Judah, p. 137.
5. Ibid., p. 501.
6. Susan S. Magoffin, *Down the Santa Fe Trail, 1846–47*, (New Haven: Yale University Press, 1926), quoted in Smith and Judah, p. 139.
7. Doniphan to Wool, March 20, 1847, Exec. Doc. No. 60, pp. 1128–29.
8. Taylor to TAG, April 4, 1847, Exec. Doc. No. 60, p. 1127.
9. Mora to Santa Anna, April 13, 1847, Exec. Doc. No. 60, p. 1088.
10. Dufour, p. 185.

CHAPTER 22
SIEGE OF VERACRUZ

1. Scott to Marcy, March 12, 1847, Exec. Doc. No. 1, p. 216.
2. Ibid., October 27, 1847, Exec. Doc. No. 59, pp. 54–55.
3. Ibid., pp. 58–59.
4. Scott to Marcy, November 16, 1846, Exec. Doc. No. 59, pp. 59–60.
5. Ibid., November 21, 1846, Exec. Doc. No. 59, p. 60.
6. Conner to Scott, January 18, 1847, Exec. Doc. No. 60, p. 892.
7. Elliot, p. 444. The informant was Alexander Barrow.
8. Justin Smith, *The War with Mexico*, vol. 2, p. 18.
9. Temple, pp. 63–64.
10. Semmes, p. 125.
11. Meade, vol. 1, p. 187.
12. Ibid. See also map in Justin Smith, *The War with Mexico*, vol. 2, p. 24.
13. Semmes, p. 129.
14. Ibid., pp. 129–30.

15. Colonel J. G. Totten, Chief Engineers of the Army.
16. Semmes, p. 132.
17. P.S.P. Conner, *The Home Squadron Under Commodore Conner in the War with Mexico*, p. 46.
18. Semmes, p. 136.
19. Alcaraz, p. 184.
20. Exec. Doc. No. 1, pp. 230–31.

CHAPTER 23
CERRO GORDO

1. Scott, GO No. 87, Exec. Doc. No. 60, p. 914.
2. Hitchcock, p. 250.
3. Freeman, pp. 235–35; Elliott, pp. 461–62.
4. Quitman to H. L. Scott, April 7, 1847, Exec. Doc. No. 60, pp. 917–18.
5. Elliott, p. 462; Scott to Jesup, March 19, 1847, Exec. Doc. No. 60, p. 913.
6. Justin Smith, *The War with Mexico*, vol. 2, pp. 3–14.
7. Ibid., p. 114; Calcott, pp. 255–56.
8. Calcott, pp. 256–57.
9. Proclamation to the public, Mexico City, March 31, 1847. Exec. Doc. No. 1, p. 260.
10. Alcaraz, p. 198; Justin Smith, *The War with Mexico*, vol. 2, p. 40.
11. *West Point Atlas*, map 15 C. Exec. Doc. No. 1, p. 264.
12. Justin Smith, *The War with Mexico*, vol. 2, p. 45.
13. Ballantine, p. 171.
14. Ibid., pp. 171–72.
15. Justin Smith, *The War with Mexico*, vol. 2, 41–42.
16. Ballantine, p. 174.
17. Ibid., pp. 174, 175.
18. Ibid., pp. 175–76.
19. Ibid., pp. 180–182.
20. Scott, GO No. 111, April 17, 1847. Exec. Doc. No. 1, p. 258.
21. Ibid., p. 59.
22. Scott to Marcy, April 23, 1847, Exec. Doc. No. 1, p. 262.
23. Justin Smith, *The War with Mexico*, vol. 2, p. 54.
24. Alcaraz, pp. 209–11.
25. Scott to Marcy, April 19, 1847, Exec. Doc. No. 1, p. 257.
26. Hitchcock, p. 251.
27. Semmes, p. 182; McClellan, p. 83.
28. McClellan, p. 87.

29. Justin Smith, *The War with Mexico*, vol. 2, p. 55.
30. Ibid.
31. Hitchcock to Scott, April 24, 1847, Exec. Doc. No. 60, pp. 1089–90. See also Hitchcock, p. 251.
32. Alcaraz, p. 214.

CHAPTER 24
''MR. POLK'S WAR''

1. *Congressional Globe Appendix*, p. 1217.
2. Polk, *Diary*, p. 138.
3. Ibid., p. 159.
4. *Boston Atlas*, May 16, 1847, quoted in Justin Smith, *The War with Mexico*, vol. 2, p. 280.
5. Justin Smith, *The War with Mexico*, vol. 1, pp. 128–29.
6. *Boston Atlas*, December 31, 1846, quoted in Justin Smith, *The War with Mexico*, vol. 2, p. 270.
7. *The Chief Executive: Inaugural Addresses*, p. 687.
8. Ibid., p. 666.
9. Ibid., pp. 690–688.
10. Justin Smith, *The War with Mexico*, vol. 2, p. 74.
11. Ibid., p. 75.
12. Polk, *Diary*, February 8, 1847, p. 195; February 10, 1847, p. 196.
13. Ibid., April 10, 1847, p. 211.
14. Ibid.
15. Ibid., pp. 212–14.

CHAPTER 25
''I BEG TO BE RECALLED''

1. Alcaraz, pp. 214–15.
2. Ibid., pp. 215–19, 221.
3. Ballantine, p. 191.
4. Ibid.
5. Ibid., pp. 192, 200.
6. Ibid., p. 197; Nevin, p. 150; Bauer, p. 268.
7. Kirby Smith, pp. 137–38.
8. Scott to Taylor, April 24, 1847, Exec. Doc. No. 60, p. 948.
9. Ibid.

10. Tennery, pp. 86, 92.
11. Ibid., p. 88.
12. Justin Smith, *The War with Mexico*, vol. 2, p. 64, gives 7113.
13. Scott to Worth, May 6, 1847, Exec. Doc. No. 60, pp. 957, 958.
14. Justin Smith, *The War with Mexico*, vol. 2, pp. 65, 66.
15. Worth to Scott, May 15, 1847, Exec. Doc. No. 60, pp. 994–95.
16. Exec. Doc. No. 60, pp. 973, 974.
17. Worth to Scott, May 19, 1847, Exec. Doc. No. 60, p. 967.
18. Scott to Marcy, June 4, 1847, Exec. Doc. No. 60, p. 993.
19. Scott, p. 466n.
20. Justin Smith, *The War with Mexico*, vol. 2, p. 128.
21. Scott to Trist, May 7, 1847, Exec. Doc. No. 60, pp. 959–60.
22. Marcy to Scott, May 31, 1847, Exec. Doc. No. 60, p. 961.
23. Scott to Trist, May 29, 1847, Exec. Doc. No. 60, p. 996.
24. Justin Smith, *The War with Mexico*, vol. 2, p. 129.
25. Scott to Marcy, June 4, 1847, Exec. Doc. No. 60, p. 994.

CHAPTER 26
"THAT SPLENDID CITY"

1. Bill, p. 245.
2. Exec. Doc. No. 60.
3. Elliott, pp. 486–87.
4. Hitchcock. See also Semmes, p. 275.
5. Ripley, vol. 2, p. 166.
6. Ibid., See also Bill, p. 259.
7. Trist Papers, quoted in Elliott, p. 491.
8. Trist to Buchanan, July 23, 1847, Exec. Doc. No. 60, p. 831.
9. Ripley, vol. 2, p. 152.
10. Ibid., p. 153.
11. Elliott, pp. 495–96.
12. Justin Smith, *The War with Mexico*, vol. 2, p. 132; Ripley, vol. 2, p. 154; Hitchcock, p. 267.
13. Justin Smith, *The War with Mexico*, vol. 2, p. 76.
14. Ibid., p. 213.
15. Alcaraz, p. 238.
16. Justin Smith, *The War with Mexico*, vol. 2, p. 87.
17. Ibid., p. 88.
18. Ibid.

19. Alcaraz, pp. 247–51.
20. Ballantine, pp. 236–37.

CHAPTER 27
BLOODY FRIDAY

1. Testimony at court-martial of Gideon Pillow, January 23, 1848, in Exec. Document No. 65, p. 523.
2. Lee to Mrs. Totten, August 22, 1847. Exhibit in Pillow court-martial, Exec. Doc. No. 65, pp. 461–62.
3. Dufour, p. 239.
4. Lee to Mason, August 14, 1847, quoted in Ripley, vol. 2, Appendix 1.
5. Duncan's report, August 14, 1847, in Ripley, vol. 2, Appendix 2.
6. Justin Smith, *The War with Mexico*, vol. 2, pp. 97–98.
7. Alcaraz, p. 256.
8. Dufour, p. 241.
9. Scott report, August 19, 1847, Exec. Doc. No. 1, p. 304.
10. Justin Smith, *The War with Mexico*, vol. 2, p. 88.
11. Letter written by a member of the Mexican Congress, August 21, 1847. Exec. Doc. No. 65, p. 417.
12. Alcaraz, p. 270.
13. Ibid., pp. 270–72.
14. Freeman, vol. 1, p. 256.
15. Ibid., p. 258.
16. Riley testimony at Pillow court-martial, Exec. Doc. No. 65, p. 182.
17. Justin Smith, *The War with Mexico*, vol. 2, p. 101.
18. Riley testimony at Pillow court-martial, Exec. Doc. No. 65, p. 147.
19. Exec. Doc. No. 65, p. 332.
20. Justin Smith, *The War with Mexico*, vol. 2, p. 106.
21. Exec. Doc. No. 65, p. 332.
22. Ibid.
23. Ibid., pp. 99–100; Justin Smith, *The War with Mexico*, vol. 2, pp. 104, 105.
24. Freeman, vol. 1, pp. 263–64.
25. Exec. Doc. No. 65, p. 101.
26. Alcaraz, p. 279.
27. Exec. Doc. No. 65, p. 102.
28. Scott report, August 28, 1847, Exec. Doc. No. 1, pp. 308–9.
29. Ibid., p. 309.
30. Worth report, August 23, 1847, Exec. Doc. No. 1, pp. 316–18.

31. Scott report, August 28, 1847, Exec. Doc. No. 1, p. 311.
32. Ibid., pp. 313, 314.

CHAPTER 28
HALLS OF MONTEZUMA

1. Alcaraz, p. 301.
2. Ibid.
3. Scott report, August 28, 1847, Exec. Doc. No. 1, p. 314.
4. Exec. Doc. No. 52, p. 308.
5. Scott, GO No. 262, Exec. Doc. No. 1, pp. 357–58.
6. Kirby Smith, p. 208.
7. Hitchcock, pp. 287–89; Alcaraz, p. 313. See also Scott report, September 11, 1847, Exec. Doc. No. 1, p. 355.
8. Dufour, p. 259; Kirby Smith, p. 216. See also Hitchcock, p. 293.
9. Scott to Santa Anna, September 6, 1847, Exec. Doc. No. 1, p. 359.
10. Steele, p. 115.
11. Ibid., p. 116.
12. Scott report, September 11, 1847, Exec. Doc. No. 1, p. 355.
13. Worth report, September 10, 1847, Exec. Doc. No. 1, p. 362.
14. Steele, p. 116.
15. Worth report, September 10, 1847, Exec. Doc. No. 1, p. 363.
16. Justin Smith, *The War with Mexico,* vol. 2, pp. 143–44.
17. Worth report, Exec. Doc. No. 1, p. 364; Steele, pp. 116–17.
18. Freeman, vol. I, p. 275.
19. Major John Smith's report, September 26, 1847, Exec. Doc. No. 1, p. 427.
20. Scott report, Exec. Doc. No. 1, p. 376; Steele, p. 117.
21. Scott report, Exec. Doc. No. 1, p. 377; Ripley, vol. 2, p. 402.
22. Alcaraz, pp. 359–60.
23. Justin Smith, *The War with Mexico,* vol. 2, pp. 153–54.
24. Scott report, September 18, 1847, Exec. Doc. No. 1, pp. 277–78. Justin Smith, *The War with Mexico,* vol. 2, p. 153.
25. Justin Smith, *The War with Mexico,* vol. 2, p. 156.
26. Ibid., p. 157.
27. Ripley, vol. 2, pp. 355–56.

CHAPTER 29
OCCUPATION

1. Justin Smith, *The War with Mexico,* vol. 2, pp. 166–67; Alcaraz, pp. 375–80.

2. Exec. Doc. No. 1, p. 386.
3. Alcaraz, pp. 422–23.
4. Ripley, vol. 2, pp. 449–504.
5. Ibid., p. 504.
6. Ibid., pp. 505–6.
7. Alcaraz, p. 403.
8. Scott to Marcy, December 14, 1847, Exec. Doc. No. 60, p. 1039.
9. Ibid., January 6, 1848, Exec. Doc. No. 60, pp. 1061–62.
10. Ripley, vol. 2, pp. 560–61.
11. GO No. 376, December 15, 1847, Exec. Doc. No. 60, p. 1050.
12. Ripley, vol. 2, p. 569.
13. Ibid., pp. 570–71.
14. Alcaraz, p. 416.
15. Scott, vol. 2, p. 416.
16. Exec. Doc. No. 65.
17. Ibid.
18. Scott to Pillow, October 3, 1847; Pillow to Scott, October 3, 1847; Scott to Pillow, October 4, 1847. Exec. Doc. No. 60, pp. 1018–20.
19. New Orleans *Delta*, September 10, 1847, reprinted in Exec. Doc. No. 65, pp. 385–89.
20. Elliott, p. 568.
21. Exec. Doc. No. 65, p. 454–55.
22. Scott, GO No. 49, November 12, 1847. Exec. Doc. No. 65, p. 455.
23. Worth to Scott, November 14, 1847, in Elliot, p. 571.
24. Elliot.
25. Manual to Scott, Scott to Manual, November 5, 1847, through December 23, 1847, Exec. Doc. No. 60, pp. 1054–57.
26. Exec. Doc. No. 60, p. 1063.
27. Hitchcock, p. 310.

CHAPTER 30
PEACE

1. Hitchcock, p. 267.
2. Marcy to Scott, October 6, 1847, Exec. Doc. No. 60, pp. 1007–8.
3. Justin Smith, *The War with Mexico*, vol. 2, pp. 234–35.
4. Ibid., p. 238.
5. GO No. 376, December 15, 1847, Exec. Doc. No. 60, p. 1050. Scott to Marcy, January 6, 1848, Exec. Doc. No. 60, p. 1062.
6. Hitchcock, p. 313.

7. Justin Smith, *The War with Mexico*, vol. 2, p. 240.
8. Hitchcock, pp. 313–15.
9. Trist to Scott, January 28, 1848, in McCormac, p. 538.
10. Marcy to Scott, January 13, 1848, Exec. Doc. No. 60, p. 1044.
11. Exec. Doc. No. 60, pp. 1218–27.
12. Justin Smith, *The War with Mexico*, vol. 2, p. 188.
13. William D. Wilkins to his father, April 22, 1848. Quoted in Smith and Judah, p. 440.
14. Scott, vol. 2, pp. 581–82.
15. McCormac, pp. 544–45.
16. Trist to Buchanan, January 25, 1848, Exec. Doc. No. 52, p. 290. See also McCormac, p. 544.
17. McCormac, p. 541.
18. Polk, *Diary*, February 28, 1848, pp. 312–13. More detail in McCormac, p. 546.
19. Exec. Doc. No. 52, quoted in McCormac, p. 548.
20. Dufour, p. 279.

EPILOGUE

1. Bill, p. 64.
2. Scott, vol. 2, pp. 586–88.
3. DeVoto, p. 464.
4. Ibid.
5. Goetzman, p. 297; DeVoto, p. 467.

BIBLIOGRAPHY

BOOKS

Adams, John Quincy. *The Diary of John Quincy Adams*. Edited by Allan Nevins. New York: Longmans, Green & Co., 1928.

*Alcaraz, Ramón, et al. *The Other Side: Notes for the History of the War Between Mexico and the United States*. Translated from the Spanish and edited by Albert C. Ramsey. New York: John Wiley, 1850.

*Ballantine, George. *An English Soldier in the US Army*. New York: Stringer and Townsend, 1853. Republished in 1860 by W.A. Townsend & Co., New York.

Bancroft, Hubert H. *History of California*, vol. XX. Santa Barbara, Calif.: Wallace Hebbard, 1966.

Barbour, Philip and Martha. *The Journals of Major Philip Norbourne Barbour and His Wife Martha Isabella Hopkins Barbour*. Edited by Rhoda Van Bibber Tanner Doubleday. New York: G.P. Putnam's Sons, 1936.

Bassett, John Spencer. *The Life of Andrew Jackson*. Hamden, Conn.: Archon Books, 1967.

Bauer, K. Jack. *The Mexican War, 1846–1848*. New York: Macmillan Publishing Co., Inc., 1974.

Bayard, Samuel John. *Life of Com. Robert F. Stockton*. New York: Derby & Jackson, 1856.

*Beauregard, Pierre G.T. *With Beauregard in Mexico: The Mexican War Reminiscences of P.G.T. Beauregard*. Edited by T. Harry Williams. Baton Rouge: Louisiana State University Press, 1956.

Benton, Senator Thomas Hart. *Thirty Years' View; or A History of the Working of the American Government for Thirty Years, from 1820 to 1850*. 2 vols. New York: D. Appleton & Co., 1854.

*Bill, Alfred Hoyt. *Rehearsal for Conflict*. New York: Alfred A. Knopf, 1947.

Brack, Gene M. *Mexican Views Manifest Destiny, 1821–1846: An Essay on the Origins of the Mexican War*. Albuquerque: University of New Mexico Press, 1975.

Brooks, Nathan Covington. *A Complete History of the Mexican War, 1846–1848*. Albuquerque: Gilberto Espinosa, 1849. Reproduced by the Rio Grande Press, Chicago, 1965.

*An asterisk denotes works of special value to this book, for background, eyewitness information or perspective.

*Calcott, Wilfrid Hardy. *Santa Anna, the Story of an Enigma Who Was Once Mexico.* Norman: University of Oklahoma Press, 1936. DeGolyer Collection.

*Calderón de la Barca, Fanny. *Life in Mexico.* Edited by Howard T. and Maron Hall Fisher. Garden City, N.Y.: Doubleday and Company, 1966.

Calhoun, John C. *Correspondence of John C. Calhoun.* Edited by J. Franklin Jameson. Annual Report of the American Historical Association, 1899, vol. II. Washington, 1900.

Callahan, James Morton. *American Foreign Policy in Mexican Relations.* New York: Macmillan, 1932.

Carson, Kit. *Kit Carson's Own Story of His Life.* Edited by Blanche C. Grant. Taos, N.M.: Kit Carson Memorial Foundation, Inc., 1955.

*Chamberlain, Samuel E. *My Confession.* New York: Harper and Brothers, 1956.

Chatfield, W. H. *The Twin Cities of the Border and the Country of the Lower Rio Grande.* New Orleans: E. P. Brandao, 1893.

The Chief Executive: Inaugural Addresses of the Presidents of the United States from George Washington to Lyndon B. Johnson. Edited by Fred L. Israel. New York: Crown Publishers, 1965.

Colton, Calvin. *The Life and Times of Henry Clay.* 2 vols. New York: A. S. Barnes, 1845.

*Colton, Rev. Walter, USN. *Three Years in California.* New York: A. S. Barnes & Co., 1850.

Connelly, William E. *War with Mexico, 1846–1847, Doniphan's Expedition and the Conquest of New Mexico and California* (Including a reprint of the work of John T. Hughes). Topeka, Kans.: published by the author, 1907.

Conner, David. *The Correspondence of Commodore David Conner, USN, During the War of 1812 and Mexican War.* Philadelphia: Henkel.

*Conner, Philip Syng Physick. "Commodore Conner: Notes on Maclay's History of the United States Navy." United Review, 1895.

———. *The Home Squadron under Commodore Conner in the War with Mexico, Being a Synopsis of Its Services, 1846–1847.* Philadelphia, 1896.

*Crittenden, John J. *The Life of John J. Crittenden, With Selections from his Correspondence and Speeches.* Edited by Mrs. Chapman Coleman. 2 vols. Philadelphia: J.B. Lippincott & Co., 1871.

Dillon, Lester R., Jr. *American Artillery in the Mexican War 1846–1847.* Austin, Tex.: Presidial Press, 1975.

*DeVoto, Bernard. *The Year of Decision, 1846.* Boston: Little, Brown and Company, 1943.

Dobie, J. Frank. *Coronado's Children.* New York: Grosset and Dunlap, 1930.

*Dufour, Charles L. *The Mexican War, A Compact History, 1846–1848.* New York: Hawthorn Books, Inc., 1968.

Dupuy, R. Ernest, and Trevor N. Dupuy. *Military Heritage of America.* New York, Toronto, London: McGraw-Hill, 1956.

Dyer, Brainard. *Zachary Taylor.* New York: Barnes & Noble, Inc., 1946.

*Eliot, Charles W. *Winfield Scott: The Soldier and the Man.* New York: Macmillan Company, 1937.

*Emory, Lt. Col. W. H. *Notes of a Military Reconnaissance from Fort Leavenworth, in Missouri, to San Diego, in California, 1848.* Executive Document No. 41, 30th Cong., 1st sess., Washington, 1848. Reprinted by Arno Press in *The United States Conquest of California,* 1976.

Estergreen, Marion. *The Real Kit Carson.* Taos, N.M.: Kit Carson Memorial Foundation, 1955.

Ferguson, Henry N. *The Port of Brownsville, A Maritime History of the Rio Grande Valley.* Brownsville, Tex.: Springman-King Press, 1976.

Folsom, George. *Mexico in 1842.* New York: Folsom, 1842.

*Freeman, Douglas Southall. *R. E. Lee,* vol. I. New York: Charles Scribner's Sons, 1949.

Frémont, John Charles. *Narratives of Exploration and Adventure.* New York, London, Toronto: Longmans, Green & Co., 1956.

*French, Samuel Gibbs. *Two Wars, An Autobiography.* Nashville, Tennessee: The Confederate Veteran, 1901.

Frost, John. *The History of Mexico and Its Wars.* New Orleans: A. Hawkins, 1882.

Fry, J. Reese. *A Life of Zachary Taylor, Comprising a Narrative of Events Connected with His Professional Career.* Philadelphia: Grigg, Elliot & Co., 1848.

Fuller, John Douglas Pitts. *The Movement for the Acquisition of All Mexico, 1846–1848.* Baltimore: Johns Hopkins Press, 1936.

*Giddings, Luther. *Sketches of the Campaign in Northern Mexico in Eighteen Hundred Forty-six and Seven.* New York: George P. Putnam and Company, 1853.

*Goetzmann, William H. *Army Exploration in the American West, 1803–1863.* Lincoln: University of Nebraska Press, 1959.

Grant, Ulysses Simpson. *The Papers of U.S. Grant,* vol. 1. Edited by John Y. Simon. Carbondale: Southern Illinois University Press, 1967.

*———. *Personal Memoirs of U.S. Grant,* vol. I. New York: Charles A. Webster & Co., 1885.

Gregg, Kate L. *The Road to Santa Fe: The Journal and Diaries of George Champlin Sibley.* Albuquerque: University of New Mexico Press, 1952.

*Griffin, John S. "A Doctor Comes to California," San Francisco, California, Historical Society Quarterly, XXI, 3, 4, and XXII, 1, 1943. Reprinted by Arno Press in *The United States Conquest of California*, 1976.

Guild, Thelma S., and Harvey L. Carter. *Kit Carson: A Pattern for Heroes*. Lincoln: University of Nebraska Press, 1984.

Hamilton, Holman. *Zachary Taylor: Soldier in the White House*. New York: Bobbs-Merrill Company, Inc., 1951.

———. *Zachary Taylor: Soldier of the Republic*. New York: Bobbs-Merrill Company, Inc., 1941.

Harlow, Neal. *California Conquered: War and Peace on the Pacific, 1846–1850*. Berkeley: University of California Press, 1982.

*Hawgood, John A., Ed. *First and Last Consul: Thomas Oliver Larkin and the Americanization of California*. Palo Alto, Calif.: Pacific Books, 1970.

Henry, Robert Selph. *The Story of the Mexican War*. New York: Frederick Unger, 1950.

*Henry, William Seaton, Captain. *Campaign Sketches of the War with Mexico*. New York: Harper Bros., 1847. Reprinted by Arno Press, N.Y., 1973.

A History of the City of Baltimore, Its Men and Institutions. Published by the Baltimore *American*, 1902.

*Hitchcock, Ethan Allen. *Fifty Years in Camp and Field*. Edited by W.A. Croffut. New York: G.P. Putnam's Sons, 1909.

Howard, George W. *The Monumental City, Its Past History and Present Resources*. Baltimore: J.D. Ehlers & Co., 1873.

Hughes, John T. *Doniphan's Expedition, Containing an Account of the Conquest of New Mexico*. New York: Arno Press, 1973.

Hutchinson, W. H. *California*. Palo Alto, Calif.: American West Publishing Company, 1969.

Jackson, Andrew. *Correspondence of Andrew Jackson*, vol. VI. Edited by John Spencer Bassett. Washington: Carnegie Institution of Washington, 1933. Reprinted by Krause Reprint Co., New York, 1969.

James, Marquis. *Andrew Jackson: Portrait of a President*. New York: Grosset & Dunlap, 1937.

———. *The Life of Andrew Jackson*. Camden: Haddon House Craftsmen, Inc., 1938.

———. *The Raven: The Life Story of Sam Houston*. Garden City, N.Y.: Blue Ribbon Books, 1929.

Johannsen, Robert W. *To the Halls of the Montezumas: The Mexican War in the American Imagination*. New York and Oxford: Oxford University Press, 1985.

Jones, Anson. *Memoranda and Official Correspondence Relating to the Republic of Texas*. New York: D. Appleton and Company, 1859. Reprinted by Arno Press, New York, 1973.

*Jones, Oakah L., Jr. *Santa Anna.* New York: Twayne Publishers, Inc., 1968.

Junior League of Washington. *The City of Washington: An Illustrated History.* Edited by Thomas Froncek. New York: Alfred A. Knopf, 1981.

*Kenly, John R. *Memoirs of a Maryland Volunteer.* Philadelphia: J.B. Lippincott and Co., 1873.

Lavender, David. *Bent's Fort.* Lincoln: University of Nebraska Press, 1954.

————. *Climax at Buena Vista: The American Campaigns in Northeastern Mexico,* 1846–47. Philadelphia and New York: J. B. Lippincott Co., 1966.

Lens, Sidney. *The Forging of the American Empire.* New York: Thomas Y. Crowell Company, 1971.

Lewis, Oscar. "California in 1846: Described in Letters from Thomas O. Larkin," in *The United States Conquest of California.* New York: Arno Press, 1976.

————. *Sutter's Fort.* Englewood Cliffs, N.J.: Prentice-Hall, Inc., 1966.

*McClellan, George Brinton. *The Mexican War Diary of General George B. McClellan.* Edited by William Starr Myers. Princeton: Princeton University Press, 1917.

*McCormac, Eugene I. *James K. Polk: A Political Biography.* New York: Russell and Russell, 1965.

McNierney, Michael, Ed. *Taos 1847: The Revolt in Contemporary Accounts.* Boulder, Colo.: Johnson Publishing Company, 1980.

Manning, William R. *Early Diplomatic Relations Between the United States and Mexico.* Baltimore: Johns Hopkins Press, 1916.

*Meade, George. *The Life and Letters of George Gordon Meade, Major-General, United States Army,* vol I. New York: Charles Scribner's Sons, 1913.

Meigs, William M. *The Life of Thomas Hart Benton.* Philadelphia and London: Lippincott Company, 1904.

The Mexican War and Its Heroes: Being a Complete History of the Mexican War, Embracing All the Operations under Generals Taylor and Scott, with a Biography of All the Officers. Philadelphia: Lippincott, Grambro, & Co., 1850.

Morgan, Robert J. *A Whig Embattled: The Presidency Under John Tyler.* Lincoln: University of Nebraska Press, 1954.

National Park Service, Department of the Interior. *Exploring the American West, 1803–1879.* Washington, D.C., 1982.

Neal, William and William A. *Century of Conflict, 1821–1913: Incidents in the Lives of William Neal and William A. Neal, Early Settlers in South Texas.* Waco, Tex.: Texian Press, 1966.

*Nevin, David. *The Mexican War.* Alexandria, Va.: Time-Life Books, Inc., 1978.

*Nichols, Edward J. *Zach Taylor's Little Army.* Garden City, N.Y.: Doubleday & Company, 1963.

Nichols, Roy Franklin. *Franklin Pierce.* Philadelphia: University of Pennsylvania Press, 1931.

Nolan Jeanette Covert. *Andrew Jackson.* New York: Julian Messner, Inc. 1949.

Oliva, Leo E. *Soldiers on the Santa Fe Trail.* Norman: University of Oklahoma Press, 1967.

Oswandel, J. Jacob. *Notes on the Mexican War, 1846–47–48.* Philadelphia, 1885.

Parton, James. *Life of Andrew Jackson.* New York: Mason Brothers, 1860. Reprinted by Johnson Reprint Corp., New York, 1967.

*Pletcher, David M. *The Diplomacy of Annexation: Texas, Oregon, and the Mexican War.* Columbia: University of Missouri Press, 1973.

Polk, James K. *Polk: The Diary of a President, 1845–1849.* Edited by Allan Nevins. London, New York and Toronto: Longmans Green and Company, 1929.

*Price, Glenn W. *Origins of the War with Mexico: The Polk-Stockton Intrigue.* Austin and London: University of Texas Press, 1967.

Prucha, Francis Paul. *The Sword of the Republic: The United States Army on the Frontier, 1783–1846.* Bloomington and London: Indiana University Press, 1969.

*Reid, Samuel C., Jr. *The Scouting Expeditions of McCullough's Texas Rangers.* New York: Books for Libraries Press, 1847. Reprinted, 1970.

Remini, Robert V. *Andrew Jackson.* New York: Twayne Publishers, Inc., 1966.

———. *Andrew Jackson and the Course of American Empire, 1767–1821.* New York: Harper & Row, 1977.

*Ripley, R.S. *The War with Mexico.* 2 vols. New York: Burt Franklin, 1970. (Originally published 1849.)

Rippy, J. Fred. *Joel R. Poinsett, Versatile American.* Durham, N.C.: Duke University Press, 1935.

Rives, George L. *The United States and Mexico.* New York: Charles Scribner's Sons, 1913. Reprinted by Kraus Reprint Co., New York, N.Y., 1969. 2 vols.

Robertson, Brian. *Wild Horse Desert: The Heritage of South Texas.* Edinburg, Tex.: New Santander Press, 1985.

Roosevelt, Theodore. *Thomas Hart Benton.* Boston and New York: Houghton and Mifflin Co., 1886.

*Santa Anna, Antonio López de. *The Eagle: The Autobiography of Santa Anna.* Edited by Ann Fears Crawford. Austin, Tex.: Pemberton Press, 1967.

*Schroeder, John H. *Mr. Polk's War: American Opposition and Dissent, 1846–1848.* Madison: University of Wisconsin Press, 1973.

*Scott, Winfield. *The Memoirs of Lieut-Gen Winfield Scott, LLD.* 2 vols. New York: Sheldon & Co., 1864.

Sears, Louis Martin. *A History of American Foreign Relations.* New York: Thomas Y. Crowell Company, 1927.

Sedgwick, John. *Correspondence of John Sedgwick,* vol. I, Stoeckle, 1902.

*Sellers, Charles. *James K. Polk, Continentalist, 1843–1846.* Princeton: Princeton University Press, 1966.

*Semmes, Raphael, Lieutenant, USN. *Service Afloat and Ashore During the Mexican War.* Cincinnati: Wm. H. Moore, 1851.

Seward, Frederick W. *William H. Seward, an Autobiography from 1801 to 1846.* New York: Derby and Miller, 1891.

Sides, Joseph C. *Fort Brown Historical.* San Antonio, Tex.: Naylor Company, 1942.

Silver, James W. *Edmund Pendleton Gaines: Frontier General.* Baton Rouge: Louisiana State University Press, 1944.

Singletary, Otis A. *The Mexican War.* Chicago: University of Chicago Press, 1960.

*Smith, E. Kirby. *To Mexico with Scott: Letters of Ephraim Kirby Smith to His Wife.* Cambridge: Harvard University Press, 1917.

Smith, Elbert B. *Magnificent Missourian; The Life of Thomas Hart Benton.* Philadelphia and New York: J. B. Lippincott Co., 1958.

Smith, George Winston, and Charles Judah. *Chronicles of the Gringos: The U.S. Army in the Mexican War, 1846–1848.* Albuquerque: The University of New Mexico Press, 1968.

Smith, Justin H. *The Annexation of Texas.* New York: AMS Press, 1971. (Reprint from the edition of 1911, New York.)

*———. *The War with Mexico.* 2 vols. Gloucester, Mass.: Peter Smith, 1963. (Originally published by the Macmillan Company, 1919.)

Soto, Miguel E. "The Monarchist Conspiracy and the Mexican War," in Douglas W. Richmond (ed.), *Essays on the Mexican War.* University of Texas at Arlington, 1986.

The State of the Union Messages of the Presidents, 1790–1966, vol. I. Edited by Fred L. Israel. New York: Chelsea House, 1966.

*Steele, Matthew Forney. *American Campaigns,* vol. I. Washington, D.C.: United States Infantry Association, 1943.

Strode, Hudson. *Timeless Mexico.* New York: Harcourt, Brace & Co., 1944.

Taylor and His Generals: A Biography of Major-General Zachary Taylor; and the Sketches of the Lives of Generals Worth, Wool, and Twiggs. Philadelphia: E.H. Butler & Co., 1847.

*Taylor, Zachary. *Letters of Zachary Taylor from the Battlefields of the Mexican War.* Rochester, N.Y.: William K. Bixby, 1908. Reprinted by Krause Reprint Company, New York, 1970.

Temple, William G. "Memoir of the Landing of the United States Troops at Vera Cruz in 1847." Appendix to P.S.P. Conner, *The Home Squadron* (q.v.).

Tennery, Thomas D. *The Mexican War Diary of Thomas D. Tennery.* Norman: University of Oklahoma Press, 1970.

*Turner, Henry Smith. *The Original Journals of Henry Smith Turner.* Norman: University of Oklahoma Press, 1966.

Tyler, Lyon G. *The Letters and Times of the Tylers,* vol. II. Richmond, Va.: Whittet and Shepperson, 1885.

*U.S. Congress. *Congressional Globe Appendix,* 29th Cong., 1st sess., 1845–46.

*U.S. Congress. Executive Document No. 1. 30th Cong., 2d sess. Message from the President of the United States to the Two Houses of Congress. With accompanying documents. Washington, D.C.: Wendell & Van Benthuysen, 1848.

U.S. Congress. Senate. Executive Document No. 52. 30th Cong., 1st sess. *The Treaty Between the United States and Mexico,* 1848.

*U.S. Congress. House. Executive Document No. 59. 30th Cong., 1st sess. Correspondence Between the Secretary of War and General Scott. Washington, D.C., 1848.

*U.S. Congress. House. Executive Document No. 60. 30th Cong., 1st sess. *Messages of the President of the United States with the Correspondence, Therewith Communicated, Between the Secretary of War and Other Officers of the Government: The Mexican War.* Washington, D.C.: Wendell and Van Benthuysen, 1848.

*U.S. Congress. Senate. Executive Document No. 65. *Message from the President of the United States Communicating, in Compliance with a Resolution of the Senate, the Proceedings of the Two Courts of Inquiry in the Case of Major General Pillow.* Washington, D.C.: 1848.

U.S. Congress. Executive Document No. 4. The President's Message to the Two Houses of Congress, December 8, 1846. 29th Cong., 2d sess. Washington, D.C.: Ritchie & Heiss, 1846.

*Upton, Bvt. Major General Emory. *The Military Policy of the United States.* Fourth Impression. Washington, D.C.: Government Printing Office, 1917. First manuscript 1881.

Van Deusen, Glyndon G. *The Jacksonian Era.* New York, Evanston, London: Harper & Row, 1959.

Wallace, Edward S. *General William Jenkins Worth, Monterey's Forgotten Hero.* Dallas, Tex.: Southern Methodist University Press, 1953.

————. *The Great Reconnaissance*. Boston: Little, Brown, 1955.

War Department, Adjutant General's Office. *Official Army Register for 1846–55*. Military History Institute, Carlisle Barracks, Pennsylvania.

Wartenburg, Count Yorck von. *Napoleon as a General*. 2 vols. The Wolseley Series. London, 1897.

*Webb, Walter Prescott. *The Texas Rangers in the Mexican War*. Austin, Tex.: Jenkins Garrett Press, 1975.

*Wilcox, General Cadmus M. *History of the Mexican War*. Washington, D.C.: Church News Publishing Co., 1892.

Williams, Frank B., Jr. *Tennessee's Presidents*. Knoxville: University of Tennessee Press, 1981.

Willson, Beckles. *John Slidell*. New York: Minto, Balch, & Co. 1932.

PERIODICALS AND NEWSPAPERS

Ames, George W., Jr. "Gillespie and the Conquest of California," *California Historical Society Quarterly*, vol. 17 (2), 1938, pp. 123–40.

————. "Gillespie and the Conquest of California," *California Historical Society Quarterly*, vol. 17 (4), 1938, pp. 325–50.

Baltimore American, May 2, 27, 28, 29, 30, June 1, 1844. Maryland Historical Society, Baltimore.

The Battery, Headquarters, Army of Occupation, Camp near Fort Brown, Texas, May 17, 1846.

Castel, Albert. "Winfield Scott, Part II," *American History Illustrated*, July 1981.

Cooling, Benjamin Franklin. "Lew Wallace and Gideon Pillow: Enigmas and Variations on an American Military Theme," *Lincoln Herald*, vol. 84, no. 2 (Summer 1981).

"The Diary and Letters of William P. Rogers, 1846–1862" (edited by Eleanor Damon Pace), *Southwestern Historical Quarterly*, vol. 30, no. 4 (April 1929), pp. 259–85.

"General Jackson on Annexation," *Niles' National Register*, Baltimore, June 15, 1844.

"George Washington Trahern: Texas Cowboy Soldier from Mier to Buena Vista" (edited by A. Russell Buchanan), *Southwestern Historical Quarterly*, vol. 63, July 1954, pp. 60–90.

Ferguson, Henry N. "The Great Western," *Westways*, December 1970.

Houston, Donald E. "The Role of Artillery in the Mexican War," *Journal of the West*, vol. II, no. 2 (April 1972), pp. 273–84.

Hussey, John A. "The Origin of the Gillespie Mission," *California Historical Society Quarterly*, vol. 19 (1).

"Intercession of Gen. Jackson on Behalf of Texan Prisoners in Mexico," *Nashville Union,* April 17, 1844.

Irey, Thomas R. "Soldiering, Suffering, and Dying in the Mexican War," *Journal of the West,* vol. 11, no. 2 (April 1972), pp. 285–98.

Oates, Stephen B. "Los Diablos Tejanos: The Texas Rangers in the Mexican War," *Journal of the West,* vol. 11, no. 2 (April 1972), pp. 487–504.

Payne, Darwin. "Camp Life in the Army of Occupation: Corpus Christi, July 1845 to March 1846," *Southwestern Historical Quarterly,* vol. 63, July 1954.

Reilly, Tom. "Jane McManus Storms: Letters from the Mexican War," 1846–1848," *Southwestern Historical Quarterly,* vol. 85, July 1981.

Remini, Robert V. "Texas Must Be Ours," *American Heritage,* February–March 1986.

Republic of the Rio Grande: And Friend of the People, vol. 1, no. 6. City of Matamoros, June 23, 1846.

Stenberg, Richard R. "Further Letters of Archibald H. Gillespie," *California Historical Quarterly,* vol. 18, no. 3 (1939), pp. 217–28.

Stonesifer, Roy P., Jr. "Gideon Pillow: A Study in Egotism," *Tennessee Historical Quarterly,* vol. 25, no. 4 (Winter 1966).

Wallace, Edward S. "General William Jennings Worth and Texas," *Southwestern Historical Quarterly,* vol. 54, October 1950, pp. 159–68.

Washington Globe, April 28, May 24, 28, 29, 30, June 4, 6, 1844.

Woodward, Arthur. "The Great Western . . . An Amazon Who Made History," Arizona Pioneers Historical Society.

"Worth Letters," *New York Times,* July 16, 1916.

ACKNOWLEDGMENTS

SPECIAL THANKS TO THE FOLLOWING:

Colonel Bruce Aiken, of Brownsville, Texas, who generously provided me with books, information, documents, and old newspapers. He and his wife, Irma, gave me a personally conducted tour of northern Mexico, to include Brownsville, Mier, Cerralvo, Monterrey, Saltillo, and Buena Vista.

Louise Arnold, historian, U.S. Army Military History Institute, Carlisle Barracks, Pa., who showed unusual interest in this project and great understanding of the resources available. My thanks for her help and enthusiasm are difficult to express fully. Thanks also to John Slonaker, Denny Vetock, and Judy Meck, of the same office.

Charlotte E. Bartlett, of West Chester University, for continuing interest and help.

The people of Brownsville, Texas, who took a special interest in this book and went to some lengths to help. Besides Bruce Aiken and Robert Vezzetti, mentioned elsewhere, I am indebted to Mr. A. A. Champion, the great authority on the battle of Palo Alto; Mr. and Mrs. Frank Yturria, erstwhile owners of the battlefield of Resaca de la Palma; Mr. Henry P. Griffin, Jr., the authority on the incident at the Arroyo Colorado; and Ms. Yolando Z. Gonzalez, of the Arnulfo Oliveira Memorial Library.

Paul Cross, of Columbia, Tenn., for great helpfulness in providing materials and insights into Gideon Pillow. And to John R. Neal, owner of Clifton, Pillow's home, for making Mr. Cross's services available.

Dr. Wayne Cutler, editor of the papers of James K. Polk, formerly of Vanderbilt University, Nashville, Tenn., who gave me much support and encouragement, including a trip to Texas in 1983.

Dr. Guadalupe Jimenez-Codinach, and her husband, Modesto Suarez-Altimarano, both citizens of Mexico and currently employed in the Latin-American Section, Library of Congress, who shared with me their invaluable insights into the Mexican viewpoint, and into the culture of present-day Mexico.

Joanne Thompson, for her help, encouragement, and keen editorial comments, particularly in the latter phases.

Robert Vezzetti, president of the Brownsville Historical Association, and his wife, Isabel, for their support.

Mrs. Jerome ("Dodie") Yentz, and Mrs. Thomas ("Judy") Hedberg, my secretaries and personal assistants. While Judy kept us administratively straight, Dodie Yentz mastered the use of the word processor and kept the various manuscripts in order, a gargantuan task. Dodie's help cut the time required to finish this book by a year, at the very least.

LIBRARIANS AND OTHERS TO WHOM I AM INDEBTED:

Mr. Jack K. Boyer, and Lorraine D. Dyson, of the Kit Carson Memorial Foundation, Taos, New Mexico.

Charles Colley, director, Jenkins Garrett Collection, Library Special Collections, University of Texas at Arlington.

Jenkins Garrett, of Fort Worth, Texas, founder of the Jenkins Garrett Library, one of the most complete collections in the country, who took me on a personally conducted tour.

Dr. William H. Goetzmann, for a very enlightening lunch and guidance on explorations in the West.

Dr. Laura Gutierrez-Witt, chief librarian, Benson Latin American Collection, University of Texas.

Dr. John Hebert, Hispanic Division, Library of Congress, and John Hobart, of the Photographic Division.

Mrs. Marcel Hull, Special Collections, University of Texas at Arlington.

William W. Hughes, University of Arkansas, for providing materials on Archibald Yell.

Dr. Harold Moser, editor of the Andrew Jackson Papers, University of Tennessee.

Colonel Jim R. ("Rod") Paschall, Director, U.S. Army Military History Institute, Carlisle Barracks, Pa. The MHI, under Rod Paschall's leadership, was my main source of research material.

Professor Roy P. Stonesifer, for providing unpublished material on Gideon Pillow.

Hannah Zeidlik, Office of the Chief of Military History, Washington, D.C., for her help.

FRIENDS WHO HAVE GIVEN HELP AND ENCOURAGEMENT:

Colonel Doniphan Carter, president of Eagle Graphics.

Detmar Finke, formerly of the Office, Chief of Military History.

Richard H. Foltz, of Los Angeles, who arranged a beneficial visit with William Mason, of the Los Angeles County Museum of Natural History.

Michael Killian, of the Chicago *Tribune*.

Sandra Myres, Department of History, University of Texas at Arlington.

Stephen Neal, of the Chicago *Sun-Times*.

Professor Louis D. Rubin, Jr., University of North Carolina at Chapel Hill.

Charles M. Tyson, for editorial comments and provision of fine original sketches.

Carol Utecht, of Brokaw, Wis., for editorial comments and research on the chapters pertaining to California.

Anne Marie Woodward, of Washington, D.C.

INDEX